Data Analysis for Social Scientists

A First Course in Applied Statistics

Lawrence C. Hamilton
University of New Hampshire

Duxbury Press
An Imprint of Wadsworth Publishing Company
I(T)P® An International Thomson Publishing Company

Belmont Albany Bonn Boston Cincinnati Detroit London
Madrid Melbourne Mexico City New York Paris
San Francisco Singapore Tokyo Toronto Washington

Statistics Editors: Curt Hinrichs, Stan Loll
Project Development Editor: Jennifer Burger
Editorial Assistant: Martha O'Connor
Production Services Coordinator: Gary Mcdonald
Production: Susan L. Reiland
Marketing Manager: Joanne M. Terhaar
Print Buyer: Barbara Britton

Permissions Editor: Peggy Meehan
Copy Editor: Robert de Freitas
Technical Illustrations: Lori Heckelman
Cover: William Reuter Design
Compositor: G & S Typesetters
Printer: Quebecor Printing/Fairfield

This book is printed on acid-free recycled paper.

I(T)P   The ITP logo is a registered trademark under license.
Duxbury Press and the leaf logo are trademarks used under license.

Printed in the United States of America
1 2 3 4 5 6 7 8 9 10

For more information, contact Duxbury Press at Wadsworth Publishing Company:

Wadsworth Publishing Company
10 Davis Drive
Belmont, California 94002, USA

International Thomson Publishing Europe
Berkshire House 168-173
High Holborn
London, WC1V 7AA, England

Thomas Nelson Australia
102 Dodds Street
South Melbourne 3205
Victoria, Australia

Nelson Canada
1120 Birchmount Road
Scarborough, Ontario
Canada M1K 5G4

Internation Thomson Editores
Campos Eliseos 385, Piso 7
Col. Polanco
11560 México D.F. México

International Thomson Publishing GmbH
Königswinterer Strasse 418
53227 Bonn, Germany

International Thomson Publishing Asia
221 Henderson Road
#05-10 Henderson Building
Singapore 0315

International Thomson Publishing Japan
Hirakawacho Kyowa Building, 3F
2-2-1 Hirakawacho
Chiyoda-ku, Tokyo 102, Japan

Library of Congress Cataloging-in-Publication Data

Hamilton, Lawrence C.
        Data analysis for social scientists : a first course in applied statistics / Lawrence C. Hamilton.
        p.   cm.
        Includes index.
        ISBN 0-534-24720-2 (casebound)
        1. Social sciences—Statistical methods.   I. Title.
HA29.H2434   1995   95-34992
519.5—dc20

Preface

A Note to Students

Data are systematically recorded information. This book offers scores of examples on topics ranging from college students to cities, gold mines, and ballistic missiles. **Data analysis** involves the application of **statistics,** the mathematical science of uncertainty, to understanding patterns in data and drawing from them wider conclusions. Statistics and data analysis form bridges across many other scientific fields, where similar analytical methods help researchers tackle seemingly quite different problems.

A course in data analysis and statistics will not ask you to memorize numerical facts such as "8.6% of Maine residents live in towns with fewer than 1,000 people," as many students seem to expect. Rather, such a course aims to convey an understanding of how statistical reasoning proceeds, and demonstrate how it helps us to discover new things about the world. That understanding has relevance whether you remain a consumer of other people's statistical claims in our "data-rich" society, or go on to do your own original research.

For this course, I assume that you have access to a computer with statistical software—not necessarily every day, but at least for major assignments. Computers open new doors for an introductory statistics course. They mean that the complexities of calculation scarcely matter at all. We can carry out a wide variety of statistical computations—going well beyond the scope of earlier generations—quickly and without much pain. This facility frees us to redirect our attention. No longer is just "getting the right (arithmetically correct) answer" the main difficulty; a computer can always do that. We can turn instead to the more interesting challenges of using our computer as a power tool for analytical thinking.

Data Analysis for Social Scientists centers around thinking about real data. The detective work of data analysis, applied to examples throughout the text, exercises, and end-of-chapter problems, really constitutes the heart of this book. I hope that the experience of exploring data yourself, and drawing conclusions about the wider universe they represent, helps to make the course both more engaging than you expect and more useful to your future educational or professional life.

Goals

Data Analysis for Social Scientists is intended as the main text for a first course in statistics. Not all of the examples represent social science, but most should be interesting and understandable to social science students—as well as students in other fields. (Moving through these examples, you may notice signs of the author's research interests in environmental social science and the far north.) The book as a whole works up to an introduction to modern regression analysis.

The title *Data Analysis* reflects an emphasis on learning about statistics through work with real data. Traditional texts tend to place greater emphasis on the mathematical logic that underlies statistical procedures, or on the calculations these procedures require. The mathematical foundations of statistics certainly constitute an important topic, central to deeper understanding. Arguments can also be made that some hand calculation is essential as a path to comprehension. But we have only so much time in any single course; more time devoted to mathematics or to calculation inevitably leaves less time for looking at data. And unfortunately, many students regard mathematics as an impenetrable, even frightening, realm. Hands-on data analysis, however, can provide a less forbidding, more curiosity-motivated entry into the world of statistical reasoning.

Over recent decades, computers—especially desktop computers—have revolutionized our field. The revolution allows cutting-edge researchers to perform more numerous, varied, and sophisticated analyses than ever before. To prepare students for this reality, an up-to-date introductory course can exploit computers in similar ways.:

1. Bypass most of the labor of hand calculation, going directly to analyzing data and interpreting the results.
2. Employ varied numerical and graphical methods to explore the data and draw conclusions.
3. Check wherever possible on the reasonableness of our assumptions, trying alternative methods when those assumptions look doubtful.

These ideas shaped the book.

Software

Almost any statistical package could be used with this book, although it was written with two particular packages in mind: StataQuest and Stata. StataQuest is a student program, easy to learn but with surprisingly advanced features. Its cousin Stata is a state-of-the-art professional package, with a full range of analytical capabilities plus a programming language that supports further expansion. Compared to other full-featured packages, Stata is remarkably fast, current, and flexible—subscribers to the *Stata Technical Bulletin* receive updates adding new features every 2 months. The StataQuest program represents a subset of Stata, with a straightforward menu interface.

The analyses in this book can be accomplished with either program, and the underlying datasets are available on disk in Stata/StataQuest, Minitab, SPSS, and ASCII format. The text gives file names of these computer datasets each time a new one appears. A companion book, *Data Analysis with StataQuest,* shows how to use Stata-

Quest to accomplish the examples, exercises, and problems of this text. More complete references on StataQuest and Stata include new books by Anagnoson and DeLeon (*StataQuest*), Hamilton (*Statistics with Stata*), and Stata Corporation (*Stata Reference Manual*).

Level and Scope

This book requires only high school algebra as mathematical background; explanations needing calculus or matrix algebra do not appear. Formal definitions have been set aside in boxes. Some students may choose to read around the boxes, returning subsequently to study them as needed. Especially in later chapters, I do not expect that many readers will want to hand-calculate from these formulas, so no computational shortcuts are given. Instead, as computers do the heavy lifting, humans remain responsible for choosing methods and making sense of the printouts. With this "division of labor" in mind, I spend more time on understanding the output tables, such as relations between the sums of squares, F statistics, and R^2 of ANOVA.

De-emphasizing mathematics does not imply that this text is easy, only that the challenge has been shifted. Real data, unlike the artificial data found in many texts, frequently are ambiguous or messy. Analytical work often takes the form of trying initial graphs or calculations, studying those results, and on that basis deciding what to try next. Such work requires thought in diagnosing what the first analysis reveals, plus a toolkit of alternative techniques with knowledge of when and how to use them.

Coverage includes most of the standard topics found in introductory social statistics courses. It also includes a few nonstandard topics, made practical by the use of computers. For example:

1. The philosophy of John Tukey's *Exploratory Data Analysis* (1977), with its focus on graphical displays, transformations, robustness, and treating assumptions suspiciously, is implicit throughout.

2. We can easily try several analytical methods, to see whether they support similar conclusions. A one-way ANOVA, for instance, might be followed up with a Kruskal–Wallis test, and with a few graphs to check out the plausibility of its normality and equal-variance assumptions.

3. Instead of leaving theoretical sampling distributions (normal, t, chi-square, etc.) as static mysteries, codified in tables at the back of the book, we can show them dynamically through simulation.

4. Computers readily provide precise binomial or other theoretical probabilities, moving beyond the limitations of tables or hand calculation.

5. Multivariate methods such as two-way ANOVA and multiple regression appear as straightforward steps up from their bivariate counterparts.

6. For the first time we can use robust regression in an introductory course. This versatile tool has, if anything, even more value for beginning analysts than for

experts; but its computational complexity has traditionally confined it to advanced courses.

Computer use not only changes what topics can be presented; it also affects their order of presentation, as discussed below.

Organization

Although the chapter outline is fairly standard, sequence within chapters is less so. In writing this book, I tried to follow the flow of data analysis, which sometimes departs from the usual sequence of introductory-course topics. For example, standard textbooks devote one chapter to "center" (mean, median, mode) and a later chapter to "spread" (variance, standard deviation, interquartile range). Instead I introduce mean, variance, and standard deviation together, to emphasize that they belong to one mathematical family and share common statistical properties. Later, median and interquartile range are introduced as members of a different family, with different properties. The analytical strategy of using mean-based and order-based statistics in parallel recurs in later chapters.

Other departures from traditional sequencing include introducing simple bivariate ideas in Chapters 1 and 2; presenting six theoretical probability distributions together in Chapter 5; alternating parametric tests with nonparametric tests in Chapters 6 and 8; and going so far as to introduce diagnostics, transformations, and robust regression along with multiple regression in Chapter 10. In each instance, the logic of data analysis and the corresponding organization of statistical software (which, for example, typically prints standard deviations together with means, and will show t, F, or chi-square statistics in many different contexts) led to a new order of presentation.

Although this text has been streamlined considerably compared with its 684-page predecessor *Modern Data Analysis* (Hamilton, 1990), it still contains more material than most classes will cover in one semester. To shorten the course and find an appropriate level of challenge, instructors might choose to omit some or all of the optional sections, indicated by asterisks in the text:

Chapter 2	Section 2.1, on graphing cumulative frequency distributions
Chapter 5	Five sections on theoretical sampling distributions (binomial, Poisson, chi-square, t, and F)
Chapter 6	Section 6.9, on sample size
Chapter 7	Section 7.7, on multiway cross-tabulation
Chapter 8	Sections 8.5 (error-bar plots) and 8.6 (two-way ANOVA)
Chapter 10	Advanced regression

The remainder of the text was written with the idea that these optional parts might have been skipped.

Exercises and Problems

Data Analysis for Social Scientists contains over 400 problems and exercises to provide hands-on experience with analyzing real data. Exercises at the end of most sections allow readers to try out the techniques that section introduced. They are meant as an integral part of working through the text; indeed some explanations are deliberately brief, where it seems that doing, rather than just reading, will more readily help understanding. Answers to selected exercises appear in Appendix I.

In addition to the within-chapter exercises, each chapter ends with 30 or so problems based on fresh data. Problems require not just routine application of the chapter's techniques, but various degrees of original thinking, troubleshooting, and pulling together conclusions from different lines of evidence. Answers to problems do not appear in this book, so selected problems could serve as assignments or exam questions.

Acknowledgments

I am grateful to many people for sharing their ideas, expertise, or data, without which *Data Analysis for Social Scientists* would not have been possible. Those who went out of their way include Bob Flewelling, Igor Krupnik, John Law, Haluk Ozkaynak, Peggy Plass, Murray Straus, Jim Taylor, George Thurston, Paul Treacy, Steve Tullar, Heather Turner, Sally Ward, and Kirk Williams. Others helped with the original research that produced some of these datasets. Christina Bellinger, Sidney Callahan, William Denkinger, Marlies Kruse, Jesse LaCrosse, Brigid Murray, Sarah Scanlan, and Patrick Yott made notable contributions. Warren Hamilton introduced me to controversies in mineral-deposit estimation, including the priceless example of Table 3.10. Thanks go also to my colleagues in recent Arctic and North Atlantic studies, Carole Seyfrit, Cynthia M. Duncan, and Nicholas Flanders. Those studies provided the broader research context for a book about data analysis.

At Duxbury Press I benefitted from the attention of two editors. Curt Hinrichs helped initiate the project, and oversaw its transformation from a straightforward revision of *Modern Data Analysis* into a whole new book. Stan Loll took over in the final months to help guide it through production, keeping pace with the ongoing software development. William Gould, James Hardin, Alan Riley, and William Sribney deserve credit for the StataQuest software, which smoothly blends power and beginner-friendliness. Many reviewers offered helpful comments on earlier drafts of the book, including J. Theodore Anagnoson, California State University, Los Angeles; Wayne Brown, California Polytechnic State University, Pomona; Richard E. DeLeon, San Francisco State University; James G. Ennis, Tufts University; Mark A. Fossett, Texas A & M University; Charles Halaby, University of Wisconsin, Madison; Daniel H. Krymkowski, University of Vermont; Michael Martin, Stanford University; Julia A. Norton, California State University, Hayward; and Dennis Palumbo, Arizona State University. Susan Reiland did her usual fine job as production editor.

Choosing a dedication was the easist part: to Leslie, for all that she has done.

Table of Contents

*Indicates optional sections that could be skipped without loss of continuity.

1

A First Look at Data

Data are systematically recorded information about the world. They provide the raw material for scientific research. To look for patterns in data, or to test whether certain theoretically expected patterns exist, researchers apply the analytical tools of statistics. Performing statistical analysis resembles detective work in which we combine knowledge, judgment, and statistical methods to gain understanding from the data. The methods of modern statistics depend on an elaborate framework of mathematical theory, but that framework is not the focus of this text. Instead, we will focus on statistics as a way to discover things about the world, through the analysis of real data.

Each chapter gives examples of such discovery, including some that you can make on your own. First, though, there is the business of learning basic vocabulary. In statistics, certain everyday words like *variable, significant*, and *population* take on special meanings. This chapter begins by showing how data are commonly organized and by introducing some of the terms needed to discuss data. We then move on to elementary ways of looking for data patterns.

1.1 A Sample Dataset

At an early stage in most research, raw data are arranged as a rectangular **dataset**. Table 1.1 gives an example based on a survey of students in an introductory statistics course. Each row in a dataset is one **case**. Cases are the entities that data describe; in Table 1.1, each case is an individual student.

The columns in this dataset represent **variables**, or specific attributes of those cases. Attributes of the students reported in Table 1.1 include their gender, age, and political-party preference. Thus Table 1.1 shows a dataset with 43 cases (individual students) and six variables:

gender	male or female
age	in years
party	political-party preference
grade	expected grade in this course
SAT	self-reported math SAT score
quiz	score on an unannounced statistics quiz

The survey took place early in the semester, before students had any information about what course grade they would actually receive.

Table 1.1
Data on 43 introductory statistics students

Student	Gender	Age	Political-party preference	Expected grade	Math SAT	Quiz score
1	male	20	Republican	B	570	0
2	female	18	Republican	C	470	5
3	male	22	Republican	C	480	1
4	female	19	Democrat	B	490	0
5	female	20	Democrat	B	540	0
6	female	21	Democrat	A	720	0
7	male	20	Republican	B	540	1
8	male	18	Democrat	A	420	4
9	female	21	Democrat	B	410	7
10	female	17	Independent	B	430	3
11	female	18	Independent	B		0
12	female	30	Independent	B		0
13	female	20	Democrat	A	610	2
14	female	20	Democrat	B		0
15	male	21	Independent	C	520	0
16	male	20	Independent	A	490	1
17	female	21	Democrat	B	540	0
18	male	25	Democrat	B	490	0
19	female	23	Democrat	B	420	2
20	male	20		B	1,000	1
21	female	43	Democrat	B		1
22	male	22	Democrat	C	370	3
23	female	21	Independent	B	540	0
24	female	19	Independent	B	510	0
25	female	19	Independent	A	610	0
26	female	20		B		0
27	male	20	Independent	B	430	5
28	female	20	Independent	C	520	4
29	female	20	Independent	A	450	0
30	female	18	Republican	A	560	3
31	female	24	Independent	B	550	0
32	female	24	Independent	B	430	3
33	female	20	Democrat	B		1
34	female	20		A		1

(*continued*)

Table 11 (*Continued*)

Student	Gender	Age	Political-party preference	Expected grade	Math SAT	Quiz score
35	female	21	Republican	B	520	0
36	female	18	Democrat	C	490	0
37	female	20	Independent	B	400	1
38	male	20	Democrat	A	600	1
39	female	20	Republican	B	630	0
40	male	22	Independent	B	550	1
41	female	19	Independent	B	460	5
42	female	18	Democrat	B	540	7
43	female	20	Democrat	B	540	3

File: *stats*

The body of Table 1.1 contains **values** for each of the six variables, for each of the 43 students. For example, "male" is the value of variable *gender* for student number 1, 20 his value on the variable *age*, and 0 his value on *quiz*. Two shorthand ways of identifying variables are popular:

1. Brief descriptive names or abbreviations, such as *age, gender,* or *quiz*. Computer programs encourage the use of such names, but typically limit them to no more than eight characters.

2. Individual symbolic letters, typically from the end of the alphabet, such as *x, y,* or *z*. Subscripts may indicate the case number. For example, if *x* stands for *gender*, x_1 = "male" (the *x* value of case 1), x_5 = "female," and so forth. If *y* stands for *quiz score*, then $y_1 = 0$, $y_{42} = 7$, and so on. Algebraic presentations favor the use of symbolic letters.

To help keep discussions concrete, we use descriptive names (in *italics*) for variables whenever possible in this book. For writing equations and mathematical definitions, however, we often use symbolic letters instead.

Several students in our survey left one or more questions blank. Their **missing values** appear as periods in Table 1.1. Missing values, common in research, complicate efforts to draw sound conclusions. Suppose we wanted to know the average SAT score of these 43 students. Did some leave this question blank because they were unhappy with their low scores? If so, an average based on the 36 who answered might overestimate the true average SAT score among these 43 students.

Measurement errors further complicate research. We do not know anyone's true SAT scores (or age, or gender), only what they reported on this survey. We do know that true SAT scores must fall in the range from 200 to 800. Student 20 reported an impossible score of 1,000. Perhaps he was joking, had a poor memory, or confused his math SAT score with his composite (math plus verbal) SAT score. We cannot now determine the explanation, but clearly we should not use his "1,000" when calculating averages or other statistics. Less obvious errors due to memory, dishonesty, or mistakes may exist with any of our other variables, or in any other survey. Even if our data came not from fallible humans but from scientific instruments such as telescopes or thermometers, those instruments too would introduce sources of error. (Have you ever weighed yourself on faulty scales?) Some degree of measurement error exists in all data.

The most troublesome errors are those with a systematic pattern, such as scales that overestimate everyone's weight by 10%, or self-reported SAT scores that tend to be exaggerated more often by students who scored poorly. Systematic measurement errors will affect not only individual values, but also averages and many other statistics calculated from the data.

1.2   Types of Variables

The variables in Table 1.1 illustrate two broad types. *Age, SAT,* and *quiz* are **measurement variables**. Their values convey numerical information, and answer questions of "How much?" A 20-year-old has lived about 20 years; someone scoring 6 on the quiz gave six correct answers.

Gender and *party* (political-party preference), on the other hand, are categorical variables. **Categorical variables** answer questions about "Which group?" or "What kind?" Researchers often assign number values to categorical variables, such as 1 = Democrat, 2 = Republican, and 3 = Independent. But these numbers convey no numerical information; they do not imply that an Independent is "more than" a Democrat or Republican. We could equally well have chosen a different coding, such as 1 = Republican, 5 = Independent, 10 = Democrat; the numbers used to represent each category are arbitrary.

The choice of analytical techniques depends partly on the nature of our variables. Averages work only with measurement variables. We might reasonably discuss the average age (21), SAT score (523), or quiz score (1.5). But the average gender (.7, if we coded 0 = male and 1 = female) or the average political party (1.975, if 1 = Democrat, 2 = Republican, 3 = Independent) seem to make little sense. Although we usually cannot average categories, we can summarize them well enough using percentages: 28% of these students are male, 42.5% are Democrats, and so forth. On the other hand, percentages work less well with measurement variables, which can take on many different values: 2.8% (one person) scored 370 on the math SAT, 2.8% scored 400, 2.8% scored 410, and so forth. We need analytical techniques that make sense with our variables.

Some texts classify variables into four "levels of measurement"—nominal, ordinal, interval, or ratio (NOIR):

nominal   Cases are classified into unordered categories or types, such as {male, female} or {Democrat, Republican, Independent}. Nominal variables represent the least informative level of measurement.

ordinal   We know the order of categories, such as {cold, cool, warm, hot}, but not the distances between them; for example, we do not know whether "warm" is as far above "cool" as "cool" is above "cold."

interval   We know the order of categories, and the intervals between them, but our variable lacks a meaningful zero point. For example, temperature in degrees Fahrenheit is an interval scale; 0°F represents an arbitrary point, so 10°F is not "twice as hot" as 5°F.

ratio   Ratio variables resemble interval variables but with a meaningful zero point. Ratios make sense only with ratio variables. For example, weight in pounds is a ratio variable; a 300-pound football player weighs three times as much as a 100-pound ballerina. Ratio measurement is the most informative level of measurement.

Statisticians have recognized drawbacks to the popular four-level NOIR scheme, however, and have proposed alternatives that include a seven-type classification (Mosteller and Tukey, 1977; Velleman and Wilkinson, 1993).

This book stays with the simplest scheme, a two-type classification of categorical or measurement variables. Categorical variables correspond to nominal-level variables, whereas measurement variables encompass both interval and ratio levels:

categorical   { nominal

                    ordinal

measurement   { interval
                    ratio

Ordinal variables fall into a gray area between categorical and measurement. Special techniques exist for analyzing ordinal variables but, in practice, it often works well enough to approach them with either categorical or measurement-variable methods. Letter grades, for example, are ordinal variables (A is better than B, but not necessarily by the same amount as D is better than F); people often reasonably describe such variables using either percentages, a categorical-variable approach ("21% of these students expect A's, and 65% expect B's") or averages, a measurement-variable approach ("the average expected grade in this class is 3.1, about a B").

EXERCISE

1.2.1 Describe four possible datasets that might be collected to study a topic that interests you. For each example, specify:
       a. the cases
       b. the variables and their types (categorical or measurement)

1.3 ▬ Frequency Distributions

The statistics quiz scores in Table 1.1 result from a question asked on the third day of class:

> "List as many as you can recall of the graphical methods or concepts intro-
> duced in Chapter 2 (assigned for today)."

Most students had not taken the reading assignment seriously, as shown by the **frequency distribution** in Table 1.2.

Table 1.2
Frequency distribution of statistics quiz scores
(number of concepts recalled)

Quiz score y	Frequency f	Proportion $p = f/n$	Percentage $100 \times p$
0	19	.44	44%
1	10	.23	23
2	2	.05	5
3	5	.12	12
4	2	.05	5
5	3	.07	7
6	0	.00	0
7	2	.05	5
	$n = 43$	1.00	100%

Frequencies, symbolized by f, count the number of times each value occurs. For example, in the first row of Table 1.2, $f = 19$, meaning that the quiz score $y = 0$ was recorded for 19 students. Proportion, p, equals the frequency divided by the number of cases, n (often called the **sample size**). The proportion of students scoring 0 on the quiz was $f/n = 19/43 = .44$. Percentages equal proportions multiplied by 100. Proportions in a frequency distribution should add to 1, and percentages should add to 100 (apart from imprecision due to rounding off).

Figure 1.1 (page 8) arranges this frequency distribution graphically as a **histogram**. A histogram's vertical axis can indicate either frequency, proportion, or percentage. Figure 1.1 shows all three axis scales, for purposes of illustration. Usually, we would show just one of them.

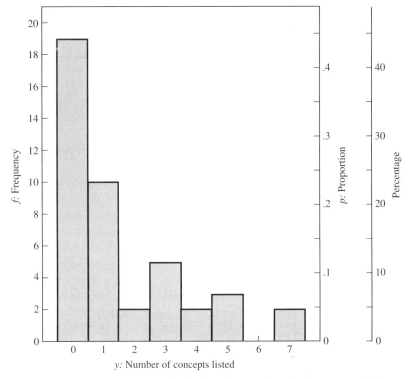

FIGURE 1.1 Histogram showing the distribution of 43 students' quiz scores, with frequency, proportion, and percentage axes

When a variable takes on only a few different values, like the statistics quiz scores (whole numbers from 0 to 7), the frequency distribution should list all possible values over the range covered by the data. Thus, Table 1.2 includes a row for $y = 6$, even though no students attained this score ($f = 0$), and it shows up as a gap in Figure 1.1.

When variables take on many different values, as math SAT scores do, we may need to employ a **grouped frequency distribution**, which counts not the number of students who scored exactly 510, for example, but the number with scores from 500 to 549, 550 to 599, and so on. To group a variable, divide its range into a manageable number of equal-width intervals. Define the intervals so that, over this range, they include all possible values; no value can fall "between" two intervals. Then, count the number of cases that have values within each interval. A table of these counts forms our grouped frequency distribution. Some groups in the table may contain no cases, or have frequencies of zero; list these too. Zero-frequency groups appear as gaps in a histogram when graphed.

Histograms display measurement-variable distributions. A similar idea called the **bar chart** displays categorical-variable distributions. Table 1.3 gives the frequency distribution for one categorical variable, political-party preference, from Table 1.1. Three of the original 43 students expressed no party preference. Their missing values are not counted in Table 1.3; instead, proportions and percentages are based on the number of nonmissing values, $n* = 40$. Alternatively, we could have included "missing" as a fourth category, and based proportions and percentages on the full sample size, $n = 43$. Either approach has analytical value, but authors and readers have to be clear about which base number was used in calculating any proportions or percentages.

Table 1.3
Frequency distribution of students' political-party preference

Political-party preference x	Frequency f	Proportion $p = f/n*$	Percentage $100 \times p$
Democrat	17	.425	42.5%
Republican	7	.175	17.5
Independent	16	.400	40.0
	$n* = 40$	1.000	100.0%

Figure 1.2 shows this distribution in bar-chart form. Bar charts resemble histograms in that bar heights correspond to frequencies (or proportions or percentages). Spaces separate each bar in a bar chart, however, unlike the bars in a histogram. This graphical convention reflects the idea that the categories are in arbitrary order, and

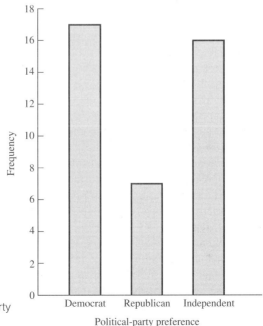

FIGURE 1.2
Bar chart showing the distribution of 40 students' political-party preferences

neighboring categories are not necessarily "close" to each other the way a quiz score of 3 is closer to a 4 than to a 7.

News and business reports often feature variations on bar charts, which replace the bars with pictures, such as stacks of coins, human figures, tall buildings, or other drawings depicting the subject. Such "picture graphs" catch the eye, but their artistry adds no new information and may distort readers' perceptions of the underlying numbers. In *The Visual Display of Quantitative Information*, perhaps the world's first coffee-table statistics book, Edward Tufte (1983) provides a richly illustrated critique of graphical excess, which he calls "chartjunk."

EXERCISE

1.3.1   Construct ungrouped frequency-distribution tables and appropriate graphs (histogram or bar chart) for the following variables from Table 1.1 (file *stats*):
   a.   *gender*
   b.   *age*
   c.   *grade*

1.4 Aggregate Data

Each case in the student survey dataset represents an individual person. In another dataset, our cases might consist of individual frogs, described by such variables as color, loudness, and jumping distance. Or the cases might be the individual moons of Saturn, with variables such as diameter, mass, and length of "day." Later in this text we encounter a dataset where cases represent the first 25 flights of the U.S. space shuttle, with launch date, temperature, and booster rocket damage as variables. In another example, the cases are individual dolphins, with tooth measurements and age as variables.

Some research employs a different kind of data, **aggregate data**, in which many individual entities are summed or combined to form each case. For example, we might collect data not on individual college students, but on whole colleges, as seen in Table 1.4. Individual data tell us about variation among students; college data, instead, tell us about variations among colleges. Individual and aggregate data address different sorts of research questions.

Individual students can be male or female, and can have a certain SAT score. These variables do not describe colleges, which neither have gender nor take the SAT. However, when aggregating all the individual students of a college together, each college does have a certain percentage of males or females, and a certain average SAT score. Thus, summary statistics, like percentages and averages, can themselves become variables in an aggregate dataset.

Table 1.4
Data on 11 U.S. Colleges and Universities (1991)

School	Full-time enrollment	Percent male	Average math SAT	Average verbal SAT
Brown Univ.	5,550	52	680	630
Univ. of Scranton	3,821	48	554	504
Univ. of N. Carolina/Asheville	2,035	47	540	480
Claremont College	849	62	660	600
DePaul Univ.	6,197	45	547	498
Thomas Aquinas College	201	54	570	570
Davidson College	1,543	55	640	590
Univ. of Michigan/Dearborn	3,541	49	485	550
Mass. College of Art	961	40	482	467
Oberlin College	2,765	46	640	600
American Univ.	5,228	40	587	550

Source: Random sample of SAT-reporting schools listed in *Barron's Compact Guide to Colleges* 1992.
File: *college1*

College enrollments can take on thousands of different values, so a readable frequency distribution for this variable requires grouping. Table 1.5 illustrates one possible grouping scheme applied to the 11-college sample.

Table 1.5
Grouped frequency distribution of 11 colleges'
full-time enrollments

Enrollment	Frequency	Proportion
0– 999	3	.27
1,000–1,999	1	.09
2,000–2,999	2	.18
3,000–3,999	2	.18
4,000–4,999	0	.00
5,000–5,999	2	.18
6,000–6,999	1	.09
	11	1.00

Figure 1.3 (page 12) shows the grouped frequency distribution as a histogram. The only formal difference between grouped and ungrouped histograms is the way we label the horizontal axis. With ungrouped data like the quiz scores in Figure 1.1, it made

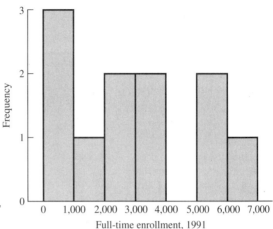

FIGURE 1.3
Grouped histogram of 11 colleges' enrollments, based on Table 1.5

visual sense to center labels (0, 1, 2, 3, etc.) under each bar. With grouped data like the enrollments in Figure 1.3, the labels (0, 1,000, 2,000, etc.) mark boundaries between the groups or bars.

For the most part, we can apply the same analytical techniques to aggregate and individual data. We could calculate the average percent male (48.9%) or the average of the average verbal SAT scores (549) for the 11 colleges in Table 1.4. Such statistics might be useful, for example, if we hoped to use this small sample of colleges to estimate the average percent male among all U.S. colleges, or the average of average SAT scores, generalizing beyond the 11 schools in Table 1.4. Note that averaging the 11 verbal SAT scores in Table 1.4 yields the average for *these 11 colleges*, which is not the same thing as the average for *the 32,691 students who attend these 11 colleges*. To obtain the latter, we would need to take into account how many students attend each school.

EXERCISE

1.4.1 Construct grouped frequency-distribution tables and histograms for the following variables from Table 1.4 (file *college1*):
a. percent male (use equal-width groups of 40–44, 45–49, 50–54, etc.)
b. average verbal SAT (use equal-width groups of 400–449, 450–499, etc.)
c. average math SAT

1.5 Sample and Population

A particular dataset often includes only a small fraction of the cases that interest a researcher. The researcher might study the dataset in hopes of drawing reasonable conclusions, not just about the data at hand but also about a much larger population of cases beyond these data, "out there" in the world. The term **population** refers to that universe of cases (people, frogs, universities, etc.) about which a researcher would like to generalize. The entire population might be huge, but even if not, it is usually unavailable for analysis. A **sample** is one subset of cases from the population, which is available for analysis. The 43 students in Table 1.1 constitute a sample from the larger population of all U.S. statistics students. But this sample is not **representative** of that larger population. Since the 43 students all came from one class, we have no reason to assume that studying them will tell us much about the larger population; these 43 students could be quite unusual.

A **simple random sample** is one for which every case in the population has an equal chance of being selected. Random sampling provides a good way to improve our chances of obtaining a representative sample, from which we *can* generalize. Students from the population of U.S. statistics students did not all have equal chances of being selected for Table 1.1. For this reason, it provides little basis for generalization to that population.

Unlike the 43 students in Table 1.1, the 11 colleges in Table 1.4 are a random sample. We used a hand calculator's random-number key to select pages in a book, *Barron's Compact Guide to Colleges*, and then chose the first college on that page (or on the following page) which provided average math and verbal SAT scores. Thus each school in the larger population (of all colleges listing SAT averages in the 1992 *Barron's Guide*) had an equal chance of selection into this sample.

Consequently, we have some basis for generalizing from the Table 1.4 sample, small though it is, back to the larger population. Of course, any such generalization involves uncertainty. It seems unlikely that the average of the average verbal SAT scores for the entire population of colleges equals exactly 549, for example, even though the population's average might be somewhere close to this value. Later chapters will introduce statistical methods for quantifying our degree of uncertainty in making such generalizations.

Note the role of a specific random device—the hand calculator's random-number function—in selecting this sample. "Random" does not mean "haphazard" or "thoughtless"; we would not necessarily obtain a truly random sample just by opening the book with our eyes closed. Selecting a random sample can be one of the most difficult and crucial stages in research, although for Table 1.4 it was fairly easy. Someone who speaks of "interviewing random people on the sidewalk," meaning passersby who happen to look approachable, is not using the word "random" in its scientific sense. Textbooks on research methods devote much space to the topic of random sampling; for example, see Babbie (1995).

EXERCISES

1.5.1   Calculate the averages (sums of the values for each college, divided by *n*) for each of the four measurement variables in Table 1.4 (file *college1*).

1.5.2   Table 1.6 (page 14; file *college2*) lists a second random sample of $n = 11$ colleges, selected using a calculator's random number key in the same manner described for Table 1.4. By chance, one college (Claremont) was selected for both samples—as sometimes happens with simple random sampling, especially when the population we draw from is not huge.

Calculate the averages for each of the four variables in this new random sample.

Table 1.6
Data on a second random sample
of 11 U.S. Colleges and Universities (1991)

School	Full-time enrollment	Percent male	Average math SAT	Average verbal SAT
Rose-Hulman Inst. Tech.	1,300	100	650	540
Washington Univ.	4,933	52	650	560
James Madison Univ.	9,311	.	578	519
Center for Creative Study	613	60	490	440
George Washington Univ.	5,593	49	600	550
Hanover College	1,060	49	535	510
Lee College	62	32	504	489
Millersville Univ.	5,371	41	530	470
Claremont College	849	62	660	600
Univ. of Texas	37,025	53	591	513
Univ. of Vermont	7,992	47	560	490

Source: Random sample of SAT-reporting schools listed in *Barron's Compact Guide to Colleges* 1992.
File: *college2*

1.5.3 Compare the corresponding averages you found for Exercises 1.5.1 and 1.5.2. Differences between these averages reflect **sampling error**. If we selected a third or fourth sample, we would almost certainly get a third and fourth set of different averages. On the basis of the two samples you now have (Tables 1.4 and 1.6), what generalizations (if any) can you suggest regarding the average enrollment, percent male, math SAT, and verbal SAT among the population of all colleges reporting SATs in the 1992 *Barron's Guide?*

1.6 ▬ Relations Between Variables

The most interesting research questions involve relations between two or more variables. Two variables are related if the distribution of one variable differs across values of the second variable. Therefore, a measurement variable's average might be different at different values of a second variable; for example, average income tends to be higher among college graduates. In addition, a categorical variable might exhibit different percentages at different values of a second variable; for example, the percentage voting Democratic often differs for men and women. Statisticians have developed a large toolkit of techniques for studying intervariable relations. Later chapters will say more about these; here, we preview some of the basic ideas.

Table 1.2 showed the frequency distribution of one categorical variable, political-party preference. To study the relation between two categorical variables such as party preference and gender, we might separately tabulate party preferences by gender. Table 1.7 illustrates this **cross-tabulation**.

Table 1.7
Cross-tabulation of political-party preference by gender

Political-party preference	Gender		Total
	Male	Female	
Democrat	4 36.4%	13 44.8%	17 42.5%
Republican	3 27.3%	4 13.8%	7 17.5%
Independent	4 36.4%	12 41.4%	16 40.0%
Total	11 100.0%	29 100.0%	40 100.0%

The *total* column in Table 1.7 lists the overall frequencies and percentages of party preference, identical to those listed earlier in Table 1.3. The *male* column tells us that there are 4 male Democrats, constituting 36.4% of the 11 males ($100 \times 4/11 = 36.4\%$). We see that women are about half as likely as men to consider themselves Republican: only 4 out of the 29 females ($100 \times 4/29 = 13.8\%$), compared with 3 out of 11 males (27.3%), chose *Republican*. During the 1990 U.S. presidential election (Democrat Bill Clinton versus Republican George Bush and Independent Ross Perot), pollsters noticed a "gender gap": the Republican candidate won a higher percentage of male votes than female votes. Although the college students of Table 1.7 appear less Republican and more Independent than the nation's voters as a whole, they do exhibit a similar gender gap.

Figure 1.4 (page 16) displays essentially the same information as Table 1.7, but in graphical form. Although this bar chart adds no new analytical information, it helps dramatize the gender difference in our sample, especially for a casual reader. Figure 1.4 also visualizes the definition of a statistical relation: The distribution of one variable (in

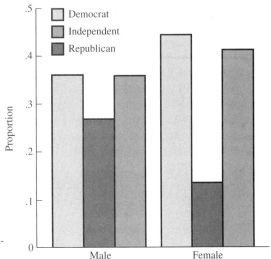

FIGURE 1.4
Bar charts of 40 students' political-party preferences by gender

this example, *party*) is different at different values of a second variable (*gender*). That is, the distribution of *party* for men (left three bars) looks different from the distribution of *party* for women (right three bars).

As noted earlier, percentages or proportions readily summarize categorical variables such as political party, but averages work better with measurement variables such as test scores. To explore the relation between a measurement variable, *quiz score*, and expected grade from Table 1.1, we might start by finding the average quiz score of students expecting A's, B's, or C's (Table 1.8). Six students expected a C in the course, and their average quiz score equals 2.17. The 28 students expecting B's earned quiz scores averaging 1.46, and the 9 students expecting A's had an average score of only 1.33. Table 1.8 suggests a surprising conclusion: The more confident students were less likely to have done any reading at this early point in the semester.

Table 1.8
Average statistics quiz score,
by grade expected in course
(second week of class)

Expected grade in statistics	Average quiz score	Frequency
C	2.17	6
B	1.46	28
A	1.33	9
Total	1.53	43

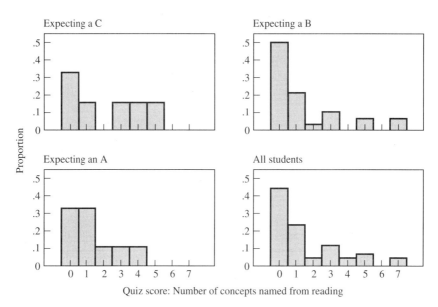

FIGURE 1.5   Histograms of students' quiz scores by what grade they expect in statistics (all students at lower right)

Figure 1.5 shows separate histograms of *quiz* for students expecting a C, B, or A, and also for all students together (lower right, which depicts the same distribution as Figure 1.1). These graphs add some detail to our findings regarding the relation between *quiz* and *grade*. We see relatively fewer good quiz scores among students expecting an A than among either of the other two grade groups. When we analyze the relation between a measurement and a categorical variable, comparing histograms in this manner provides a graphical accompaniment to comparing means as in Table 1.8.

Tables 1.7–1.8 and Figures 1.4–1.5 illustrate, in small ways, the power of statistics to teach us new things about the world, and illustrate general analytical approaches that will be developed in upcoming chapters. To understand a relation between two categorical variables, we use cross-tabulations such as Table 1.7 to show percentages of one variable at different levels of a second. Bar charts graphically display differences among these percentages (or proportions). When one of the two variables of interest is a measurement, on the other hand, average comparisons such as Table 1.8, supplemented by histogram comparisons such as Figure 1.5, conveniently summarize their relation.

Relations between two measurement variables, each taking on many different values (such as average math SAT and average verbal SAT in Table 1.4) require a third general approach. Chapter 2 provides an introductory look at this method.

EXERCISES

1.6.1   Cross-tabulate students' expected statistics grade by gender, using the data of Table 1.1 (file *stats*). Place gender as the column variable, as in Table 1.7. Calculate what percentage of the women expect A's, what percentage of the men expect A's, and so forth. Write a paragraph describing your findings.

1.6.2 Calculate average math SAT scores of students expecting A's, B's, or C's in Table 1.1 (file *stats*). Write a paragraph describing your findings.

1.7 Statistics and the Social Sciences

The analytical methods and ideas presented in this book form a common language across the social sciences. If you glance through the scholarly journals that publish cutting-edge research, you will find that many articles—perhaps the majority—are unreadable without up-to-date statistical training. The same is true for other fields as well, from business to zoology. A statistical background enables you to read critically the research of others, while opening possibilities for conducting original studies of your own. It also permits you to browse through unfamiliar disciplines, where scientists may employ similar analytical methods to answer a wide variety of different research questions.

Although statistics forms a common language of science, within individual disciplines it tends to have local "dialects," which emphasize methods suited to the particular kinds of data that each discipline confronts. For example, many psychologists conduct experiments, including some that use introductory psychology students. A simple experiment might involve seeing how one or two categorical treatment variables, controlled by the experimenter, affect some measured response variable. Data from such experiments are easily analyzed by a method called **analysis of variance** (ANOVA), described in Chapter 8. Psychologists also often work with sophisticated methods built upon **correlations** (Chapter 9), which help analyze complicated scales used to measure intelligence, self-confidence, and other mental phenomena that cannot be directly observed. The influence of psychological statistics can be seen in several other fields, notably education, medicine, and health-care research, when their data involve experiments or scales.

Sociologists, political scientists, and economists, in contrast, conduct experiments less often. The variables of most interest to them (such as social class, voting, or income) lie outside the researchers' control. Consequently, people in these fields experience greater difficulties in differentiating between cause and effect. To work around such difficulties, economists have pioneered a wide variety of **regression** methods (Chapters 9–10) for analyzing relations among measurement variables. They emphasize regression methods designed to deal with measurements obtained at many successive times (**time series** data), such as daily stock prices or monthly unemployment rates. The methods developed by economic statisticians have influenced other fields, including sociology and environmental science, where researchers work with nonexperimental measurement data.

Sociologists and political scientists commonly work with survey data, collected at a single time but encompassing dozens or hundreds of variables. Since survey questions often produce categorical variables, cross-tabulation-based methods (Chapter 7) prove useful. More elaborate studies of phenomena with many causes, such as voting behavior or social status, may employ some form of **multiple regression** (Chapter 10). Multiple regression helps sociologists test theories called **causal models**, which appear in journal articles as diagrams with arrows indicating cause and effect.

Of course, there are exceptions to these broad generalizations within each discipline. Researchers freely borrow and adapt methods appropriate for their own particular research questions. When psychologists or sociologists confront time-series data, for instance, they may turn to economic texts for advice. And all of the social sciences follow developments in statistics, where new ideas such as **robust regression** (Chapter 10) are constantly being refined. In each social science's main journals, and in its textbooks, however, certain methods and traditions tend to have more prominence than others.

Summary

This chapter introduced five central concepts of statistics: case, variable, distribution, sample, and population. Cases are the "units of analysis," or the entities about which we have information. Variables record attributes of the cases, and may be of several different types, which require different analytical approaches. For example, percentages work best to summarize categorical-variable distributions, whereas averages serve better to summarize measurement-variable distributions. Extensions of these simple ideas allow us to examine relations between two variables.

Graphs such as histograms (for measurement variables) and bar charts (for categorical variables) display distributions visually. Particularly with measurement variables, graphs can show complex information in an easily understood form. This strength, together with the ease of drawing graphs on computers, has given graphical methods a much larger role in modern data analysis than they played a decade or two ago. Chapter 2 presents more graphical tools.

Data analysis, like this chapter, begins with a dataset in hand. Our purpose in data analysis is to learn what we can from those data, to help us draw conclusions about our broader research questions. Our research questions determine what sort of data we need in the first place, and how we ought to go about collecting them. Unless data collection has been done carefully, even a brilliant analyst may be unable to reach valid conclusions regarding the original research questions.

As its title suggests, this book concentrates on data *analysis*. Although they lie outside our main focus, two topics in data *collection* deserve particular mention: **sampling** and **experiments**. Sampling refers to the process of selecting a subset of cases from the population for analysis, when that population is too large or otherwise inaccessible for direct study. Our ability to generalize about the population may depend on whether we actually have a random sample: one for which every case in the population theoretically had an equal chance of selection. A nonrandom sample could easily be unrepresentative of the population, and hence would provide us with little basis for generalization.

Experiments address a different issue: our ability to draw conclusions about cause and effect. An experimenter directly controls the values of a suspected "cause" variable, then observes the "effect" variable to see what if anything results. This is done in such a way as to minimize the possibility that some other, extraneous variable is producing the effects we see. Nonexperimental researchers, lacking direct control over their variables, instead try to adjust statistically for the effects of extraneous variables. (Chapters 7, 8, and 10 discuss some ways to accomplish statistical adjustment.) Although statistical adjustment gives nonexperimental researchers a powerful tool, it provides much less conclusive evidence about cause and effect than can be obtained from experiments.

PROBLEMS

1.1 Suppose you planned to conduct a survey regarding illegal drug use among college students.
   a. Suggest two questions you might ask about drug use that would produce categorical variables. How might the categories be coded? How could you summarize your findings about these two variables?
   b. Suggest two further questions about drug use that would produce measurement variables. How could your findings with these measurement variables be summarized?
   c. Distinguish between sample and population in your study.

Problems 1.2–1.5 refer to Table 1.9, which contains aggregate data on a sample of U.S. cities. These 20 cities were chosen randomly from the population consisting of all U.S. cities with 1980 populations over 100,000. Variables are:

city	city
region	geographical region
divorce	yearly divorces per 1,000 people 15–59 years of age
educ	median years of education, population over 25 years of age
inequal	an index of inequality; higher values indicate greater inequality (a small fraction of households have a relatively large fraction of the city's wealth)
change	percent change in population from 1970 to 1980

Table 1.9
Data on 20 U.S. cities

city	region	divorce	educ	inequal	change
1. Tulsa	South	13.60	12.8	.42	9.3
2. Columbus	South	12.61	12.3	.43	9.3
3. Dallas	South	11.96	12.7	.45	7.1
4. Virginia Beach	South	7.71	12.8	.36	52.3
5. Fullerton	West	9.98	13.2	.41	18.7
6. Berkeley	West	9.29	16.1	.50	-9.4
7. Honolulu	West	8.11	12.7	.44	12.4
8. Portland	West	10.60	12.8	.43	-3.6
9. Albuquerque	West	13.97	12.9	.40	35.7
10. Salt Lake City	West	10.27	12.9	.45	-7.3
11. Tempe	West	12.72	14.0	.38	68.0
12. Concord	West	9.29	12.9	.33	21.2
13. Sunnyvale	West	10.10	13.2	.35	11.1
14. Rochester	N.East	6.39	12.3	.42	-18.1
15. Allentown	N.East	5.60	12.3	.39	-5.6
16. Erie	N.East	6.61	12.3	.39	-7.8
17. Independence	Midwest	10.08	12.5	.35	.2
18. Peoria	Midwest	9.93	12.6	.43	-2.2
19. Milwaukee	Midwest	6.66	12.6	.39	-11.3
20. Sterling Hts.	Midwest	7.46	12.6	.28	77.6

Source: Williams and Flewelling (1988).
File: *urban*

1.2 Construct frequency tables (grouped if necessary) including percentages, and draw corresponding graphs (bar chart or histogram) for these variables from Table 1.9:
   a. *region*
   b. *divorce*
   c. *educ*
   d. *inequal*
   e. *change*

1.3 Write a brief paragraph comparing the average divorce rates of cities in the four different regions. Suggest two possible explanations for the regional differences you see. Do you think you would find similar regional differences if you had data on all U.S. cities, and not just these 20? Why or why not?

1.4 Write a brief paragraph comparing the average inequality index within each of the four regions.

1.5 Write a brief paragraph comparing the average of population change within each of the four regions.

Sometimes missing values become an object of study in their own right, instead of just a nuisance to research. Seven of the 43 students in Table 1.1 (file *stats*) did not report a math SAT score. Define a new categorical variable called *missat* for each student in Table 1.1. If his or her math SAT score is missing, set *missat* equal to 1. If math SAT is not missing, *missat* equals 0. Problems 1.6–1.11 analyze this new variable to learn more about who left the math SAT question blank, and why.

1.6 Construct a frequency distribution for *missat*, showing frequency and percentage.

1.7 Compare the average quiz scores of *missat* = 0 (nonmissing) and *missat* = 1 (missing) students.

1.8 Compare the average ages of *missat* = 0 and *missat* = 1 students.

1.9 Compare the average expected statistics grades of *missat* = 0 and *missat* = 1 students.

1.10 Cross-tabulate *missat* by gender.

1.11 Write a paragraph based on Problems 1.6–1.10, giving a profile of students who tended to leave the math SAT question blank.

Table 1.10 (file *jobrisk*) contains data on U.S. occupational fatality rates (average number of job-related deaths per 100,000 workers in that occupation, per year), in selected occupations classified either as "blue collar" or "white collar." Problems 1.12–1.16 refer to these data.

Table 1.10
Occupational fatality rates in selected
blue- and white-collar occupations

Occupation	Status	Annual deaths per 100,000 workers
1. oiler	blue	22.5
2. weigher	white	7.1
3. driller	blue	38.8
4. truck driver	blue	39.6
5. metal worker	blue	72.0
6. assessor	white	5.2
7. butcher	blue	13.8
8. geologist	white	9.5
9. advertising agent	white	3.6
10. cable installer	blue	50.7

Table 1.10
(*Continued*)

Occupation	Status	Annual deaths per 100,000 workers
11. restaurant manager	white	5.1
12. public administrator	white	7.2
13. forge operator	blue	14.2
14. surveyor's apprentice	blue	33.3
15. shipfitter	blue	14.2
16. farm-machine operator	blue	14.2
17. engraver	blue	16.6
18. physicist	white	7.6
19. taxicab driver	blue	34.0
20. police officer	blue	17.5
21. veterinarian	white	5.2
22. garbage collector	blue	40.0
23. office worker	white	14.5
24. pilot	white	97.0
25. baker	blue	16.9
26. firefighter	blue	48.8
27. ticket agent	white	3.7
28. bulldozer operator	blue	39.3
29. craftsman	blue	37.5
30. tailor	blue	15.0
31. inspector	white	3.9
32. school administrator	white	4.2
33. technician	white	6.7
34. crane operator	blue	19.3
35. millwright	blue	15.5
36. editor	white	3.6
37. roofer	blue	31.9
38. flight attendant	blue	23.0
39. sheriff	blue	32.4
40. miller	blue	33.3
41. engineer	white	7.3
42. grader	blue	20.9
43. sawyer	blue	15.4
44. logger	blue	129.0
45. boilermaker	blue	35.0
46. coach	white	6.6

(*continued*)

Table 1.10
(*Continued*)

Occupation	Status	Annual deaths per 100,000 workers
47. sales manager	white	4.7
48. manager	white	6.6
49. miner	blue	37.5
50. office manager	white	7.4
51. pharmacist	white	6.5
52. chemist	white	4.2
53. surveyor	white	6.1
54. agricultural scientist	white	9.0
55. architect	white	4.3
56. asbestos worker	blue	78.7
57. loom operator	blue	12.5
58. plasterer	blue	14.2
59. construction worker	blue	33.5
60. union official	white	4.6
61. funeral director	white	4.5
62. computer operator	white	5.0
63. superintendent	white	5.8
64. insurance sales	white	4.9
65. molder	blue	26.6
66. sales manager	white	12.3
67. realtor	white	6.6
68. dispatcher	white	8.3
69. construction inspector	white	7.6
70. athlete	white	6.5

Source: Ubell (1989).
File: *jobrisk*

1.12 Construct a grouped frequency distribution for these occupational death rates, using groups of 0–9.9, 10–19.9, 20–29.9, etc., up to 120–129.9. Include:
   a. a frequency distribution table showing the frequency and percent within each group, including groups such as 60–69.9 that have 0 frequency
   b. a histogram
   c. a brief summary of what the histogram shows about occupational fatality rates

1.13   Separate the occupations and fatality rates of Table 1.10 into blue- and white-collar categories. Construct frequency distributions and histograms as described in Problem 1.12, for the occupational fatality rates within each status (use the same scales in both graphs). Describe what these graphs show about the risks of blue- and white-collar occupations.

1.14   Compare the average fatality rate among blue-collar occupations with the average among white-collar occupations. Do these results support your conclusions in Problem 1.13?

1.15   Status, as defined in Table 1.10, is a categorical variable, and fatality rates are measurements. We can create categorical variables from any measurement variable, however, as illustrated in this problem.

Divide fatality rates into "low" (less than 15 deaths per 100,000 per year) and "high" (15 or more deaths per 100,000 per year) categories. Fill in the following cross-tabulation, including both frequencies and percentages (based on the total number within each column):

Fatality rate	Status		
	blue	white	total
low			
high			
total			

1.16   Use percentages from Problem 1.15 to write a brief statement comparing fatality rates in blue- and white-collar jobs.

1.17   Jorgensen (1990) published a comparison, excerpted in Table 1.11 (page 26; file *gambell*), of food prices in Newport Beach, California, and in Gambell, Alaska, a small community on an island in the Bering Sea. For both economic and cultural reasons, many Gambell families rely on their own hunting, fishing, and gathering efforts to provide themselves with sufficient food.

Construct a bar chart that graphically compares the prices in both communities. The vertical axis of this chart should indicate price. One possible arrangement is to do side-by-side (Newport and Gambell) bars for each commodity, distinguished by different shading.

Table 1.11
Market basket prices in Newport Beach, California,
and in Gambell, Alaska (1988)

Commodity	Newport price	Gambell price
1 pound onions	$ .29	$ 1.70
10 pounds sugar	3.15	7.15
10 pounds flour	1.57	14.45
18 ounces corn flakes	.99	3.25
3 pounds coffee	7.19	10.57
48 ounces cooking oil	1.89	9.95
6-pack cola	1.39	4.74

Source: Jorgensen (1990).
File: *gambell*

2

Graphing Measurement Variable Distributions

This book emphasizes two kinds of analytical tools. **Numerical summaries** are statistics that summarize important features of variable distributions. Averages and percentages are the best-known examples of numerical summaries, but many others exist. Statisticians often employ more elaborate summaries involving mathematical equations, called **models**, which are meant to represent the causal processes that we suspect created the data. In classical statistics, we seek to understand and describe data largely through the appropriate numerical summaries and models.

Recent years have seen new emphasis on a second kind of analytical tool: methods for displaying distributions in **graphical** form. A well-constructed graph can show several features of the data at once. Some graphs contain as much information as the original data, and so (unlike numerical summaries) do not actually simplify the data; rather, they express it in visual form. Unexpected or unusual features, which are not obvious within numerical tables, often jump to our attention once we draw a graph. Because the strengths and weaknesses of graphical methods are opposite those of numerical summary methods, the two work best in combination.

This chapter introduces basic graphical displays that help researchers see variable distributions. We focus on displays for measurement variables. Categorical-variable distributions can also be graphed, but such displays (notably bar charts and pie charts) serve mainly to present results to an audience, and have less importance in data analysis. The information contained in most pie charts, for example, could easily be read from a brief table. Since they convey information that we could not easily grasp by scanning tables of numbers, graphs offer substantial help in analyzing measurement variables.

2.1 Histograms

Histograms display frequency distributions of measurement variables; they show bars covering an area proportional to the frequency, proportion, or percentage of each value. Examples appeared in Figures 1.1, 1.3, and 1.5. If the variable takes on many different values, then we may need grouping to produce a readable table or graph. For graphical purposes, this usually involves grouping data values into a number of equal-width classes or **bins**. Some classes (bins) may contain no cases.

Table 2.1 lists data compiled by the environmentalist League of Conservation Voters, reflecting the percentage of "pro-environment" votes (according to the League) cast by each state's U.S. House of Representatives and Senate delegations in 1990. House voting percentages range from 0% agreement with the environmentalists' positions (Alaska) to 100% agreement (Vermont). The 101 possible values in this range are too many to tabulate in an ungrouped frequency distribution. Table 2.2 (page 30) employs one obvious grouping scheme.

Table 2.1
Average pro-environment voting percentages of
U.S. States' House and Senate delegations, 1990

State	House voting	Senate voting	Region
1. Alabama	39	17	other
2. Alaska	0	13	West
3. Arizona	25	38	West
4. Arkansas	35	54	other
5. California	52	79	West
6. Colorado	53	55	West
7. Connecticut	79	84	New England
8. Delaware	75	71	other
9. Florida	59	55	other
10. Georgia	46	55	other
11. Hawaii	63	59	other
12. Idaho	13	17	West
13. Illinois	70	63	other
14. Indiana	73	25	other
15. Iowa	52	54	other
16. Kansas	63	25	other
17. Kentucky	39	17	other
18. Louisiana	35	25	other
19. Maine	88	84	New England
20. Maryland	68	88	other
21. Massachusetts	81	92	New England
22. Michigan	63	54	other
23. Minnesota	64	42	other
24. Mississippi	28	0	other
25. Missouri	49	21	other
26. Montana	25	25	West
27. Nebraska	38	59	other
28. Nevada	38	96	West
29. New Hampshire	82	46	New England
30. New Jersey	75	100	other
31. New Mexico	29	63	West
32. New York	75	71	other
33. North Carolina	72	33	other
34. North Dakota	38	42	other
35. Ohio	56	67	other
36. Oklahoma	36	8	other

(continued)

Table 2.1 (*Continued*)

State	House voting	Senate voting	Region
37. Oregon	45	84	West
38. Pennsylvania	62	54	other
39. Rhode Island	94	75	New England
40. South Carolina	61	33	other
41. South Dakota	75	63	other
42. Tennessee	54	75	other
43. Texas	42	25	other
44. Utah	29	8	West
45. Vermont	100	80	New England
46. Virginia	32	34	other
47. Washington	57	71	West
48. West Virginia	50	58	other
49. Wisconsin	68	67	other
50. Wyoming	13	8	West

Source: League of Conservation Voters (1990).
File: *envote*

Table 2.2
Grouped frequency distribution of House
"pro-environment" voting percentages

House voting	Frequency	Percentage
x	f	$100 \times f/n$
0–9	1	2%
10–19	2	4
20–29	5	10
30–39	9	18
40–49	4	8
50–59	8	16
60–69	8	16
70–79	8	16
80–89	3	6
90–99	1	2
100–109	1	2
Totals	$n = 50$	100%

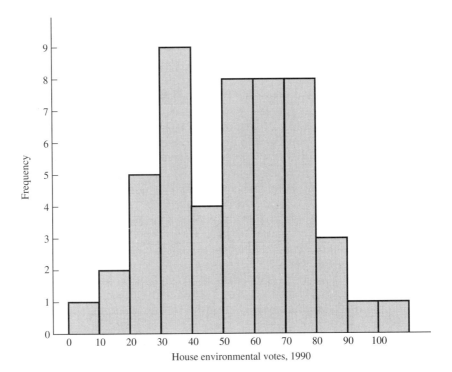

FIGURE 2.1
Histogram of environmental voting scores of 50 state delegations to the U.S. House of Representatives

Figure 2.1 shows a histogram based on the grouping of Table 2.2. The area under a histogram's bars corresponds to the proportion of cases having those values. Table 2.2 indicates that 10% of the U.S. states had voting scores in the 20–29 class; the corresponding bar in Figure 2.1 covers 10% of the graph's total shaded area.

About half the states' delegations voted in the 50's, 60's, and 70's; we see a slight gap, then another peak in the 30's. Only two states' delegations (Rhode Island and Vermont) voted "pro-environment" more than 90% of the time, and three (Alaska, Idaho, and Wyoming) voted "pro-environment" less than 20% of the time.

Notice that the two highest are both in New England, and the three lowest are all in the mountain West. Perhaps environmental voting varies by region? Histograms provide a quick way to investigate. Figure 2.2 (page 32) displays separate histograms for House voting in New England, the mountain West, and other states. For comparison, at lower right it also shows the 50-state distribution, identical to Figure 2.1. The height of each bar in the histogram at the lower right is equal to the sum of the heights of the respective bars in the other three histograms.

We see that the six New England delegations all had pro-environment records (although politically they ranged from liberal Democrats to conservative Republicans).

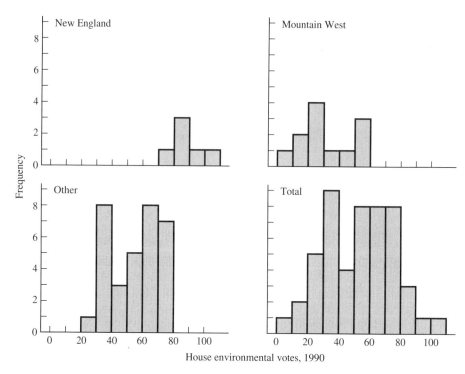

FIGURE 2.2

Histograms of environmental voting scores by region (all states at lower right)

All of Figure 2.1's values above 80% came from New England; Connecticut is the lowest New England state, at 79%. In contrast, most of Figure 2.1's values below 30% come from the mountain West, where many people make their living from resources (such as oil, mines, grazing, or timber) on federal lands. Western states appear less homogeneous than New England, however. Several Western states with diverse nonresource economies have environmental voting records near the national average (California, Colorado, Washington).

Figure 2.1 graphs the distribution of one measurement variable, House environmental voting. We might also draw histograms that display one measurement variable's distribution at specific values of a second variable. For example, Figure 2.2 shows the distribution of environmental voting among New England, Mountain West, and other states. These separate histograms illustrate a concept called **conditional distributions**: distributions of one variable (in this example, environmental voting) at specific values of a second variable (here, region = "New England," region = "Mountain West," and region = "other"). Conditional distributions provide information about whether, and how, two variables are related. Figure 2.1 and the "Total" graph at the lower right in Figure 2.2 represent unconditional distributions.

EXERCISES

2.1.1   Construct a histogram to show the distribution of Senate environmental voting from Table 2.1 (file *envote*). Briefly describe what you see.

2.1.2   Create separate histograms for Senate voting by region, in the manner of Figure 2.2. Describe what you see. Are these results consistent with our earlier conclusions about the relation between region and environmental voting?

*2.2   **Graphing Cumulative Distributions**

Cumulative frequency distributions report the frequency, proportion, or percentage of cases at a certain value *or less*. Table 2.3 illustrates these using the House voting data. Its first two columns copy Table 2.2. Since one state voted in the 0–9 class, and two in the 10–19 class, a total of three states (cum(f) = 3) voted 10–19 or less. Eight states (cum(f) = 8) voted 20–29 or less, and so on. Ninety percent voted 70–79 or less; 100% voted 100–109 or less.

Table 2.3
Cumulative grouped frequency distribution
of House pro-environment voting percentages

House voting	Frequency	Cumulative frequency	Cumulative proportion	Cumulative percent
x	f	cum(f)	cum(f)/n	100 × cum(f)/n
0–9	1	1	.02	2%
10–19	2	3	.06	6
20–29	5	8	.16	16
30–39	9	17	.34	34
40–49	4	21	.42	42
50–59	8	29	.58	58
60–69	8	37	.74	74
70–79	8	45	.90	90
80–89	3	48	.96	96
90–99	1	49	.98	98
100–109	1	50	1.00	100

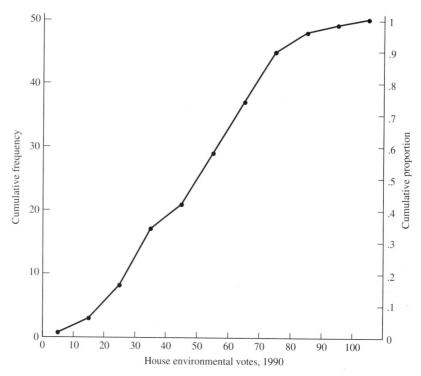

FIGURE 2.3

Grouped cumulative distribution of 50 state delegations' environmental voting scores, with cumulative frequency and cumulative proportion axes

Figure 2.3 graphs the cumulative distribution of Table 2.3, with vertical axes labeled to show both frequency (at left) and proportion (at right). We could have drawn histogram-style bars, but cumulative frequency distributions are more often graphed by curves. The curve in Figure 2.3 simply connects points at the midpoint of each class interval. That is, we connected the points (4.5, 1), (14.5, 3), (24.5, 8), and so on. Frequency distributions that have roughly "bell-shaped" histograms (as in Figure 2.1) produce somewhat "S-shaped" cumulative frequency curves. Such curves rise steeply in the middle but flatten out toward the lower-left and upper-right corners of the graph.

Grouping, as in Table 2.2, is often necessary for histograms but not needed for cumulative frequency graphs. Since grouping takes effort and reduces accuracy, a better way to proceed (especially if we have a computer) is to calculate the proportion of cases at or below each individual case in an ordered list, as seen in Table 2.4. Since each state constitutes $1/50 = .02$ of these data, the *proportion at or below* rises by .02 with each successive case. Notice that for this graphical purpose, we assigned cumulative proportions to the tied cases as if they were not tied. The order of such tied cases (for example, Wyoming before Idaho or vice versa) does not matter.

Table 2.4
Proportion of cases at or below each value of House voting

State	House voting	Proportion at or below
	x	cum(f)/n
1. Alaska	0	.02
2. Wyoming	13	.04
3. Idaho	13	.06
4. Arizona	25	.08
5. Montana	25	.10
6. Mississippi	28	.12
7. Utah	29	.14
8. New Mexico	29	.16
9. Virginia	32	.18
10. Arkansas	35	.20
11. Louisiana	35	.22
12. Oklahoma	36	.24
13. Nevada	38	.26
14. North Dakota	38	.28
15. Nebraska	38	.30
16. Kentucky	39	.32
17. Alabama	39	.34
18. Texas	42	.36
19. Oregon	45	.38
20. Georgia	46	.40
21. Missouri	49	.42
22. West Virginia	50	.44
23. Iowa	52	.46
24. California	52	.48
25. Colorado	53	.50
26. Tennessee	54	.52
27. Ohio	56	.54
28. Washington	57	.56
29. Florida	59	.58
30. South Carolina	61	.60
31. Pennsylvania	62	.62
32. Michigan	63	.64
33. Hawaii	63	.66
34. Kansas	63	.68

(*continued*)

Table 2.4 (*Continued*)

State	House voting	Proportion at or below
	x	cum(f)/n
35. Minnesota	64	.70
36. Wisconsin	68	.72
37. Maryland	68	.74
38. Illinois	70	.76
39. North Carolina	72	.78
40. Indiana	73	.80
41. Delaware	75	.82
42. South Dakota	75	.84
43. New Jersey	75	.86
44. New York	75	.88
45. Connecticut	79	.90
46. Massachusetts	81	.92
47. New Hampshire	82	.94
48. Maine	88	.96
49. Rhode Island	94	.98
50. Vermont	100	1.00

Figure 2.4 shows a cumulative distribution based on Table 2.4: It simply connects the points (0, .02), (13, .04), (13, .06), (25, .08), and so on. Tied cases produce vertical steps in the curve, where the cumulative proportion increases but x value (voting) remains the same. Graphs such as Figure 2.4 allow readers to estimate the proportion of cases at or below any given value, without referring back to the original data. For example, from Figure 2.4 we can see that about half of the states have voting indexes in the mid-50's or less.

Graphs based on cumulative height and weight distributions often appear in doctors' offices where, for example, they are used to look up the proportion of 12-year-olds who weigh less than 80 pounds. Other common applications for cumulative distributions occur in educational testing where, for example, they are used to determine the proportion of students that scored below 650 on a certain test.

EXERCISES

*2.2.1 Construct a grouped cumulative frequency distribution table from the Senate voting data (file *envote*), employing classes of 0–9, 10–19, etc. Graph this grouped cumulative frequency distribution.

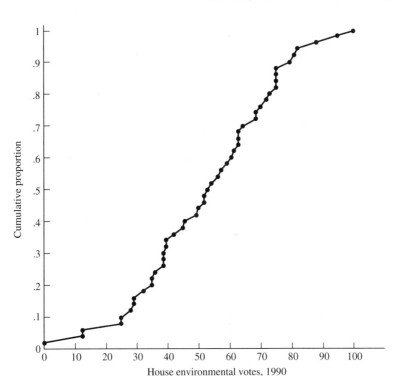

FIGURE 2.4
Ungrouped cumulative distribution of 50 state delegations' environmental
voting scores

*2.2.2   Construct an ungrouped cumulative frequency distribution graph in the manner
of Table 2.4 and Figure 2.4, using the math SAT variable in Table 1.1 (file
stats). Include only those 35 students with nonmissing and reasonable (less
than 800) math SAT values.

2.3   Graphs and Distribution Shape

The shapes of variable distributions commonly fall into one of several broad types. One
type, **symmetrical** distributions, encompasses any shape in which the left half looks
like a mirror image of the right. Symmetry implies equal proportions of cases at any
given distance above and below the center. Figure 2.5 (page 38) illustrates with four
histograms that show approximately symmetrical distributions. At lower right in
Figure 2.5 is an important kind of symmetrical distribution called "bell shaped." Many

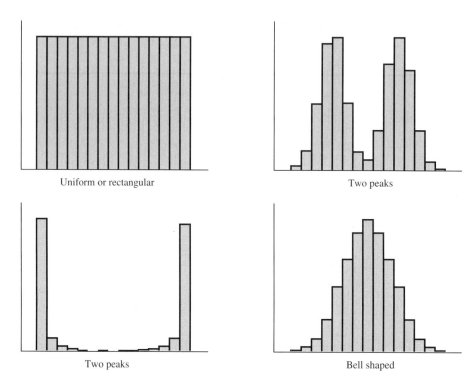

Uniform or rectangular

Two peaks

Two peaks

Bell shaped

FIGURE 2.5
Four examples of symmetrical distributions

variables, including scores on standardized tests such as IQ and SAT, tend to have bell-shaped distributions.

Distributions that are not symmetrical are called **skewed**. Skewed distributions having a drawn-out left tail, like the two at the left in Figure 2.6, are termed **negatively skewed**. **Positively skewed** distributions, like the two at the right in Figure 2.6, possess drawn-out right tails. Either positive or negative skewness is a matter of degree; some distributions are more skewed than others. Skewed distributions complicate the job of statistical analysis.

Although statisticians may hope for symmetry, what they often get instead with real data is positive skew. In positively skewed distributions, most of the cases have low or middling x values, but some cases with much higher values produce the drawn-out right-hand tail, perhaps ending with one or more **high outliers** (exceptionally high values). Positive skew occurs frequently in variables that have a lower limit of zero, but no definite upper limit—such as income, air pollution, or anything counted (family size, number of arrests, population density, and so forth). Skew complicates analysis because such distributions have no unambiguous center, and because the long right or left tail tends to affect the average and other statistics. A too-hard final exam might result in a positively skewed grade distribution: most students scoring low, but a few scoring high and pulling the class average up (perhaps to their peers' dismay).

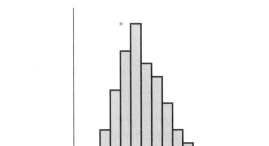

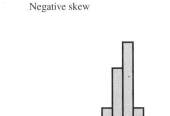

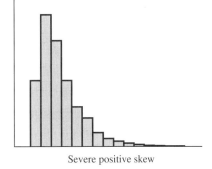

FIGURE 2.6
Four examples of skewed distributions

Negative skew occurs when most cases have middling or high values of *x*, but a few are very much lower. Consequently, we see a longer left tail, perhaps ending with one or more **low outliers** (exceptionally low values). Negative skew leads to the same analytical complications as positive skew, but in the opposite direction. A too-easy final exam might produce negatively skewed grades: most students earning high scores, but a few who forgot to study pulling the class average down.

Multiple peaks sometimes warn us that we have mixed two or more dissimilar kinds of cases together. Two of the symmetrical distributions in Figure 2.5 exhibit multiple peaks, which can also occur in skewed distributions. The one at top right in Figure 2.5 was produced by mixing values from two bell-shaped distributions with different centers. The original bell-shaped distributions would be easy to analyze separately; it is less simple, however, to summarize a multipeaked distribution. An average could be misleading. Exam scores might exhibit two peaks if a class contains two kinds of students, those who "get it" and those who do not, but with few students in between. Multiple peaks invite further study, to identify and individually examine the subpopulations.

Figure 2.7 (page 40) depicts several differently shaped distributions in cumulative form. Cumulative distribution curves climb steeply in regions with lots of data, such as the middle of a bell-shaped distribution, and climb slowly in regions with sparse data.

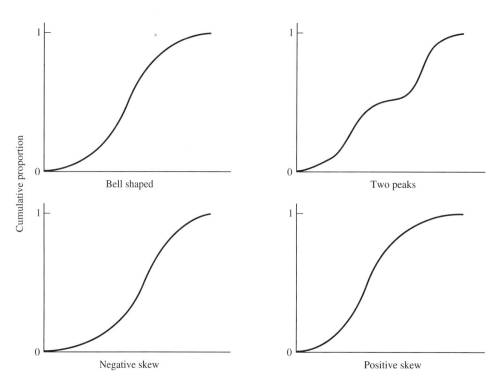

FIGURE 2.7
Four cumulative distributions with different shapes

The cumulative proportion (height of the curve) equals .5 at the x variable's average, which lies near the midpoint of the horizontal scale. Positive skew produces a cumulative curve that takes off steeply, then gradually flattens. The cumulative proportion reaches .5 (mid-height) well before the x average (mid-horizontal). Negative skew causes the opposite: a cumulative curve that takes off gradually, but then flattens abruptly. The curve reaches .5 well after passing the x average. Gaps between multiple peaks produce local flat sections, so the curve resembles several simpler curves stacked together (upper right in Figure 2.7).

Many statistical techniques work best when variables have bell-shaped distributions. Before trusting such techniques, however, it is necessary to check on the actual shapes of the data distributions. Graphs provide the simplest way to do so.

EXERCISES

2.3.1 Describe the shapes of the following distributions, and explain in real-world terms what those shapes tell us:
    a. statistics quiz scores (Figure 1.1)
    b. college enrollments (Figure 1.3)
    c. House environmental voting (Figure 2.1)

2.3.2 Sketch and describe the shapes you would expect for these distributions:

a. weights, for a sample consisting of equal numbers of Olympic marathon runners and sumo wrestlers

b. house values, for all houses in the state of Florida

c. final exam scores, in a class where most of the students understood the material, but a few did not

d. number of brothers and sisters, for all students at your school

2.4 Stem-and-Leaf Displays

Imaginative statisticians continually invent new methods for graphical analysis. One of these, called the **stem-and-leaf display**, went from being an unfamiliar concept in 1977—one of many new ideas in John Tukey's (1977) influential book *Exploratory Data Analysis*—to a tool so obvious it now appears in sixth-grade math textbooks. Stem-and-leaf displays modify the histogram by replacing bars with numbers from the data. Histograms and cumulative frequency distributions are most easily graphed with computers, and they can represent infinitely large datasets. Stem-and-leaf displays, in contrast, provide a wonderful paper-and-pencil method for analyzing small datasets, without much effort, even on the back of an envelope.

Figure 2.8 shows a stem-and-leaf display of the House environmental voting data. Stems, the column of numbers at the left, are the data's initial digits. Here they represent the tens digit of each voting value. For example, any state with an environmental voting score in the 30's belongs on the 3 stem (meaning 3 tens). Leaves, to the right of the display's vertical line, show the data's second digits. In Figure 2.8, leaves represent ones. Virginia's representatives agreed with environmentalists on 32% of their votes; we show this 32 as a 2 leaf (meaning 2 ones) on the 3 stem (3 tens). The Arkansas and Louisiana delegations both sided with environmentalists on 35% of their votes, so the next two leaves on the 3 stem are a pair of 5's. These are followed by a 6 representing Oklahoma's 36, and so on. Putting the leaves in ascending order (as in 3 | 2556 . . .) requires an extra step if we did not begin with an ordered list like Table 2.4.

FIGURE 2.8
Stem-and-leaf display for House environmental voting (compare with Figure 2.1). Stems digits are 10's, leaves are 1's; 9 | 4 means 94% of votes cast along "pro-environment" lines.

0	0
1	3 3
2	5 5 8 9 9
3	2 5 5 6 8 8 8 9 9
4	2 5 6 9
5	0 2 2 3 4 6 7 9
6	1 2 3 3 3 4 8 8
7	0 2 3 5 5 5 5 9
8	1 2 8
9	4
10	0

Figure 2.8 has the same shape as the histogram in Figure 2.1, only turned on its side. Thus stem-and-leaf displays convey exactly the same information about distributional shape as histograms. But where a histogram has bars, stem-and-leaf displays show individual data values—information that is lost in a histogram. We can reconstruct the raw data exactly from Figure 2.8, but not from Figure 2.1. Both Figures 2.1 and 2.8 tell us that three states scored in the 80's, but only Figure 2.8 gives their individual values as 81, 82, and 88. A further advantage is that by using initial digits to define the stems, stem-and-leaf displays simplify the work of grouping data.

If the data contain more than two digits, leaves are **truncated** rather than rounded off. For example, 15.9 would appear as 1 | 5, a 5 leaf on the 1 stem (that is, truncated to 15), rather than rounded off to 16. This speeds hand preparation of stem-and-leaf displays, and makes it easier to refer back and forth between display and data.

Figure 2.9 illustrates a **double-stem** version of a stem-and-leaf display, using the math SAT scores from Table 1.1. Most of the 35 scores begin with the numbers 4 or 5 (400's or 500's). Double-stem versions allow us to spread the display out a bit by creating two stems for each initial digit, marking the first with an asterisk and the second with a period. For example:

> 4*   initial digit 4, second digit of 0–4
> 4.   initial digit 4, second digit of 5–9

Thus scores from 400 to 449 (after truncating 449 to 4* | 4) would appear on the 4* stem in Figure 2.9; scores from 450 to 499 (truncating 499 to 4. | 9) would appear on the 4. stem. Similarly:

> 5*   initial digit 5, second digit of 0–4
> 5.   initial digit 5, second digit of 5–9
> and so on.

FIGURE 2.9
Stem-and-leaf display for students'
self-reported math SAT scores.
Double-Stem version: Stems digits
are 100's, leaves are 10's; 3. | 7
means a math SAT score of 370
points.

3.	7
4*	0 1 2 2 3 3 3
4.	5 6 7 8 9 9 9 9
5*	1 2 2 2 4 4 4 4 4 4
5.	5 5 6 7
6*	0 1 1 3
6.	
7*	2

To spread a display further we could resort to a **five-stem** version, creating five stems for each initial digit as illustrated with student ages (from Table 1.1) in Figure 2.10. The symbols denote, for example:

> 2*   initial digit 2, second digit zero or one
> 2t   initial digit 2, second digit **t**wo or **t**hree
> 2f   initial digit 2, second digit **f**our or **f**ive
> 2s   initial digit 2, second digit **s**ix or **s**even
> 2.   initial digit 2, second digit eight or nine

For some purposes, Figure 2.10 appears too spread out; we might improve readability by listing the 43-year-old separately, and showing the display only from 1s | 7 (a 17-year-old) to 3* | 0 (a 30-year-old). As it is, however, the display dramatizes the large age-gap separating one or two nontraditional students from the rest of their classmates.

```
1s  │  7
1.  │  8 8 8 8 8 8 9 9 9 9
2*  │  0 0 0 0 0 0 0 0 0 0 0 0 0 0 0 0 0 1 1 1 1 1 1
2t  │  2 2 2 3
2f  │  4 4 5
2s  │
2.  │
3*  │  0
3t  │
3f  │
3s  │
3.  │
4*  │
4t  │  3
```

FIGURE 2.10
Stem-and-leaf display for students' ages. *Five-stem version*: Stems digits are 10's, leaves are 1's; 4t | 3 means 43 years old.

▓▓ EXERCISES ▓▓

2.4.1   Construct a stem-and-leaf display for the Senate voting variable of Table 2.1 (file *envote*). Include a label explaining what the stems and leaves represent. Briefly describe the distribution's shape.

2.4.2   Construct a double-stem stem-and-leaf display for the inequality index of Table 1.9 (file *urban*). Use stems of 2., 3*, 3., 4*, 4., and 5* where stems digits are 0.1's, leaves are 0.01's. Include a label. Briefly describe the distribution's shape.

2.4.3   Construct a five-stem stem-and-leaf display for the divorce rates of Table 1.9. Use stems of 0f, 0s, 0., 1*, and 1t, where stems digits are 10's, leaves are 1's. Include a label. Briefly describe the distribution's shape.

2.5 ▲ **Time Plots**

Time plots graphically track one or more variables over time. Figure 2.11 (page 44) shows an example. Canada's easternmost province, Newfoundland, was settled largely for its cod fishing. Until quite recently, fishing remained the main pillar of Newfoundland's economy and culture. The people in hundreds of fishing villages around Newfoundland's rocky coast have no other livelihood. Figure 2.11 depicts dramatic changes from 1960 to 1991. During the 1960s and early 1970s, ships from many coun-

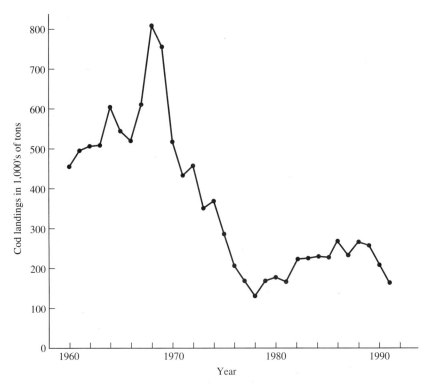

FIGURE 2.11
Time plot showing the total codfish catch off Newfoundland from 1960 to 1991

tries took huge quantities of cod in the waters around Newfoundland, driving fish populations down to levels from which they have not recovered. After a decade of fluctuation, codfish landings fell drastically again in the early 1990s.

Table 2.5
Northern codfish landings (in thousands of metric tons)
off Newfoundland, 1960–1994

Year	Total catch	Canadian catch	Quota
1960	459	165	.
1961	498	124	.
1962	503	143	.
1963	509	149	.

(*continued*)

Table 2.5 (*Continued*)

Year	Total catch	Canadian catch	Quota
1964	603	142	.
1965	545	118	.
1966	524	119	.
1967	612	115	.
1968	810	123	.
1969	754	116	.
1970	520	91	.
1971	440	75	.
1972	458	67	.
1973	355	44	666
1974	373	36	657
1975	288	42	554
1976	214	63	300
1977	173	80	160
1978	139	102	135
1979	167	131	180
1980	176	148	180
1981	171	147	200
1982	230	208	237
1983	232	214	260
1984	233	203	266
1985	231	187	266
1986	267	199	266
1987	236	200	256
1988	266	240	266
1989	253	215	235
1990	219	191	199
1991	171	120	190
1992	.	21	120
1993	.	9	0
1994	.	0	0

Source: Statistics Canada (1991).
File: *newfcod*

One strength of time plots is their ability to show how several variables change together; this helps us both to learn from the data and to tell a story. Figure 2.12 (page 46) graphs all three of the time series from Table 2.5. In 1977, Canada declared a 200-mile fishing limit, within which it began enforcing quotas meant to protect fish popula-

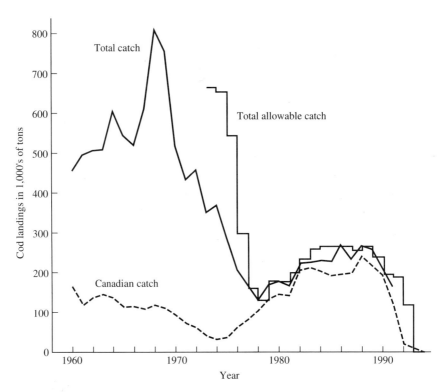

FIGURE 2.12
Time plot showing the collapse of Newfoundland's codfish industry: total catch,
Canadian catch, and total allowable catch (official quota)

tions and supply Canadian fishers first. The Canadian share of the total catch grew larger
as Canadians took over where foreigners had been. Meanwhile the foreign fleets re-
treated scarcely beyond Canada's 200-mile limit. Under continuing pressure, the fish did
not recover as hoped. In 1992, Newfoundland's codfish populations collapsed. Besides
the decades of overfishing, some people blamed North Atlantic temperature changes and
the growth of Newfoundland's fish-eating seal population after animal rights activists
had ruined the international market for furs. To protect the few remaining fish, the government had to ban northern cod fishing altogether. Over 26,000 people immediately
lost their jobs, and a centuries-old way of life came to an end.

EXERCISE

2.5.1   Table 2.6 (file *whales*) lists the annual worldwide catch of three species of
       whales, at 5-year intervals from 1920 to 1985. Blue, fin, and sei whales are re-

lated species: blues the largest and commercially most valuable, fins the second largest, and sei whales third. Today all three species survive precariously, with only small fractions of their prehunting populations. Construct a time plot showing all three time series of Table 2.6. What story does this plot tell?

Table 2.6
Worldwide catch of three whale species
at 5-year intervals, 1920–1985

Year	Blue	Fin	Sei
1920	2,274	4,946	1,120
1925	7,548	9,121	1,093
1930	19,079	14,281	841
1935	16,834	14,078	962
1940	11,559	19,924	541
1945	1,111	2,653	218
1950	6,313	22,902	2,471
1955	2,495	32,185	1,940
1960	1,465	31,064	7,035
1965	613	12,351	25,454
1970	0	5,057	11,195
1975	0	1,634	4,975
1980	0	472	102
1985	0	218	38

Source: Council on Environmental Quality (1987).
File: *whales*

Scatterplots

2.6

Scatterplots provide basic tools for visualizing the joint distribution of two measurement variables. Figure 2.13 (page 48) illustrates a scatterplot using the voting data from Table 2.1. By convention, we refer to the horizontal axis (House voting in Figure 2.13) as x and the vertical axis (Senate voting) as y. Each state appears as a point, with (x, y) coordinates given by its House and Senate voting percentages. Thus Alabama has co-ordinates (39, 17), Alaska (0, 13), Arizona (25, 38), Arkansas (35, 54), and so on. If one variable causes another, that "cause" variable (also called the **independent variable**) goes on the x-axis, and the "effect" (**dependent variable**) goes on the y-axis. With House and Senate voting, however, our choice of x and y seems arbitrary.

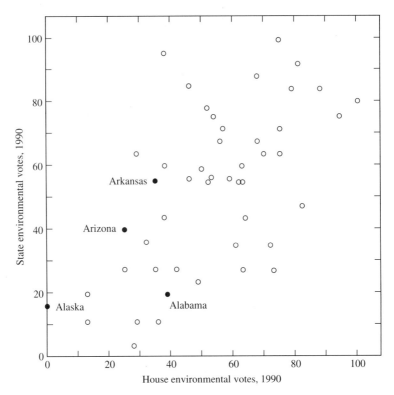

FIGURE 2.13
Scatterplot of 50 states' Senate environmental voting scores (y, or vertical axis) versus House environmental voting scores (x, or horizontal axis)

The scatter of points in Figure 2.13 tends vaguely upward, left to right. This indicates that, on average, states with higher House environmental voting scores tended also to have higher Senate scores. The relationship is far from perfect; some states' delegations (for example, Nevada or Indiana) exhibit considerable disagreement. More often, however, we see at least moderate consistency.

Many variations on scatterplots enhance their ability to convey complex information. For example, Figure 2.14 modifies Figure 2.13 by using different symbols to distinguish three subgroups of states: New England (solid squares), Western (open squares), and others (circles). Five of the six New England states cluster toward upper right, with high scores for both Senate and House delegations. (New Hampshire's Senators had noticeably lower scores than their House colleagues.) Western states appear to fall into two groups: one group (Alaska, Arizona, Idaho, Montana, Utah, and Wyoming) with low scores for both Senate and House delegations; the other group with more moderate House scores and moderate to high Senate scores.

Figure 2.14 displays visually the joint distribution of three variables at once: Sen-

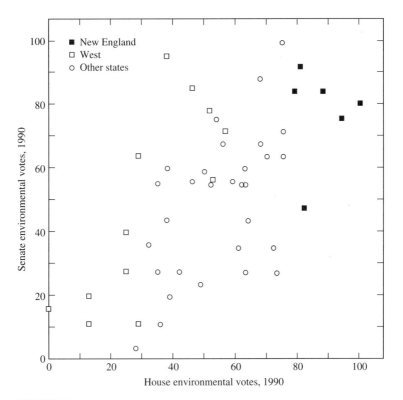

FIGURE 2.14
Scatterplot of Senate and House environmental voting, showing New England, Western, and other states

ate voting score, House voting score, and region. In principle, we could reconstruct the original dataset of Table 2.1 by reading carefully from the scatterplot in Figure 2.14. Therefore, Figure 2.14 must contain as much information as the original table, although organized in a different form.

EXERCISES

2.6.1 Using data from Table 1.4 (file *college1*), draw a scatterplot of the schools' average verbal SAT scores (arbitrarily, as *y*) versus their average math SAT scores (*x*). Include school names in this plot. Describe the general pattern you see. Do any schools seem not to fit this general pattern?

2.6.2 Draw a scatterplot involving the percent male and the average math SAT score for the schools in Table 1.4. Decide for yourself which variable should be *y*, and explain why. What, if any, overall pattern do you see?

Summary

This chapter introduced some basic techniques for analytical graphing. Analytical graphs are visual displays employed by researchers to gain insights into their data. Such displays differ in design and purpose from presentation graphics, such as pie or bar charts, which researchers might use to present conclusions to an audience after analysis is complete. A few types of graphs, notably time plots, serve both analytical and presentation purposes.

Histograms and stem-and-leaf displays show us a distribution's shape—for example, whether it appears symmetrical, skewed, or has multiple peaks. Stem-and-leaf displays are particularly useful for a quick analysis of small datasets by hand; computers can easily draw histograms from datasets of any size, or draw separate histograms to compare subgroups of the sample. Cumulative distribution graphs allow us to read what proportion of the cases fall below any particular value.

A distribution's shape can reveal interesting things about the real world. Furthermore, departures from the "ideal" bell shape can complicate data analysis, or easily distort the results. As we will see in Chapter 3, even simple statistics, such as averages, become problematic when applied to skewed distributions. Such problems emphasize the importance of graphs. If we fail to notice important features of distributional shape at an early stage in our analysis, we risk drawing nonsensical conclusions later on.

Scatterplots are among the most versatile and important tools of analytical graphics. Chapters 9 and 10 return to this topic, with statistical methods for summarizing what a scatterplot shows.

What We Learn from Measurement-Variable Graphs

Histograms

Histograms reveal a distribution's shape, including its approximate center, symmetry or skew, and the presence of any multiple peaks, gaps, or outliers. Areas under a histogram's bars correspond to the proportion of cases having that value or range of values.

Cumulative Frequency Graphs

Cumulative frequency graphs are most useful for seeing how a particular *y* value compares with the rest of the distribution: We can read what proportion of a distribution is above or below that *y* value; or conversely, what *y* value is higher than a certain proportion (such as 50%, 75%, or 99%) of the data.

Stem-and-Leaf Displays

Like histograms, stem-and-leaf displays show a distribution's shape, but they are quicker to draw by hand and provide a more detailed picture, especially in small samples.

Time Plots

Time plots visualize how a measurement variable changed over time, or whether several such variables changed together.

Scatterplots

Scatterplots graph the joint distribution of two measurement variables. As we look from left to right, does the cloud of points exhibit any systematic upward or downward drift, or other pattern? That is, does y tend to change as x increases?

PROBLEMS

The dataset on Boston-area beach pollution in Table 2.7 forms the basis for Problems 2.1–2.3.

Table 2.7
Coliform bacteria counts from water
of 21 Boston-area beaches, summer 1987

Beach	Average bacteria count per ml	Highest measured bacteria count per ml
Carson Beach	45	>4,000
Constitution Beach	35	2,080
Houghton's Pond	9	40
Kings Beach	22	>4,000
Lovell Island	13	268
Lynn Beach	22	2,000

(*continued*)

Table 2.7 (*Continued*)

Beach	Average bacteria count per ml	Highest measured bacteria count per ml
Malibu Beach	16	275
Nahant Beach	14	375
Nantasket Beach	12	148
Pearce Lake	15	95
Peckem Pond	18	150
Pleasure Bay	30	242
Revere Beach	13	262
Sandy Beach	10	40
Short Beach	8	32
Stacey Brook Outlet	10	>4,000
Swampscott Beach	21	>4,000
Tenean Beach	52	2,260
Winthrop Beach	13	138
Wollaston Beach	88	>4,000
Yirrel Beach	8	48

Source: Lehman (1988).
File: *beach*

2.1   Draw a histogram of average coliform bacteria count, and briefly describe what it shows.

*2.2   For average coliform bacteria count, draw a cumulative distribution curve, such as Figure 2.4, with the vertical axis indicating cumulative proportion. Show how to read this curve, if it were published alone without the supporting data, to determine:
   a.   whether the frequency distribution is symmetrical, skewed, or has multiple peaks
   b.   what proportion of beaches have average counts below 20 bacteria/ml
   c.   what proportion of beaches have average counts above 40 bacteria/ml
   d.   what bacteria count falls in the middle of this distribution, with 50% of the beaches higher and 50% lower

2.3   Draw a scatterplot based on the Boston beach data, with:

y variable   highest measured counts (plotting >4,000 values as if they equaled 4,000)

x variable   average counts

Describe what the plot tells us about these 21 beaches.

2.4   In the 1994 Winter Olympics at Lillehammer, Norway, 44 skiers completed the women's downhill ski race. Table 2.8 (file *downhill*) lists their times.

     a.   Construct a grouped frequency histogram showing skiers' race times; describe the shape of this distribution.
     b.   Construct a scatterplot of place (*y* axis) versus time (*x* axis).
     c.   What do your histogram and scatterplot reveal about these 44 skiers?

Table 2.8
Times of downhill racers in 1994 Winter Olympics

Place	Skier	Country	Time (sec.)
1	Katja Seizinger (gold)	Germany	95.93
2	Picabo Street (silver)	United States	96.59
3	Isolde Kostner (bronze)	Italy	96.85
4	Martina Ertl	Germany	97.10
5	Catherine Pace	Canada	97.17
6	Melanie Suchet	France	97.34
7	Hillary Lindh	United States	97.44
8	Varvara Zelenskaia	Russia	97.48
9	Pernilla Wiberg	Sweden	97.61
10	Katja Koren	Slovenia	97.69
11	Jeanette Lunde	Norway	97.80
12	Miriam Vogt	Germany	97.86
13	Florence Masnada	France	97.92
14	Morena Gallizio	Italy	97.94
14	Veronic Stallmaier	Austria	97.94
16	Alenka Dovzan	Slovenia	98.07
17	Svetlana Gladischeva	Russia	98.10
18	Katharina Gutensohn	Germany	98.14
19	Kerrin Lee-Gartner	Canada	98.22
20	Megan Gerety	United States	98.24
21	Emi Kawabata	Japan	98.29
22	Heidi Zurbriggen	Switzerland	98.46
23	Spela Pretnar	Slovenia	98.50
24	Olga Vediacheva	Kazakhstan	98.58
25	Barbara Merlin	Italy	98.65

(*continued*)

Table 2.8 (*Continued*)

Place	Skier	Country	Time (sec.)
26	Regine Cavagnoud	France	98.69
27	Krista Schmidinger	United States	98.76
28	Heidi Zeller-Baehler	Switzerland	98.78
29	Nathalie Bouvier	France	98.85
30	Michelle Ruthven	Canada	98.88
31	Anja Haas	Austria	98.98
32	Lucia Medzihradska	Slovakia	99.22
33	Vreni Schneider	Switzerland	99.35
34	Erika Hansson	Sweden	99.40
35	Natalia Buga	Russia	100.93
36	Mihaela Fera	Romania	101.07
37	Olga Loginova	Ukraine	103.07
38	Mira Goloub	Russia	103.21
39	Szvetlana Kesthlyi	Hungary	103.33
40	Maria Zarug	Romania	105.73
41	Francisca Steverlynck	Argentina	106.76
42	Kristina Podhrushna	Ukraine	106.96
43	Gabriela Quijano	Argentina	109.26
44	Jennifer Taylor	Argentina	109.53

File: *downhill*

2.5 Biologists studying islands have observed that biodiversity, or the number of different kinds of animals and plants present, tends to increase with island size. Larger islands usually have a greater variety of habitats, and thus support a greater variety of life. Table 2.9 (file *islands*) contains data illustrating this relation. The cases are eight Pacific island groups; for each group we have the land area, number of bird genera, and number of angiosperm or flowering plant genera. (*Genera*, plural of genus, are biological classifications including one or more related species.) Construct two scatterplots, and describe what they show about island biodiversity and land area.

    a. Construct a scatterplot showing the number of bird genera (*y*) versus land area (*x*), and describe what it reveals.

    b. Graph the number of flowering plant genera (*y*) versus land area (*x*), and describe what this reveals.

    c. Why should the biodiversity measures appear as the *y* (vertical axis) variables in parts **a** and **b**?

Table 2.9
Land area and the number of bird genera and non-endemic
angiosperm (flowering plant) genera on some Pacific island groups

Island	Land area (km²)	Bird genera	Flowering plant genera
Solomon Islands	40,000	126	654
New Caledonia	22,000	64	655
Fiji Islands	18,500	54	476
New Hebrides	15,000	59	396
Samoa group	3,100	33	302
Society Islands	1,700	17	201
Tonga group	1,000	18	263
Cook Islands	250	10	126

Source: Cox and Moore (1993).
File: *islands*

2.6 Construct stem-and-leaf displays for the three variables in Table 2.10 (file *airline*), and describe what they show:
   a. baggage complaints per 1,000 passengers
   b. percentage of flights arriving on time (double-stem version)
   c. consumer complaints per 100,000 passengers (five-stem version)

Table 2.10
Data on 14 major airlines during October and November 1987

Airline	Consumer complaints per 100,000 passengers	Percentage of flights arriving on time	Baggage complaints per 1,000 passengers
American	4.0	86.1	7.3
Southwest	1.6	85.2	3.9
Continental	17.2	84.4	7.1
Piedmont	2.2	83.2	6.5
Eastern	12.4	83.0	2.9
United	5.1	80.7	10.3

(*continued*)

Table 2.10 (*Continued*)

Airline	Consumer complaints per 100,000 passengers	Percentage of flights arriving on time	Baggage complaints per 1,000 passengers
United	5.1	80.7	10.3
Trans World	9.5	79.4	7.4
Pan American	11.8	79.2	4.0
Delta	1.9	77.5	6.0
USAir	3.4	77.3	5.5
Northwest	19.1	76.5	10.6
Alaska	2.6	75.2	7.4
America West	2.5	74.9	7.2
Pacific Southwest	2.5	60.3	4.1

Source: *Boston Globe*, December 3, 1987.
File: *airline*

2.7   Table 2.11 (file *parks*) contains data on overnight tent and recreational vehicle (RV) camping in U.S. national parks from 1960 to 1989. Draw a time plot of these data. Do you know of any socioeconomic trends that might explain:
   a.   the rise of tent camping in the early 1960s
   b.   the subsequent rise of RV camping
   c.   the decline in tent camping after 1970
   d.   the decline in RV camping during the 1980s

Table 2.11
Number of overnight campers (in millions)
in U.S. national parks, 1960–1989

Year	Tent nights	RV nights
1960	3.59	1.26
1961	3.59	1.47
1962	4.31	1.81
1963	4.62	2.15
1964	5.04	2.41
1965	5.10	2.98
1966	5.06	3.94

(*continued*)

Table 2.11 (*Continued*)

Year	Tent nights	RV nights
1967	4.72	4.59
1968	4.79	4.62
1969	4.39	4.66
1970	4.68	4.34
1971	3.48	4.45
1972	3.65	4.73
1973	3.80	4.88
1974	3.79	4.62
1975	3.74	5.08
1976	3.87	5.40
1977	3.97	5.35
1978	3.78	5.35
1979	3.42	4.45
1980	3.93	4.38
1981	4.22	4.66
1982	4.15	4.60
1983	3.60	4.23
1984	3.75	3.94
1985	3.59	3.76
1986	3.36	3.79
1987	3.95	4.05
1988	3.85	3.92
1989	3.93	3.89

Source: U.S. National Park Service (1991).
File: *parks*

2.8 Table 2.12 (page 58; file *sunspot*) lists time series data on:

sunspot relative number   a measure of the amount of sunspot activity; higher numbers indicate more solar storms

melanoma cases   age-adjusted number of malignant melanoma (skin cancer) cases in Connecticut, per 100,000 people

Construct two separate time plots, or one plot with two different vertical axis scales, to visually display these data.
    a. Describe the general pattern you see in sunspot activity.
    b. Describe the general patterns in melanoma incidence.
    c. Do you see any relation between sunspot activity and melanoma incidence? If so, describe it.

Table 2.12
Sunspot activity and age-adjusted melanoma incidence in Connecticut, 1936–1972

Year	Sunspot relative number	Melanoma cases per 100,000
1936	40	.9
1937	115	.8
1938	100	.8
1939	80	1.3
1940	60	1.4
1941	40	1.2
1942	23	1.7
1943	10	1.8
1944	10	1.6
1945	25	1.5
1946	75	1.5
1947	145	2.0
1948	130	2.5
1949	130	2.7
1950	80	2.9
1951	65	2.5
1952	20	3.1
1953	10	2.4
1954	5	2.2
1955	10	2.9
1956	60	2.5
1957	190	2.6
1958	180	3.2
1959	175	3.8
1960	120	4.2
1961	50	3.9
1962	35	3.7
1963	20	3.3
1964	10	3.7
1965	15	3.9
1966	30	4.1
1967	60	3.8
1968	105	4.7
1969	105	4.4
1970	105	4.8
1971	80	4.8
1972	65	4.8

Source: Houghton, Munster, and Viola (1978).
File: *sunspot*

2.9 Construct either a histogram or a stem-and-leaf display for the sunspot numbers in Table 2.12, and describe the shape of this distribution.

*2.10 Graph the cumulative frequency distribution of sunspot numbers (without grouping) from Table 2.12. How does this cumulative graph reflect the distribution shape you saw in Problem 2.9?

*2.11 Graph the cumulative frequency distribution of melanoma rates (without grouping) from Table 2.12, showing cumulative proportion on the vertical axis. Demonstrate how reading the graph helps to estimate the proportion of years that had melanoma rates below 1, below 2, below 4.

Table 2.13 (file *lottery*) lists data on the 10 largest state-run U.S. lotteries in 1985. These data appeared in a newspaper article suggesting that Massachusetts' lottery was less efficient than those in other states. Variables are

employ	number of lottery employees
sales	gross sales in millions of dollars
advert	advertising expenditures in millions of dollars
prizes	percent of gross sales awarded as prizes
admin	percent of gross sales spent on administration

Problems 2.12–2.20 refer to these data.

Table 2.13
Data on the 10 largest state-run U.S. lotteries, 1985

State	employ	sales	advert	prizes	admin
1. Connecticut	105	344.5	2.7	52	11
2. Illinois	185	1,207.6	8.4	49	9
3. Maryland	109	681.1	2.8	54	8
4. Massachusetts	430	1,235.3	10.4	59	9
5. Michigan	194	891.2	8.7	48	12
6. New Jersey	250	936.1	4.5	49	9
7. New York	210	1,299.1	15.1	43	11
8. Ohio	288	855.6	7.2	50	11
9. Pennsylvania	210	1,336.5	7.5	45	8
10. Washington	153	150.0	3.5	47	18

Source: *Boston Globe*, October 6, 1986.
File: *lottery*

2.12 Graph *employ* (number of lottery employees) from Table 2.13 as a single-stem stem-and-leaf display. Which state stands apart as an outlier?

2.13 Construct a grouped frequency distribution and histogram for *advert* (advertising expenditures in millions) from Table 2.13. Describe the shape of this distribution.

*2.14 Construct an ungrouped cumulative graph (proportions on the vertical axis) for *advert*. What information does this graph convey?

2.15 Construct two histograms for *sales*, using groups of 100–199, 200–299, 300–399, etc. Show proportion on the vertical axis of one histogram, and frequency on the vertical axis of the other histogram (or draw one histogram with both scales).

2.16 Draw a double-stem stem-and-leaf display of *prizes*. Which state awards the largest percentage of its gross sales as prizes? Which state awards the least?

2.17 Whatever money (from gross sales) a lottery does not spend on administration or give away in prizes, it returns to the state as profit. Generate a new variable equal to the percentage of gross sales returned to the state, for each of the 10 lotteries in Table 2.13. Which lottery returned the highest percentage to the state? Which returned the lowest?

2.18 Does advertising pay off? Draw a scatterplot of gross sales (*y*-axis) versus dollars spent on advertising (*x*-axis), and describe the general trend of the data. What do you conclude from this graph?

2.19 Do larger lotteries tend to have larger or smaller profit margins? Construct a scatterplot depicting percent returned to state (*y*-axis, from Problem 2.17) versus gross sales in millions (*x*-axis). Most of the data points follow a general up-to-right trend. What does this trend suggest about profits and size? Sketch in a straight line that summarizes this general trend. Which state lottery appears to be an exception to the overall "rule"? In what way is this lottery exceptional?

2.20 The Massachusetts lottery employs many people, but it is also one of the larger lotteries in gross sales. Does the Massachusetts lottery employ an unusually large number of people *considering its size*? Construct a scatterplot showing number of employees (*y*-axis) versus gross sales (*x*-axis), labeling each state in this plot. Refer to this scatterplot to discuss whether the Massachusetts lottery's employment appears unusual even among lotteries with similar sales.

2.21 Many atmospheric scientists believe that air pollution is changing the earth's climate. For example, the buildup of carbon dioxide that results from burning fossil fuels may contribute to global warming. Proving this hypothesis has been difficult because the earth's climate also warms or cools for natural reasons, such as solar variation and volcanic eruptions. Most governments want more scientific certainty before they take expensive or unpopular steps to reduce fossil fuel use. Unfortunately, "playing it safe" by waiting for scientific certainty actually entails grave risks: We continue polluting and find out what happens.

Table 2.14 (file *warming*) contains time series data relevant to the global warming debate: global mean temperature in degrees centigrade (°C) and atmospheric carbon dioxide concentration (parts per million) from 1960 to 1993.

    a.   Graph these data either as two separate time plots, or as one combined time plot with two different vertical scales (one for temperature and one for CO_2). The vertical scale for temperature should range from 14.7 to 15.5°C. The vertical scale for CO_2 should range from 310 to 360 parts per million.

    b.   What do we learn from these time plots?

    c.   What difficulties do the plots suggest, for determining whether CO_2 causes warming?

Table 2.14
Global mean temperature and atmospheric carbon
dioxide (CO_2) concentration from 1960 to 1993

Year	Mean global temperature, °C	Carbon dioxide, parts per million
1960	14.98	316.8
1961	15.08	317.5
1962	15.02	318.3
1963	15.02	318.8
1964	14.74	·
1965	14.85	319.9
1966	14.91	321.2
1967	14.98	322.0
1968	14.88	322.8
1969	15.03	323.9
1970	15.04	325.3
1971	14.89	326.2
1972	14.93	327.3
1973	15.19	329.5
1974	14.93	330.1
1975	14.95	331.0
1976	14.79	332.0
1977	15.16	333.7
1978	15.09	335.3
1979	15.14	336.7
1980	15.28	338.5
1981	15.39	339.8
1982	15.07	341.0
1983	15.29	342.6
1984	15.11	344.3
1985	15.11	345.7
1986	15.16	347.0
1987	15.32	348.8
1988	15.35	351.4
1989	15.25	352.8
1990	15.47	354.0
1991	15.41	355.4
1992	15.13	356.2
1993	15.20	357.0

Source: Brown, Kane, and Rodman (1994).
File: *warming*

In his book *Inuit Youth*, anthropologist Richard Condon (1988) describes everyday life among adolescents in the remote Canadian Arctic settlement of Holman Island. He learned about their lives through conversation, observation, surveys, and interviews while he lived in the community. Table 2.15 (file *holman*) lists data from a household survey Condon conducted. He found that many adolescent children were given their own rooms to sleep in, even if this crowded other family members. Problems 2.22–2.25 refer to these data.

Table 2.15
Holman Island adolescents' age, gender, and whether they share
a room with siblings or sleep in their own room

Respondent	Age	Gender	Sleep in own room or share
1	13	male	share
2	16	male	share
3	10	male	share
4	11	male	share
5	14	male	share
6	11	male	share
7	14	male	share
8	16	male	share
9	13	male	share
10	18	male	share
11	15	male	share
12	19	male	share
13	15	male	share
14	16	male	share
15	11	male	share
16	12	male	share
17	15	male	share
18	18	male	share
19	13	male	share
20	17	male	share
21	18	male	share
22	16	male	share
23	17	male	share
24	16	male	own
25	16	male	own
26	17	male	own

(*continued*)

Table 2.15 (*Continued*)

Respondent	Age	Gender	Sleep in own room or share
27	19	male	own
28	19	male	own
29	12	male	own
30	19	male	own
31	16	male	own
32	17	male	own
33	13	male	own
34	13	female	share
35	11	female	share
36	12	female	share
37	14	female	share
38	15	female	share
39	15	female	share
40	15	female	share
41	13	female	share
42	11	female	share
43	12	female	share
44	11	female	share
45	12	female	share
46	14	female	share
47	13	female	share
48	11	female	share
49	14	female	share
50	16	female	share
51	16	female	share
52	14	female	share
53	14	female	share
54	18	female	share
55	11	female	share
56	13	female	share
57	10	female	share
58	12	female	share
59	20	female	own
60	17	female	own
61	13	female	own
62	12	female	own

(*continued*)

Table 2.15 (*Continued*)

Respondent	Age	Gender	Sleep in own room or share
63	19	female	own
64	16	female	own
65	19	female	own
66	17	female	own
67	13	female	own
68	16	female	own
69	19	female	own
70	15	female	own
71	13	female	own

Source: Condon (1988).
File: *holman*

2.22   Construct two separate ungrouped frequency distributions, including proportions and percentages, one for the ages of adolescents who share a room, and one for the ages of adolescents who have their own rooms. Graph these distributions as histograms and comment on what they show.

2.23   Construct two separate frequency distributions, one for the ages of females who share a room, and one for the ages of females who have their own rooms. Compare these two graphs.

2.24   Construct two separate frequency distributions, one for the ages of males who share a room, and one for the ages of males who have their own rooms. Compare these two graphs.

2.25   (*review*) Cross-tabulate own/share room by gender. What percentage of the girls have their own room? What percentage of the boys have their own room?

2.26   In 1992, the U.S. population was about 256 million people. The birth rate had dropped near replacement levels, but the population continued to grow about .75% per year due to immigration. (A .75% growth rate means that each year's population is 1.0075 times the previous year's population.) Assuming that this same growth rate continues, calculate what the U.S. population will be for the years 1993–2030, and draw a time plot showing your results. How long would it take the population to double from its 1992 value?

2.27   In 1992, the population of Brazil was about 151 million people. Although birth rates had declined in recent decades, so had death rates, and the population was growing at roughly 2% per year. Assuming that this same growth rate continues, project Brazil's population for the years 1993–2030 and plot your results. How soon would the population double from its 1992 value?

A 1989 medical-journal article by Thomas Hornbein and others (1989) examined the possibility that climbing extremely high mountains might lead to oxygen deprivation that injured the brain. (The article does not mention that its senior author himself was one of the first Americans to climb Mt. Everest, a story well told in Dr. Hornbein's 1966 book *Everest: The West Ridge*.) The researchers found some evidence that high-altitude exposure affected climbers' speech, coordination, and long-term memory. One unexpected finding involved the association between a physiological measure called hypoxic ventilatory response and the increase in frequency of mountaineers' speech (aphasic) errors after they descended. Problems 2.28–2.30 refer to Table 2.16 (file *high*).

Table 2.16
Hypoxic ventilatory response and increase
in the number of speech errors among
members of American Medical Research
Expedition to Everest

Climber	Hypoxic ventilatory response	Increase in speech errors
1	.21	-1
2	.13	0
3	.76	0
4	1.00	0
5	.16	1
6	.52	1
7	.58	1
8	.75	1
9	.67	2
10	.77	2
11	1.30	3

Source: Adapted from Hornbein et al. (1989).
File: *high*

2.28 Analyze hypoxic ventilatory response in Table 2.16:
   a. Construct a grouped frequency distribution table for this variable. (Use groups of 0–.19, .20–.39, etc.) Include proportions in your table.
   b. Graph the grouped frequency distribution as a histogram and describe its shape.

*2.29   Graph the ungrouped cumulative frequency distribution of hypoxic ventilatory response. (Place the cumulative proportion on the vertical axis.) Indicate how to read the value of hypoxic ventilatory response that falls in the middle, with 50% of the climbers higher and 50% lower, from the graph.

2.30   Graph increase in speech errors (y) versus hypoxic ventilatory response (x) in a scatterplot. Describe any pattern you see.

3

Summarizing Center and Spread

$\mathbf{C}$enter is an imprecise term, as this chapter will show. Although an average summarizes the center of a measurement variable's distribution, there are other ways to define "center" besides the familiar "average." The various definitions all converge on the same location when applied to a bell-shaped distribution like the one in Figure 2.5 but, with other shapes, the center's location depends on the definition used. This chapter presents three alternative measures of center, all of them useful in data analysis: the mean, the median, and the mode.

"Spread" is another imprecise term with several alternative definitions. In general, spread refers to how much a variable varies. The best-known measure of spread, the **range** (distance from lowest to highest value) has limited use in statistics. Other measures, based on variation around the center of a distribution, prove more useful.

This chapter begins a theme followed through much of the rest of the book. The most important measures of center and spread belong to one of two broad mathematical families, each with its own characteristic merits and disadvantages. We begin with the family that includes the familiar "average."

3.1 Arithmetic Mean

You already know how to calculate an average: Add up data values, then divide by the number of cases. Statisticians call this statistic the **arithmetic mean**, often shortened just to **mean** (although other types of means exist). A formal definition, given in the box, employs the summation operator Σ (the uppercase Greek letter *sigma*). Σ means "add up what follows." For example, Σy_i means add up values of y_i, from $i = 1$ to n:

$$\Sigma y_i = y_1 + y_2 + y_3 + \cdots + y_n$$

where y_1 denotes the value of variable y for case number 1, y_2 the value of y for case number 2, and y_n the value of y for the nth or last case in the data. In some instances, the start and endpoint of the summation are written below and above the Σ:

$$\sum_{i=1}^{n} y_i$$

meaning the summation of y_i from $i = 1$ to $i = n$.

Arithmetic mean

The sample **arithmetic mean** of a variable y, written $\bar{y}$, is defined:

$$\bar{y} = \frac{\Sigma y_i}{n} \qquad (3.1)$$

The symbol μ (Greek letter *mu*) denotes the arithmetic mean of a population, which is often unknown. The sample mean, $\bar{y}$, is an **estimator** of the unknown parameter μ.

If we cut an ungrouped sample histogram out of a block of wood, the arithmetic mean corresponds to that point along its base where the histogram will balance. For this reason, we could term the arithmetic mean a *center of gravity*. The quiz score variable from Table 1.1, for example, has a mean and therefore a balance point equal to 1.535, as illustrated in Figure 3.1.

To examine measures of center and spread more closely, we will move on to a new example. Table 3.1 (page 70) lists data from an observational study of preschool children. The researchers watched 26 children over several days, counting the number of times each child got involved in mildly aggressive rough-and-tumble play, or in more seriously aggressive fighting and chasing.

Were the boys more aggressive than the girls? To investigate this deceptively simple question, we might begin, following the advice of Chapter 2, with a graphical display. Quick visual comparisons between two distributions can often be made with **back-to-back stem-and-leaf displays**, like the one in Figure 3.2. Boys' fighting and chasing episodes are graphed on the display's right-hand side, in usual stem-and-leaf fashion. Girls' fighting and chasing episodes are graphed, reading from right to left, on the left-hand side of the display. Figure 3.2 (page 70) reveals positive skew in both distributions, and also shows that two boys were more aggressive than any girls.

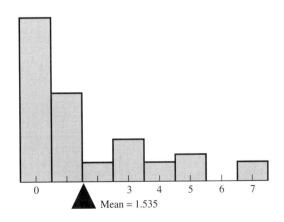

FIGURE 3.1
The mean is a distribution's center of gravity, or the point at which a histogram would balance (student quiz scores)

Table 3.1
Number of rough-and-tumble play episodes or
aggressive fighting-and-chasing episodes,
observed in 26 preschool children

Gender	Age in months	Rough and tumble	Aggressive fighting
1. Girl	50	4	0
2. Girl	50	3	0
3. Girl	50	8	1
4. Girl	47	10	2
5. Girl	51	6	3
6. Girl	56	13	3
7. Girl	47	9	4
8. Girl	52	25	4
9. Girl	48	21	8
10. Girl	51	42	9
1. Boy	51	1	0
2. Boy	54	5	0
3. Boy	50	18	1
4. Boy	47	4	1
5. Boy	54	5	1
6. Boy	48	3	1
7. Boy	53	22	2
8. Boy	49	25	2
9. Boy	51	19	3
10. Boy	48	19	3
11. Boy	54	40	4
12. Boy	53	42	4
13. Boy	55	25	4
14. Boy	48	36	7
15. Boy	51	61	13
16. Boy	51	19	20

Source: Smith and Lewis (1985).
File: *play*

FIGURE 3.2
Back-to-back stem-and-leaf
displays comparing aggressive
fighting episodes of 26 preschool
boys and girls. Stems are 10's,
leaves are 1's; 1* | 3 indicates 13
episodes of fighting and chasing.

girls			boys
4 4 3 3 2 1 0 0	0*		0 0 1 1 1 1 2 2 3 3 4 4 4
9 8	0.		7
	1*		3
	1.		
	2*		0

Two boys were very aggressive, but what should we say about these 26 children as a whole? Arithmetic means provide one way to compare the 10 girls with the 16 boys. Among girls, the mean equals 3.4 fighting-and-chasing episodes:

$$\Sigma y_i = 0 + 0 + 1 + 2 + 3 + 3 + 4 + 4 + 8 + 9$$

$$= 34 \text{ episodes}$$

$$\bar{y} = \frac{\Sigma y_i}{n}$$

$$= \frac{34}{10}$$

$$= 3.4 \text{ episodes}$$

(Table 3.1 lists the values in order, but for calculating a mean order does not matter.) The boys have a higher mean, $\bar{y} = 4.125$ episodes. Thus we might conclude, based on the mean number of fighting-and-chasing episodes, that the boys ($\bar{y} = 4.125$) tended to behave more aggressively than the girls ($\bar{y} = 3.4$). There is nothing wrong with our calculations, but this conclusion will nonetheless prove to be premature.

EXERCISES

3.1.1   Construct back-to-back stem-and-leaf displays or separate histograms, and calculate means, to compare the rough-and-tumble play episodes of boys with girls (file *play*). Write a paragraph summarizing your findings.

3.1.2   Do the boys and girls of Table 3.1 differ with respect to age? Use graphs and means to compare them.

3.2 Variance and Standard Deviation

The defining characteristic of a variable is that it varies from case to case. Variation centers around the mean, but the mean by itself tells us nothing about how much variation exists. Some distributions spread out widely; in others, most of the data lie close to the mean. To describe the different degrees of spread, we need a new type of statistic. Researchers often employ one called the **standard deviation** to summarize a distribution's spread around its mean.

Calculating a standard deviation is more complicated than calculating a mean, but each step makes sense if you look at it closely. To illustrate, we continue with the preschoolers' fighting-and-chasing example. Each preschooler's fighting-and-chasing value lies a certain distance from the mean. For example, the first girl listed in Table 3.1 did no fighting or chasing ($y_1 = 0$), so she is 3.4 episodes below the mean:

$$y_1 - \bar{y} = 0 - 3.4 = -3.4$$

The girl last listed in the table was involved in 9 episodes ($y_{10} = 9$), placing her 5.6 episodes above the mean:

$$y_{10} - \bar{y} = 9 - 3.4 = 5.6$$

If we calculate **deviations from the mean** in this manner for each of the 10 girls, then add them together, positive (above the mean) and negative (below the mean) deviations cancel each other out. The same holds true for boys' deviations from their mean.

In fact it is always the case, for any variable y

$$\Sigma\, (y_i - \bar{y}) = 0$$

This fact, called the **zero-sum property of the mean**, prevents us from using sums of deviations to measure variation around the mean. No matter how much or how little variation there is, the sum of deviations from the mean equals zero.

Squaring deviations eliminates negative values, and provides a quantity that can be used to measure variation. The most elementary statistic based on squared deviations is called the **variance**. Although variance has many uses in more advanced analyses, for the present we can view it as just another step along the way to finding a standard deviation.

Variance

The sample **variance**, written s^2, is defined as

$$s^2 = \frac{\Sigma(y_i - \bar{y})^2}{n - 1} \qquad\qquad (3.2)$$

s^2 is an estimator of the population variance σ^2 (lowercase *sigma* squared), which we usually do not know.

Applying equation (3.2) to the girls' fighting-and-chasing episodes from Table 3.1,

$$s^2 = \frac{\Sigma(y_i - \bar{y})^2}{n - 1}$$

$$= \frac{(0 - 3.4)^2 + (0 - 3.4)^2 + (1 - 3.4)^2 + \cdots + (9 - 3.4)^2}{10 - 1}$$

$$= \frac{84.4}{9}$$

$$= 9.38 \text{ episodes}^2$$

Note the squared units: Since y is measured in episodes, s^2 is measured in episodes squared. If a variable measured weight in pounds, its variance would be a certain number of squared pounds, and so forth. Similar calculations for boys yield $s^2 = 28.25$ episodes^2.

The variance is measured in unnatural squared units, such as episodes^2 or pounds^2. To return to more understandable units, we might find the square root of variance, which is called the **standard deviation**.

Standard deviation

The **sample standard deviation**, symbolized by **s**, equals the square root of the sample variance:

$$s = \sqrt{s^2}$$

$$= \sqrt{\frac{\Sigma(y_i - \bar{y})^2}{n - 1}}$$

(3.3)

A standard deviation measures spread around the mean, in the variable's natural units; s is an estimator of the population standard deviation σ (*sigma*).

For Table 3.1, the standard deviations are

Girls: $\quad s = \sqrt{s^2} = \sqrt{9.38}$ episodes^2 = 3.06 episodes

Boys: $\quad s = \sqrt{s^2} = \sqrt{28.25}$ episodes^2 = 5.32 episodes

These standard deviations indicate that the boys' distribution ($s = 5.32$) is more spread out around its center than the girls' ($s = 3.06$), a finding visually confirmed by Figure 3.2. Put another way, the boys were more varied or unalike than the girls, in terms of their fighting-and-chasing behavior.

Our calculations so far yield two conclusions regarding the number of aggressive fighting-and-chasing episodes among 26 preschool boys and girls:

1. By comparing the means, we know that the boys on average took part in more aggressive episodes.

2. By comparing the standard deviations, we know that the boys exhibited more variation or spread around their mean.

The next sections take a different approach, leading to somewhat different conclusions about center and spread in these data.

Students sometimes wonder why the term $n - 1$, rather than just n, appears as the denominator for sample variance in equation (3.2). To calculate a sample mean, we add up n independent values; any $n - 1$ of them, such as the first nine girls' fighting-and-chasing episodes in Table 3.1, does not indicate what the one remaining value will be. But to calculate a sample variance, we must already know the mean. Knowing the mean and any $n - 1$ values, we could deduce the one remaining value by simple arithmetic. Consequently the variance involves only $n - 1$ independent values, not n. Statisticians describe this as starting out with n **degrees of freedom**, then using up 1 degree of freedom to estimate the mean; so only $n - 1$ degrees of freedom remain to estimate the variance. Dividing by degrees of freedom in equation (3.2) theoretically makes s^2 a better estimate of the unknown population variance σ^2.

EXERCISES

3.2.1   Find the standard deviation for rough-and-tumble play episodes, separately for the boys and girls in Table 3.1 (file *play*). Include units with your answers. What do you learn by comparing the standard deviations of boys and girls? Are these results consistent with earlier findings regarding aggressive fighting and chasing?

3.2.2   Find the standard deviation for age, separately for the boys and girls in Table 3.1. Include units with your answers. What do you learn from these two standard deviations?

3.3 Median

The mean has theoretical advantages that make it very useful in statistical analysis. It also has a weakness, however: The mean can be drastically affected by even one extremely high or low value. The median, an alternative measure of center, lacks the mean's theoretical advantages but also lacks this weakness. Medians are **resistant**, meaning they are less easily affected by extreme values. One billionaire enrolled among the students in your class could raise the class's mean income into the millions, but she would not much affect the median. In that situation the mean paints a misleading picture of the class's wealth, but the median still provides a reasonable summary. Analysts thus often prefer to work with medians, when the data contain a few values much higher or lower than the rest.

If we order all cases in a dataset from lowest to highest, the **median (Md)** is that value in the middle. Half of the cases lie above a median, and the other half below. This provides an alternative definition of center—the *center of position*—distinct from the mean's *center of gravity*. Figure 3.3 illustrates this definition, again using the quiz score variable from Table 1.1. There are $n = 43$ students, so the median equals the score of

FIGURE 3.3
The median is a distribution's
positional center: that value
midway through the data when
cases are ordered from lowest to
highest (student quiz scores)

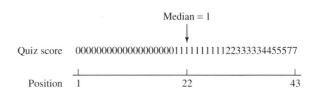

Median = 1

Quiz score 00000000000000000001111111111122333334455577

Position 1   22   43

the 22nd student when scores are put in order from lowest to highest. The 22nd student is among those scoring 1, so the median equals 1.

Median

Given an ordered list of *n* values, the **sample median** equals the value at position (*n* + 1)/2. We call this position the **median depth**:

$$\text{median depth} = \frac{n + 1}{2} \tag{3.4}$$

If *n* is odd, a single value occupies this position. If *n* is even, the median equals the mean of the two middle values.

Among the 10 girls in Table 3.1

$$\text{median depth} = \frac{10 + 1}{2} = 5.5$$

indicating that the median value lies halfway between the 5th and 6th from lowest (or highest) values. The 5th girl participated in 3 episodes, and so did the 6th girl, so the median is

$$Md = \frac{3 + 3}{2} = 3 \text{ episodes}$$

Among the 16 boys,

$$\text{median depth} = \frac{16 + 1}{2} = 8.5$$

so the median itself lies halfway between the 8th boy (2) and the 9th (3):

$$Md = \frac{2 + 3}{2} = 2.5 \text{ episodes}$$

Judging from their medians, the boys tended to be *less* aggressive than the girls. This seems to contradict the earlier conclusion, based on means, that the boys were more aggressive.

Neither conclusion is wrong; each just reflects different definitions of center, and hence different understandings of what it means to say that one gender is more aggressive than the other. The apparent contradiction warns us that "Were boys more aggressive than girls?" is not the straightforward question it seemed: It is too vague, and so permits multiple answers.

EXERCISES

3.3.1 Find medians for the following:
   a. college enrollments (Table 1.4, file *college1*)
   b. divorce rates (Table 1.9, file *urban*)
   c. Senate environmental voting (Table 2.1, file *envote*)
   d. Canadian codfish catch (Table 2.5, file *newfcod*)

3.3.2 Find the median number of rough-and-tumble play episodes for boys and girls separately, using the data of Table 3.1 (file *play*). Do these medians lead to the same conclusion as the means (Exercise 3.1.1)?

3.3.3 Table 2.7 (file *beach*) contains data on "highest measured" bacteria counts. In several instances values of "> 4,000" were recorded because the bacteria were too numerous to count. What does this measurement imprecision do to our ability to calculate the actual mean? The median? Find both, if you can.

3.4 Median, Mean, and Shape

In perfectly symmetrical distributions, the mean equals the median. In skewed distributions, the mean and median differ systematically:

approximate symmetry	mean ≈ median
positive skew	mean > median
negative skew	mean < median

Few real data distributions are perfectly symmetrical, but they may be approximately symmetrical; skewness is a matter of degree. The more severe the skew, the larger the mean–median difference.

Figure 3.4 graphs the locations of the mean and median in approximately symmetrical, positively skewed, and negatively skewed distributions. The long right-hand tail of a positively skewed distribution pulls the mean up relative to the median, thus mean > median. Similarly, the long left-hand tail of a negatively skewed distribution pulls the mean down, thus mean < median.

In general, means are **not resistant** to the pull of a few extreme values. Medians,

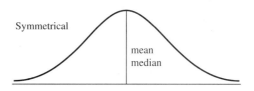

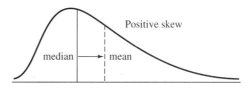

FIGURE 3.4
Relative locations of mean and
median in symmetrical, positively
skewed, and negatively skewed
distributions

on the other hand, are highly **resistant**. Consider three arbitrary numbers {1, 2, 12}. Their mean is 5 and their median is 2; since mean > median, these values are positively skewed. Now suppose we replace the 12 with a wild value, 12,000,000. The mean then jumps from 5 to about 4,000,000—illustrating its lack of resistance. But the median of {1, 2, 12,000,000} is still 2. We could shift the first and last values all the way to negative and positive infinity without changing the median. Resistance is an important property because many variables have skewed distributions, or distributions with a few extreme outliers (sometimes due to measurement errors). In these instances medians often provide more reasonable measures of "center" than means do.

Variables that reflect wealth, for example, tend to have positively skewed distributions; mean incomes or mean house values are pulled up by the millionaires and billionaires among us. Consequently, economic analysts often prefer medians for discussing these variables, and news reports mention that "the *median* family income rose .1% this year" or "the *median* price of new houses in this town declined for the third year in a row."

Figure 3.2 revealed positive skew in the distributions of girls' and boys' aggressive behavior. In both distributions, a few ill-behaved children pulled the mean up:

$$\text{Girls: } \bar{y} = 3.4 \qquad Md = 3$$

$$\text{Boys: } \bar{y} = 4.125 \qquad Md = 2.5$$

The mean–median difference is greater among the boys because that distribution is more severely skewed. Two boys behaved much worse than any of the other children, pulling the boys' mean up farther. Most boys and most girls were relatively peaceful, and the middle point among boys is actually a bit lower than the middle point among girls.

To answer the question "Were boys more aggressive than girls?" we therefore need to be specific about what we mean by "more aggressive." Means reflect the entire distributions, including any extreme values. Medians reflect only middle points of the distributions, ignoring extreme values. Which statistic best summarizes these data? Analysts often prefer medians when working with skewed distributions, but a mean–median difference warns us that differences in center are not the whole story.

EXERCISES

3.4.1   Compare the mean and median for the following distributions. What do these comparisons tell us?
  a.   math SAT scores (Table 1.1, file *stats*)
  b.   student ages (Table 1.1, file *stats*)
  c.   median education (Table 1.9, file *urban*)
  d.   Senate environmental voting (Table 2.1, file *envote*)
  e.   average bacteria counts (Table 2.7, file *beach*)

3.4.2   One student claimed an impossible value, 1000, as his math SAT score for Table 1.1 (file *stats*).
  a.   What is the mean of the math SAT scores, with and without this value?
  b.   What is the median of the math SAT scores, with and without this value?
  c.   Suppose he had maliciously written not 1000 but 1,000,000, and the data analyst was too careless to notice. What would be the mean, with and without his 1,000,000? What would be the median, with and without?
  d.   Describe in your own words the general principle illustrated by parts a–c.

3.5 Quartiles and Boxplots

Medians belong to a family called **order statistics**: statistics defined from the position of values within an ordered list. A median divides an ordered list in half. Other order statistics, called **quartiles,** divide ordered lists into quarters:

Q_1, the **first quartile,** separates the lowest quarter from the upper three-quarters of the data.

Md, the median (same as the **second quartile**) separates the lower and upper halves of the data.

Q_3, the **third quartile,** separates the lowest three-quarters from the top quarter of the data.

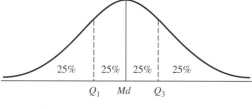

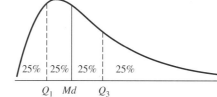

FIGURE 3.5
The median divides a distribution
in half and quartiles divide it
further, into quarters

Figure 3.5 schematically illustrates these divisions in symmetrical (upper) and positively skewed (lower) distributions. Twenty-five percent of the area under these curves lies to the left of the first quartile (Q_1), and 25% lies to the right of the third quartile (Q_3).

Quartiles

Since most datasets do not divide evenly into quarters, **sample quartiles** must be approximate. One simple way to find approximate quartiles by hand is

$$\text{quartile depth} = \frac{\text{truncated median depth} + 1}{2} \qquad (3.5)$$

Truncating the median depth involves dropping any fractional part (10.5 becomes 10, and so forth). Other quartile approximation methods (about seven are widely used) may lead to slightly different results.

For the 10 girls in Table 3.1, median depth is $(10 + 1)/2 = 5.5$, which truncates to 5. Consequently equation (3.5) gives us:

$$\text{quartile depth} = \frac{\text{truncated median depth} + 1}{2}$$
$$= \frac{5 + 1}{2}$$
$$= 3$$

The first quartile for the girls thus equals the third-from-lowest value:

$$Q_1 = 1 \text{ episode}$$

and the third quartile is the third-from-highest value:

$$Q_3 = 4 \text{ episodes}$$

Similar calculations for the 16 boys yield a median depth of $(16 + 1)/2 = 8.5$, and hence a quartile depth of $(8 + 1)/2 = 4.5$. The quartiles are halfway between the 4th and 5th from lowest (both 1's) and the 4th and 5th from highest (both 4's):

$$Q_1 = 1 \text{ episode}$$

$$Q_3 = 4 \text{ episodes}$$

Approximately the middle 50% of any dataset should lie between Q_1 and Q_3. The distance between these two quartiles is called the **interquartile range (IQR)**. Boys and girls have the same interquartile ranges in our example:

$$IQR = Q_3 - Q_1 = 4 - 1 = 3 \text{ episodes}$$

Roughly the "middle 50%" of the boys, and also the middle 50% of the girls, were involved in one to four episodes of aggressive fighting and chasing. By this measure the two distributions are equally spread out. Recall that the boys' standard deviation (a mean-based measure of spread) indicated the boys' distribution is more spread out. Standard deviations, like means, summarize entire distributions including any extreme values. Interquartile ranges, like medians, summarize only the central part of a distribution, ignoring the extremes.

Interquartile range

The **interquartile range** or **IQR** equals the third quartile minus the first quartile:

$$IQR = Q_3 - Q_1 \tag{3.6}$$

Boxplots are graphical displays based on median, quartiles, and IQR, as shown at the bottom of Figure 3.6. The "box" extends from the first to the third quartile, with the median in between. Outside the box, we see the tails of a distribution, with outliers marked individually. Boxplots provide one simple definition for the imprecise term "outlier."

Boxplots

The **box** in a **boxplot** indicates the location of Q_1, Md, and Q_3. This box spans the middle 50% of the data; its length shows the IQR.

    Whiskers extend outward to the last data point not more than $1.5IQR$ above Q_3, or not more than $1.5IQR$ below Q_1. Any data value higher than $Q_3 + 1.5IQR$, or lower than $Q_1 - 1.5IQR$, is considered an **outlier**, and plotted separately.

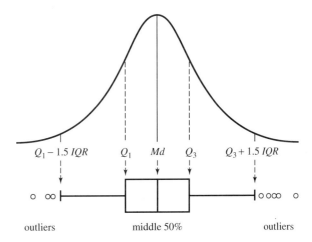

FIGURE 3.6
A boxplot uses median, quartiles, and interquartile range (IQR) to graphically summarize the distribution (symmetrical example)

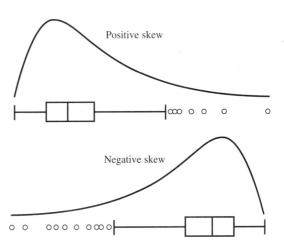

FIGURE 3.7
Two examples of boxplots showing skewed distributions

The boxplot in Figure 3.6 portrays a symmetrical distribution. Figure 3.7 shows boxplots for positively and negatively skewed distributions: Medians are off-center within the boxes, and one tail in each plot is noticeably longer than the other. Outliers often appear in the longer tail of a skewed distribution.

Figure 3.8 (page 82) compares boxplots of the preschool boys' and girls' aggression. Both exhibit positive skew. The girls' median is slightly higher, but both have identical quartiles and IQRs. Among either:

$$Q_1 - 1.5 \; IQR = 1 - 1.5(3) = -3.5 \text{ episodes}$$

$$Q_3 + 1.5 \; IQR = 4 + 1.5(3) = 8.5 \text{ episodes}$$

No child had fewer than 0 episodes, so the lower whiskers just extend down to 0 in both plots. Among girls, the upper whisker extends to 8 episodes (the highest value is not more than 8.5); among boys, the upper whisker extends to only 7 episodes (again, the

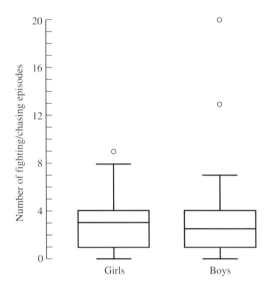

FIGURE 3.8
Boxplots of numbers of fighting-
and-chasing episodes by preschool girls and boys

highest value is not more than 8.5). Beyond this point, we see one high outlier among
the girls and two among boys: the girl with 9 episodes, and the boys with 13 and 20
episodes.

Boxplots are another versatile idea from John Tukey, the inventor of stem-and-
leaf displays. With practice they become easy to read. They provide an unmistakable
warning when distributions are skewed, contain outliers, or have greatly different
spreads. Such features cause problems for many statistical techniques, especially those
based on means, variances, and standard deviations. Careful analysts often use boxplots for their first look at any new data, so that they learn about potential problems
early on.

Figure 3.8 helps pull together what we learned in this chapter about the preschool children's aggression. Three-fourths of the kids were involved in four or fewer
episodes; the middle 50% ranged from one to four. Thus we see little difference between
most of the boys and most of the girls. However, two of the boys were very aggressive,
more so than any girl. Those two draw the boys' mean up, and increase their standard
deviation.

EXERCISES

3.5.1   Examine boxplots comparing boys' and girls' rough-and-tumble play from
Table 3.1 (file *play*). Write a description of what these plots show. How do features visible in the plots help explain differences between the two distributions'
means (Exercise 3.1.1) and medians (3.3.2)? How do these results fit with findings from Figure 3.8?

3.5.2   Draw a boxplot showing population change rates in the 20 cities of Table 1.9
(file *urban*). Indicate the median, quartiles, and IQR, and identify the two out-
lying cities on this plot. Also show the position of the mean, explaining why it
differs from the median.

3.6   Modes

The mean is a distribution's center of gravity; we could think of it as a histogram's
balance point (Figure 3.1). The median is the value at its central position—the midpoint
when cases are listed from low to high (Figure 3.3). A third measure of center, the **mode**,
has traditionally been defined as the most frequent value. Four of the 16 boys in
Table 3.1 were involved in 1 episode each of aggressive behavior. Since no other value
occurs more than three times, the mode among boys equals 1 episode.

This simple definition of mode is most useful with categorical variables, or with
other variables that take on only a small number of different values. Many measurement
variables, however, can take on so many different values that no single "most frequent"
value stands out. If we consider the number of aggressive episodes among girls in
Table 3.1, for instance, the values 0, 3, and 4 each occur twice, and other values occur
only once. If we measured the children's weights, rather than number of aggressive episodes, we might find that no single weight occurred more than once. We could still easily
find the median or mean, but what about the mode?

A more useful but vaguer definition of the mode is the value or class of values
producing a peak in graphs of the frequency distribution. By this definition, the mode
for both boys and girls, judging from Figure 3.2, is 0–4 episodes. A distribution can
have a graphical mode even if no value occurs more than once. Some distributions have
more than one graphical peak, and hence more than one mode.

Figure 3.9 (page 84) illustrates some descriptive applications of this concept. The
two upper distributions have single peaks and hence are **unimodal** (one mode). In the
unimodal distribution at the top left, the modal value(s) appear to be much more common than any other values. We could call this example **strongly modal**. The other unimodal distribution, at top right, has a less distinct peak; we could call this **weakly modal**. The lower graphs in Figure 3.9 illustrate **bimodal** (two peaks, not necessarily of
equal height) and **multimodal** distributions.

The appearance of two or more distinct peaks sometimes tells us that we have
mixed together several dissimilar kinds of cases that really ought to be analyzed separately. For example, a distribution of heights for a sample of preschoolers and their
parents would produce a distinctly bimodal histogram. The mean or median height in
such a mixed sample might be around 4 feet, even though none of the preschoolers is
this tall, and none of the adults this short! It makes more sense to first separate the two
groups, before attempting further analysis. In serious research, the explanations for multiple modes tend to be less obvious but well worth the trouble of investigating.

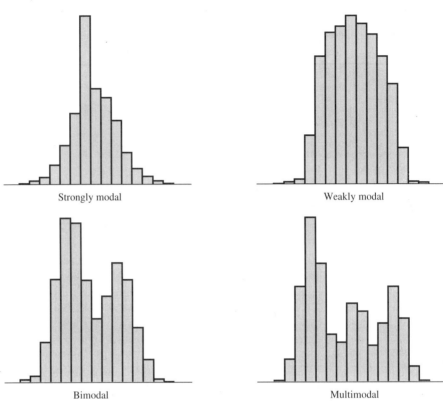

Strongly modal

Weakly modal

Bimodal

Multimodal

FIGURE 3.9
Four examples of modality as an aspect of distribution shape

EXERCISE

3.6.1 Identify and describe how you found the mode(s) for the following distributions. Would you characterize any of them as strongly modal, weakly modal, bimodal, or multimodal?

    a.   student ages (Table 1.1, file *stats*)

    b.   expected statistics grade (Table 1.1, file *stats*)

    c.   inequality index (Table 1.9, file *urban*)

    d.   divorce rates (Table 1.9, file *urban*)

Summary

Mean, median, and mode offer three alternative definitions of where a distribution's "center" lies. These three definitions converge on the same location with symmetrical, unimodal distributions, which have a single, obvious center. Difficulties arise with other distributional shapes, where the concept of "center" becomes ambiguous. Multiple peaks (bimodality or multimodality) sometimes alert us that the distribution mixes cases from several dissimilar populations. We should try to separate these out before proceeding further. Mean–median differences reflect the direction and degree of skew. Outliers can pull a mean far away from the median. Its lack of resistance to outliers makes the mean a poor choice for describing the center of severely skewed distributions; medians work better in such instances.

Variance and its square root, the standard deviation, summarize the amount of spread around the mean, or how much a variable varies. Outliers influence these statistics too, even more than they influence the mean. On the other hand, the variance and standard deviation have important mathematical advantages that make them (together with the mean) the foundation of classical statistics. If a distribution appears reasonably symmetrical, with no extreme outliers, then the mean and standard deviation or variance are the summaries most analysts would use.

The interquartile range, a distance spanning the middle 50% of the data, provides a measure of spread that has greater resistance to outliers. Its resistance makes the IQR useful in identifying which cases *are* outliers, as done visually in a boxplot. Boxplots permit quick comparisons of several distributions at once, in terms of their centers (medians), spreads (IQR), symmetry, and outliers. If a boxplot reveals severe skew or outliers, then analysts tend to consider the median and IQR as better summaries than the mean and standard deviation.

The main example in this chapter involved data on 26 preschool children; the aggressiveness of these particular boys and girls was compared. To what extent might we generalize our conclusions to larger populations, and describe similar-age children in other schools, other years, or other countries? Surely other children are not exactly like these 26, but some broad similarities may exist.

Statisticians often symbolically distinguish between sample statistics and their population counterparts, called **population parameters**, by using Greek letters to represent the latter (Table 3.2). We employ the sample mean, $\bar{y}$, as an estimator of the unknown population mean μ. Similarly, the sample standard deviation, s, serves as an estimator of the unknown population standard deviation, σ.

Table 3.2
Symbols commonly used to represent sample statistics
and corresponding population parameters

Concept	Sample statistic	Population parameter
mean	$\bar{y}$	μ (mu)
variance	s^2	σ^2 (lowercase sigma)
standard deviation	s	σ

To address systematically the issue of generalizing about unknown population parameters on the basis of known sample statistics, we need a mathematics of uncertainty: probability theory. Subsequent chapters introduce probability theory, and show how we can apply this theory to answer research questions.

What We Learn from Measures of Center and Spread

Mean-Based Measures

Mean: The location of a distribution's center of gravity. Useful for simply summarizing or comparing distributions.

Variance: The average variation around the mean, based on squared deviations and therefore measured in squared units. Chapters 8–10 introduce several important methods that focus on variance.

Standard deviation: The distribution's spread around its mean, in natural units. Often used to compare several distributions (which distribution is more spread out?) or as a measure of distance (a certain point lies z standard deviations from the mean).

Order Statistical Measures

Median: The value dividing the distribution into top and bottom halves, a positional center. Used like the mean to simply summarize or compare distributions. The median often works better than the mean when a distribution is skewed or has outliers.

Interquartile range (IQR): The distance spanning the middle 50% (from first quartile to third quartile) of the data. Like standard deviation, this provides a natural-units measure of spread, but unlike standard deviation, the IQR is not much affected by outliers.

Boxplot: Graphical display based on median and IQR. Reveals at a glance the center, spread, symmetry or skew, and any outliers in a distribution. Especially useful for making quick yet fairly detailed comparisons of two or more distributions.

PROBLEMS

3.1   Figure 3.10 contains boxplots of life expectancy (mean age at death) among the populations of 142 countries, somewhat arbitrarily grouped into four "continents" [data from Sivard (1985)]. A horizontal line shows the overall median, 62 years. The highest and lowest countries within each continent are noted; these include two outliers, Turkey and Mauritius. Write a paragraph comparing the distributions of life expectancy on

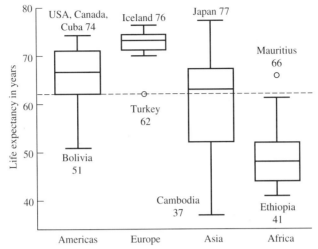

FIGURE 3.10
Boxplots of life expectancies in 142 countries, grouped by
continent

these four continents in terms of both centers (medians) and spread (IQR). Why do
Turkey and Mauritius appear so unusual?

Problems 3.2–3.3 analyze data from Table 3.3 (file *trees*), on the lead concentration of
tree leaves sampled in Lagos, Nigeria. The trees' locations are classified here as having
either low-to-medium or high vehicle traffic. Like many countries, Nigeria does not
restrict the sale of cars that run on leaded gasoline. Problems 3.2–3.3 refer to these data.

Table 3.3
Traffic density and lead concentration in tree leaves
(micrograms per 100 square centimeters of leaf)
sampled in Lagos, Nigeria

Sample	Traffic density	Lead concentration
1	low–medium	12.3
2	low–medium	10.6
3	low–medium	8.0
4	low–medium	8.7
5	low–medium	11.1
6	low–medium	13.3

(*continued*)

Table 3.3 (*Continued*)

Sample	Traffic density	Lead concentration
7	high	16.0
8	high	15.4
9	high	17.4
10	high	17.2
11	high	21.1
12	high	24.9

Source: Adapted from Fatoki (1987).
File: *trees*

3.2   Find and compare the mean lead concentrations of low-to-medium and high traffic areas. Also find and compare the two standard deviations. What do these comparisons tell you?

3.3   Find the median lead concentrations of low-to-medium and high traffic areas. Do the medians support the same conclusion you reached with means in Problem 3.2?

Table 3.4 (file *britu*) gives historical data on unemployment rates among graduates of 44 British universities. Other variables are average exam scores (on the British A-level exams, taken by university-aspiring 17- or 18-year-olds), an index of the per-student cost of academic staff, and the ratio of male-to-female (M/F) full-time undergraduates. Ten of these universities were formerly Colleges of Advanced Technology (CATs), emphasizing technical and scientific vocational training; the others are more general universities (other). Problems 3.4–3.8 refer to these data.

Table 3.4
Data on 44 British universities

University	Type	Graduate unemployment	Average exam scores	Staff cost index	M/F ratio
Bath	CAT	8.8	10.5	102.6	1.87
Brunel	CAT	8.3	7.1	102.5	3.48
Loughborough	CAT	10.4	9.1	111.2	2.38
Aston	CAT	6.8	7.2	104.5	2.54

(*continued*)

Table 3.4 (*Continued*)

University	Type	Graduate unem-ployment	Average exam scores	Staff cost index	M/F ratio
Bradford	CAT	13.0	7.9	104.5	1.94
Strathclyde	CAT	10.1	7.7	104.4	1.89
City	CAT	8.5	8.4	106.3	3.64
Heriot-Watt	CAT	10.6	8.7	102.0	3.20
Surrey	CAT	11.7	8.2	103.2	1.54
Salford	CAT	9.1	6.8	102.7	2.86
Warwick	other	18.4	9.0	97.4	1.15
Kent	other	19.9	7.9	96.3	1.40
East Anglia	other	23.6	7.3	95.8	1.23
London	other	14.4	9.7	99.5	1.45
Ulster	other	28.8	9.7	98.5	.77
Sussex	other	23.4	9.4	97.6	1.15
Hull	other	16.8	7.9	96.6	1.05
Aberdeen	other	11.4	8.5	97.1	1.12
Cambridge	other	9.1	13.6	98.5	2.42
Dundee	other	9.2	8.2	97.9	1.89
Bristol	other	14.0	12.1	98.7	1.46
Sheffield	other	12.9	10.0	102.7	1.47
Edinburgh	other	15.1	10.7	98.3	1.11
Leicester	other	16.5	9.2	97.8	1.20
Durham	other	12.9	11.8	97.7	1.21
St. Andrews	other	16.9	10.5	96.0	.87
Stirling	other	21.0	7.8	96.8	1.16
Nottingham	other	15.3	10.3	101.5	1.47
Leeds	other	13.6	9.7	102.0	1.40
Wales	other	16.1	7.8	99.0	1.38
Southampton	other	11.5	10.8	100.2	1.64
Liverpool	other	10.7	9.5	100.5	1.74
Oxford	other	10.4	13.1	98.0	2.12
Lancaster	other	20.4	8.1	98.7	1.28
Birmingham	other	9.8	10.3	100.6	1.50
Exeter	other	13.5	9.6	98.2	1.07
Newcastle	other	11.4	8.6	102.0	1.55
York	other	18.4	10.2	96.2	1.13
Keele	other	21.0	7.0	97.4	1.19

(*continued*)

Table 3.4 (*Continued*)

University	Type	Graduate unemployment	Average exam scores	Staff cost index	M/F ratio
Essex	other	18.1	6.3	96.7	1.63
Reading	other	16.4	9.8	101.8	1.18
Glasgow	other	8.7	9.2	98.7	1.25
Queens	other	11.5	9.7	99.5	1.58
Manchester	other	13.0	10.4	101.6	1.66

Source: Taylor (1984).
File: *britu*

3.4   Use boxplots and summary statistics (means, standard deviations, medians, IQRs) to compare the unemployment rates among graduates of former CATs and other universities. Can you think of any specific reason why graduates from the one outlier school experienced such high unemployment?

3.5   Use boxplots and summary statistics to compare the average exam scores of students enrolled at the two types of schools. What do they suggest about the students attracted to CATs and other universities?

3.6   Compare the academic cost per student across the two university types. What economic realities could explain the difference in median costs?

3.7   Boxplots and mean or median comparisons help us understand relations between one categorical variable (e.g., university type) and one measurement variable (e.g., unemployment rate or M/F ratio). To study relations between pairs of measurement variables, we need other tools such as scatterplots, introduced in Chapter 2. Construct a scatterplot of unemployment rate (y) versus M/F ratio (x) for all 44 schools in Table 3.4. Sketch a straight line or a curve on this scatterplot to summarize what you see as the general trend of the data. Describe your findings.

3.8   Construct a scatterplot of the staff cost index (y) versus M/F sex ratio (x), using different symbols to represent CAT and other universities. Sketch a straight line or a curve on this scatterplot to summarize what you see as the overall trend. Describe your findings.

3.9   Table 3.5 (file *smoke*) contains data on nicotine concentrations measured in the cabin air of 75 commercial airline flights. These data were collected during a period when the Federal Aviation Administration was considering whether seating segregation (smoking and nonsmoking sections) adequately protected nonsmoking passengers.
    Explore the relation between nicotine concentration (measured in micrograms per

cubic meter of air) and seating section (smoking, boundary, nonsmoking) on the 75 flights in Table 3.5. The means differ, of course, but in what other ways did air quality differ among these three seating sections? Write a report summarizing your conclusions, including appropriate graphs and discussion of means, standard deviations, medians, and interquartile ranges.

Table 3.5
Smoking and cabin air nicotine concentration on 75 commercial airline flights

Plane type	Seating section	Number of smokers	Cigarettes smoked	Nicotine concentration in cabin air
1. 727-200	Nonsmoking	20	49	.03
2. 737-200	Nonsmoking	15	20	.5
3. 737-300	Nonsmoking	12	17	.8
4. 737-200	Nonsmoking	25	63	1.7
5. 737-300	Nonsmoking	.	.	2.1
6. 737-300	Nonsmoking	.	.	2.7
7. 737-200	Nonsmoking	6	7	4.4
8. 737-300	Nonsmoking	.	.	8.1
9. 737-200	Nonsmoking	.	.	10.1
10. 727-200	Boundary	35	76	.03
11. 737-200	Boundary	20	30	.04
12. 737-300	Boundary	5	8	.4
13. 727-200	Boundary	12	26	.6
14. 737-200	Boundary	30	45	.8
15. 737-300	Boundary	.	.	1.5
16. 737-200	Boundary	.	.	1.6
17. 737-200	Boundary	1	1	1.8
18. 727-200	Boundary	20	49	1.9
19. 727-200	Boundary	20	49	2.3
20. 737-200	Boundary	25	44	2.3
21. 727-200	Boundary	.	.	2.4
22. 727-200	Boundary	.	.	2.7
23. 737-200	Boundary	.	.	3.3
24. 727-200	Boundary	14	16	3.4
25. 737-300	Boundary	7	13	4.3
26. 737-200	Boundary	.	.	6.4
27. 737-200	Boundary	.	.	6.4

(*continued*)

Table 3.5 (*Continued*)

Plane type	Seating section	Number of smokers	Cigarettes smoked	Nicotine concentration in cabin air
28. 737-200	Boundary	.	.	6.8
29. 737-200	Boundary	.	.	7.2
30. 737-200	Boundary	20	30	10.0
31. 737-200	Boundary	.	.	10.1
32. 737-200	Boundary	7	12	11.2
33. 737-300	Boundary	20	11	11.7
34. 737-200	Boundary	15	56	12.8
35. 737-200	Boundary	6	8	14.3
36. 737-200	Boundary	25	29	14.6
37. 727-200	Boundary	40	88	14.6
38. 737-200	Boundary	8	15	15.4
39. 737-200	Boundary	30	48	16.6
40. 737-300	Boundary	10	15	16.7
41. 737-300	Boundary	.	.	17.2
42. 737-200	Boundary	5	8	17.9
43. 737-200	Boundary	16	30	19.5
44. 737-200	Boundary	.	.	21.5
45. 737-200	Boundary	14	18	23.3
46. 727-200	Boundary	54	128	24.2
47. 737-200	Boundary	.	.	24.4
48. 737-200	Boundary	15	24	32.7
49. 737-200	Boundary	.	.	40.2
50. 737-200	Smoking	13	26	.03
51. 737-200	Smoking	.	.	.08
52. 727-200	Smoking	25	88	.4
53. 737-200	Smoking	20	37	.6
54. 737-300	Smoking	22	37	.7
55. 727-200	Smoking	21	50	.7
56. 737-200	Smoking	.	.	2.1
57. 737-200	Smoking	.	.	2.3
58. 737-200	Smoking	10	17	3.1
59. 727-200	Smoking	.	.	4.5
60. 737-200	Smoking	24	20	8.6
61. 737-300	Smoking	10	17	8.8
62. 727-200	Smoking	10	23	10.2
63. 727-200	Smoking	17	32	10.5

(*continued*)

Table 3.5 (*Continued*)

Plane type	Seating section	Number of smokers	Cigarettes smoked	Nicotine concentration in cabin air
64. 727-200	Smoking	.	.	11.0
65. 727-200	Smoking	.	.	14.9
66. 737-300	Smoking	35	123	18.7
67. 737-200	Smoking	11	6	22.1
68. 737-200	Smoking	7	11	30.2
69. 737-300	Smoking	15	19	39.5
70. 727-200	Smoking	20	48	42.2
71. 737-300	Smoking	22	30	45.0
72. 737-200	Smoking	20	17	57.1
73. 737-300	Smoking	22	84	59.8
74. 737-300	Smoking	23	38	76.7
75. 737-200	Smoking	23	31	112.4

Source: Oldaker and Conrad (1987).
File: *smoke*

3.10 Return to the occupational fatality dataset in Table 1.11 (file *jobrisk*) of Chapter 1. Construct boxplots comparing the occupational fatality rates of blue- and white-collar occupations. Which jobs are outliers?

3.11 Analyze the occupational fatality data of Table 1.11 to fill in the following table:

Fatality rate

	mean	median
blue collar		
white collar		

In what respect do the medians paint a different picture here than the means? Refer to your graphs to explain why this occurs.

Table 3.6 (page 94) contains data on 59 portable computers, including processing speed and battery life tests conducted by the staff of *Byte* magazine. Variables are

cpu	central processing unit (CPU) chip type
speed	processing speed test index (higher numbers mean faster)

battery   battery life in minutes (higher numbers mean the batteries lasted longer)
price   list price in dollars
screen   screen type (color or monochrome)

Problems 3.12–3.19 refer to these data.

Table 3.6
Data on 59 notebook computers

Vendor	cpu	speed	battery	price	screen
1. Micro	SLC	1.91	140	1,599	mono
2. CAF	SLC	1.74	167	2,099	mono
3. Epson	SLC	1.4	152	1,699	mono
4. Hyperdata	SLC	1.83	124	3,395	color
5. KingTech	SLC	1.2	90	1,695	mono
6. Panasonic	SLC	.	. .	2,699	mono
7. Xinetron	SLC	1.51	152	1,580	mono
8. Noteable	SLC	1.47	136	1,886	mono
9. Samsung	SLC	1.48	150	2,978	mono
10. NEC	SL	3.06	175	5,538	color
11. Compaq	SL	2.21	235	2,949	mono
12. Zenith	SL	2.34	194	3,999	color
13. Zenith	SL	2.34	217	2,999	color
14. IBM	SL	2.41	187	2,800	color
15. AST	SL	2.18	229	4,758	color
16. Acer	SL	2.22	268	3,988	color
17. Zenith	SL	2.34	327	2,599	mono
18. NEC	SL	2.52	160	4,888	color
19. AMS	SL	2.2	178	3,290	color
20. Toshiba	SL	2.69	232	4,699	color
21. Ergo	SL	2.17	196	3,795	mono
22. Compaq	SL	2.71	140	5,419	color
23. Compaq	SL	2.21	426	4,339	mono
24. Texas	SX	2.28	143	3,278	color
25. Toshiba	SX	2.03	197	2,700	color
26. Mitsuba	SX	1.87	153	3,895	color
27. CompuAdd	SX	2.32	204	3,890	color
28. AST	SX	2.14	135	2,748	color
29. Chaplet	SX	2.29	115	3,399	color
30. Chaplet	SX	2.3	159	1,999	mono

(*continued*)

Table 3.6 (*Continued*)

Vendor	cpu	speed	battery	price	screen
31. CompuAdd	SX	2.29	250	2,090	mono
32. AST	SX	2.15	196	1,948	mono
33. IBM	SLC2	2.7	240	4,900	color
34. Hyperdata	DLC	2.82	172	2,295	mono
35. AMS	DX	2.66	131	2,495	color
36. CAF	DX	2.29	184	3,259	color
37. Twinhead	DX	2.74	174	3,895	color
38. CAF	DX	2.8	274	2,559	mono
39. Aspen	DX	2.88	99	2,595	color
40. Sager	DX	2.99	172	3,750	color
41. Aero	DX	2.45	152	1,699	mono
42. CAF	DX	2.8	196	4,650	color
43. Texas	DX	2.48	286	2,678	mono
44. Jetta	DX	2.34	175	1,995	mono
45. Twinhead	DX	2.51	172	2,195	mono
46. CompUSA	DX	2.51	150	2,728	mono
47. MicroInt	DX2	3.96	158	4,305	color
48. MicroInt	DX2	3.92	153	3,535	color
49. CompUSA	DX2	3.31	247	3,228	mono
50. Amrel	DX2	4.13	90	5,249	color
51. AMS	DX2	3.39	172	3,895	color
52. CompUSA	DX2	3.5	137	4,728	color
53. Ergo	DX2	3.12	159	4,295	color
54. Texas	DX2	3.5	241	3,499	mono
55. MicroInt	DX2	3.84	212	2,805	mono
56. Primax	DX2	2.15	121	2,640	mono
57. Hyperdata	DX2	3.33	79	5,495	color
58. Texas	DX2	3.62	156	5,278	color
59. Twinhead	DX2	3.41	158	4,399	color

Source: "Lab tests of 59 notebook computers." *Byte*, October 1993.
File: *notebook*

3.12 Refer to means, medians, and appropriate graphical displays to describe the shapes of the following distributions:
  a. processing speed
  b. battery life
  c. price

3.13 On average, how much more do notebook computers with color displays cost? Find the mean and standard deviation of price for computers with color screens, and compare these with the mean and standard deviation for those with monochrome screens. What do you learn by comparing the two standard deviations?

3.14 Color displays tend to consume more electricity than monochrome displays. Computer manufacturers often try to compensate for this by putting more advanced power-saving technology or more expensive batteries into their top-of-the-line color systems. Do these efforts succeed? Use means, standard deviations, and boxplots to compare the battery life of computers with color and monochrome screens.

3.15 Do you "get what you pay for" in speed? Construct a scatterplot of *speed* (*y*-axis) versus *price* (*x*-axis) to investigate whether more expensive computers also tend to be faster. Identify in this plot several individual computers that appear notably faster than others in their price range, or notably slower than others in their price range.

3.16 Seven different CPU types appear in Table 3.6. For each type, find the mean and standard deviation of processing speed. Which CPU has the highest mean speed? Which type has the most varied speeds, as indicated by standard deviations?

3.17 Construct boxplots showing processing-speed distributions for each of the seven types of CPU. Which CPU has the highest median speed? Which type has the most varied speeds, as indicated by the boxplots' interquartile ranges?

3.18 Several of these CPU types were advertised as providing longer battery life for notebook computers. Compare boxplots of battery life for each type to identify which CPU appears most successful at conserving power. Analyze its battery-life performance compared with that of the other CPU types.

3.19 Find median prices for each CPU and identify the two most expensive types. Review your analyses of Problems 3.15–3.17 to answer the question, Why might buyers be willing to pay more for computers with these two types of CPU?

3.20 On September 20, 1993, the mean age of the 43 statistics students in Table 1.1 was 21, and the standard deviation was 4.1 years. Assuming that they all survive, what was or will be their mean age on September 20th of the current year? The standard deviation of their ages?

3.21 Table 3.7 (file *skijump*) lists distances from the 90-meter ski jump competition at the 1994 Winter Olympics in Lillehammer, Norway. Competitors each took two jumps. Did these competitors as a group tend to jump farther on their first or their second try? Use means, standard deviations, and graphical displays (boxplots and histograms) to compare the distributions of first and second jump distances. Write two paragraphs summarizing your findings.

Table 3.7
Distances jumped by competitors in the 90-meter ski jump,
1994 Winter Olympics

Place	Skier	Country	First jump in meters	Second jump in meters
1	Espen Bredesen	Norway	110.5	104.0
2	Lasse Ottesen	Norway	102.5	98.0
3	Dieter Thoma	Germany	98.5	102.5
4	Jens Weissflog	Germany	98.0	96.5
5	Noriaki Kasai	Japan	98.0	93.0
6	Jani Markus Soininen	Finland	95.0	100.5
7	Andreas Goldberger	Austria	98.0	93.5
8	Jinya Nishikata	Japan	99.0	94.0
9	Takanobu Okabe	Japan	95.0	95.5
10	Christian Moser	Austria	92.0	95.0
11	Gerd Siegmund	Germany	94.5	92.0
12	Stefan Horngacher	Austria	92.0	95.0
13	Jaroslav Sakala	Czech Republic	86.5	94.5
14	Nicolas Dessum	France	95.5	88.0
15	Robert Meglic	Slovenia	93.0	88.5
16	Ari-Pekka Nikkola	Finland	90.0	89.0
17	Didier Mollard	France	91.5	90.0
18	Christof Duffner	Germany	88.5	92.5
19	Jiri Parma	Czech Republic	92.0	87.0
20	Matjaz Kladnik	Slovenia	92.5	87.5
21	Roberto Cecon	Italy	90.5	88.5
22	Nicolas Jean-Prost	France	89.5	89.0
23	Mikael Martinsson	Sweden	87.0	90.0
24	Andrei Verveikine	Kazakhstan	85.0	92.0
25	Heinz Kuttin	Austria	89.5	82.0
26	Sylvain Freiholz	Switzerland	94.0	79.5
27	Martin Svagerko	Slovakia	81.5	90.0
28	Samo Gostisa	Slovenia	86.5	85.5
29	Wojiciech Skupien	Poland	84.5	86.5
30	Janne Vaeaetaeinen	Finland	89.5	80.5
31	Ivo Pertile	Italy	89.5	80.0
32	Ivan Lunardi	Italy	84.0	84.5
33	Tad Langlois	United States	87.5	78.0

(*continued*)

Table 3.7 (*Continued*)

Place	Skier	Country	First jump in meters	Second jump in meters
34	Staffan Taelberg	Sweden	81.0	82.0
35	Bob Holme	United States	83.0	82.0
36	Zbynek Krompolc	Czech Republic	86.0	75.5
37	Janne Petteri Ahonen	Finland	88.0	73.0
38	Alexander Siniavski	Belarus	81.0	76.5
39	Bjorn Myrbakken	Norway	87.0	84.5
40	Martin Trunz	Switzerland	88.5	68.5
41	Dejan Jekovec	Slovenia	74.0	82.0
42	Stanislav Pokhilko	Russia	81.0	74.0
43	Fredrik Johansson	Sweden	86.5	70.0
44	Randy Weber	United States	77.0	78.0
45	Alexei Solodiankine	Russia	75.0	78.5
46	Alexander Kolmakov	Kazakhstan	79.0	69.0
47	Steve Delaup	France	74.5	79.0
48	Jim Holland	United States	77.5	71.0
49	Kairit Biekenov	Kazakhstan	79.0	69.0
50	Kakha Tsakadze	Georgia	75.5	71.0
51	Miroslav Slusny	Slovakia	80.5	66.5
52	Oyvind Berg	Norway	89.0	59.0
53	Magnus Westman	Sweden	78.5	67.5
54	Dmitri Tchelovenko	Russia	68.0	72.5
55	Masahiko Harada	Japan	92.0	54.5
56	Vasyl Grybovich	Ukraine	64.0	59.0

File: *skijump*

3.22 Table 2.15 (file *holman*) contained data from a study of adolescents in a Canadian Arctic village. This study also involved a survey question asking young people to list their friends. Table 3.8 gives means and standard deviations of the number of friends they listed, broken down by respondent age and gender.

    a. Use means and standard deviations to describe how the number of friends listed by the older boys differs, if at all, from the number of friends listed by the younger boys. Make a similar comparison between older and younger girls.

    b. Use means and standard deviations to describe how the number of friends listed by young boys differs, if at all, from the number of friends listed by young girls. Make a similar comparison between older boys and older girls.

c. Considering boys and girls together, how do the older respondents differ from the younger respondents in number of friends listed?

d. Considering older and younger respondents together, how do the boys differ from the girls in number of friends listed?

Table 3.8

Means and standard deviations of the number of friends listed by Holman Island adolescents, by respondent age and gender

Gender of respondents	Age of respondents		
	11–13	*14–19*	*All*
Males	$\bar{y} = 5.7$ $s = 1.6$ $n = 7$	$\bar{y} = 5.8$ $s = 2.4$ $n = 13$	$\bar{y} = 5.8$ $s = 2.1$ $n = 20$
Females	$\bar{y} = 7.3$ $s = 2.9$ $n = 12$	$\bar{y} = 7.4$ $s = 5.2$ $n = 9$	$\bar{y} = 7.4$ $s = 3.9$ $n = 21$
All	$\bar{y} = 6.7$ $s = 2.6$ $n = 19$	$\bar{y} = 6.5$ $s = 3.8$ $n = 22$	$\bar{y} = 6.6$ $s = 3.2$ $n = 41$

Source: Condon (1988).

3.23 In Table 3.8, the mean number of friends increases slightly with age among boys, and likewise among girls. But the mean number of friends *decreases* slightly with age when we look at boys and girls together. Mathematically, how is that possible?

When policymakers consider whether certain lands should be set aside as wilderness, they may first ask geologists to estimate the probability that valuable undiscovered mineral deposits exist on those lands. To supply such estimates, some geologists begin with data on known mineral deposits from other areas that have been well explored. Table 3.9 (page 100; file *goldmine*) lists an example, describing 29 known Chugach-type gold-quartz vein deposits. For each deposit, the table lists the deposit's estimated size (in millions of metric tons of ore) and the percent of that ore believed to consist of gold or silver. Problems 3.24–3.30 refer to these data.

Table 3.9
Grade and tonnage data on 29 Chugach-type gold-quartz vein deposits

Deposit	Millions of metric tons of ore	Gold concen-tration (%)	Silver concen-tration (%)
1. Cliff-Sealy	78,000	.000081	.000016
2. Crown Pt-Fall Ck	43,000	.000830	.000210
3. Granite-Snowball	32,000	.002700	.000270
4. Hirshey-Lucky	13,500	.001500	.000510
5. Ramsay-Rutherford	10,000	.001600	.000360
6. Gold King	10,000	.000610	.000058
7. Monarch-Bahrenburg	9,110	.001900	.000380
8. Nearhouse	8,800	.000140	.000004
9. Hercules-Big Four	7,960	.000540	.000160
10. Cameron-Johnson	6,500	.000400	.000038
11. Mineral King	6,100	.002070	.000620
12. Donohue	4,400	.001300	.000340
13. Hirshey-Carlson	3,900	.000370	.000022
14. Tomboy-Lansing	3,430	.000350	.000039
15. Imperial	3,300	.000071	.000017
16. Primrose	2,900	.001150	.000240
17. Rough & Tough	1,400	.000170	.000044
18. Alaska Homestake	1,300	.000210	.000083
19. Granite Lake (1)	1,000	.002900	.000460
20. Granite Lake (2)	974	.003400	.000530
21. Seward Bonanza	910	.000220	.001250
22. Mayfield	582	.000950	.000340
23. Little Giant	500	.002300	.000950
24. Heaston-James	15,000	.001700	0
25. Cube	7,800	.000029	0
26. McMillan	526	.000150	0
27. Downing	240	.002000	0
28. Kana	170	.001400	0
29. Kenai Lu	160	.000510	0

Source: Root, Menzie, and Scott (1992).
File: goldmine

3.24 Use a histogram, boxplot, and mean–median comparison as the basis for describing the shape of the ore tonnage variable in Table 3.9.

3.25   Using histogram, boxplot, and mean–median comparison, analyze the distribution of gold concentration.

3.26   Using histogram, boxplot, and mean–median comparison, analyze the distribution of silver concentration.

3.27   (*review*) By hand, construct and label stem-and-leaf displays of each of the three mineral-deposit variables in Table 3.9:
   a.   tons of ore, single-stem version (stems 10,000 million tons)
   b.   gold concentration, double-stem version (stems .001%)
   c.   silver concentration, five-stem version (stems .001%)

3.28   The mineral-deposit variables in Table 3.9 plainly do not have symmetrical distributions. For purposes of estimating undiscovered deposits, however, some geologists assume that the **logarithms** (powers of 10) of such variables do follow a certain type of bell-shaped, symmetrical distribution: a **normal distribution**, defined in Chapter 5. Other geologists question whether this assumption is justified. This assumption of normality has played a role in policy decisions regarding whether certain U.S. areas should be set aside as wilderness, or kept open to mining (Hamilton, 1993b).
   Investigate this issue yourself using the data of Table 3.9. Create a new variable equal to the logarithm of tonnage. Examine the mean, median, boxplot, and histogram of log tonnage. Does this variable have a symmetrical distribution?
   Optional: Graph the histogram together with a superimposed normal curve. In what ways does the histogram's shape differ from the outline of the theoretical normal curve?

3.29   Calculate log gold concentration, and examine its mean, median, boxplot, and histogram. Does log gold concentration's distribution appear approximately symmetrical?
   Optional: Do you see any systematic differences between the histogram and a normal curve?

3.30   Calculate log silver concentrations, and analyze as in Problems 3.28–3.29. Comment on the distribution's shape. In view of your analysis in Problems 3.28–3.29, does the symmetry assumption seem to fit these data well?
   Optional: Does the assumption of normality seem to fit these data well?

3.31 What is wrong with Table 3.10 (page 102)? In 1992, the U.S. Geological Survey's Branch of Resource Analysis (BORA) supplied a similar table to members of a Senate committee debating wilderness designation for the East Mojave National Scenic Area (EMNSA), California. The table contains medians, 90th percentiles (values below which 90% of the data lie), and means summarizing 4,999 different computer estimates of the value, in millions of dollars, of undiscovered mineral deposits within the proposed wilderness area. Focusing on the means column at right, BORA's report told Congress that "The mean gross-in-place value of estimated undiscovered mineral deposits of 10 types in the EMNSA is **$6.2 billion**." This sounds like a strong economic argument against designating the EMNSA as wilderness and closing it to mining. But what can we learn from this table about the *distributions* of value estimates for each type of mineral? And what does that suggest about the appropriateness of using means, rather than medians, as a measure of center?

Table 3.10

Estimates of the gross-in-place value, in millions of dollars, of undiscovered mineral deposits of 10 types in the East Mojave National Scenic Area

Commodity	Median of estimated values	90th percentile of estimated values	Mean of estimated values
Rare-earth oxide	0	0	229
Niobium	0	3,240	1,853
Copper	165	1,350	776
Gold	362	2,210	814
Silver	169	833	323
Tungsten	0	0	3
Zinc	218	1,530	541
Lead	107	530	210
Molybdenum	0	0	84
Iron	0	1,570	1,295
Total			6,152

Source: Adapted from "Undiscovered metallic mineral resources in the East Mojave National Scenic Area, southern California," a 3-page document prepared by U.S. Geological Survey's Branch of Resource Analysis for Senate Minority staffers, April 1992.

4

Introduction to Probability

In previous chapters, we considered only sample data. Since sample data are known, we can analyze them directly. Typically our sample includes just a small fraction of some much larger population of cases, and this population remains mostly unknown. What we learn from a sample guides us in drawing conclusions about the population. But when we cannot analyze the population itself, such conclusions inevitably contain a degree of uncertainty.

Probability theory allows us to quantify and speak precisely about the "degree of uncertainty" inherent in our conclusions about a population. This chapter starts by introducing some basic concepts and rules of probability theory. Originally derived for the study of gambling, probability rules today are applied to a wide variety of topics for which outcomes are uncertain—from election forecasts to nuclear power plant design. Probability provides new tools for thinking about categorical and measurement-variable distributions.

The chapter concludes with a look at **random sampling**, a concept of great importance in statistics. Random sampling helps in selecting samples that are representative of the larger population.

4.1 Reasoning with Probability

Any phenomenon where the outcomes are uncertain, such as tossing a coin or contracting a disease, we can view as a **statistical experiment**. An **event** consists of one particular outcome, or set of outcomes, from such an experiment. *An event's **probability** is the proportion of times that event would occur, if the experiment were repeated an infinite number of times.* Although we cannot actually repeat experiments an infinite number of times (or sometimes, even twice), we may be able to deduce probabilities through mathematical reasoning.

For example, consider a young couple who plan to start a family. They are not sure how many children they want, but they hope to have at least one girl, and at least one boy. What is the probability of one boy and one girl among their first two children? Among their first three children, or four? Although we might try to answer this question by surveying a large number of families, or by experimentally tossing coins (described at the end of this section), thinking about the probabilities provides the simplest and most accurate solution.

Assume, for the moment, that the probability of their first child being a girl is .5. Let G1 stand for the event "first child is a girl," and $P(G1)$ stand for "probability that first child is a girl":

$$P(G1) = .5$$

We might sketch the two possible outcomes for the experiment "have one child" as a simple **tree diagram** with two branches:

girl $P(G1) = .5$

boy $P(B1) = .5$

The first child's gender does not affect probabilities regarding a second child, so we can assume similar probabilities that the second child is a girl: $P(G2) = .5$. The tree diagram for two consecutive experiments, "have one child" and "have second child," looks like this:

girl $P(G1) = .5$
    girl $P(G2) = .5$ $P(G1 \text{ and } G2) = .25$
    boy $P(B2) = .5$ $P(G1 \text{ and } B2) = .25$

boy $P(B1) = .5$
    girl $P(G2) = .5$ $P(B1 \text{ and } G2) = .25$
    boy $P(B2) = .5$ $P(B1 \text{ and } B2) = .25$

There exist four possible outcomes: first child a girl, second also a girl (G1 and G2); first a girl, second a boy (G1 and B2); first a boy, second a girl (B1 and G2); or first a boy, second also a boy (B1 and B2). These four outcomes are equally likely, which is to say they all have the same probability: $\frac{1}{4} = .25$. Two of the four outcomes include one child of each gender, so the probability of the outcome "one child of each gender" must be $.25 + .25 = .5$. Thus there is a .5 probability, or 50% chance, that a couple's first two children will include one boy and one girl.

What if they have three children? The tree diagram grows another step, now encompassing the eight possible outcomes:

girl $P(G1) = .5$
  girl $P(G2) = .5$
    girl $P(G3) = .5$
    $P(G1 \text{ and } G2 \text{ and } G3) = .125$
    $P(G1 \text{ and } G2 \text{ and } B3) = .125$
    boy $P(B3) = .5$

  boy $P(B2) = .5$
    girl $P(G3) = .5$
    $P(G1 \text{ and } B2 \text{ and } G3) = .125$
    $P(G1 \text{ and } B2 \text{ and } B3) = .125$
    boy $P(B3) = .5$

boy $P(B1) = .5$
  girl $P(G2) = .5$
    girl $P(G3) = .5$
    $P(B1 \text{ and } G2 \text{ and } G3) = .125$
    $P(B1 \text{ and } G2 \text{ and } B3) = .125$
    boy $P(B3) = .5$

  boy $P(B2) = .5$
    girl $P(G3) = .5$
    $P(B1 \text{ and } B2 \text{ and } G3) = .125$
    $P(B1 \text{ and } B2 \text{ and } B3) = .125$
    boy $P(B3) = .5$

Each of the eight outcomes is equally likely, meaning that each has probability $\frac{1}{8}$ = .125. Six of these eight include at least one boy and at least one girl, so the probability of having at least one child of each gender, in a family of three, is $\frac{6}{8}$ = .75.

We might carry on in this fashion to diagram possible outcomes with four, five, or six children. The probability of having at least one of each gender increases with family size, but never quite reaches 1 (certainty). It remains theoretically possible, though improbable, to have a large family of only sons, or only daughters.

Tree diagrams remain useful for more complicated problems, where events are not equally probable or where probabilities depend on what has happened previously. This very simple example serves to introduce some basic ideas. Our tree diagrams illustrate several probability concepts:

> **Multiplication rule:** We can obtain the probability of a particular combination of events by multiplying probabilities along that sequence of branches. For example, $P(\text{G1 and B2 and G3}) = P(\text{G1}) \times P(\text{B2}) \times P(\text{G3}) = .5 \times .5 \times .5 = .125$.
>
> **Addition rule:** We can obtain the probability that either of several branches occur by adding their respective probabilities. For example, what is the probability of all girls or all boys? $P\{(\text{G1 and G2 and G3}) \text{ or } (\text{B1 and B2 and B3})\} = P(\text{G1 and G2 and G3}) + P(\text{B1 and B2 and B3}) = .125 + .125 = .25$. (This rule applies here because the paths in a tree diagram represent *mutually exclusive events,* as defined in Table 4.1 on page 108.)
>
> **Sample space:** Since the paths at each step represent nonoverlapping (mutually exclusive) events, and together they encompass all possible outcomes (are *exhaustive*), the probabilities at each step (each "experiment") add up to 1. For example, $P(\text{B1}) + P(\text{G1}) = .5 + .5 = 1$. A set of mutually exclusive and exhaustive events is called a *sample space.*

The next section gives a more formal statement of these rules, and other properties of probability.

Exercises

4.1.1 Unlike the boy/girl example, many probability questions are too complex to allow statisticians to find clear theoretical solutions. We sometimes resort instead to **Monte Carlo** methods (named after the European gambling resort), and watch what happens as a computer repeats some numerical experiment a very large number of times. Here is a simple classroom Monte Carlo experiment:

a. Everyone takes out a coin. We agree that heads = "girl," tails = "boy." To simulate having a family with three children, toss three times and record each outcome as B or G.

b. Repeat step **a** ten times. Each person now has ten simulated families, recorded in codes such as GGB or BGB.

c. For the entire class, tabulate the number of simulated families in each of the eight possible types; then calculate the observed proportions.

    d.   Compare your observed proportions of GGG, GGB, etc. families with their theoretical probabilities. What do you think would happen if you repeated the whole experiment? If you repeated it with only one family per student, instead of ten? If you repeated it with 100 families per student? An infinite number of families?

4.1.2   The boy/girl example began by assuming that $P(G) = P(B) = .5$. In fact, because slightly more boys are born than girls, a more realistic value might be $P(G) = .49$. Using this value, draw tree diagrams and apply the appropriate multiplication and addition rules to obtain:

    a.   the probability of one boy and one girl, if the couple has exactly two children

    b.   the probability of at least one boy and at least one girl, if the couple has exactly three children

4.2   Basic Concepts of Probability

Events are specific outcomes or collections of outcomes to an experiment. We will denote different events by capital letters such as *A, B,* or *C.* An event that must occur every time an experiment is repeated has a probability of 1, meaning certainty. An event that can never occur has a probability of 0, meaning impossibility. All probabilities lie somewhere in the range from 0 to 1, inclusive. The probability that at least one of all possible events occurs is 1. If two events cannot both occur on a single trial of the experiment, those events are **mutually exclusive**. The probability that both will occur is 0. A sample space, written *S*, is a set of mutually exclusive and exhaustive events.

    For every event *A,* we can define a second, mutually exclusive event called its **complement**, that is, not *A*: the set of all outcomes that are in *S,* but are not in the event *A*. If *A* does not occur, then not *A* must; conversely, if not *A* does not occur, then *A* must. Put another way, the probability of either *A* or not *A* occurring equals 1 (certainty). You already understand this as common sense: If the probability of rain tomorrow is .3 (30%), then the probability of no rain tomorrow must be .7 (70%). Table 4.1 (page 108) summarizes this and other basic properties of probability.

    Having a daughter as a first child does not alter the probability of having a son as a second child. These two events are **independent**. On the other hand, a heavy cloud buildup does alter the probability of rain; those two events are **not independent**. To define independence, we need the idea of **conditional probability**: the probability of one event, given that another event has occurred. Suppose a city experiences rain on about 10% of all its days each summer. On those days with heavy clouds, however, it rains about half the time. Then the unconditional probability of rain is $P(R) = .1$, but the conditional probability of rain *given clouds* is $P(R|C) = .5$. Two events are **independent** only if the conditional probability equals the unconditional probability, which is not the case with clouds and rain.

Table 4.1
Basic properties of probabilities

Property	Symbols
If event *A* must always occur, its probability is 1.	$P(A) = 1$
If event *A* can never occur, its probability is 0.	$P(A) = 0$
Probabilities are always between 0 and 1, inclusive.	$0 \le P(A) \le 1$
The probability that one of the sample space's events will occur is 1.	$P(S) = 1$
Events *A* and *B* are **mutually exclusive** if they cannot both occur together.	$P(A \text{ and } B) = 0$
Since *A* and not *A* are mutually exclusive and between them include all possible outcomes, $P(A)$ plus $P(\text{not } A)$ equals 1.	$P(A) + P(\text{not } A) = 1$ $P(A) = 1 - P(\text{not } A)$ $P(\text{not } A) = 1 - P(A)$

To pick a more dramatic example, what is the probability of contracting AIDS from a single unprotected heterosexual encounter? A controversial 1988 U.S. study by Hearst and Hulley estimated this probability at .0000002—that is, 2 chances in 10 million (or 1 chance in 5 million; see box on the **1/$P(A)$ rule**)—*if* your partner does not belong to a high-risk group such as homosexual/bisexual, injection drug user, female prostitute, transfusion recipient, coming from country where heterosexual AIDS is common, and so forth. Hearst and Hulley estimated the probability of contracting AIDS

1/P(A) rule

We can re-express any probability as "1 chance in . . . " by taking the inverse of the probability. That is, if event *A* occurs with probability $P(A)$, then *A* has 1 chance in 1/$P(A)$ of occurring, so that over the long run *A* should occur about once in every 1/$P(A)$ trials.

For example, if $P(A) = .0000002$, then *A* should occur about once in 1/.0000002, or once in 5 million times. Such calculations are easily accomplished with a calculator's 1/*x* key, which divides any number into 1.

from a single heterosexual encounter, if your partner *does* belong to a high-risk group, as .001, or 1 in 1,000. According to these estimates, the conditional probability of contracting AIDS given a high-risk partner, $P(A|R)$, is 5,000 times higher than $P(A|\text{not } R)$. Clearly the events "contract AIDS" and "partner is from a high-risk group" are not independent.

Multiplication rule

The general **multiplication rule** for probabilities states that the probability of *both A and B occurring* equals the probability of *B* times the probability of *A if B* occurs:

$$P(A \text{ and } B) = P(B) \times P(A|B) \tag{4.1}$$

where $P(A|B)$ stands for "the probability of *A* given *B*."

Earlier, we saw how the multiplication rule applies to tree diagrams: Final outcome probabilities equal the product of probabilities along a given sequence of branches.

For independent events, $P(A|B) = P(A)$, so equation (4.1) simplifies to:

$$P(A \text{ and } B) = P(B)P(A) \tag{4.1a}$$

Since equation (4.1a) holds only if *A* and *B* are independent, it provides us with a way to test for independence in data.

The multiplication rule, equation (4.1), gives probabilities for the combined event (*A* and *B*). The general **addition rule** yields the probability of (*A* or *B*). This rule states that the probability of either *A* or *B* occurring equals the probability of *A* plus the probability of *B*, minus the probability that they both occur.

Addition rule

For any two events *A* and *B*, the probability that *either A or B will occur* is given by the **addition rule**:

$$P(A \text{ or } B) = P(A) + P(B) - P(A \text{ and } B) \tag{4.2}$$

How likely are we to get a jack or a diamond in one draw from a deck of 52 playing cards? There are four jacks, so $P(J) = \tfrac{4}{52}$. There are 13 diamonds, so

$P(D) = {}^{13}\!/_{52}$. And there is one card that is both a jack and a diamond, so $P(J \text{ and } D) = {}^{1}\!/_{52}$. To avoid counting this jack of diamonds twice, we subtract as indicated by the addition rule:

$$P(J \text{ or } D) = P(J) + P(D) - P(J \text{ and } D)$$

$$= \frac{4}{52} + \frac{13}{52} - \frac{1}{52}$$

$$= \frac{16}{52}$$

Sometimes we cannot obtain the probability of an event such as $(A \text{ and } B)$, which we need to solve equation (4.2). Even so, we can use the addition rule to define the **upper bound** of the probability of $(A \text{ or } B)$. Since any probability, including $P(A \text{ and } B)$, must be a number from 0 to 1, knowing that

$$P(A \text{ or } B) = P(A) + P(B) - P(A \text{ and } B)$$

implies that

$$P(A \text{ or } B) \leq P(A) + P(B) \tag{4.2a}$$

By definition, for mutually exclusive events $P(A \text{ and } B)$ equals 0. Then for mutually exclusive events only, equation (4.2) simplifies to

$$P(A \text{ or } B) = P(A) + P(B) \tag{4.2b}$$

The simplified addition rule, equation (4.2b), works with tree diagrams because their branches represent mutually exclusive events.

Table 4.2 summarizes the rules just described. Although in principle these rules are straightforward, in practice they are often misunderstood—especially the multiplication rule, as shown in the next section.

Table 4.2
Some rules about probabilities for any events *A* and *B*

Rule	Symbols
The **conditional probability** of *A* given *B* is the probability of event *A*, if event *B* occurs.	$P(A\|B)$
A is independent of B if the conditional probability of *A* given *B* is the same as the unconditional probability of *A*.	$P(A\|B) = P(A)$

Table 4.2 (*Continued*)

Rule	Symbols
Multiplication rule:	
The general multiplication rule for probabilities	$P(A \text{ and } B) = P(B)P(A|B)$
For *independent events* only, the multiplication rule becomes simpler.	$P(A \text{ and } B) = P(B)P(A)$
Addition rule:	
The general addition rule for probabilities	$P(A \text{ or } B)$ $= P(A) + P(B) - P(A \text{ and } B)$
The addition rule implies an upper bound for the probability of (A and B).	$P(A \text{ or } B) \leq P(A) + P(B)$
For *mutually exclusive events* only, the addition rule becomes simpler.	$P(A \text{ or } B) = P(A) + P(B)$

EXERCISES

4.2.1   For an experiment consisting of a single draw from a well-shuffled deck of playing cards, give examples of:
a.   an event and its complement
b.   two events that are mutually exclusive but not complementary
c.   two independent events
d.   two events that are neither independent nor mutually exclusive

4.2.2   A deck of playing cards consists of 52 cards, including an ace, king, queen, jack, and 2 through 10 in each of four suits (diamonds, hearts, clubs, spades). Write the following probabilities symbolically and find their numerical value, for the experiment of drawing a single card from a shuffled deck:
a.   drawing a queen
b.   drawing anything but a queen
c.   drawing a face card (jack, queen, king)
d.   drawing the 10 of hearts (use the multiplication rule)
e.   drawing either a face card or a jack (apply the addition rule)

4.2.3   Define events X and Y for the single-card draw experiment such that:
a. $P(X) = 0$
b. $P(Y) = 1$

A Note on Risks and the Multiplication Rule

Consider a nuclear power plant with four backup cooling pumps. Any one of these pumps, by itself, could theoretically keep the reactor core from melting down in an emergency. The plant's designers built in such redundancy because like any machines, the pumps are not perfectly reliable. Suppose we have engineering data suggesting that single pumps fail about 5% of the time. How likely is it that all four could fail at once? We might reason that, if the probability pump #1 fails is $P(F1) = .05$, and the probability pump #2 fails is likewise $P(F2) = .05$, then the probability of both failing is low: $.05 \times .05 = .0025$. By similar reasoning, a disastrous four-pump failure seems even less likely:

$$P(\text{F1 and F2 and F3 and F4}) = P(\text{F1}) \times P(\text{F2}) \times P(\text{F3}) \times P(\text{F4})$$

$$= .05 \times .05 \times .05 \times .05$$

$$= .00000625$$

or about 1 failure in every 160,000 emergencies. But our answer is probably wrong. The reassuringly low probability in this hypothetical example illustrates a common mistake: applying the multiplication rule for independent events, equation (4.1a), to events that are not really independent.

Consider just the first two pumps. Suppose #1 has just failed, and demand now falls on #2. Independence requires that pump #2 be equally reliable, whether #1 just failed on not: $P(\text{F2}|\text{F1}) = P(\text{F2})$. But why did #1 fail? Some possible causes such as operator error, faulty design, or power loss could equally well affect all of the pumps, so that the probability of #2 failing is actually much higher than .05 if #1 has already failed. We call it a **common-mode failure** when multiple components fail for similar reasons. For example, a 1974 Atomic Energy Commission study noted that one possible cause of emergency pump failure is the operators' forgetting to turn any of them on. If the operators forget to turn on the pumps, then having two pumps or four pumps is no safer than having one.

If, for whatever reason, $P(\text{F2}|\text{F1}) > P(\text{F2})$, then the two failures are not independent and we cannot find their joint probability by applying equation (4.1a). Instead we need equation (4.1), which in turn requires knowing the conditional probability $P(\text{F2}|\text{F1})$:

$$P(\text{F1 and F2}) = P(\text{F1})P(\text{F2}|\text{F1})$$

Extending equation (4.1) further:

$P(\text{F1 and F2 and F3 and F4})$
$$= P(\text{F1})P(\text{F2}|\text{F1})P(\text{F3}|\text{F1 and F2})P(\text{F4}|\text{F1 and F2 and F3})$$

Experimentally estimating such conditional probabilities would involve testing entire systems rather than their individual components. System tests under emergency conditions are dangerous to perform with nuclear power plants, and difficult or expensive with any complex system. Most likely, the conditional probabilities remain unknown.

The situation creates two pressures toward improperly applying the multiplication rule:

1. Applying the proper rule, equation (4.1), requires conditional probabilities that we often have no way of knowing, whereas the wrong rule, equation (4.1a), assuming independence, requires only the easier-to-obtain unconditional probabilities.

2. Due to common-mode failures, the conditional probabilities may be higher than unconditional probabilities. If so, improperly applying equation (4.1a) will make a system sound safer than it really is.

Controversies over risk estimation have occurred with respect to spacecraft, airplanes, oil tankers, food processing, railroads, chemical plants, and many other systems. Sociologist Charles Perrow (1984) coined the term "normal accidents" to express the idea that despite redundant safety features, complex systems often do fail, in ways that result from deficiencies in a system as a whole and not just in its component parts.

EXERCISES

4.3.1   Describe circumstances that might make the following conditional probabilities much different from the corresponding unconditional probabilities.
  a.   The probability that a ship's radar does not work, given that the ship's radio does not work
  b.   The probability that a space shuttle's fourth redundant onboard computer will give the wrong answer, given that the other three onboard computers are wrong

4.3.2   Hearst and Hulley (1988) estimated the probability of a female contracting AIDS from a single episode of unprotected intercourse with an infected male as .002. (Critics object that their estimate concerns only the "average" infectivity, and individuals vary widely in their susceptibility to AIDS. For some people, the probability of infection is apparently much higher.) Assuming for the moment that Hearst and Hulley's estimate is correct, and also that the probability remains unchanged through successive episodes (so that the multiplication rule for independent events applies), what is the probability of contracting AIDS from 100 such encounters? [*Hint:*   First, find the probability of *not* contracting AIDS in one, then in 100, encounters.]

4.4 Probabilities and Cross-Tabulation

Data collection often resembles one particular kind of statistical experiment: selecting cases at random from a population and observing the value(s) of one or more variables for those cases. (Mathematically, this is the same idea as dealing cards from a shuffled deck.) The probability that, for a single randomly selected case, variable y has a certain value c, $P(y = c)$, is the same as the population proportion of cases for which $y = c$. This correspondence provides a foundation for drawing conclusions about the population on the basis of sample data.

Chapter 1 introduced the idea of **cross-tabulation**, a table displaying the joint distribution of two categorical variables. Cross-tabulations serve well to illustrate the concepts of conditional probability and independence. Table 4.3 cross-tabulates number of heterosexual partners by gender, for 4,229 British 16–24-year-olds. The table indicates that 250 men and 123 women reported having three or more partners within the past year.

Table 4.3
Cross-tabulation of number of heterosexual partners within the past year
by gender, among 4,229 British 16–24-year-olds (frequencies)

Heterosexual partners in past year	Gender		total
	male	female	
none	534	537	1,071
one	917	1,359	2,276
two	284	225	509
three or more	250	123	373
total	1,985	2,244	4,229

Source: Adapted from Johnson et al. (1992).
File: *tab4_3*

The survey sample includes 4,229 people in this age group, 373 of whom reported having three or more partners. The proportion with three or more partners is therefore $^{373}/_{4,229} = .09$. This proportion also equals the probability that a randomly selected individual from the sample had three or more partners:

$$P(\text{three or more partners}) = .09$$

Table 4.4 shows this and other proportions calculated from the frequencies of Table 4.3.

Table 4.4
Cross-tabulation of number of heterosexual partners within the past
year by gender, among 4,229 British 16–24-year-olds (proportions)

Heterosexual partners in past year	Gender		total
	male	female	
none	.27	.24	.25
one	.46	.61	.54
two	.14	.10	.12
three or more	.13	.05	.09
total	1.00	1.00	1.00

The unconditional probability of three or more partners thus equals .09. Table 4.4 also shows conditional probabilities. The 4,229 respondents included 1,985 men and 2,244 women. Of the 1,985 men, 250 reported three or more sexual partners, so the conditional probability of three or more partners given that the respondent is male is

$$P(\text{three or more}|\text{male}) = \frac{250}{1,985} = .13$$

Among the 2,244 women, 123 reported three or more partners, so the conditional probability of three or more partners given that the respondent is female is

$$P(\text{three or more}|\text{female}) = \frac{123}{2,244} = .05$$

The conditional probability for men is almost 3 times that for women. Since conditional probabilities differ substantially from the unconditional probability, we can conclude that gender and number of partners are not independent:

$$P(\text{three or more}|\text{male}) \neq P(\text{three or more}|\text{female})$$

$$\neq P(\text{three or more})$$

In this sample, men were more likely to report having three or more heterosexual partners.

EXERCISES

Table 4.5 (page 116) presents another cross-tabulation from the Johnson et al. sexual behavior study. Exercises 4.4.1–4.4.3 refer to this table.

Table 4.5
Cross-tabulation of number of heterosexual
partners in lifetime by gender, among
5,068 British 25–34-year-olds (frequencies)

Heterosexual partners in lifetime	Gender	
	male	female
none	67	61
one	325	893
two	199	531
three or more	1,575	1,417

Source: Adapted from Johnson et al. (1992).
File: *tab4_3*

4.4.1 Construct a table of proportions similar to Table 4.4, based on the frequencies in Table 4.5.

4.4.2 In this age group, is having three or more partners in a lifetime independent of gender? Answer with reference to the appropriate conditional and unconditional probabilities.

4.4.3 Using your proportions from Exercise 4.4.1, discuss how male and female respondents differ (or appear similar) with respect to:
   a. having no partners in lifetime
   b. having one partner in lifetime
   c. having two partners in lifetime

▪ ▪ ▪ ▪ ▪ ▪ ▪ ▪ ▪ ▪ ▪ ▪ ▪ ▪ ▪ ▪

4.5 Randomness and Sampling

Games often rely on procedures that produce chance outcomes, such as throwing dice, dealing from a shuffled deck of cards, spinning a wheel, tossing coins, or drawing names from a hat. Specific outcomes from such **random generators** should be impossible to predict or control. Scientists employ their own kind of random generator: Certain computer-executed equations produce series of numbers that can be taken as random for most practical purposes. Strictly speaking, these are not truly random because we can predict them if we know which equation is being used.

Table 4.6 lists 1,800 random digits produced by one such equation. The digits 0 through 9 are equally probable anywhere in a random series. For example, the unconditional probability of a 6 appearing at any one point equals $\frac{1}{10}$ or $P(6) = .1$. But what if we just saw an extremely unlikely sequence of twenty 6's in a row? The conditional probability that the 21st value is a 6, given twenty previous 6's, is the same as it always was: $P(6|\text{twenty previous 6's}) = P(6) = .1$.

Table 4.6
Random number table containing 1,800 digits

24679	24655	75970	85292	24429	22660	41106	66621	62724	15055
11896	05212	02348	95800	16874	51650	73357	78654	15313	88811
98182	94875	94573	71509	12832	29303	29270	93421	87824	52745
85760	30078	95351	79073	18351	69546	60569	03328	53840	07491
08425	65259	19137	99585	95462	18381	60672	85371	85743	51832
70880	29136	73527	63465	68509	58548	72900	55802	45819	06653
78709	46697	97289	18568	48303	99486	61650	15469	98139	57038
08168	67125	78084	77402	40905	06494	31908	75149	85052	89520
12779	95960	25920	39177	14051	42682	10086	17736	89177	95177
61548	27226	04191	53097	13739	56957	77947	18478	05516	93751
80867	95863	18035	23682	95091	98410	49819	07466	26695	16051
07117	12800	93806	57732	55399	33934	87499	93185	19549	95323
27915	84750	49209	38778	95994	06563	37001	29319	90226	12374
84873	27112	62544	05360	78041	12484	55030	62900	79534	76345
09937	27206	86478	10230	15254	80380	14984	65773	99356	98091
59182	94429	66156	22286	24137	17464	63664	18631	46772	57673
52752	43666	65773	18843	24232	26588	27596	89245	44133	50300
31860	71017	84848	98844	98596	67631	91669	16769	48893	82375
46865	73631	78551	09330	40849	70234	25205	23207	18820	76956
55599	85987	82556	26868	12953	23818	30625	02007	11059	27472
93046	85481	04042	96948	56314	40960	43739	40909	61024	10864
55662	99590	33478	44850	18292	97511	76301	05921	06369	69068
45182	15390	30568	01297	55227	96988	93883	24866	30293	99963
34155	20448	49537	41653	19973	80100	44705	90817	37281	79858
10273	68675	97678	62451	32659	63858	35923	86010	73540	14727
53857	33405	40138	54814	39871	13209	13371	43638	82524	48184
09961	98872	10364	51633	06370	97010	85276	48494	69194	75488
27477	06045	39464	90883	70779	86912	41929	66129	72883	24210
33778	43186	77412	26928	98078	90568	44487	94363	67743	65809
23380	14608	96725	42895	02735	75318	36074	05101	44384	71415
71301	87437	57967	54039	64744	99224	39547	81872	03390	92552
90226	08936	91174	33972	42484	47902	35536	70547	08831	80569
48723	09442	13678	62898	49099	65893	01621	52000	89803	29062
50608	71223	56361	26225	44910	80112	79255	49521	29280	38441
64846	56778	08310	92965	38200	04849	29849	69743	82468	84927
67705	64777	27013	50516	79205	78204	79893	90100	41967	84957

File: *random* (Since *n* = 1,800, this file may be too large to access with student software versions.)

Many people misunderstand this aspect of randomness. They believe that if some unlikely event has just occurred, a mysterious force of "probability" now makes it even more unlikely that this event will repeat. No such force exists, however. A coin cannot "remember" that it came up heads on the last five tosses; it still has exactly 1 chance in 2 of coming up heads on the next toss. Similarly, each digit in a series of random numbers appears completely independently of whatever has gone before.

Statistical analysis helps us judge whether a supposedly random process is indeed producing random outcomes. For example, as one test of a table of random numbers like Table 4.6, we can check whether each of the digits from 0 to 9 occurs about equally often, making up $1/10$ of the total. Since there are 1,800 digits in this table, we expect each digit to show up about 180 times. As Figure 4.1 shows, the actual counts range from 163 (1's) to 202 (9's). Such minor variations around the expected frequencies could easily be due to chance, as we will prove in Chapter 7.

A distribution in which all possible values of the variable are equally probable is called a **uniform distribution**. Histograms of uniformly distributed variables appear generally rectangular, like the histogram in Figure 4.1.

Samples represent subsets of cases selected from a larger population. To draw conclusions about the population, on the basis of what we see in a sample, it is important

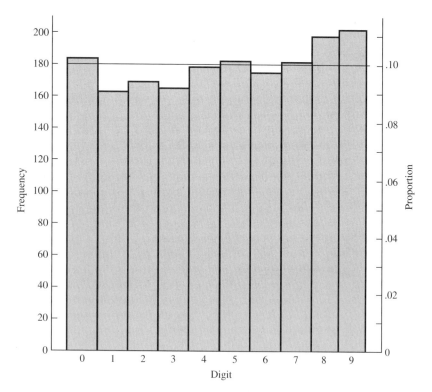

FIGURE 4.1
Histogram showing the distribution of 1,800 random digits from Table 4.6

that the selection be random. Random-number generators or tables like Table 4.6 provide basic tools for random sampling. A **simple random sample** is a subset consisting of n cases, selected randomly (each with an equal and independent chance of inclusion) and without replacement (no case can be selected twice), from a larger but finite population. Many basic statistical techniques assume that the data were produced by simple random sampling. Tables 1.4 and 1.6 in Chapter 1 are examples of simple random samples, selected by the method described on page 13.

Telephone surveys often select simple random samples (from the population of all telephones) by a process of random-digit dialing. For example, suppose we wish to contact people in that mythical community where all telephone numbers start with 555. Using Table 4.6, our first attempt might be dialing 555-2467. The next would be 555-2465, followed by 555-7597, and so on. Many such randomly selected telephone numbers may not exist, in which case we just choose another and move on. (Professional pollsters or direct-marketing salespeople may speed things up by using a computer to generate and dial the random telephone numbers.) All phone numbers that exist have an equal chance of being called, regardless of whether that number is listed or unlisted. Pollsters sometimes add further levels of selection, such as calling at varied times or proceeding with the interview only if the random telephone turns out to be residential. They may also randomly select whom they ask to talk to, after tossing a coin or using even/odd random numbers to select the "male head of household" or the "female head of household," and so forth.

Random number tables allow simple random sampling from population lists as well. Suppose the population of interest consists of 14,000 students at one university; we have a list of their names (in any order) and wish to select a simple random sample. To do so, we could assign each student an identification number with the same number of digits, from 00001 to 14000. Since the identification numbers have five digits, we would read five digits at a time from a table of random numbers. Then, if the random digits correspond to a student's identification number, he or she gets selected for the sample; if not, we would go on to the next five random digits. Reading across the rows of Table 4.6, the first randomly selected student would be the one with identification number 11,896, followed by 05212, 02348, and 12832.

Some other sampling methods offer theoretical or practical advantages over simple random sampling. When the population of interest can be divided into convenient groups, we might start by randomly selecting a subset of groups rather than individuals—a method called **cluster sampling.** For example, suppose we wish to survey U.S. college students. No list of these students exists, and drawing a simple random sample from this huge and dispersed population would be virtually impossible. Lists of colleges do exist, however, making it relatively easy to select a random sample of colleges. Often, cluster sampling forms the first stage in a **multistage sampling** design. For example, after randomly selecting colleges, we could then (using enrollment lists) draw simple random samples, within each college, of the students to be interviewed. The probability of individuals' selection within each school should be adjusted to avoid overrepresenting students from small colleges in our final sample.

Stratified sampling involves grouping the population not for convenience, as with cluster sampling, but rather according to certain theoretically important characteristics. To continue the college example, we might divide our list of colleges into types such as research universities, liberal arts colleges, community colleges, and so forth. We then randomly select schools within each type, roughly in proportion to their numbers in the population of all colleges. The goal is to improve confidence that our sample is representative with respect to type of college. Sometimes researchers deliberately over-sample a less numerous type, such as military schools, to provide enough cases to draw generalizations. To compensate for such oversampling, however, they must subse-quently apply careful readjustments (termed *weighting*) in all their statistical analyses.

Computerized equations can produce apparently random number lists of unlim-ited size, for any statistical purpose—including the creation of artificial random data, like the Monte Carlo experiment in Exercise 4.1.1. Computers also can automatically select random samples from stored data files. Many hand calculators also have random number keys. Statisticians study the results from such pseudo-random generators to en-sure that they truly behave randomly, for all practical purposes. Not all generators are suitable for demanding scientific applications. But the modern availability of these de-vices much reduces the need scientists formerly had for tables like Table 4.6, or for their larger cousins such as the Rand Corporation's 1955 classic, *A Million Random Digits with 100,000 Normal Deviates.*

EXERCISES

4.5.1   If we generate five genuinely random digits, what is the probability that:
   a.   all five of them will be 3's?
   b.   the sequence will be 2, 4, 6, 7, 9?
   c.   none of the five will be a 0?
   d.   all five will be odd numbers?
4.5.2   Use the random number key of a statistical calculator, a computer program, or another random device to construct your own table of 100 random digits.
4.5.3   Draw a histogram similar to Figure 4.1 for the digits in your table from Exercise 4.5.2. Comment on how closely your histogram resembles the uniform distri-bution we would theoretically expect.
4.5.4   How could Table 4.6 simulate rolls from a single six-sided die, if we wanted to play a dice-based game without the dice? How could the table be used to simu-late rolls from a pair of six-sided dice?

4.6 — Sampling Distributions

Table 3.5 (file *smoke*), at the end of Chapter 3, lists data from 75 commercial airline flights. These particular flights actually represent a sample selected from some larger population of airline flights. For purposes of this section, however, let's assume that *the 75 flights constitute the whole population of interest, and we must make guesses about the mean nicotine concentration in this "population" based on a smaller random sample.*

We can use pairs of digits from Table 4.6 to select a simple random sample of n = 5 flights. Starting at top left, Table 4.6 gives us 24, 67, 92 (ignored because no such flight exists), 46, 55, and 75. (If the same flight's number had come up twice, we could have counted it twice—a process called **sampling with replacement**.) Our random sample therefore consists of these flights:

flight	nicotine			
24	3.4			
46	24.2		mean:	$\bar{y} = 32.56$
55	.7	standard deviation:		$s = 45.88$
67	22.1			
75	112.4			

Mean nicotine concentration in our five-flight sample equals 32.56 micrograms per cubic meter of air. Can we therefore conclude that the mean in our 75-flight population likewise equals 32.56? Obviously not, but we might hope more realistically that our sample mean is "close" to the unknown population mean. Probability theory will eventually help us to consider the question, "How close?"

If we select other samples, we will get other sample means. For example, starting with the second row of Table 4.6, we have the digit pairs 11, 89 (ignore), 60, 52, 12, 02, leading to this new sample:

flight	nicotine			
2	.5			
11	.04		mean:	$\bar{y} = 1.99$
12	.4	standard deviation:		$s = 3.70$
52	.4			
60	8.6			

The second sample's mean, 1.99, is much smaller than that of the first sample. This sample might lead us to make quite different guesses about the population mean.

We could continue in this fashion, selecting sample after sample and finding a new sample mean for each one. Eventually we might assemble a distribution consisting of the means from many different samples. The theoretical probability distribution of means from *all possible* random samples of size n = 5, drawn from this population, illustrates what we call a **sampling distribution**. More generally, a sampling distribution is the theoretical probability distribution of a particular statistic (such as mean, median, or proportion) across all possible random samples of size n. Chapter 5 introduces some important theoretical sampling distributions.

Before moving on to theoretical sampling distributions, we can illustrate this general idea with data from a statistical experiment. Figure 4.2 (top) shows the distribution of mean nicotine concentrations in 200 samples of $n = 5$ cases each, drawn by random sampling with replacement from the 75-case "population" of Table 3.5. That is, this distribution depicts 200 means, ranging from about 1 to 47. The mean of the 200 sample-specific means equals 12.97, not far from the true "population" mean of 13.84 (indicated by the vertical dashed line).

Other things being equal, the larger the samples, the less variation in the mean we expect from one sample to the next. The lower histogram in Figure 4.2 shows the distribution of means in 200 samples of $n = 35$ cases each, again sampling with replacement

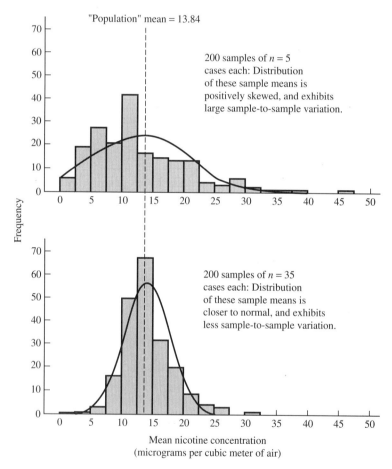

FIGURE 4.2
Results from two computer experiments: Distributions of sample means across 400 random samples taken from the airline smoking data of Table 3.5

from Table 3.5. The mean of these 200 samples equals 13.98, closer still to the "population" mean 13.84. Means in the $n = 35$ samples range only from about 5 to 28, compared with a range from 1 to 47 for the $n = 5$ sample means.

The top ($n = 5$) distribution in Figure 4.2 has a standard deviation of about 8; the lower ($n = 35$) distribution has a standard deviation of about 5. Standard deviations measure spread around the center. The larger the size of the samples, the smaller the standard deviation of the sampling distribution. The standard deviation of a theoretical sampling distribution is called its **standard error**.

The smooth curves superimposed on the observed distributions shown in Figure 4.2 depict **normal distributions**, one important kind of theoretical sampling distribution. The $n = 35$ histogram appears more nearly "normal" than the $n = 5$ histogram does. In general, the larger the size of the samples, the more closely the sampling distribution of the means resembles a normal distribution. Both sampling distributions look much more "normal" than the nicotine concentration variable's original frequency distribution, shown in Figure 4.3.

The previous three paragraphs introduce a mathematical idea called the **Central Limit Theorem**. Figure 4.2 illustrated the Central Limit Theorem in action, as sample size increased from $n = 5$ to $n = 35$.

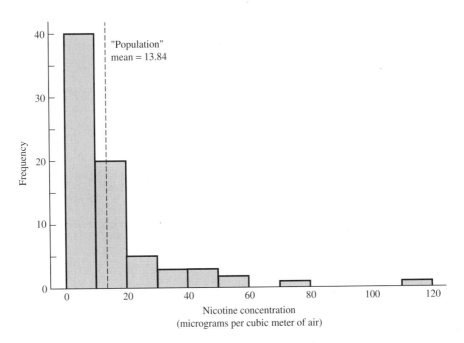

FIGURE 4.3
Histogram of nicotine concentration on 75 airline flights

Central Limit Theorem

According to the Central Limit Theorem, as sample size (n) becomes large:

1. The sampling distribution of the mean becomes approximately normal, regardless of the shape of the variable's frequency distribution.
2. This sampling distribution will center on the population mean. That is, the mean of the sample means will approach the population mean.
3. The standard deviation of this sampling distribution, which is called its **standard error** ($\sigma_{\bar{y}}$), approaches the population standard deviation σ divided by the square root of the sample size:

$$\sigma_{\bar{y}} = \frac{\sigma}{\sqrt{n}} \tag{4.3}$$

The next chapter presents normal and other theoretical distributions in greater detail. Chapters 6–10 describe applications of these distributions, and of such concepts as standard errors.

EXERCISES

4.6.1   Use your own example to illustrate the distinction between the sample distribution of a variable and the sampling distribution of a statistic.

4.6.2   Use rows 3–7 of Table 4.6 to select five samples of $n = 4$ cases each from Table 3.5 (file *smoke*). Find the mean for each of your five samples, and calculate the standard deviation of these five means.

4.6.3   Use the 8th and later rows of Table 4.6 to select five samples of $n = 16$ cases each from Table 3.5. Find the mean for each of these five samples, and calculate the standard deviation of these five means.

4.6.4   Compare your results from Exercises 4.6.2 and 4.6.3 with each other, and with the Central Limit Theorem's predictions. According to the Central Limit Theorem, how should the theoretical standard error for $n = 4$ samples differ from the standard error for $n = 16$ samples?

Summary

This chapter began by introducing some basic ideas and rules of probability. The concepts of statistical experiments, outcomes, and events; the relative frequency definition of probability; the ideas of independence and conditional probability; and rules for deducing some probabilities from others are of central importance. Tree diagrams provide a visual aid for thinking about possible combinations of events. A simple version of the multiplication rule sometimes gets used inappropriately to calculate risks in complex systems, where events are not really independent.

Cross-tabulations provide a data-based illustration of what we mean by independence and conditional probability. Chapter 7 will return to this topic and address what a sample cross-tabulation tells us about the population.

Random sampling ensures that, over the long run, our samples should reasonably well represent their population. Tables of random numbers, and random devices including computers' and calculators' pseudo-random equations, assist in drawing truly random samples. Simple random sampling requires that every possible random sample of size n has an equal chance of selection.

Repeatedly drawing random samples and calculating a summary statistic, such as the mean, for each one would eventually give us a sampling distribution—the distribution of our sample statistic across all possible random samples. Standard errors describe the spread of a sampling distribution, or the amount of sample-to-sample variation. The Central Limit Theorem asserts that as sample size increases, the mean's sampling distribution becomes approximately normal, centered on the population mean, and with standard error $\sigma/\sqrt{n}$. The next chapter has more to say about normal and other theoretical sampling distributions.

Elementary Tools for Reasoning with Probability

Tree Diagrams

Tree diagrams are visual tools for thinking through the outcomes of a brief sequence of experiments.

Multiplication Rule

The multiplication rule gives the probability that several events will all occur: $P(A$ and B and C . . .). A simplified version of the multiplication rule applies only if the events are independent of each other.

Addition Rule

The addition rule gives the probability that any one of several events will occur: $P(A$ or B or C . . .). A simplified version of the addition rule applies only if the events are mutually exclusive.

Conditional Probability

Conditional probability is the probability of event A, given that event B has occurred. By comparing conditional with unconditional probability, we learn whether and how two events are related.

Random Sampling

In random sampling, each case in the population has an equal chance of selection. This helps to ensure a representative sample, from which we can draw conclusions about the population. Many techniques in subsequent chapters assume random sampling.

Sampling Distribution

Sampling distribution refers to the theoretical distribution of a statistic over all possible random samples. This theory guides us in drawing conclusions based on the one sample we have in hand.

PROBLEMS

4.1   Set up tree diagrams and find probabilities for
   a.   drawing at least one diamond on two consecutive draws (without replacement) from a deck of 52 cards
   b.   drawing first a king, then a queen on two consecutive draws (without replacement) from a deck of 52 cards
   c.   drawing one king and one queen (in any order) on two consecutive draws (without replacement) from a deck of 52 cards

4.2   A simple lottery involves spinning a pointer on a colored wheel marked with numbers from 1 to 32. The pointer is spun four times to select four numbers; any number can be chosen more than once. When you pay $1 to buy a ticket, you are entitled to guess what the four numbers will be.
   a.   What is the probability that with a single guess you correctly specify all four numbers, in order?
   b.   Over the long run, how often could you expect to guess the winning lottery numbers correctly (once in every _____ spins)? How large would the jackpot need to be, to equal the amount of money an average player would spend before winning?

A Las Vegas-type slot machine or "one-armed bandit" commonly has three dials, each with 20 different symbols. Suppose that hitting the jackpot on such a machine pays $100, and requires that a bar symbol shows up on all three dials. Below are the numbers of bars and other symbols on each dial:

	Dial 1	Dial 2	Dial 3
# of bar symbols	1	3	1
# of other symbols	19	17	19
total # of symbols	20	20	20

Problems 4.3–4.4 refer to this slot machine. Assume that the machine is fair, the dials are independent, and that each of the 20 symbols on each dial is equally likely to be showing at the end of a spin.

4.3   Construct a tree diagram for possible outcomes from one play of this slot machine.
    a.   What is the probability of three bars showing?
    b.   What is the probability of at least two bars showing?
    c.   What is the probability of at least one bar showing?
    d.   Show how your answers to parts **b** and **c** can be used to find the probability of exactly one bar showing.
    e.   Show how your answer to part **c** can be used to find the probability of no bars showing.

4.4   How often should we expect the jackpot (three bars showing) to occur with the slot machine described above? If each trial costs $.25, how much money would be spent, over the long run, for each $100 jackpot won?

4.5   An aircraft manufacturer conducted studies of the following accident scenario: (1) its plane loses engine power, (2) slats on leading edges of the wing become damaged, and (3) this occurs during takeoff. The studies concluded that the probability of all three events occurring together was less than 1 in 1 billion. Yet this sequence of events actually happened four times during 1977–1981 (once causing a crash that killed 273 people), before the manufacturer made modifications to the aircraft (Perrow, 1984). Support your answers to the following questions using the symbols E for loss of engine power, S for slat damage, and T for takeoff, and refer to the appropriate probability rules.
    a.   The "1 chance in 1 billion" estimate was evidently in error. What assumptions about probability likely contributed to this very low figure?
    b.   Can you suggest reasons why the assumptions in part **a** might be unrealistic?

4.6   M. L. Murray and others (1987) studied possible health risks from Canadian uranium-mill tailings piles, which contain radioactive sand and clay wastes from the processing of uranium ore. These wastes remain potentially hazardous for thousands of years, and they could be spread into the environment by a variety of natural processes. For example, a forest fire or drought could send radioactive dust into the air; a flood could wash it into a nearby lake. Over a period of 1,000 years, these events were judged to have the following probabilities of occurring at least once to a given tailings pile:

Event	P(one or more in 1,000 years)
Flood	.049
Drought	.095
Forest fire	.865

Assume for the moment that occurrences of flood, drought, or fire are independent events. Construct a tree diagram based on these probabilities, and use it to determine the following:
    a.   What is the probability that none of these three types of events will disturb the pile in 1,000 years?

b. What is the probability that at least one dust-causing event (drought or fire) will occur?

c. Confirm your answer to part **b** by applying the multiplication and addition rules directly to the probabilities in the table above. Assume that drought and fire are independent events.

d. How likely is it that both air contamination (due to fire or drought) and water contamination (due to flood) will occur? Show how the answer can be obtained either by using the tree diagram, or by applying the multiplication and addition rules.

4.7   The probabilities given in Problem 4.6 refer to occurrences in 1,000 years. For purposes of this exercise, suppose that the 1-year probabilities equal 1/1,000 of the 1,000-year probabilities. Find the probability that in any one year, a forest fire occurs at the tailings site. Apply the $1/P(A)$ rule to estimate how often (once every _____ years) forest fires occur over the long run.

4.8   Following the reasoning of Problem 4.7, how often are floods expected to occur at a given uranium tailings site? How often are droughts expected to occur?

4.9   The probability that none of the three types of events will occur to a given tailings pile in 1,000 years is about $P = .116$ (Problem 4.6.**a**). Use this probability to solve the following:

a. The probability that at least one contaminating event will occur to a given pile in 1,000 years

b. Uranium mining areas may contain hundreds of separate tailings piles. Suppose we expand our consideration from just one pile to two. Under the optimistic assumption that events affecting the two piles are independent, what is the probability that either of two tailings piles will experience one or more contaminating events in 1,000 years?

c. Explain why the independence assumption of part **b** is "optimistic."

4.10   Since the early 1980s, space shuttles have been the principal vehicles of the U.S. manned space program. The *Challenger* disaster in 1986 set this program back several years, and raised questions about the risks of relying on shuttles for future projects such as establishing a space station. Prior to the *Challenger* loss, National Aeronautics and Space Administration (NASA) officials had estimated the probability of disaster as about 1 failure per 10,000 shuttle flights, or $P(F) = .0001$. After *Challenger*, it appeared that a more realistic estimate might be about 1 failure per 25 flights, or $P(F) = .04$, similar to that for other U.S. rocket vehicles. The *Challenger* accident forced NASA to look harder at its statistical assumptions; even with post-*Challenger* safety improvements, NASA now estimates the probability of shuttle failure around 1 in 50, or .02. Using this $P(F) = .02$ value, the federal Office of Technology Assessment in 1991 stated that there was at least a 50% chance of losing an orbiter before the first space station assembly flight (63 flights later), and an 88% chance of losing an orbiter before space station assembly was completed after 42 more flights (reported in the *Boston Globe*, April 20, 1991).

a. Show how they might have calculated "at least a 50% chance" (actually, closer to 72%!) of losing an orbiter over the next 63 flights.

b.   Show how they calculated an "88% chance" of loss within the next 105 flights (63 + 42 = 105).
c.   On what assumptions do these calculations depend?
d.   Suppose shuttle reliability doubles, so that $P(F) = .01$. What then would be the probability of at least one failure over the next 105 flights?

4.11   A 1985 study looked at the geographical knowledge of college students who were training to become elementary and secondary school teachers (Herman et al., 1985). Among the students in this study, 90% were elementary-school education majors, and the remainder were secondary-school social studies education majors. In general, the geographical knowledge of these students turned out to be poor. For example, only 44.7% of them could locate England on a map of the world.
   Use the following symbols to represent events in the experiment of selecting one student at random from this group:

E randomly chosen student is training to become an elementary-school teacher

S randomly chosen student is training to become a secondary-school social studies teacher

L randomly chosen student is able to locate England on a map of the world

a.   What is the probability that a student selected at random from this group would be an elementary-education major? That a randomly selected student could correctly locate England?
b.   If geographical knowledge and major (elementary vs. secondary/social studies) were independent, what would be the probability that a randomly chosen student is both an elementary-education major and able to locate England? A secondary/social studies major, and able to locate England?
c.   Do you think it is likely that geographical knowledge and major actually are independent? Explain why or why not.
d.   State your answer to part **c** in terms of what you would expect to find if you compared the unconditional and conditional probabilities.

4.12   The study described in Problem 4.11 involved 282 students.
a.   How many of these were elementary education majors? How many were able to locate England on a map?
b.   If major and ability to locate England were independent, how many of the 282 students would you expect to be both elementary majors and able to locate England?
c.   In the actual study, 99 students were both elementary majors and able to locate England. Compare this with the number expected under independence (part **b**), and comment on what the difference suggests.

4.13   Imagine a large lecture course with an enrollment of 140 students, including 80 women and 60 men. Fifteen percent of the 140 students are seniors. To facilitate random selection, we write down each student's name on a scrap of paper and mix the papers thoroughly in a fishbowl.

Apply the appropriate probability rules and show how the following probabilities may be calculated. Use the symbols

S student is senior

M student is male

F student is female

a. If gender and class (junior, senior, etc.) are independent, then what is the probability that a single student drawn at random will be both female and a senior?

b. Assuming that gender and class are indeed independent, what is the probability that a student drawn at random will be female or a senior?

c. If we draw a name, write it down, mix it back into the fishbowl, and then repeat this process, we will have a list of two names that may or may not be different. What is the probability that both of these students will be male?

d. What is the probability that five students drawn with replacement, as described in part **c**, will all be male?

4.14 Refer to Problem 4.13. What is the probability that both students will be seniors, if we make two drawings without replacing either of the drawn names (so the two must be different)? What is the probability that at least one of the students will be a senior? Construct a tree diagram to illustrate your reasoning.

The probabilities below are based on census estimates of the distribution of household income (in dollars) for the U.S. population in 1985:

$$P(y < 5,000) = .077$$

$$P(y < 10,000) = .201$$

$$P(y < 15,000) = .316$$

$$P(y < 20,000) = .425$$

$$P(y < 25,000) = .525$$

$$P(y < 35,000) = .695$$

$$P(y < 50,000) = .853$$

Problems 4.15–4.16 refer to these probabilities.

4.15 In answering the following questions, include both the appropriate symbolic expression [for example, $P(y \geq 25,000)$] and the numerical answer. What is the probability that a household selected at random from this population has an income

a. of at least $10,000?

b. of at least $50,000?

c. of at least $5,000, but less than $20,000?

d. either less than $5,000 or at least $50,000?

e. either less than $10,000, or from $20,000 to $34,999, or at least $50,000?

4.16 If the probabilities given above were applied to a population of 88,458,000 households, how many households would you expect with incomes:

     a.   of at least $50,000?
     b.   of at least $35,000, but less than $50,000?

4.17 In November 1984, there was an outbreak of intestinal illness at a Caribbean resort club. Among one group of 411 tourists who had visited the resort during this period, 300 reported that they became ill; 349 of the 411 tourists in this group had been drinking bottled water (Spika et al., 1987).
     a.   What is the probability that a tourist selected at random from this group became ill? Had been drinking bottled water?
     b.   If drinking bottled water and becoming ill were independent events, what would be the probability that a randomly selected tourist was a bottled-water drinker who became ill?
     c.   In fact, 261 of the bottled-water drinkers in this group became ill. What is the conditional probability of a bottled-water drinker becoming ill?
     d.   Contrast the conditional probability found in part **c** with the unconditional probability found in part **a.** Does drinking bottled water seem to have provided much protection against illness?
     e.   Apply the multiplication rule to find the actual probability that a randomly selected individual is both ill and a bottled-water drinker. Compare this probability with the probability expected under independence (part **b**), and explain why they are or are not very different.

4.18 Many of the 411 resort club tourists of Problem 4.17 had been taking medication (chloroquine) to protect themselves from malaria. Of 380 taking chloroquine, 282 became ill. Calculate the conditional probability of illness given chloroquine, and compare this with the unconditional probability of illness. Does this evidence suggest that the chloroquine protected people against intestinal illness? (Problems 4.17–4.18 illustrate **epidemiological** research, in which statistical analysis helps identify the causes of disease in an uncontrolled, real-world setting. This particular disease was spread by ill North American food handlers; factors such as eating raw hamburger or having an ill roommate increased the tourists' chances of becoming ill themselves.)

The probabilities below are based on census estimates of the years of schooling completed by people 25 years old and over in the U.S. population in 1985. Let x stand for the number of years of schooling a randomly selected individual has completed: If $x < 5$, he or she completed less than 5 years; if $x < 12$, he or she is not a high school graduate, and so forth:

$$P(x < 5) = .027$$

$$P(x < 8) = .075$$

$$P(x < 9) = .139$$

$$P(x < 12) = .261$$

$$P(x < 13) = .643$$

$$P(x < 16) = .806$$

Problems 4.19–4.20 refer to these probabilities.

4.19 In answering the following questions, include the appropriate symbolic expression [for example, $P(x \geq 13)$] with your numerical answer. What is the probability that a person selected at random from this population

    a. has at least an eighth-grade education?
    b. is at least a college graduate?
    c. has exactly 12 years of education?
    d. has at least an eighth-grade education, but did not finish high school?
    e. has some college education, but did not graduate?

4.20 If we apply the probabilities given for Problem 4.19 to a population of 124,905,000 people, how many people would we expect

    a. with less than an eighth-grade education?
    b. with at least some college education?

4.21 Describe and illustrate how Table 4.6 could be used to do the following:

    a. Simulate the experiment of flipping a coin ten times.
    b. Simulate the experiment of drawing one of 30 names from a hat.
    c. Randomly choose one page in this book.
    d. Grade a stack of student papers by randomly assigning grades of A, B, C, D, or F.

Table 4.7 (file *teva180*) contains a dataset in which the cases are 118 college classes. The variables are class size (number of students); percentage of these students receiving A's or B's as their final grade in the class; percentage of the students who rated the instructor highly on end-of-semester teaching evaluations; and the instructor's status, whether regular faculty or teaching assistant (T.A.). The data were originally collected to examine the question of whether teaching evaluations were higher in courses where the instructor gave out a higher proportion of good grades. Problems 4.22–4.26 treat these 118 cases as if they constitute a population, too large to study directly.

Table 4.7
Data on class size, grading, teaching evaluations
and instructor status (regular faculty or
teaching assistant) in 118 college classes

Class	Size	Percent A's and B's	Percent high evaluations	Instructor status
1	96	75	48	faculty
2	60	45	61	faculty
3	86	41	43	faculty
4	58	53	51	T.A.
5	29	66	61	T.A.
6	43	74	73	faculty
7	75	43	56	faculty

Table 4.7 (*Continued*)

Class	Size	Percent A's and B's	Percent high evaluations	Instructor status
8	53	68	9	T.A.
9	63	70	23	faculty
10	42	60	72	T.A.
11	51	67	68	T.A.
12	33	52	48	T.A.
13	57	56	31	T.A.
14	24	51	26	T.A.
15	16	69	93	faculty
16	26	65	11	T.A.
17	21	76	95	faculty
18	36	46	65	faculty
19	44	34	51	faculty
20	17	65	77	faculty
21	56	39	58	faculty
22	36	91	68	T.A.
23	86	61	70	faculty
24	16	69	50	T.A.
25	38	66	28	T.A.
26	43	63	61	faculty
27	52	29	38	faculty
28	44	57	60	faculty
29	72	63	39	faculty
30	38	53	65	faculty
31	89	62	52	faculty
32	95	38	61	faculty
33	53	47	51	T.A.
34	27	37	9	T.A.
35	97	44	73	faculty
36	38	63	50	T.A.
37	89	54	67	T.A.
38	51	67	19	T.A.
39	39	64	32	T.A.
40	37	51	23	faculty
41	43	93	81	faculty
42	17	52	21	faculty
43	62	51	31	faculty
44	53	75	32	T.A.
45	55	67	32	T.A.

(continued)

Table 4.7 (*Continued*)

Class	Size	Percent A's and B's	Percent high evaluations	Instructor status
46	24	66	70	T.A.
47	33	54	37	faculty
48	32	56	25	faculty
49	28	35	78	faculty
50	60	36	73	faculty
51	91	60	0	T.A.
52	58	60	5	T.A.
53	123	60	16	T.A.
54	67	79	55	faculty
55	68	44	35	faculty
56	69	68	82	faculty
57	24	58	100	faculty
58	164	68	84	faculty
59	87	66	30	faculty
60	51	41	50	faculty
61	82	32	33	faculty
62	39	33	19	faculty
63	35	57	56	faculty
64	23	83	95	faculty
65	36	64	45	T.A.
66	55	42	5	faculty
67	47	68	90	T.A.
68	74	50	47	faculty
69	77	52	60	faculty
70	14	57	61	T.A.
71	96	37	77	faculty
72	59	51	62	faculty
73	25	56	33	T.A.
74	57	86	98	T.A.
75	53	60	36	faculty
76	33	70	42	faculty
77	59	58	33	T.A.
78	34	62	33	T.A.
79	44	48	33	T.A.
80	49	39	33	T.A.
81	19	53	33	faculty
82	38	74	46	faculty
83	31	77	17	T.A.

Table 4.7 (*Continued*)

Class	Size	Percent A's and B's	Percent high evaluations	Instructor status
84	17	65	44	faculty
85	31	32	13	T.A.
86	32	53	88	faculty
87	80	33	45	faculty
88	85	61	45	faculty
89	114	67	15	T.A.
90	132	66	18	T.A.
91	90	59	55	faculty
92	54	35	29	faculty
93	15	47	73	faculty
94	15	67	36	T.A.
95	15	40	25	faculty
96	85	47	47	faculty
97	52	83	74	T.A.
98	54	35	37	faculty
99	66	30	20	faculty
100	91	59	45	faculty
101	22	55	78	T.A.
102	42	50	71	faculty
103	75	40	56	faculty
104	52	73	83	T.A.
105	48	48	29	faculty
106	32	41	17	faculty
107	50	80	81	faculty
108	66	79	28	T.A.
109	58	76	37	T.A.
110	32	69	65	T.A.
111	32	50	53	T.A.
112	33	67	58	faculty
113	35	69	58	T.A.
114	40	42	6	faculty
115	24	50	87	faculty
116	62	18	61	faculty
117	30	67	89	T.A.
118	30	73	44	faculty

Source: Hamilton (1980).
File: *teval80*

4.22 Use the random number table (Table 4.6) or a computer to select a simple random sample of $n = 15$ from the population in Table 4.7. For the 15 cases in your sample, find the sample mean, median, and standard deviation of class size.

4.23 Select nine additional random samples of $n = 15$ cases each from Table 4.7. (Cases selected for each sample may be chosen again later.) For each sample, record the sample mean, median, and standard deviation of class size.

4.24 Graph the distribution of the ten sample means from Problems 4.22–4.23. Find their mean and standard deviation.

4.25 Graph the distribution of the ten sample medians from Problems 4.22–4.23. Find their mean and standard deviation. Which exhibits more sample-to-sample variation, the mean or the median?

4.26 According to the Central Limit Theorem, how would you expect the appearance of your graph in Problem 4.24 to differ if
  a. samples had contained $n = 5$ cases each instead of $n = 15$?
  b. samples had contained $n = 25$ cases each instead of $n = 15$?

Political scientist Lawrence Miller (1986) studied the characteristics of male and female candidates for municipal offices in 303 cities of nine U.S. states. He divided candidates into three categories of political ambition, with "progressive" being the most ambitious category:

progressive	a politician who aspires to higher office
static	a politician who seeks to make this particular office his or her long-run career
discrete	a politician who wants this particular office for a specified term only

Male (305) and female (161) candidates were distributed among these ambition categories as shown in Table 4.8. Problems 4.27–4.28 refer to this cross-tabulation.

Table 4.8
Political ambition of 464 male and female
candidates for municipal offices

Ambition	Gender	
	Men	Women
Progressive	144	56
Static	82	50
Discrete	79	55

Source: Miller (1986).
File: *ambition*

4.27 Calculate the following probabilities:

    a. *P*(female), the unconditional probability that a candidate chosen at random from this sample would be female

    b. *P*(progressive), the unconditional probability that a candidate chosen at random from this sample would have ambitions for higher office ("progressive")

    c. *P*(female and progressive), the theoretical probability, based on the multiplication rule, that a randomly chosen candidate would be both female and progressive *assuming that ambition and gender are independent*

4.28 Use the data of Table 4.8 to find:

    a. *P*(progressive|male), the conditional probability that a randomly chosen candidate would be progressive given that he is male

    b. *P*(progressive|female), the conditional probability that a randomly chosen candidate would be progressive given that she is female

    c. *P*(female and progressive), the observed probability based on the table's data that a randomly chosen candidate would be both female and progressive

    d. Comparing your answers to Problem 4.27**b** with 4.28**a** and 4.28**b**, does the evidence suggest that ambition and gender really are independent? Explain.

    e. *If* the two variables were independent as assumed for Problem 4.27**c**, how many progressive females should you expect in this sample? Compare this number with the number actually observed, and comment on the difference.

Table 4.9 contains further results from Miller's study of municipal election candidates. He explored whether election success was related to candidates' wealth. Problems 4.29–4.31 refer to this table.

Table 4.9
Family income and election success of male and female candidates for municipal offices

Election success	Male candidate's annual family income			
	Under $15,000	*$15,001– $25,000*	*$25,001– $50,000*	*Over $50,000*
Winners	5	31	83	28
Losers	18	40	63	20

Election success	Female candidate's annual family income			
	Under $15,000	*$15,001– $25,000*	*$25,001– $50,000*	*Over $50,000*
Winners	7	18	40	19
Losers	16	20	29	3

Source: Miller (1986).
File: *success*

4.29 Calculate conditional probabilities of winning given income level [*P*(winner| income under $15,000), *P*(winner|income $15,001–$25,000), and so forth] for the *male candidates* in Table 4.9.

4.30 Calculate conditional probabilities of winning given income level, for the *female candidates* in Table 4.9.

4.31 Compare your findings from Problems 4.29 and 4.30. What generalization about income and winning applies to both male and female candidates? In which income group are men's and women's probabilities most different?

5

Theoretical Distributions

C hapters 1–3 examined distributions of variables across many different cases within one sample. Chapter 4 introduced the idea of a **sampling distribution**: the distribution a sample statistic would theoretically have if we calculated it repeatedly from all possible random samples of size *n*. Researchers typically have only one sample to work with, which is not enough to determine the true sampling distribution. But they also have statistical theories that suggest how that sampling distribution might look. Under certain conditions, it will resemble one of several theoretical distributions. The best-known of these distributions is called the **normal distribution**. Many other theoretical distributions are mathematically related to the normal distribution.

Theoretical sampling distributions provide the probabilities needed to answer questions like this:

> If we could draw random samples repeatedly from a population with certain **hypothesized** characteristics, how often would these samples resemble the sample we actually have?

Two answers are possible:

1. A high probability means that we could "fairly often" draw samples like ours from a population with the hypothesized characteristics. Therefore, we cannot rule out that our sample really did come from such a population.

2. A low probability means that we should "hardly ever" draw samples like ours from a population with the hypothesized characteristics. Since we did draw the sample, the population most likely does not have the hypothesized characteristics.

As our cutoff between "high" and "low" probability, we often choose a low probability such as .05 (a 5% chance). This use of sampling distributions, called **hypothesis testing**, plays a central role in statistical analysis.

A small number of theoretical distributions suffice for many different kinds of hypothesis tests, and for other statistical purposes as well. Optional sections of this chapter introduce five other distributions: the binomial, Poisson, chi-square (χ^2), Student's *t*, and *F*. The binomial and Poisson are theoretical distributions of **discrete variables**—variables that can take on only a limited number of specific values, such as how many children in a family of six are girls (the only possibilities are 0, 1, 2, 3, 4, 5, or 6). The normal, chi-square, *t*, and *F* distributions, on the other hand, are theoretical distributions of **continuous variables**—variables that can take on an infinite number of different values, such as mean temperature or weight.

This chapter introduces sampling distributions in theory, noting their general characteristics and the mathematical connections between various distributions. Except for two key sections on normal distributions, less mathematically oriented classes may choose to skip most of this chapter. The normal, chi-square, *t*, and *F* distributions all reappear in subsequent chapters, as practical tools for performing statistical tests.

*5.1 Binomial Distribution

What is the likelihood of having five or more daughters, in a family of six children? Chapter 4 suggested tree diagrams as a tool for simple problems of this sort, but a six-trial tree diagram would end with $2^6 = 64$ branches—beyond the practical limitations of diagrams. The **Binomial Theorem** provides a less limited mathematical alternative. It generalizes the reasoning of the multiplication rule to any number (n) of trials.

> **Binomial probabilities**
>
> The probability that an event will occur exactly f times out of n independent trials, assuming the same probability p that the event will occur on each trial, is given by the **binomial** equation:
>
> $$P(f) = \frac{n!}{f!(n - f)!} \, p^f (1 - p)^{n-f} \qquad (5.1)$$
>
> where "!" denotes a **factorial**; for example $4! = 1 \times 2 \times 3 \times 4 = 24$; $n! = 1 \times 2 \times 3 \times \cdots \times n$. By definition $0! = 1$; $1!$ also equals 1.
> For a straightforward demonstration of how this equation arises from binomial experiments with $n = 1, 2,$ or 3, see Mendenhall (1987).

By defining the probability for each possible value of f, from 0 to n, equation (5.1) yields the complete binomial distribution for any combination of sample size (n) and event probability (p). A binomially distributed variable is one that counts the number of times (zero, once, twice, . . .) a binomial event occurs. Such binomial variables have mean

$$\mu = np \qquad (5.2)$$

and standard deviation

$$\sigma = \sqrt{np(1 - p)} \qquad (5.3)$$

A different binomial distribution exists for every combination of n and p.

Applying equation (5.1), the probability that exactly five out of six children are daughters, assuming constant probability $p = .49$ of female births, equals about .086:

$$P(5) = \frac{6!}{5!(6 - 5)!} \, .49^5 (1 - .49)^{6-5}$$

$$= \frac{720}{120(1)} \, (.49)^5 \, (.51)^1$$

$$= .086$$

Since having exactly five and exactly six daughters (among six children) are mutually exclusive events, we can find the probability of five *or more* daughters by addition:

$$P(f \geq 5) = P(5) + P(6)$$

$$= .086 + .014$$

$$= .100$$

Figure 5.1 graphs the complete binomial distribution for $n = 6$ and $p = .49$. About 10% of the area under this histogram, corresponding to the probability of five or more daughters $[P(f \geq 5) = .100]$, is shaded in the right tail of this distribution.

Since the binomial distribution is discrete, we graph it as a histogram. The bars in Figure 5.1 represent each possible value of this binomial variable. In contrast, theoretical distributions for continuous variables (seen later in Figures 5.4–5.13) are graphed using smooth curves rather than histograms.

A study commissioned by a computer-chip manufacturer provides a second binomial example. Among women who worked with chemicals in the company, there seemed to be an unusually high rate of miscarriages: 7 out of 18 pregnancies. The researchers found that among hundreds of women who did not work with chemicals, the proportion of pregnancies that ended in miscarriage was $p = .178$. It is possible, of course, that the higher miscarriage rate among exposed workers could be due solely to chance. How likely is that?

Stating the question more formally: If the probability of miscarriages among individual exposed workers were the same as it is among unexposed workers, $p = .178$, then what is the probability that 7 or more of the 18 exposed women would suffer miscarriages? Equation (5.1) gives us the probability of exactly 7 miscarriages:

$$P(7) = \frac{18!}{7!(18 - 7)!} .178^7 (1 - .178)^{18-7}$$

$$= .021$$

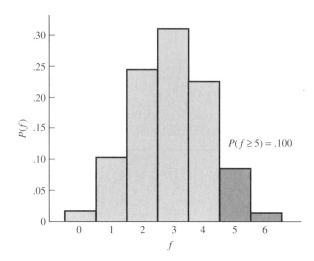

FIGURE 5.1
Binomial distribution for the probability that an event with probability $p = .49$ occurs f times out of $n = 6$ trials

Further calculations or a computer program yield the probability of 7 or more:

$$P(f \geq 7) = .029$$

Thus, there is less than a 3% chance we would see 7 or more miscarriages out of 18 pregnancies, if the miscarriage rate among exposed workers were the same as among unexposed workers. Such a low probability suggests that the rates are not the same: Chemically exposed workers are *significantly more likely* to experience miscarriages.

   Figure 5.2 displays this conclusion graphically. In a binomial distribution with $n = 18$ and $p = .178$, seven or more occurrences would be very unlikely—less than 3% of the total area falls this far out in the right-hand tail.

   For any given value of p, as sample size (n) increases, binomial distributions increasingly resemble normal distributions. As a rule of thumb, binomial distributions become approximately normal when both $np/(1 - p)$ and $n(1 - p)/p$ exceed 9. For the $n = 6$, $p = .49$ binomial distribution graphed in Figure 5.1:

$$\frac{np}{1 - p} = 5.76$$

$$\frac{n(1 - p)}{p} = 6.24$$

For the $n = 18$, $p = .178$ distribution in Figure 5.2:

$$\frac{np}{1 - p} = 3.90$$

$$\frac{n(1 - p)}{p} = 83.12$$

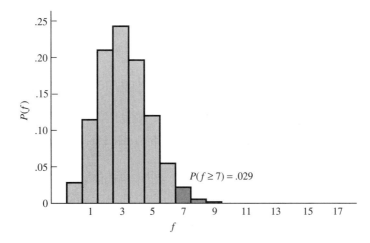

FIGURE 5.2
Binomial distribution for the probability that an event with probability $p = .178$ occurs f times out of $n = 18$ trials

In neither example do both quantities exceed 9, so we cannot consider either distribution to be approximately normal. With larger samples, however, the normal approximation provides a useful shortcut around binomial calculations.

EXERCISES

*5.1.1 If we toss a fair coin eight times, what is the probability of six or more heads?

*5.1.2 A certain basketball player usually scores on 47% of his shots. If this probability remains constant throughout a game, how likely is he to score on all of his first five shots? On at least four of these first five shots? At least three?

*5.2 ━━ Poisson Distribution

The **Poisson distribution**, named after a 19th-century French mathematician, provides an approximation for the binomial distribution when p (event probability) is small and n (sample size, or number of trials in which the event could have occurred) is large. Specifically, if

$$n > 50, \quad p < .05, \quad \text{and} \quad np < 5$$

then a Poisson distribution with mean $\mu = np$ reasonably substitutes for the more precise, but sometimes hard to calculate, binomial distribution. Poisson distributions also have other important statistical applications. Many variables that are counts of random events follow Poisson distributions. Poisson variable values are nonnegative integers, 0, 1, 2, 3, ... Calculating the probability of each value requires only the Poisson variable's mean, μ.

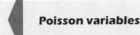

Poisson variables

y represents a count of events that occur randomly but with constant probability. The probability that this count equals some specific number c is

$$P(y = c) = \frac{\mu^c e^{-\mu}}{c!} \tag{5.4}$$

where μ represents the mean of y (the rate at which the event occurs); e is a mathematical constant, approximately 2.72.

The shape of a Poisson distribution depends on its mean, μ. Poisson distributions with low means exhibit severe positive skew, but they become less skewed as μ increases. A Poisson distribution's variance equals its mean:

$$\sigma^2 = \mu$$

$$= np \qquad (5.5)$$

which also implies that the standard deviation equals the square root of the mean:

$$\sigma = \sqrt{\mu}$$

$$= \sqrt{np} \qquad (5.5a)$$

Thus the higher the mean of a Poisson variable, the greater its spread or variation.

An environmental-health example, somewhat like the miscarriages study described earlier, serves to illustrate Poisson hypothesis testing. Suppose that a rare illness strikes apparently at random in the general population. Any one person has a probability of $p = .0001$ (1 chance in 10,000) of contracting this illness over a 10-year period. Water contamination has been discovered in a community of 30,000 people, where six cases of the illness occurred over a 10-year period. The average number of cases for a community of this size should be

$$\mu = np$$

$$= 30,000 \times .0001$$

$$= 3$$

How often might communities of 30,000 people experience six cases, strictly by chance? If such apparent "outbreaks" often occur randomly, it will be hard to make a case that water contamination is to blame here.

Since $n = 30,000 > 50$, $p = .0001 < .05$, and $np = 3 < 5$, we can apply equation (5.4) (with $\mu = np = 3$) to calculate the probability of zero cases of illness:

$$P(y = 0) = \frac{3^0 e^{-3}}{0!}$$

$$= \frac{1 \times .0498}{1}$$

$$= .0498$$

Similar calculations yield probabilities for one through five events.

c	$P(y = c)$
0	.0498
1	.1494
2	.2240
3	.2240
4	.1680
5	.1008
less than 6	.9160

By the addition rule for mutually exclusive events, $P(y < 6)$ equals the sum of the probabilities for 0, 1, 2, 3, 4, and 5 occurrences:

$$P(y < 6) = P(y = 0 \text{ or } y = 1 \text{ or } y = 2 \text{ or } y = 3 \text{ or } y = 4 \text{ or } y = 5)$$
$$= P(y = 0) + P(y = 1) + P(y = 2) + P(y = 3) + P(y = 4)$$
$$+ P(y = 5)$$
$$= .9160$$

Therefore the probability of six or more occurrences must equal .084:

$$P(y \geq 6) = 1 - P(y < 6)$$
$$= .084$$

Figure 5.3 depicts a Poisson distribution with $\mu = 3$. The shaded area in the right-hand tail indicates the region of the distribution that corresponds to $P(y \geq 6)$. Since Poisson variables are discrete, we graph their distributions with histograms.

Although communities of this size average three cases of the illness, by chance we would expect about 8.4% of such communities to experience six or more cases. Thus the six-case outbreak under study could easily be random, and not due to chemical contamination. Our calculations have not proven the contamination "innocent"; rather, they show only that we lack evidence to judge it "guilty."

Another type of Poisson application appeared in a study regarding the distribution of hits by V-1 "buzz bombs" launched against London during World War II (Clarke, 1946). The V-1, a precursor of modern cruise missiles, was a very inaccurate weapon intended to demoralize a civilian population with random strikes from the sky. Clarke

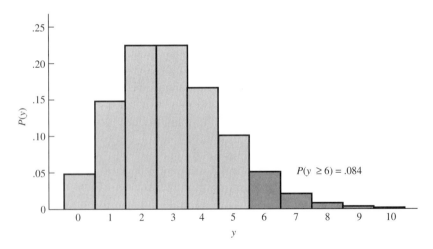

FIGURE 5.3
Poisson distribution for experiments having *y* events, when the mean number of events per experiment is $\mu = 3$

divided a map of south London into 576 small areas, each ¼ of a square kilometer (km²), and counted the number of V-1 hits in each area. A total of 535 V-1's hit this part of the city, or an average of slightly less than one hit for each ¼-km² area: $\mu = {}^{535}\!/_{576} = .929$ hit/area. Two hundred twenty-nine of the 576 areas were not hit at all, but some unfortunate areas received three, four, or even five bomb hits. These counts appear in the first two columns of Table 5.1.

Table 5.1
Distribution of V-1 buzz bomb hits in 576 areas
of South London during World War II ($\mu = .929$)

Number of hits c	Actual count of areas with c hits	Poisson probability of c hits $P(y = c)$	Poisson predicted count of areas with c hits $P(y = c)n$
0	229	.3949	227.5
1	211	.3669	211.3
2	93	.1704	98.2
3	35	.0528	30.4
4	7	.0123	7.1
5	1	.0023	1.3

Source: Clarke (1946).

If the probability that any given area got hit by an incoming V-1 was independent of whether it had ever been hit before (the bombs' targeting was not accurate enough to hit any particular area on purpose), we might expect that counts of hits per area should follow a Poisson distribution. The third column of Table 5.1 gives probabilities of exactly c hits, as predicted by equation (5.4), given that $\mu = .929$. Multiplying these theoretical probabilities by the actual number of areas (576) yields the predicted counts in the right-hand column. Poisson predictions closely resemble the actual counts of how many areas received 0, 1, 2, 3, 4, or 5 V-1 bomb strikes. The uncanny accuracy of these mathematical predictions became a literary metaphor in Thomas Pynchon's strange novel *Gravity's Rainbow* (1973).

Other researchers have found the Poisson distribution to be a good model for phenomena as diverse as deaths by horse kick in the Prussian army or the incidence of race riots. These phenomena all involve counting an event that occurs within a given area or time interval with a small probability p. Occurrences of this event are **independent** if their probability remains unchanged by previous occurrences, as with V-1 bombs falling on London. The probability that the event occurs 0, 1, 2, 3 . . . times in a given area or time interval then follows a Poisson distribution.

EXERCISES

*5.2.1 Demonstrate how equation (5.4) yields the Poisson probabilities for one through five hits given in Table 5.1.

*5.2.2 For the chemical-contamination example, we calculated the Poisson probability of six or more cases of illness, given that the mean equals 3. For this same example, find the probabilities of

    a.   four or more cases of illness

    b.   eight or more cases of illness

5.3 ▬ Normal Distribution

The **normal distribution** is one specific type of bell-shaped probability distribution, defined by equation (5.1). The term "normal distribution" sometimes misleads people into thinking that such distributions must be "typical" or "usual." Not necessarily so; few of the sample distributions graphed in Chapters 1–3 resemble the bell shape of a normal distribution (see Figure 5.4). (Normal distributions extend horizontally from negative to positive infinity; Figure 5.4 depicts only the central part.) To avoid confusion, many statisticians prefer the term **Gaussian distribution**, named after the German mathematician Karl F. Gauss (1777–1855). By either name, normal or Gaussian distributions play a key role in statistics.

Normal (or *Gaussian*) *distributions*

Normal distributions have probability density functions $f(y)$:

$$f(y) = \frac{1}{\sigma\sqrt{2\pi}}\, e^{-(y-\mu)^2/(2\sigma^2)} \qquad\qquad (5.6)$$

where μ represents the population mean and σ the population standard deviation; π and e are mathematical constants, approximately equal to 3.14 and 2.72, respectively.

    Graphing $f(y)$ against y produces a bell shape called the **normal curve**. Not all bell-shaped distributions are normal, however—only those defined by equation (5.6).

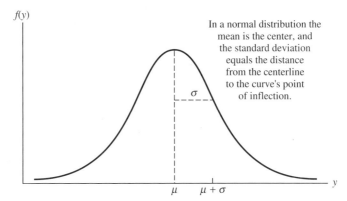

$f(y)$

In a normal distribution the
mean is the center, and
the standard deviation
equals the distance
from the centerline
to the curve's point
of inflection.

σ

μ $\mu + \sigma$

y

FIGURE 5.4
Normal or Gaussian distribution, showing mean (μ) and standard
deviation (σ)

The importance of normal distributions results from two practical observations:

1. Many measurement variables have approximately normal distributions.

2. Given large enough samples, many sample statistics have approximately normal
    sampling distributions.

Both observations reflect the theoretical fact that variables that are themselves sums of
many independent, identically distributed random variables should follow normal distributions. Sums of the random digits from many tables like Table 4.6, for example,
would appear approximately normal. Other statistics also meet this description, including the sample mean—which equals the sum of values, one for each case, divided
by the number of cases. Consequently, as the Central Limit Theorem states, with large
enough samples, a mean should follow an approximately normal sampling distribution. With large samples, proportions also follow approximately normal sampling
distributions.

There exists a unique normal distribution for every possible combination of mean
(μ) and standard deviation (σ). Notationally, $y \sim N(\mu, \sigma)$ indicates that "y follows a
normal distribution with mean μ and standard deviation σ." The mean identifies the
distribution's center, and standard deviation measures spread around this center. Graphically, the standard deviation equals the distance from the centerline (the mean) to the
curve's points of inflection, where it shifts from convex to concave. Figures 5.5–5.7
(page 150) illustrate how μ and σ determine the location and spread of a normal curve.

A **standard normal** variable has a mean equal to 0 and a standard deviation
of 1 (see Figure 5.8, page 151). Values of a standard normal variable indicate distance
from the mean, in standard deviations. A value of 2, for example, falls two standard
deviations above the mean. A value of -1.5 falls one-and-one-half standard deviations
below the mean.

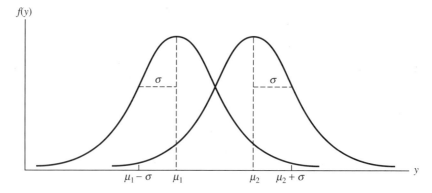

FIGURE 5.5
Two normal distributions with different means ($\mu_1 < \mu_2$) but identical standard deviations (σ)

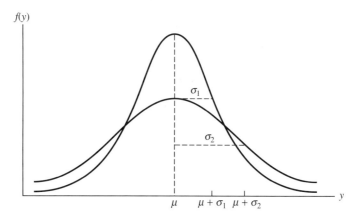

FIGURE 5.6
Two normal distributions with identical means (μ) but different standard deviations ($\sigma_1 < \sigma_2$)

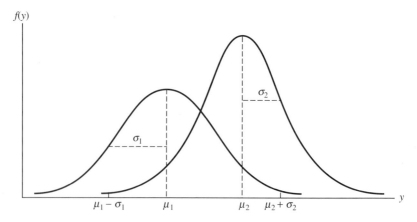

FIGURE 5.7
Two normal distributions with different means ($\mu_1 < \mu_2$) and different standard deviations ($\sigma_1 > \sigma_2$)

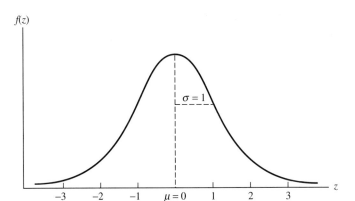

FIGURE 5.8
Standard normal distribution, with mean $\mu = 0$ and standard deviation $\sigma = 1$

Standard normal distribution

If y is distributed normally with mean μ and standard deviation σ:

$$y \sim N(\mu, \sigma)$$

then

$$z = \frac{y - \mu}{\sigma} \qquad (5.7)$$

follows a standard normal distribution with mean 0 and standard deviation 1:

$$z \sim N(0, 1)$$

We can convert any normally distributed variable into a standard normal variable by applying equation (5.7). For example, suppose y represents normally distributed achievement test scores, with mean $\mu = 500$ and standard deviation $\sigma = 75$. An exceptional student who scored a 725 on this test has a standard score of

$$z = \frac{725 - 500}{75}$$
$$= 3$$

indicating that he or she is three standard deviations above average. Similarly, a student whose test score is 350 has a standard score of

$$z = \frac{350 - 500}{75}$$
$$= -2$$

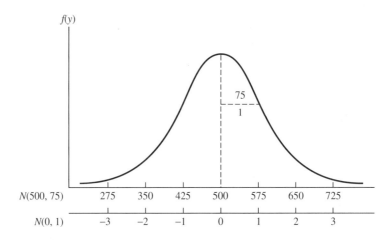

FIGURE 5.9
Correspondence between a normal distribution with mean 500 and standard deviation 75, $N(500, 75)$, and a standard normal distribution, $N(0, 1)$

or two standard deviations below the mean. Figure 5.9 illustrates the correspondence between $N(500, 75)$ and $N(0, 1)$ or standard normal values.

How exceptional are scores three standard deviations above the mean, or two standard deviations below? The next section illustrates what standard normal scores tell us about probability.

EXERCISES

5.3.1 Sketch normal curves to represent the following trios of normal distributions. Label each mean and standard deviation on your figures.
  a. $\mu_1 > \mu_2 > \mu_3$, $\sigma_1 = \sigma_2 = \sigma_3$
  b. $\mu_1 = \mu_2 = \mu_3$, $\sigma_1 > \sigma_2 > \sigma_3$
  c. $\mu_1 < \mu_2 < \mu_3$, $\sigma_1 < \sigma_2 < \sigma_3$
  d. $\mu_1 > \mu_2 = \mu_3$, $\sigma_1 = \sigma_2 > \sigma_3$
5.3.2 What can you guess about the means and standard deviations of achievement test scores among high school seniors in the following types of classes:
  a. "advanced" classes consisting only of seniors who are academically above average
  b. "general" classes for which seniors are chosen randomly, without regard to academic achievement
  c. "remedial" classes consisting only of seniors who are academically below average

Use the symbols μ and σ, subscripted by a (advanced), g (general), or r (remedial) to summarize your answer.

5.3.3 Convert the following y values to standard scores, and write out an interpretation of each score:

    a. $y = 800$, given $\mu = 500$, $\sigma = 75$

    b. $y = 275$, given $\mu = 500$, $\sigma = 75$

    c. $y = 22$, given $\mu = 17$, $\sigma = 2$

    d. $y = 1{,}250$, given $\mu = 2{,}000$, $\sigma = 1{,}500$

    e. $y = .8$, given $\mu = .6$, $\sigma = .2$

    f. $y = -24$, given $\mu = -6$, $\sigma = 9$

5.4   Normal Distribution Probabilities

Unlike binomial or Poisson distributions, normal distributions are continuous. This means that between any two normal values such as $y = 1$ and $y = 2$ lie an infinite number of other possible values. The probability of obtaining any one single value such as $y = 1.000 \ldots$ in drawing from this continuous distribution equals zero. More formally, for a normally distributed variable y and any constant c:

$$P(y = c) = 0$$

Instead, we focus on the probabilities of a range of values, such as $P(y > c)$ or $P(1 < y < 2)$, both of which exceed 0.

Area under a normal curve corresponds to probability. The total area equals 1.0— the probability for all possible values of the variable. About 68% of this total area or probability falls within one standard deviation of the mean (see Figure 5.10, top; page 154). In other words, if y follows a normal distribution, about 68% of all cases should have values greater than $\mu - \sigma$, but less than $\mu + \sigma$:

$$P(\mu - \sigma < y < \mu + \sigma) = .6826$$

For a standard normal variable z, this simplifies to

$$P(-1 < z < 1) = .6826$$

Since the total area equals 1.0, we can deduce that about 32% falls more than one standard deviation below or above the mean:

$$P(y < \mu - \sigma \text{ or } \mu + \sigma < y) = P(z < -1 \text{ or } 1 < z)$$

$$= 1 - .6826$$

$$= .3174$$

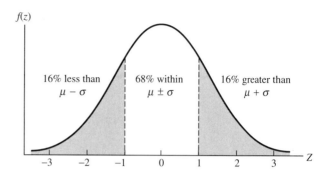

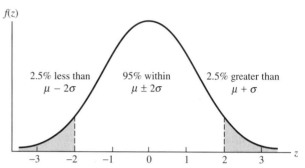

FIGURE 5.10
Approximately 68% of the area under a normal curve is within plus or minus one standard deviation of the mean (top); approximately 95% is within plus or minus two standard deviations (bottom).

If both tails together contain about 32% of the area, since the normal distribution is symmetrical, either one alone must have about 16%. That is, 16% of the cases in a normal distribution have values more than one standard deviation above the mean. Another 16% have values more than one standard deviation below the mean.

Approximately 95% of the total area under a normal curve falls within two standard deviations of the mean (Figure 5.10, bottom):

$$P(\mu - 2\sigma < y < \mu + 2\sigma) = .9544$$

or, in terms of standard scores:

$$P(-2 < z < 2) = .9544$$

This leaves about 2.5% of the area two standard deviations or more above the mean, plus another 2.5% of the area two standard deviations or more below the mean:

$$P(y < \mu - 2\sigma \text{ or } \mu + 2\sigma < y) = P(z < -2 \text{ or } 2 < z)$$

$$= 1 - .9544$$

$$= .0456$$

We can look up probabilities for normally distributed variables by using tables like Appendix Table A.1. This table lists the first two digits of standard normal values in its left-hand column, and their third digit along the top row. [If a variable is normal but not standard normal, we first re-express it as standard normal using equation (5.7).] A z value of 2.34, for instance, is found by reading down the left-hand side to the row for 2.3, then moving across that row to the column for .04. The value in the cell for 2.34 is .4904. This number equals the probability of z values between 0 and 2.34. A graph at the top of Table A.1 illustrates that the probabilities correspond to area between the mean (0) and some positive value c, in the right half of the standard normal distribution. Since the distribution is symmetrical, and its total area equals 1.0, we can calculate other probabilities from the right-tail values in Table A.1.

For example, suppose we need to find the probability of values within plus or minus 2.34 standard deviations of the mean. From Table A.1 we obtain

$$P(0 < z < 2.34) = .4904$$

The probability of values between -2.34 and 2.34 equals twice the one-tail probability:

$$P(-2.34 < z < 2.34) = 2 \times .4904$$
$$= .9808$$

Or, to find the probability of values less than 2.34, add the probability of values below 0 (.5) to the probability of values between 0 and 2.34:

$$P(z < 2.34) = .5 + P(0 < z < 2.34)$$
$$= .5 + .4904$$
$$= .9904$$

Other normal-distribution probabilities can be found in this manner. Sketching and shading areas under the curve helps clarify the thinking involved.

Table A.2 presents a simplified tabulation of the standard normal distribution, listing only certain **critical values** of z corresponding to round-number probabilities such as .1, .2, .3, and so forth. Shaded curves at the top of Table A.2 indicate whether these probabilities refer to central, two-tail, or one-tail areas.

Statistical computer programs can give us normal distribution probabilities with less effort and more precision than tables like Table A.1 or A.2. As introductory statistics courses follow the lead of modern data analysis in becoming more computer-based, probability tables become less important. They remain useful for understanding the distributions, however, and are not quite ready to disappear as have the tables of square roots, logarithms, and similar functions that, before calculators, filled the back pages of math textbooks.

A word of caution regarding the standard score (also called z **score**) transformation, equation (5.7): If we substitute the sample mean and standard deviation, this transformation will change any variable into one with sample mean 0 and standard deviation 1. The transformation does not change distributional shape, however. If y's sample distribution looks approximately normal, then so will that of the transformed variable y^*. But if y is skewed, for example, then y^* will be skewed to the same degree. A standard score transformation does not "normalize" any variable.

> **Standard score transformation**
>
> For any variable y, with sample mean $\bar{y}$ and standard deviation s, the standard score transformation
>
> $$y^* = \frac{y - \bar{y}}{s} \qquad\qquad (5.7a)$$
>
> creates a new variable y^* that has sample mean 0, standard deviation 1, and a distribution with the same shape as the original variable y.

EXERCISES

5.4.1 Find the following probabilities, assuming that x follows a normal distribution. Sketch shaded curves to illustrate each answer.
  a. $P[(x < \mu - 3\sigma) \text{ or } (x > \mu + 3\sigma)]$
  b. $P(x < \mu - 2\sigma)$
  c. $P[(x < \mu - 1\sigma) \text{ or } (x > \mu + 2\sigma)]$
  d. $P[(x < \mu - 3\sigma) \text{ and } (x > \mu + 3\sigma)]$

5.4.2 Assuming that y follows a normal distribution, find (and sketch curves showing) values of a constant c for which
  a. $P(y > \mu + c\sigma) = .5$
  b. $P(y < \mu + c\sigma) = .8413$
  c. $P(y > \mu + c\sigma) = .9772$

5.4.3 A distribution of grade point averages is approximately normal, with $\mu = 2.58$ and $\sigma = .62$.
  a. What GPA would be required for a student to be in the top 2.28% of this distribution? Draw a curve illustrating your answer.
  b. What proportion of the students have GPAs below 1.34? Draw a curve illustrating your answer.

*5.5 Chi-Square (χ^2) Distribution

If z_1 follows a standard normal distribution (normal with mean $\mu = 0$ and standard deviation $\sigma = 1$), then its square, z_1^2, follows a **chi-square** distribution with 1 **degree of freedom**, denoted $\chi^2[1]$:

$$z_1^2 \sim \chi^2[1] \qquad\qquad (5.8a)$$

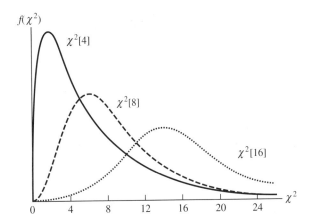

FIGURE 5.11
Chi-square (χ^2) distributions with
4, 8, and 16 degrees of freedom

If z_2 is a second standard normal variable, independent of z_1, then the sum of both variables' squares follows a chi-square distribution with 2 degrees of freedom, $\chi^2[2]$:

$$z_1^2 + z_2^2 \sim \chi^2[2] \tag{5.8b}$$

We can continue in this manner to define chi-square distributions with 3, 4, or more degrees of freedom as sums of three, four, or more squared independent standard normal variables. "Degrees of freedom" refers simply to the number of independent, squared standard normal variables making up the chi-square.

Chi-square distributions range continuously from 0 to positive infinity; there are no negative values. Unlike normal distributions, chi-square distributions vary in shape, depending on their degrees of freedom. All chi-square distributions exhibit positive skew, but this lessens with increasing degrees of freedom. Figure 5.11 depicts chi-square distributions with 4, 8, and 16 degrees of freedom.

Chi-square (χ^2) distribution

If each z_d is an independent standard normal variable ($d = 1, 2, 3, \ldots, df$), then the sum of squared z_d values follows a chi-square distribution with df degrees of freedom:

$$z_1^2 + z_2^2 + z_3^2 + \cdots + z_{df}^2 \sim \chi^2[df] \tag{5.9}$$

A chi-square variable's theoretical mean equals the degrees of freedom:

$$\mu = df \tag{5.10}$$

Its variance equals twice the degrees of freedom:

$$\sigma^2 = 2df \tag{5.11}$$

Chi-square distributions have many statistical applications. The best-known of these involves comparing how often a particular event actually occurred with how often we might expect that event to occur if a certain hypothesis were true. Examples appear in Chapter 7.

Equation (5.9) also implies that the sum of two chi-square variables will itself follow a chi-square distribution [equation (5.12)]. This property proves useful in more advanced applications.

Sums of chi-square distributions

If $\chi^2[d]$ is distributed as chi-square with d degrees of freedom, and $\chi^2[e]$ is distributed as chi-square with e degrees of freedom, and is independent of $\chi^2[d]$, then their sum follows a chi-square distribution with $d + e$ degrees of freedom:

$$\chi^2[d] + \chi^2[e] \sim \chi^2[d + e] \tag{5.12}$$

Table A.3 in the Appendix tabulates critical values for chi-square distributions. Degrees of freedom appear down the left-hand column, chi-square values in the body of the table, and corresponding right-tail probabilities along the top. At any given degrees of freedom, the larger a chi-square value, the lower the probability of still greater values. For example, Table A.3 informs us that in a chi-square distribution with 1 degree of freedom:

$$P(\chi^2[1] > .455) = .500$$

$$P(\chi^2[1] > 10.83) = .001$$

Similarly, in a chi-square distribution with 20 degrees of freedom:

$$P(\chi^2[20] > 28.41) = .100$$

$$P(\chi^2[20] > 31.41) = .050$$

and so on.

We can look up only the approximate probabilities corresponding to chi-square values that are not listed in the table. With 1 degree of freedom, the largest chi-square value listed is 10.83; the probability of a value greater than 10.83 is given as .001:

$$P(\chi^2[1] > 10.83) = .001$$

The probability of a value greater than 12, for example, must therefore be less than .001:

$$P(\chi^2[1] > 12) < .001$$

Chi-square values greater than the rightmost one in a given row cut off tail probabilities below .001. Similarly, chi-square values less than the leftmost one in a given row cut off probabilities above .500. Chi-square values between any two values within a row correspond to probabilities between those two values' probabilities. For example, since

$$P(\chi^2[1] > 3.841) = .050$$

and

$$P(\chi^2[1] > 5.024) = .025$$

we can surmise that although $\chi^2[1] > 4$ does not appear in the table, its probability must lie between the probabilities for 3.841 and 5.024, which do appear in the table:

$$.025 < P(\chi^2[1] > 4) < .050$$

As they do for normal probabilities, computers now readily estimate more precise chi-square probabilities, thereby relieving us of the work of table-reading. This makes it simple to carry out a widely used chi-square test for cross-tabulations, described in Chapter 7.

EXERCISES

*5.5.1   Read Table A.3 to estimate the following probabilities:
      a. $P(\chi^2[4] > 50)$
      b. $P(\chi^2[2] > .5)$
      c. $P(\chi^2[13] > 20)$
      d. $P(\chi^2[100] > 131)$
      e. $P(\chi^2[25] > .2)$
      f. $P(\chi^2[3] > 5)$
      g. $P(\chi^2[9] > 400)$
      h. $P(\chi^2[30] > 50)$

*5.5.2   Use a computer program to estimate more precise probabilities for the chi-square values of Exercise 5.5.1. *Note:*   Some of these probabilities may round off to 0 but, no matter what the computer says, they do not exactly equal 0.

*5.6   *t* Distribution

A third important family of continuous theoretical sampling distributions, called *t* **distributions** or **Student's *t***, is closely related to the normal distribution. Like the standard normal distribution, *t* distributions are bell shaped, center on zero, and range from negative infinity to positive infinity. Unlike normal distributions, *t* distributions do not all have exactly the same shape. Instead, their shape is governed by a degrees-of-freedom

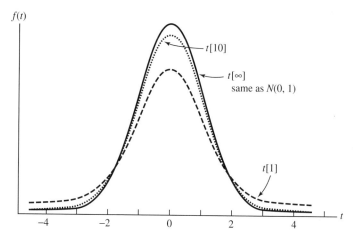

FIGURE 5.12
t distributions with 1, 10, and ∞ (infinite) degrees of freedom

(*df*) parameter; *t* distributions with few degrees of freedom possess noticeably heavier-than-normal tails. Figure 5.12 depicts *t* distributions with 1, 10, and infinite degrees of freedom. As degrees of freedom increase, *t* distributions approach normality. A *t* distribution with infinite degrees of freedom is the same as a standard normal distribution.

t distributions

If *z* is a standard normal variable and χ^2 is a chi-square variable, independent of *z* and with *df* degrees of freedom, then

$$t[df] = \frac{z}{\sqrt{\chi^2/df}}$$

(5.13)

follows a **t distribution** with *df* degrees of freedom.

    t distributions are widely used with means and related statistics, when we wish to evaluate how far our statistic lies from a particular value of the corresponding population parameter. Equations of the general form

$$t = \frac{\text{sample statistic } - \text{ population parameter}}{\text{estimated standard error of statistic}}$$

are known as **t tests**. Chapters 6 and 8–10 contain a variety of specific examples.

As will be seen in later chapters, *t* distributions figure in many simple tests involving means and related statistics. We can look up critical *t* values in tables like Table A.4 in the Appendix. The left-hand column of Table A.4 lists degrees of freedom (*df*) from 1 to ∞ (infinity). Specific *t* values in the body of this table correspond to probabilities listed at the top. Notice the identity between *t*[∞] critical values (Table A.4) and their standard normal counterparts (Table A.2). Table A.4, like Table A.2, gives probabilities for central, two-tail, or one-tail areas. At any given *t* value, the central plus two-tail probabilities equal 1.0, and the one-tail probability equals half of the two-tail probability.

For example, in a *t* distribution with 1 degree of freedom, 90% of the area falls between $t[1] = -6.314$ and $t[1] = 6.314$:

$$P(-6.314 < t[1] < 6.314) = .90$$

Ten percent falls in the two tails beyond -6.314 and 6.314:

$$P\{(t[1] < -6.314) \text{ or } (.6314 < t[1])\} = .10$$

so either of these two tails alone contains 5%:

$$P(t[1] < -6.314) = .05$$

$$P(t[1] > 6.314) = .05$$

Only positive *t* values appear in Table A.4. Since a *t* distribution is symmetrical, we do not need to tabulate negative *t* values. The negative values and their left-hand tail probabilities mirror those of positive *t* values and the right-hand tail. For instance, the probability of *t* values below -1.5 equals the probability of *t* values above 1.5.

Applications of the *t* distribution typically involve one of two kinds of questions:

1. What range of *t* values encompasses the central 95% of a *t* distribution with, for example, 25 degrees of freedom? Table A.4 answers this directly: 2.060 is the *t* value in the *df* = 25 row, .95 confidence interval (central probability) column. Therefore

$$P(-2.060 < t[25] < 2.060) = .95$$

2. How probable are values greater than 2.5, if our statistic follows a *t* distribution with 12 degrees of freedom? The *df* = 12 row of Table A.4 does not include $t[12] = 2.5$, but it does include two surrounding values, $t[12] = 2.179$ and $t[12] = 2.681$. The corresponding one-tail probabilities are

$$P(t[12] > 2.179) = .025$$

$$P(t[12] > 2.681) = .01$$

A *t* value of 2.5 lies between 2.179 and 2.681, so its probability must lie between .025 and .01:

$$.01 < P(t[12] > 2.5) < .025$$

How we use *t* distributions to answer such questions will be explained in Chapter 6.

EXERCISES

*5.6.1 Use Table A.4 to find the critical values, c, for each of the following probabilities:
  a. $P(t[5] > c) = .05$ 　　　　　　b. $P(t[60] > c) = .001$
  c. $P(|t[13]| > c) = .02$ 　　　　　d. $P(|t[1]| > c) = .50$
  e. $P(|t[17]| < c) = .998$ 　　　　f. $P(|t[9]| < c) = .95$

*5.6.2 Use Table A.4 to find approximate probabilities for each of the following t values. State your answer symbolically, as in $.01 < P(t[12] > 2.5) < .025$.
  a. $P(t[3] > 5)$ 　　　　　　　　b. $P(t[120] > .3)$
  c. $P(|t[\infty]| > 1.7)$ 　　　　　　d. $P(|t[7]| > 2.5)$
  e. $P(|t[24]| < 3)$ 　　　　　　　f. $P(|t[9]| < 23)$

*5.6.3 Use a computer to help obtain more precise probabilities for the t values of Exercise 5.6.2. Think carefully; the computer may supply only part of your answer.

*5.7 　 F Distribution

F distributions help in analyzing the ratio of one variance to another. These positively skewed distributions range continuously from 0 to positive infinity. Two different degrees-of-freedom parameters, df_1 and df_2, control the distribution's shape. We call df_1 the **numerator degrees of freedom**, and df_2 the **denominator degrees of freedom**, referring to their positions in equation (5.14). Figure 5.13 shows an F distribution with $df_1 = 4$ and $df_2 = 16$, written $F[4, 16]$.

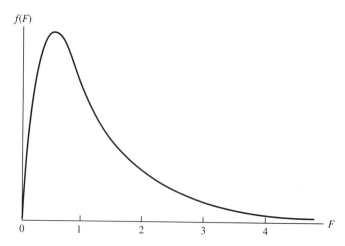

FIGURE 5.13
F distribution with 4 and 16 degrees of freedom

F distributions

If $\chi^2[df_1]$ is a chi-square variable with df_1 degrees of freedom, and $\chi^2[df_2]$ is a second, independent chi-square variable with df_2 degrees of freedom, then the ratio

$$F[df_1,\ df_2] = \frac{\chi^2[df_1]/df_1}{\chi^2[df_2]/df_2}$$ (5.14)

follows an **F distribution** with df_1 and df_2 degrees of freedom. *F* distributions help us in comparing variances. One important application, introduced in Chapter 8, compares the variance of a measurement variable within particular subgroups of cases to the variance between the groups as a whole.

Table A.5 in the Appendix gives critical values for *F* distributions. Numerator degrees of freedom appear along the top, and denominator degrees of freedom down the left-hand column. The body of the table lists the *F* values that cut off five specific right-tail probabilities: $P = .25, .10, .05, .01,$ and $.001$. Table A.5 helps us answer questions such as

What is the probability of an $F[1, 8]$ value of 5.0 or greater?

To answer, find the column for $df_1 = 1$, and the row for $df_2 = 8$. At their intersection, we see this information:

	P	$df_1 = 1$
$df_2 = 8$	.25	1.54
	.10	3.46
	.05	5.32
	.01	11.26
	.001	25.42

The table tells us that 10% of the area ($P = .10$) under an $F[1, 8]$ curve falls to the right of $F[1, 8] = 3.46$, and 5% ($P = .05$) falls to the right of $F[1, 8] = 5.32$. Therefore the probability of an $F[1, 8]$ value greater than 5.0 must be

$$.05 < P(F[1, 8] > 5.0) < .10$$

Similarly, we might find the probability of values greater than 12.0, given an *F* distribution with 3 and 5 degrees of freedom, by reading the $df_1 = 3$ column, $df_2 = 5$ row in Table A.5:

$$.01 < P(F[3, 5] > 12.0) < .05$$

Ratio-of-variances questions, requiring the use of *F*-distribution probabilities, occur often in analyses with measurement variables. Here is a simple example. Chapter 3 analyzed data on the playground behavior of 26 preschool children. Counts of the number of fighting-and-chasing episodes had a variance of $s_1^2 = 28.25$ among boys and

$s_2^2 = 9.38$ among girls. Thus boys in this sample appear much more varied or diverse than girls in their fighting-and-chasing behavior, because several boys were exceptionally aggressive. How likely is it that we would observe such a large difference between the two variances, if these 26 children represented a random sample from a population of children in which boys' and girls' variances were the same? If that were true, then the variance ratio (VR)

$$VR = \frac{28.25}{9.38}$$

$$= 3.01$$

should approximately follow an $F[15, 9]$ distribution. Table A.5 suggests about a 5% probability, $P(F[15, 9] > 3.01) \approx .05$, for F values this large or larger.

Before looking at the data, we did not know that boys' variance would be larger, so we must also consider the possibility of an equally large difference in the opposite direction:

$$VR = \frac{9.38}{28.25}$$

$$= .33$$

We need a computer to determine the probability of F values this small or smaller, $P(F[15, 9] < .33) = .0281$. Thus there is a $.05 + .028 = .078$ or roughly 8% chance of seeing gender differences this great, in drawing samples of $n = 26$ children from populations in which boys' and girls' variances are equal.

Equations (5.15)–(5.16) more formally describe this test for the equality of two variances or, equivalently, for the equality of two standard deviations.

F test for the equality of two variances

We have the following information:

	n of cases	**variance of y**
Group 1	n_1	s_1^2
Group 2	n_2	s_2^2

and $s_1^2 > s_2^2$. If both samples were drawn randomly from populations with equal variances, in which y follows a normal distribution, then the variance ratio

$$VR = \frac{s_1^2}{s_2^2} \tag{5.15}$$

follows an F distribution with $n_1 - 1$ and $n_2 - 1$ degrees of freedom. For a two-tail test of the hypothesis of equal population variances, find the probability

$$P(F[n_1 - 1, n_2 - 1] > VR) + 1 - P(F[n_1 - 1, n_2 - 1] > 1/VR) \tag{5.16}$$

Typically, if the result of expression (5.16) is below .05, researchers decide to **reject** or disbelieve the hypothesis that population variances are equal.

Unfortunately, tests based on equation (5.16) become untrustworthy if y's distribution possesses heavier-than-normal tails. Our sample data appear positively skewed (Figure 3.2), and similar skewness almost certainly characterizes the population as well. Therefore we cannot fully trust this particular test; Cleves (1995) describes one alternative. Later chapters return to the issue of normality assumptions in statistical tests.

Although this example makes a questionable assumption, it serves to introduce the general concept of **hypothesis testing**. We formulate a hypothesis, such as equal variances in the population, then calculate a test statistic and its probability. If this probability is low, then we can reject the hypothesis and believe its complement instead—for example, that the population variances are *un*equal.

EXERCISES

*5.7.1 Find, write symbolically, and sketch a diagram to illustrate the following probabilities:

    a. $P(F[4, 30] > 8.3)$ b. $P(F[3, 30] > 3.1)$

    c. $P(F[2, 13] > 14.6)$ d. $P(F[10, 120] > 45.3)$

    e. $P(F[8, 10] > .5)$ f. $P(F[5, 18] > 4.3)$

*5.7.2 In which of the following instances should we reject the hypothesis of equal population variances, because probabilities from equation (5.16) are below .05? (Where necessary, use the fact that standard deviation equals the square root of variance.)

    a.   Group 1 has 21 cases and variance 9. Group 2 has 13 cases and variance 4.

    b.   Group 1 has 41 cases and variance 81. Group 2 has 121 cases and variance 64.

    c.   Group 1 has 70 cases and variance 625. Group 2 has 150 cases and variance 400.

    d.   Group 1 has 4 cases and *standard deviation* 1. Group 2 has 3 cases and standard deviation 10.

    e.   Group 1 has 7,000 cases and standard deviation 13.1. Group 2 has 9,000 cases and standard deviation 13.3.

    f.   Group 1 has 27 cases and standard deviation 8. Group 2 has 12 cases and standard deviation 7.

Summary

This chapter described six types of theoretical probability distribution that have broad applications in statistics. Four types are continuous: normal, chi-square (χ^2), t, and F. A particular mathematical equation defines normal distributions; the word *normal* here does not have its ordinary English meaning of "usual" or "typical." Variables that represent sums of many small identically distributed random influences often follow normal distributions. This property makes normal distributions a good model for the sampling distribution of means and related statistics. All normal distributions have the same shape, and are easily transformed into standard normal distributions with mean 0 and standard deviation 1.

Chi-square, t, and F distributions derive from the standard normal distribution. Details of shape depend on parameters called degrees of freedom, which reflect how many independent pieces of information contribute to a particular statistic. Researchers use theoretical distributions to test hypotheses. We saw one simple hypothesis test (equality of two variances) involving the F distribution. Later chapters present many others. Hypothesis tests estimate what the probability of certain sample results would be, *if* some hypothesis about the population were true. Low probabilities (usually below .05, or 5%) suggest that we should not believe the hypothesis.

The discrete binomial and Poisson distributions provide models for counts of categorical variables. Exact binomial probabilities become difficult to calculate unless samples are small. Poisson distributions, for larger samples combined with low probabilities, or normal distributions, for larger samples combined with higher probabilities, then provide reasonable approximations. Like the other theoretical distributions, binomial and Poisson distributions can also be used in testing hypotheses.

Subsequent chapters look more systematically at sampling distributions in research. We begin Chapter 6 with a discussion of how t distributions help us draw conclusions about an unknown population mean.

Characteristics and Common Applications of Theoretical Sampling Distributions

Distribution	Characteristics	Common applications
binomial	discrete; shape determined by sample size (n) and event probability (p); approximately normal if both $np/(1 - p)$ and $n(1 - p)/p$ exceed 9	drawing conclusions about the frequency of some event that occurs with constant probability p at each trial
Poisson	discrete; shape determined by mean, which equals sample size times event probability ($\mu = np$)	drawing conclusions about the frequency of some event that occurs with constant probability p at each trial, or the number of occurrences of an event in a given time period; approximation for binomial when n is large and p is small

Distri-bution	Characteristics	Common applications
normal (Gaussian)	continuous, symmetric; mean (μ) indicates the center; standard deviation (σ) indicates the spread around this center	drawing conclusions about a population mean, if population standard deviation known; also used as a large-sample approximation for certain other distributions
standard normal	normal distribution with mean 0 and standard deviation 1	transformation of any normally distributed variable to $N(0, 1)$, allowing comparison with standard tables
chi-square (χ^2)	continuous; positive skew especially at low degrees of freedom (df); more nearly symmetrical at higher df	drawing conclusions about a population variance, or testing the fit between observed and expected frequencies in cross-tabulations
Student's t	continuous, symmetric; heavier-than-normal tails at low df; becomes approximately normal at higher df	drawing conclusions about a population mean, difference of means, or regression coefficient, if population standard deviation is unknown
F	continuous; shape controlled by two parameters, the numerator and denominator degrees of freedom (df_1 and df_2)	drawing conclusions about the equality of two population variances; allows tests for differences among several means (ANOVA) or for the proportion of variance explained (regression)

PROBLEMS

5.1 Sketch and label curves to show the following normal distributions:
 a. $x \sim N(0, 15)$
 b. $x \sim N(25, 5)$; $y \sim N(25, 10)$
 c. $x \sim N(1{,}000, 500)$; $y \sim N(2{,}000, 1{,}000)$

5.2 Express the following x values as standard scores:
 a. $x = 34$, given $x \sim N(28, 16)$ b. $x = 943$, given $x \sim N(1{,}236, 89)$
 c. $x = -6$, given $x \sim N(12, 10)$ d. $x = 400$, given $x \sim N(400, 65)$

5.3 Intelligence quotient (IQ) tests are commonly designed so that scores follow an approximately normal distribution with a mean of 100 and a standard deviation of 15.
    a.   Sketch a normal curve representing such a distribution.
    b.   Add a second horizontal scale to this curve, showing IQ in standard-score form.
    c.   What standard score corresponds to an IQ of 100? 75? 145? Explain what these standard scores tell us, beyond what we know from the IQ scores themselves.

5.4 For an IQ test as described in Problem 5.3:
    a.   What proportion of the population should score above 124?
    b.   What is the probability that a single individual, selected at random from the population, will score above 124?
    c.   What is the probability that a single randomly selected individual will score above 115, but below 148?
    d.   What is the probability of scores between 64 and 94?
    e.   If the population consists of 200 million people, how many could be expected to score above 160 points on the test?
    f.   What is the probability that a randomly selected individual will score between 85 and 130?
    g.   What score would an individual need to be in the top 5% of the population? Top 1%? Top .05%?

5.5 The third quartile (Q_3) of a distribution lies above 75% of the cases, and below the remaining 25%. Use Table A.1 to determine:
    a.   What is the third quartile of a standard normal distribution?
    b.   What is the first quartile? How wide, in standard deviations, is the interquartile range, $IQR = Q_3 - Q_1$?
    c.   Find Q_1, Q_3, and IQR for a $N(100, 15)$ distribution.
    d.   Use your answer to part **b** to derive an equation for estimating the standard deviation of a normal distribution, if we know only its IQR. (This equation defines a useful statistic called the **pseudo standard deviation**.)

5.6 Boxplots (Chapter 3) define an "outlier" as any case with a value below $Q_1 - 1.5IQR$, or above $Q_3 + 1.5IQR$. What is the proportion of outliers in a normal population?

5.7 Use a computer to generate an artificial dataset with $n = 150$ cases and four variables named a, b, c, and d, drawn from normal distributions as follows:
    a. $a \sim N(0, 1)$ b. $b \sim N(100, 15)$
    c. $c \sim N(500, 75)$ d. $d \sim N(-20, 3)$

5.8 Compare the actual means and standard deviations of a, b, c, and d from Problem 5.7 with the theoretical population parameters. Why are the sample statistics and population parameters not identical?

5.9   Graph each of your sample variables from Problem 5.7 as a histogram, indicating the mean and one standard deviation on the graph. Compare these histograms with theoretical normal curves.

5.10   In a theoretical normal distribution, about 5% of the cases fall more than two standard deviations from the mean. What proportion of the cases in your artificial data of Problem 5.7 fall more than two standard deviations from the mean? Use the theoretical mean and standard deviation (e.g., 0 and 1; 100 and 15; etc.) of each distribution rather than the sample mean and standard deviation.

*5.11   Estimate the probability of chi-square values greater than:

  a.   .7, given $df = 19$ b.   18.1, given $df = 8$
  c.   24.4, given $df = 16$ d.   12.8, given $df = 1$
  e.   27.5, given $df = 10$ f.   34, given $df = 18$

*5.12   Use a computer to generate a random dataset of $n = 150$, containing three variables named $x1$, $x3$, and $x6$, drawn from the following chi-square distributions. Compare the means and variances of your variables with the theoretical population parameters.

  a. $x1 \sim \chi^2[1]$
  b. $x3 \sim \chi^2[3]$
  c. $x6 \sim \chi^2[6]$

*5.13   For each theoretical chi-square distribution of Problem 5.12, look up the critical value c such that $P(\chi^2 \geq c) = .05$. What proportion of sample values of each of your variables actually falls above the critical value?

*5.14   Graph each of the variables in Problem 5.12 as a histogram, and describe its shape. What trend in shape appears, as degrees of freedom increase?

*5.15   Sketch the shape you would expect to see in a $\chi^2[800]$ distribution, and indicate the mean and standard deviation.

*5.16   Estimate the probability of t values greater than

  a.   .79, given $df = 60$ b.   4.35, given $df = 120$
  c.   2.38, given $df = 5$ d.   1.02, given $df = 74$
  e.   2.7, given $df = 29$ f.   1.63, given $df = 34$

*5.17   Generate a dataset of $n = 150$ with variables named $t1$, $t5$, and $tinf$, randomly generated from these three theoretical distributions:

$$t1 \sim t[1]$$

$$t5 \sim t[5]$$

$$tinf \sim t[\infty] \sim N(0, 1)$$

All three variables' theoretical distributions center on 0, but $t[1]$ has the heaviest tails. Does this difference show up in your samples? Graph your variables as boxplots and compare the proportions and severity of outliers in each plot.

*5.18 Theoretically, what proportion of values should fall between -12.706 and $+12.706$ in a $t[1]$ distribution? What proportion of the sample values of $t1$, from Problem 5.17, fall within this range?

*5.19 Theoretically, what proportion of values should exceed 2.015 in a $t[5]$ distribution? What proportion of sample values of $t5$, from Problem 5.17, exceed this value?

*5.20 Estimate the probability of F values greater than
    a. 3.05, given $df_1 = 4$ and $df_2 = 5$
    b. 7.7, given $df_1 = 20$ and $df_2 = 7$
    c. 28.1, given $df_1 = 2$ and $df_2 = 30$
    d. 1.0, given $df_1 = 5$ and $df_2 = 12$
    e. 4.4, given $df_1 = 2$ and $df_2 = 500$
    f. 3.9, given $df_1 = 9$ and $df_2 = 19$

*5.21 For each of the pairs of samples below, calculate probabilities [equation (5.16)] to test the hypothesis that the samples come from populations with equal variances. State whether you "reject" (disbelieve) or "do not reject" the equal-variances hypothesis, applying this rule: Reject if the F statistic's probability is less than .025. For the purposes of this exercise, assume that the variables' distributions are approximately normal, although in several instances they actually are not.
    a. Based on the sample in Table 1.1 (file *stats*), are female and male statistics students equally diverse, in terms of their math SAT scores?

	n of cases	variance
females	24	5,999
males	11	4,805

    b. Based on the sample in Table 1.1, are female and male statistics students equally diverse, in terms of their ages?

	n of cases	variance
females	31	22.5
males	12	3.1

    c. Based on the sample in Table 3.5 (file *smoke*), are nicotine concentrations equally varied in the air of the two types of Boeing 737 jets (737-200s and 737-300s)? Among the 40 Boeing 737-200 aircraft, the standard deviation of nicotine content equals 20.1. Among the 17 Boeing 737-300s, the standard deviation equals 23.0
    d. Based on the data of Table 3.1 (file *play*), we concluded earlier that boys exhibit more variation than girls in their aggressive fighting-and-chasing behavior. Do boys and girls likewise exhibit a different degree of variation in their rough-and-tumble play?

e.   Again use the data of Table 3.1 to test the hypothesis that the population variance for the boys' ages is equal to the population variance for the girls' ages.

*5.22   Calculate and graph binomial probabilities for $f = 0, 1, 2, 3, 4$ if $n = 4$ and $p = .3$. What is $P(f \geq 3)$?

*5.23   Calculate and graph binomial probabilities for $f = 0, 1, 2, 3, 4, 5, 6, 7, 8, 9$ given $n = 9$ and $p = .1$. What is $P(f \geq 2)$?

*5.24   The Census Bureau reported that in 1980 about 6.7% of the 287,806 lawyers in America were women. If a certain law firm hired six lawyers that year, all of them male, could it plausibly claim this had happened just "by chance"? To address this question, find the binomial probability of hiring exactly zero women out of six if gender were not a factor, given $n = 6$ and $p = .067$.

*5.25   Referring to Problem 5.24, what is the probability of the firm hiring three or more women "by chance"? Five or more?

*5.26   On July days in the high country of Rocky Mountain National Park, there is about a 40% chance of thunderstorms ($p = .40$). Assume that the occurrence of a storm one day does not change the probability of a storm the following day. A hiker is planning a 7-day trip. Use the binomial distribution to estimate the probability that she will encounter no storms. What is the probability that she will have storms on at most 2 days?

*5.27   A quiz consists of 10 true–false questions, half of them false. If an unprepared student answers each question by flipping a coin, what is the probability that he will earn a passing grade (at least 7 correct)? What is the probability he will earn an A (at least 9 correct)?

*5.28   Calculate probabilities for the following Poisson distributions:
   a. $y = 0, 1, 2, 3, 4$, given $\mu = 2.5$
   b. $y = 0, 1, 2, 3, 4, 5, 6$, given $\mu = 4$

*5.29   An insurers' association released the following information about malpractice suits against the physicians they insured. During an 8-year period, there had been a total of 2,131 malpractice suits among the 9,683 physicians. About 3% of the physicians received 31.7% of these lawsuits.

   This information seems to imply that a few physicians are especially prone to lawsuits, perhaps to the detriment of the whole profession. Before jumping to this conclusion, though, you should consider that even if lawsuits were totally random events, unrelated to physicians' characteristics, some physicians would have the bad luck to be sued more than once.

   If lawsuits were distributed randomly among these 9,683 physicians, we could expect them to follow a Poisson distribution with a mean (μ) equal to $2,131/9,683 = .22$ suit per physician during the 8-year period. Use equation (5.4) to find the following probabilities, if lawsuits were indeed random:
   a. $P(y = 0)$, the probability a physician is not sued during the 8-year period

    b. $P(y = 1)$, the probability a physician is sued only once during the 8-year period

    c. $P(y = 2)$, the probability a physician is sued only twice during the 8-year period

    d. $P(y \geq 3)$, the probability a physician is sued three or more times during the 8-year period

*5.30   Use your answers to Problem 5.29 to determine the expected number of physicians sued never, once, twice, or three or more times during the 8-year period, if lawsuits were a random (Poisson) process. What percentage of the physicians would be expected to receive one or more of the lawsuits?

*5.31   Your analysis in Problems 5.29–5.30 shows that even if lawsuits were random, the unluckiest 2.1% of the physicians (those sued more than one time) would be the targets of nearly 20% of suits, since $2{,}131 - 1{,}710 = 421$ of the 2,131 lawsuits are against physicians who get sued more than once. Thus a completely random process in which everyone has the same chance of being sued could still produce results that superficially look like evidence of "bad apples" among physicians. How might these percentages be different if some physicians really were more likely to be sued than others?

*5.32   A fire department planner calculates that the department receives an average of .51 alarm per day. Assuming that fire alarms follow a Poisson distribution, what is the probability of three or more alarms in a given day?

6

One-Sample Confidence Intervals and Tests

S uppose we selected 100 voters, using a random-number table like Table 4.6, from the 20,000 names on a town's list of registered voters. We then contact each of these 100 people and ask, "Do you favor or oppose the plan to locate a new state prison in your town?" Of the 100 people in our sample, 34 say they favor, 57 oppose, and 9 do not know. We can accurately claim that 57% of the voters we surveyed oppose the prison. But that has limited interest: What about the other 19,900 voters? Should state officials conclude that 57% of all the town's voters oppose the prison? Or even that a majority oppose it? These more interesting questions require a step called **inference**: moving from what we know about the sample at hand, to some broader, but uncertain, conclusions about the population as a whole. The theoretical distributions introduced in Chapter 5 provide a framework for inference. Statistical inferences usually take one of two forms: confidence intervals or hypothesis tests.

Confidence intervals represent our "best guess" about the true value of an unknown parameter such as the proportion of all voters opposing the prison. We state this guess not as a single number like 57% (a **point estimate**), which would probably be wrong, but rather as an **interval estimate**: We suspect that the true proportion equals 57% *plus or minus* 10%, for instance. This chapter introduces methods for constructing such intervals so that, over the long run, our interval estimates should be correct (i.e., include the true value of the parameter) about 95% of the time.

Hypothesis tests follow related but more elaborate reasoning, starting from a pair of specific statements about the population—our hypotheses. These two hypotheses are complementary (as defined in Chapter 4), so that if one hypothesis is false, the other must be true. We apply probability reasoning to the evidence from our sample, with the aim of deciding which of the two hypotheses to believe. If this reasoning casts doubt on one hypothesis, then there is good reason to believe the other hypothesis instead. **One-sample hypothesis tests**, discussed in this chapter, test pairs of hypotheses about one proportion, mean, or median.

In Chapter 3 we noted the contrasting behavior of the mean and the median in the presence of outliers. Outliers can drastically affect a mean, while having little or no impact on the median. Furthermore, medians often work better as summaries for skewed distributions. As we now consider hypothesis tests for means and medians, these properties become relevant again. If our data contain outliers or exhibit a high degree of skew, then mean-based tests may perform poorly, and we should consider a median-based test instead. This chapter concludes with an example of a median-based test.

All of the inferential methods described in this book assume that we have a random sample from the population of interest. If not, then our conclusions may apply only to a population that is much narrower than we think, perhaps so narrow it includes only the sample itself. Suppose we had selected our 100-voter sample not randomly from a voters' list, but by interviewing people who walked past a table we had set up outside the elementary school. Then, instead of generalizing about the whole population of voters, we could generalize only about the population consisting of people who were walking past the elementary school at that particular time, and happened to make contact with the interviewer. Very likely, these are mostly parents of young children in that particular neighborhood. If 57% of them said they opposed the prison, this tells us nothing much about the town's voters as a whole, unlike the random sample.

6.1   Student Grades Dataset

Table 6.1 (page 176) lists part of the dataset forming this chapter's central example. The complete sample includes 160 undergraduate students taking sociology courses at one university. To save space, only the first 16 students appear in Table 6.1. For each of the 160 students in this sample, we know:

gender	male or female
degree	lifetime degree goals (bachelor's, master's, or doctorate/professional) as reported by the student
rankp	high school class rank percentile (higher numbers are better) from university records
gpa	cumulative college grade point average (GPA) from university records
gpar	cumulative college GPA as reported by the student
gpaerr	error in GPA, equal to self-reported GPA minus true GPA from university records

These data were originally assembled to study patterns of errors in self-reports—a topic of great importance to survey researchers.

Summary statistics at the bottom of Table 6.1 summarize this 160-student dataset. We can describe this sample with as much precision as we want, but these students represent only a small fraction of the thousands of students taking sociology courses at the university in that particular year. What conclusions should we draw about that larger population, on the basis of this sample? In addressing this question, we depend on the important—and in this instance, reasonable—assumption that the 160 students represent a random sample from the population of all sociology students enrolled at the university at that time.

The following sections introduce some widely used statistical techniques that help to answer this question. Distinct but mathematically related techniques apply to categorical and measurement variables. With categorical variables such as gender and degree goals, we most often focus on proportions or percentages. Means and standard deviations, on the other hand, work better with measurement variables such as percentile rank and GPA.

Table 6.1

Student academic data—the first 16 students in a sample of $n = 160$

	gender	degree	rankp	gpa	gpar	gpaerr
1	male	bachelor's	80.0	2.42	2.40	−.02
2	male	master's	79.3	3.03	3.00	−.03
3	female	master's	66.5	2.72	3.40	.68
4	male	master's	80.6	2.14	2.10	−.04
5	male	master's	56.0	3.22	3.28	.06
6	female	bachelor's	82.4	2.75	2.70	−.05
7	female	master's	86.3	3.28	3.67	.39
8	male	master's	23.5	1.25	2.50	1.25
9	female	master's	70.0	2.57	2.39	−.18
10	female	master's	89.6	2.78	2.90	.12
11	male	master's	66.4	2.77	2.87	.10
12	male	master's	74.4	3.49	3.48	−.01
13	female	bachelor's	85.2	3.46	3.50	.04
14	female	master's	92.2	3.47	3.66	.19
15	female	doctorate	33.5	3.42	3.35	−.07
16	female	bachelor's	60.2	1.45	2.00	.55
.						
.						
.						
160						

Summary statistics based on $n = 160$:

60%	34.4%	$\bar{y}$:	75.8	2.64	2.83	.20
female	bach.	s:	17.2	.53	.47	.38

Source: Hamilton (1981).
File: *selfrep*

EXERCISE

6.1.1 Write a paragraph describing the student grades data, using the summary statistics at the bottom of Table 6.1.

6.2 ▬ Large-Sample Confidence Intervals for Proportions

When our samples consist of cases drawn independently from a large population, proportions such as "the proportion of women" or "the proportion expecting a bachelor's degree" should follow binomial sampling distributions (described in Section 5.1). Binomial probabilities are awkward to calculate with large samples, however. Fortunately, binomial distributions become approximately normal if $np/(1 - p)$ and $n(1 - p)/p$ exceed 9—as is the case in most survey research. The proportion of students in Table 6.1 who expect bachelor's degrees (34.4%, or $p = .344$) comfortably meets this criterion for approximate normality. Given $n = 160$ and $p = .344$:

$$\frac{np}{1 - p} = 83.9$$

$$\frac{n(1 - p)}{p} = 305.1$$

Large-sample sampling distribution and standard error of a proportion

In large samples the sampling distribution of a proportion p becomes approximately normal, with mean:

$$\mu_p = \pi \tag{6.1}$$

variance:

$$\sigma_p^2 = \frac{\pi(1 - \pi)}{n} \tag{6.2a}$$

and standard error:

$$\sigma_p = \sqrt{\frac{\pi(1 - \pi)}{n}} \tag{6.2b}$$

where π (pi) represents the true population proportion.
    We can estimate this standard error by substituting a sample proportion p for the true (but unknown) population proportion π in equation (6.2b):

$$s_p = \sqrt{\frac{p(1 - p)}{n}} \tag{6.3}$$

Let π stand for the population proportion of students expecting bachelor's degrees, and p the proportion of such students in one random sample of $n = 160$. A normal sampling distribution implies that if we collected many $n = 160$ random samples, and calculated p for each one, those many values of p should follow a normal distribution centered on π. We call the standard deviation of this sampling distribution, σ_p, the **standard error** of p. By the definition of a normal distribution, about 68.26% of all random samples should have p values in the range $\pi \pm \sigma_p$; about 95.44% should have p values in the range $\pi \pm 2\sigma_p$; and so forth (see Figure 6.1).

For most studies, we have just one sample and do not know the true values of either π or σ_p. Instead, we must estimate σ_p from our single sample by using the sample proportion p in place of the unknown population proportion π, as in equation (6.3). Note that different symbols represent the true (but usually unknown) standard error σ_p and its estimated value s_p.

For the degree goals example, equation (6.3) yields the estimated standard error

$$s_p = \sqrt{\frac{.344(1 - .344)}{160}}$$

$$= .038$$

A principal use for such estimated standard errors is forming **confidence intervals**— intervals within which we have a certain degree of confidence that the true population proportion lies.

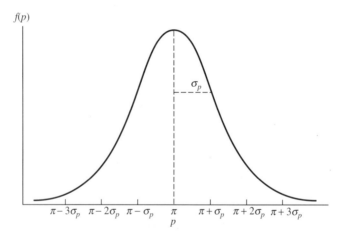

FIGURE 6.1
Theoretical sampling distribution of a sample proportion p, obtained from many random samples of size $n = 160$ each: Approximately normal with mean π and standard error σ_p

Large-sample confidence interval for a proportion

To form a confidence interval for any proportion π, based on a sample large enough for the normal approximation to hold, find

$$p \pm zs_p \tag{6.4a}$$

or

$$p \pm z \sqrt{\frac{p(1 - p)}{n}} \tag{6.4b}$$

where z is chosen from a theoretical **standard normal distribution**. The left-hand column of Table A.2 in Appendix II lists z distribution values needed to obtain the desired degree of confidence.

Section 5.4 gave the z distribution's theoretical definition. Here, we concentrate simply on using this distribution as it appears in Table A.2. To obtain a 95% confidence interval, or central-area probability of .95, requires a critical value of $z = 1.96$ (found by reading down the left-hand or confidence interval column to .95, then reading across to the right-hand column to find the corresponding value of z). This tells us that a 95% confidence interval must cover a width equal to plus and minus 1.96 standard errors.

Applied to the degree goals example, equation (6.4) gives us the 95% confidence interval:

$$.344 + 1.96(.038) = .418$$

$$.344 - 1.96(.038) = .270$$

Thus we are 95% confident (based on our 160-student sample) that $.270 < \pi < .418$. That is, our sample leads us to believe that the true population proportion of students expecting bachelor's degrees falls somewhere between .270 and .418. The "95% confident" phrase stands for this more technical claim: If we collected many random samples of size $n = 160$ and constructed confidence intervals in this fashion from each one, about 95% of those intervals should actually contain π.

To construct a 99% confidence interval, Table A.2 indicates we should use $z = 2.576$:

$$.344 + 2.576(.038) = .442$$

$$.344 - 2.576(.038) = .246$$

We are 99% confident, based on this sample, that the population proportion falls between .246 and .442:

$$.246 < \pi < .442$$

In a similar fashion, we could form intervals for any other degree of confidence. By convention, most research articles report just the 95% interval.

If you follow political campaign news, you may notice that opinion poll results are often announced with phrasing like this:

> In our survey of 600 registered voters, we found that 54% favored presidential candidate Bill Clinton. This survey has a margin of error of plus or minus 4%.

The "margin of error" mentioned derives from a 95% confidence interval. The pollsters are at least 95% confident that in the population of all voters, the true percentage favoring Clinton falls between $54 - 4 = 50\%$ and $54 + 4 = 58\%$. Most use "margin of error" instead of the more technical-sounding term "confidence interval" when presenting their conclusions to the public.

Standard errors [equation (6.3)] are largest, and hence confidence intervals [equation (6.4)] widest, when $p = .5$. Thus if a survey of $n = 600$ people reports many different proportions (proportion favoring Clinton, proportion favoring Ross Perot, and so forth), the largest possible standard error for any proportion must be

$$\sigma_p(\text{max}) = \sqrt{\frac{.5(1 - .5)}{600}}$$

$$= .02$$

This implies that given any sample proportion p, and $n = 600$, we have *at least* 95% confidence that the true proportion π falls within about plus or minus .04 of the sample proportion p:

$$p \pm 1.96(.02) = p \pm .04$$

Multiplying by 100 translates these proportions into percentages, and gives us the pollster's "plus or minus 4%" margin of error. Instead of applying equations (6.3) and (6.4) to calculate a separate confidence interval for the percentage favoring Clinton, the percentage favoring Perot, and so forth, the pollster simply reports one overall confidence interval width that is large enough to provide 95% confidence with any percentage in the survey.

Opinion-poll "margins of error"

Opinion polls often report percentages with a "margin of error," which they base on the 95% confidence interval [equation (6.4b)] when $p = .5$ or 50%:

$$\text{sample percentage} \pm 1.96 \sqrt{\frac{50(100 - 50)}{n}} \qquad \textbf{(6.5a)}$$

or, rounding off the 1.96 to 2 and then simplifying algebraically:

$$\text{sample percentage} \pm \frac{100}{\sqrt{n}} \qquad\qquad\qquad \textbf{(6.5b)}$$

Equations (6.5a) or (6.5b) provide "at least 95% confidence" intervals for the true population percentage.

The "large-sample" methods described in this section provide only approximate confidence intervals. Exact confidence intervals for proportions require binomial calculations that are difficult to work through by hand. Computer programs, however, perform these binomial calculations more easily and provide the exact confidence intervals.

EXERCISES

6.2.1 Sixty percent of the 160 students (Table 6.1, file *selfrep*) are women. Find and interpret the 90%, 95%, and 99% confidence intervals for the percentage of women among the larger population of students from which this sample was drawn.

6.2.2 Of the 160 students in Table 6.1, 8.75% say they expect to obtain a doctorate degree. Find and interpret the 80%, 95%, and 98% confidence intervals based on this percentage.

6.2.3 Demonstrate that, according to the rule of thumb, the normal approximation applies in Exercise 6.2.2.

6.2.4 A survey measured support for three political candidates among a random sample of 300 registered voters:

Lee   51%
Smith   44%
Jones   5%

   a. Find the actual 95% confidence interval [using equations (6.3) and (6.4)] for each candidate's support in the population of all registered voters.
   b. Does Lee look like the winner, or is this election still "too close to call" with 95% confidence?
   c. Find the pollster's "margin of error" (or "at least 95% confidence" interval) using equation (6.5b). Write a brief paragraph summarizing these poll results as if for a newspaper article.
   d. Compare the "margin of error" you obtained in part **c** with the actual confidence intervals from part **a**.

6.3 — The Logic of Hypothesis Testing

A statistical **hypothesis** is a statement about the true value of an unknown population parameter. **Hypothesis tests** work with pairs of hypotheses: the **null hypothesis** (H_0) and its complement, the **research** or **alternative hypothesis** (H_1). We test the null hypothesis because statistical theory suggests how samples should behave, and therefore how likely or unlikely our particular sample results would be, *if the null hypothesis were true.*

For example, a null hypothesis might assert that a certain coin is fair, meaning that in the population of all possible tosses of that coin the proportion of heads (π) equals .5:

$$H_0: \pi = .5$$

The alternative hypothesis simply states that the coin is not fair:

$$H_1: \pi \neq .5$$

Generally the null hypothesis is the simpler of the two, in that it involves an equality (e.g., $\pi = .5$), whereas the research hypothesis specifies an inequality (e.g., $\pi \neq .5$ or $\pi > .5$).

Hypothesis tests use sample data, such as 100 sample coin tosses, to assess whether the null hypothesis is plausible. When sample evidence weighs against the null hypothesis, that strengthens the case for believing the alternative hypothesis instead, since H_1 must be true if its complement H_0 is not.

Typically H_1, the research hypothesis, is more interesting to the researcher. It may stand for ideas (like "students taught by my method learn more" or "meditation lowers blood pressure") for which the researcher hopes to find support. The null hypothesis then represents a negation of the researcher's hypothesis (as in "students taught by my method do not learn more" or "meditation does not lower blood pressure"). Although the researcher may hope that the evidence favors H_1, hypothesis tests are set up to test H_0. The research hypothesis will be accepted only if sample evidence argues strongly against H_0.

Statistical hypothesis tests involve several steps:

1. We specify the two complementary hypotheses, H_0 and H_1.

2. Analyzing our data, we ask: What would be the probability of results that are this favorable to H_1, if this sample had been drawn randomly from a population in which H_0 is true? This probability we call a *P*-value.

3a. A low *P*-value (such as $P < .05$) makes it appear unlikely that our sample came from a population where H_0 is true. We therefore have reason to *reject the null hypothesis,* and accept (believe) H_1 instead. The evidence supporting H_1 is **statistically significant**.

4a. Sometimes, in rejecting H_0, we are mistaken. A **Type I error** occurs if we reject a null hypothesis that is actually true.

3b. On the other hand, a high *P*-value (such as $P \geq .05$) gives us no reason to disbelieve H_0; we *fail to reject the null hypothesis*. Our sample might well have come from a population where H_0 is true. The evidence supporting H_1 is **not statistically significant**. (This does not mean that the null hypothesis *is* true; but we cannot rule it out.)

4b. This decision might also be mistaken. Failure to reject a false H_0 constitutes a **Type II error**.

A predetermined cutoff called the **significance level**, symbolized by the Greek letter α (alpha), defines what we consider a "low *P*-value." Typically, researchers choose a cutoff such as $\alpha = .05$ or $\alpha = .01$. Choosing $\alpha = .05$, for example, means that we decide to reject H_0 only when $P < .05$. Table 6.2 summarizes the relation between significance level and error types.

Table 6.2
Significance level (α), power ($1 - \beta$), and Type I and Type II errors

Fact	Decision, based on significance level α	
	Not reject H_0	*Reject H_0*
H_0 *is true*	correct decision: P(not reject H_0 when H_0 true) $= 1 - \alpha$	**Type I error**: P(reject H_0 when H_0 true) $= \alpha$
H_1 *is true*	**Type II error**: P(not reject H_0 when H_1 true) $= \beta$	correct decision: P(reject H_0 when H_1 true) $= \mathbf{1 - \beta}$ $= \mathbf{power}$

If we reject H_0, we have an α probability of making an error (Type I), and therefore a $1 - \alpha$ probability of not making an error. That is, if we follow a rule of rejecting H_0 whenever $P < .05$ (the $\alpha = .05$ significance level), then over the long run our decisions to reject H_0 should be correct about 95% of the time, and wrong about 5% of the time.

A Type I error is possible only if we reject H_0. The Greek letter β (beta) represents the probability of a Type II error when we *fail to reject H_0*. The probability of making a correct decision by rejecting H_0 equals $\mathbf{1 - \beta}$, called the **power** of a test.

Since the significance level controls the likelihood of a Type I error, it may seem best to choose a very low level, such as $\alpha = .0001$ or $.00001$. Unfortunately there is a trade-off. Simply lowering the cutoff point at which H_0 is to be rejected does reduce the probability of mistaken H_0 rejection (Type I error), but it simultaneously increases the likelihood of mistakenly not rejecting H_0 (Type II error). We trade the risk of one kind of error for another.

Depending on the research question, the two types of errors may have quite different consequences. In several examples discussed in Chapter 5, researchers investigated whether chemical contamination was harming people's health. The null and alternative hypotheses in such research have the general form:

H_0: Illness rates among people exposed are no higher than normal

H_1: Illness rates among people exposed are higher than normal

Researchers then collect data and apply statistical tests to obtain P-values.

If the obtained P-value is low, then we may decide to reject H_0, concluding instead that exposed people do have abnormally high illness rates, possibly due to contamination. This conclusion might be mistaken—a Type I error. In that case, our mistake will needlessly alarm people, and perhaps cause the expenditure of millions of dollars for environmental cleanup, health monitoring, and other steps to remove a nonexistent problem.

On the other hand, if the obtained P-value is high, then we would fail to reject H_0, concluding instead that the observed illness rates could be due to chance. This conclusion too might be mistaken—a Type II error. In that case, we may be falsely reassuring people that nothing is wrong, when in fact they are being poisoned.

Should our study try to minimize the probability of a Type I error (in these examples, a false alarm), or a Type II error (a false sense of security)? Although $\alpha = .05$ is the most widely used cutoff point, we could choose a lower level if we consider Type I errors much worse than Type II. An accused polluter might want α set very low, perhaps .01 or .001. But someone who considers a Type II error worse, such as parents worried about their children's health, might gladly accept the higher risk of a Type I error by increasing α to .10 or even .20. Selecting the cutoff level α thus becomes not just a technical decision; it also depends on how results will be used, and ultimately on the values motivating the research.

EXERCISES

6.3.1 For each of the following research hypotheses, state both research and null hypotheses symbolically, and explain specifically what the symbols represent (use π for a population proportion, or μ for a population mean).
  a. Less than 10% of the parachutes we manufacture are defective.
  b. More than half of all U.S. college students are women.
  c. Students who receive coaching do better than the national average of 18.1 on this test.
  d. The claim that 60% of small businesses pay no taxes is inaccurate.
  e. Due to the greenhouse effect, the average July temperature in Seattle this year will be higher than 64.8°F.

6.3.2 For each of the hypothesis pairs in Exercise 6.3.1, describe the meaning of Type I and Type II errors.

6.3.3 Imagine yourself in the role of a manufacturer who makes thousands of auto-mobile airbags each month, and is concerned about product quality. Since the bags work only once, you cannot test them all for defects; instead you rely on random sampling to estimate the rate of defects. Describe in general terms the steps required to test the hypothesis that less than 1 in 100 airbags is defective. Discuss null and alternative hypotheses, sampling, obtained P-value, and deci-sion regarding H_0 and H_1.

6.3.4 Referring to Exercise 6.3.3, discuss the nature and consequences of Type I and Type II errors, as viewed by the airbag manufacturer. Would it be better here to choose $\alpha = .05$ or $\alpha = .001$ as the significance level for testing the null hypothe-sis H_0: $\pi \geq .01$? Why?

Large-Sample Hypothesis Tests

6.4 — for Proportions

Table 6.1 introduced a sample consisting of 160 students enrolled in sociology courses. Sixty percent of these students are women. Among all the university's undergraduates, however, women made up only 56%. Is the proportion of women among sociology students significantly higher than it was in the university's population as a whole? We can address this question by testing the null hypothesis that the 160 sociology students came randomly from a population in which the true proportion of women equals .56:

$$H_0: \pi = .56$$

The alternative hypothesis states that the sociology sample did not come from a popu-lation with 56% women:

$$H_1: \pi \neq .56$$

Next we ask, what is the probability of obtaining a sample containing 60% or more (or 52% or less) women, if we selected 160 students at random from a population that is 56% female ($\pi = .56$)? Since proportions have approximately normal sampling dis-tributions for samples this large, we can employ a statistical test based on the standard normal distribution [equation (6.6) page 186].

One-sample z test for a proportion

Let p represent one sample's proportion, and π_0 the hypothesized population proportion. If the null hypothesis

$$H_0: \pi = \pi_0$$

(continued)

is true, then given large enough samples, the test statistic:

$$z = \frac{p - \pi_0}{\sqrt{\pi_0(1 - \pi_0)/n}} \qquad (6.6)$$

follows an approximately standard normal distribution. The normal tail probability associated with z gives the P-value associated with the hypothesis H_0: $\pi = \pi_0$. Low P-values suggest that we can reject H_0.

Applying equation (6.6) to the student gender example results in the following:

$$z = \frac{.60 - .56}{\sqrt{.56(1 - .56)/160}}$$

$$= \frac{.04}{.0392}$$

$$= 1.02$$

Thus the sample proportion is .04, or 1.02 estimated standard errors (since the estimated standard error equals .0392) distant from the null-hypothesis proportion of .56.

Figure 6.2 illustrates this distance graphically, based on the assumption that the true population proportion equals .56 (as claimed by the null hypothesis), and that the sample proportion p follows a normal sampling distribution with standard error equal to .0392. Then the sample proportion $p = .60$ is 1.02 standard errors from $\pi = .56$.

The shaded areas in the tails of Figure 6.2 correspond to the probability of normal-

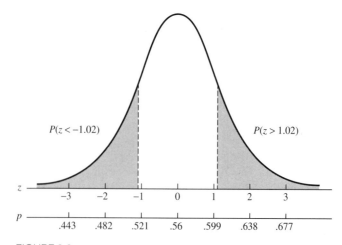

FIGURE 6.2
Theoretical sampling distribution of p, assuming that $\pi = .56$ and $\sigma_p = .039$; shaded area shows two-tailed probability $P(|z| > 1.02)$ = .308.

distribution values more than 1.02 standard deviations from the center. A computer calculates this probability as

$$P(|z| > 1.02) = .308$$

or about 30.8% of the area under the curve. If we consult instead the "two-tailed tests" column in Table A.2, we obtain the less precise statement that the probability of absolute z values larger than 1.02 falls between .30 and .40, but very close to .30:

$$.30 < P(|z| > 1.02) < .40$$

Either way, since our obtained P-value is well above the usual $\alpha = .05$ cutoff level, we must conclude that the sample proportion $p = .60$ does not differ significantly from the hypothesized population proportion $\pi_0 = .56$. Even if the null hypothesis were true, we could fairly often obtain $n = 160$ samples with 60% or more women.

  In some situations, before looking at our sample, we already have a directional research hypothesis. For example, if we had begun with a theory that sociology classes include higher proportions of women than the student body as a whole, our research hypothesis H_1 would have been stated

$$H_1: \pi > .56$$

and the complementary null hypothesis becomes

$$H_0: \pi \leq .56$$

A directional research hypothesis, if it appears consistent with the data, calls for a one-tailed test. Since normal distributions are symmetrical, one-tail probabilities equal half their two-tailed counterparts. For example,

$$P(z > 1.02) = \frac{P(|z| > 1.02)}{2}$$

$$= \frac{.308}{2}$$

$$= .154$$

or, simply consulting the one-tailed test column of Table A.2:

$$.15 < P(z > 1.02) < .20$$

A one-tailed test reflects probabilities from only one tail of the sampling distribution, as illustrated in Figure 6.3 (page 188).

  Suppose we had begun instead with a belief that sociology classes include *lower* proportions of women than the student body as a whole. This implies a different pair of directional hypotheses:

$$H_1: \pi < .56$$
$$H_0: \pi \geq .56$$

Since the sample proportion, $p = .60$, agrees with the null hypothesis $\pi \geq .56$, there is no point in running this hypothesis test; it cannot possibly reject H_0.

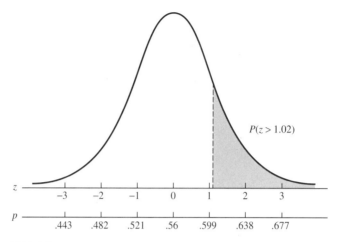

FIGURE 6.3
Theoretical sampling distribution of p, assuming that $\pi = .56$ and $\sigma_p = .039$; shaded area shows one-tailed probability $P(z > 1.02) = .154$.

One-tailed hypothesis tests are justified only if

1.   We have a clearly formed directional research hypothesis before seeing the data, *and*
2.   The data agree with the direction of this previously formed research hypothesis.

Statistical computer programs often automatically provide two-tailed tests. Users who need a one-tailed test instead can simply divide the printout's two-tail P-value by 2.

EXERCISES

6.4.1   Fifty-nine percent of the 160-student sample reported grade point averages somewhat accurately, within plus or minus .2 of their true values. Test the null hypothesis that this sample came from a population in which half the students would accurately report their GPA:

$$H_0: \pi = .5$$

$$H_1: \pi \neq .5$$

Show the steps in testing; state your final conclusion in terms of the problem.

6.4.2   Among nonsmoking adult U.S. males, about 95% survive to at least age 55. In one sample of 7,500 smokers, only 88% survived to at least age 55. Is the proportion of smokers surviving significantly lower than the proportion surviving among nonsmokers? A one-tailed hypothesis test

$$H_0: \pi \geq .95$$

$$H_1: \pi < .95$$

is appropriate here, because the researchers expected to find harmful effects from smoking.

6.4.3   Local governments in many communities organize special pickup days to help residents dispose of their hazardous household wastes—paint thinner, pesticides, and so forth. Observers have noted that young adults seem to participate less often than older adults.

One survey of 170 participants at a pickup day in Dover, New Hampshire, found that 37% were between the ages of 20 and 39. According to U.S. Census estimates, 20–39-year-olds comprise 49% of Dover's adult population. Test whether the proportion of young adults participating in Dover's pickup was significantly lower than the proportion in Dover's population. State the null and research hypotheses symbolically and in terms of the problem; justify your choice of one- or two-tailed test; perform the appropriate test; and summarize your conclusion.

6.5   Confidence Intervals for Means

Figure 6.4 graphs the distribution of high school class rank (percentiles) among the 160 students of Table 6.1. The median rank equals 79.2, and most of these students were above 70, or in the top 30% of their high school class. A handful of other students had weaker high school records, resulting in a drawn-out lower tail that pulls the overall mean down to 75.8, represented by the vertical line in Figure 6.4.

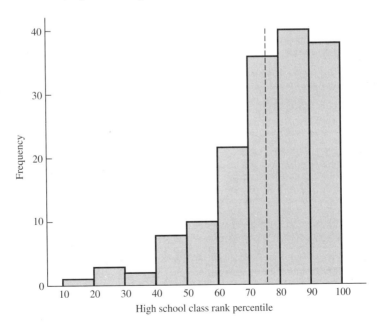

FIGURE 6.4
Distribution of high school class rank percentiles among 160 students

Although the distribution of high school ranks exhibits clear negative skew, according to the Central Limit Theorem the sampling distribution of mean ranks, across many such samples, should nonetheless be approximately normal. Therefore we can apply the normal distribution, and the related t distribution, to draw inferences about the population of students from which this sample came.

Section 6.3 described confidence intervals for proportions: intervals within which we suspect, with a specified degree of confidence, that the population proportion lies. Similar logic leads to confidence intervals based on sample means.

Estimated standard error of a mean

The **estimated standard error** of a mean, written $s_{\bar{y}}$, is

$$s_{\bar{y}} = \frac{s}{\sqrt{n}} \qquad (6.7)$$

where s represents the sample standard deviation of variable y, and n equals sample size.

To form a **confidence interval for a mean**, assuming we have either

1. a reasonably large sample, or

2. a normally distributed variable y

find

$$\bar{y} \pm ts_{\bar{y}} \qquad (6.8a)$$

or

$$\bar{y} \pm \frac{ts}{\sqrt{n}} \qquad (6.8b)$$

choosing t from the t distribution (see Table A.4) with degrees of freedom

$$df = n - 1 \qquad (6.9)$$

to obtain the desired degree of confidence.

In the high school records example, $n = 160$ cases yield 159 degrees of freedom, according to equation (6.9). To use Table A.4 we must round df off to 120; the table indicates that with 120 degrees of freedom, we need a t value of 1.98 for a 95% confidence interval. Given $\bar{y} = 75.8$ and $s = 17.2$, a 95% confidence interval for high school class rank is

$$75.8 \pm \frac{1.98 \times 17.2}{\sqrt{160}}$$

$$75.8 \pm 2.7$$

so we have 95% confidence that the mean high school rank among the population our sample represents falls somewhere between $75.8 - 2.7 = 73.1$ and $75.8 + 2.7 = 78.5$:

$$73.1 < \mu < 78.5$$

A 90% confidence interval is somewhat narrower: $t = 1.658$, yielding

$$75.8 \pm \frac{1.658 \times 17.2}{\sqrt{160}}$$

so that, based on this sample, we can be 90% confident that

$$73.5 < \mu < 78.1$$

If we insist on 99.9% confidence, our interval must become relatively wide: $t = 3.373$, yielding

$$75.8 \pm \frac{3.373 \times 17.2}{\sqrt{160}}$$

$$71.2 < \mu < 80.4$$

For larger samples—say, $n = 250$ or more—the $t[\infty]$ distribution (bottom row in Table A.4) provides a close approximation. As noted in Chapter 5, the t distribution with infinite degrees of freedom is identical to the standard normal or z distribution. Consequently, for large enough samples equation (6.8) becomes nearly the same thing as

$$\bar{y} \pm \frac{zs}{\sqrt{n}} \qquad \textbf{(6.10)}$$

In theory, we can legitimately use the z distribution (Table A.2) instead of t to form confidence intervals from samples of any size if we know the true population standard deviation σ:

$$\bar{y} \pm \frac{z\sigma}{\sqrt{n}} \qquad \textbf{(6.11)}$$

In practice, however, if we need a confidence interval to estimate an unknown population mean μ, we probably do not know the true population standard deviation σ either. Therefore most researchers employ t tables and equation (6.8) to form confidence intervals for a mean.

   If we collected many random samples and constructed 95% confidence intervals according to equation (6.8) from each one, about 95% of those intervals should contain the true population mean μ. This is what we really mean when we say we are "95% confident" that the true mean lies within our interval. Figure 6.5 (page 192) illustrates with data from a computer experiment. One hundred artificial samples of $n = 120$ cases each were generated from a normal distribution having mean $\mu = 500$ and standard deviation $\sigma = 75$. The sample means varied from 483 to 519, and sample standard deviations from 65 to 84. Using these sample means and standard deviations, 95% confidence intervals were calculated from each of the 100 samples. Each line in Figure 6.5 represents one of these intervals. Over the long run, all but 5% of such intervals ought

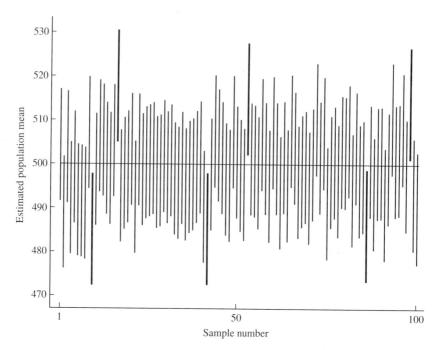

FIGURE 6.5
Results from a computer experiment: In 94 out of these 100 random samples, the
95% confidence interval does include the true population mean $\mu = 500$

to contain $\mu = 500$. In this particular experiment we came quite close: Only 6 of the
100 intervals in Figure 6.5 do not include 500.

EXERCISES

6.5.1   Tobacco leaves often contain measurable amounts of heavy metals, which find
their way into cigarettes and from there into smokers' blood. One European
study of 44 different cigarette brands reported a mean cadmium content of
1.4 micrograms/gram, with a standard deviation of .4 (Mussala-Rauhamaa et al.,
1986). Assume that these 44 brands represent a random sample from all available
cigarette brands.
   a.   Estimate the standard error of the mean cadmium content.
   b.   Construct and interpret an 80% confidence interval for the true population
mean.
   c.   Construct and interpret a 95% confidence interval for the true population
mean.
   d.   Construct and interpret a 99% confidence interval for the true population
mean.

e.   Which of your intervals is narrowest? Over the long run, which size of interval will most often contain the true population mean?

6.5.2   A survey of 110 elementary schools found that microcomputer use averaged 39.1 hours per week, with a standard deviation of 15.7 hours per week (McGee, 1987). Construct a 95% confidence interval around this mean. If the 110 schools comprised a random sample from the population of all U.S. elementary schools, how would we interpret this interval?

6.6   One-Sample *t* Tests for Means

The mean GPA among the 160 sociology students of Table 6.1 is $\bar{y} = 2.64$ (standard deviation $s = .53$). Among all undergraduates at that time, the mean GPA was somewhat lower: $\mu = 2.58$. Could the higher mean in our sample be due to chance, or does it indicate that sociology students get systematically better grades? To answer, we need a test of hypotheses:

$$H_0: \mu = 2.58$$
$$H_1: \mu \neq 2.58$$

This test should be two tailed because, before seeing the data, we had no theoretical reason to expect that sociology students would fare better or worse than other students.

One-sample *t* test for a mean

Let $\bar{y}$ represent one sample's mean, and μ_0 the hypothesized population mean. If the null hypothesis

$$H_0: \mu = \mu_0$$

is true, and if either

1.   the sample is reasonably large, *or*
2.   variable *y* follows a normal distribution,

then the test statistic

$$t = \frac{\bar{y} - \mu_0}{s_{\bar{y}}}$$ (6.12)

$$= \frac{\bar{y} - \mu_0}{s/\sqrt{n}}$$

follows approximately a *t* distribution with $df = n - 1$.

   If the *t* distribution tail probability corresponding to our *t* statistic is small (e.g., below .05), we can reject H_0. For a one-tailed test, divide the two-tailed *P* value in half.

Applying equation (6.12) to the student GPA example, we have

$$t = \frac{2.64 - 2.58}{\frac{.53}{\sqrt{160}}}$$

$$= \frac{.06}{.042}$$

$$= 1.4$$

Like the z test for a proportion, the t test for a mean measures distance between sample statistic and (null) hypothesized population parameter *in standard errors*. Our sample mean is $2.64 - 2.58 = .06$ grade point from the hypothesized population mean. Its estimated standard error equals .042, so the distance between sample and hypothesized means equals $.06/.042 = 1.4$ standard errors. According to Table A.4, the two-tail probability corresponding to $t = 1.4$, with 120 degrees of freedom, is

$$.10 < P < .20$$

This probability is too high for us to reject the null hypothesis. A random sample of $n = 160$ with $\bar{y} = 2.64$ ($s = .53$) could easily have come from a population in which $\mu = 2.58$. Therefore we conclude that the mean grade point average of sociology students does not significantly differ from the mean GPA of all students.

EXERCISES

6.6.1   Among the sociology student sample ($n = 160$), the mean mathematics Scholastic Aptitude Test (MSAT) score equals 525, with a standard deviation of 95. Is this mean significantly different (at $\alpha = .05$) from the mean of 536 for the college's undergraduates as a whole?

6.6.2   Health researchers have tracked trends in national fitness by collecting data on such variables as the amount of body fat in schoolchildren. One simple test of body fat uses skinfold thickness: The thicker the skinfold (measured at back of arm and at shoulder blade), the more body fat. In 1960 a large study estimated the mean skinfold thickness of 9-year-old boys at 14 millimeters. Twenty years later, a study of 475 boys found $\bar{y} = 17$, $s = 4$. Test whether the mean body fat of 9-year-old boys in 1980 differed significantly from the 1960 value.

6.6.3   Test whether the mean body fat of 9-year-old girls in 1980 differed significantly from the 1960 mean, estimated as 17 millimeters. The 1980 statistics are $n = 502$, $\bar{y} = 21$, and $s = 4$.

···············
Paired-Difference Intervals
6.7 —— and Tests for Means

Table 6.1 includes one variable defined as the difference between two others: GPA error, equal to self-reported GPA minus true GPA. Figure 6.6 shows the distributions of true GPA, self-reported GPA, and GPA error. The true GPA distribution exhibits a drawn-out lower tail of students with poor grades, missing from the self-reported GPA distribution. The self-report distribution, in contrast, shifts noticeably to the right; its mean (2.83) is almost .2 higher than the true GPA mean (2.64). The error distribution shows that almost 60% of the students reported GPAs within plus or minus .2 of their true values. A substantial minority, however, made larger errors, almost all in an upward direction (reporting higher GPAs than they had actually earned).

Such variables, called **difference scores**, provide a natural way to approach the study of survey errors. Difference scores also occur in before-and-after studies, where the same variable is measured across the same set of cases, but at two different times.

We often wish to form confidence intervals for a mean difference, or to test whether the mean difference equals 0. The same confidence interval and one-sample *t*

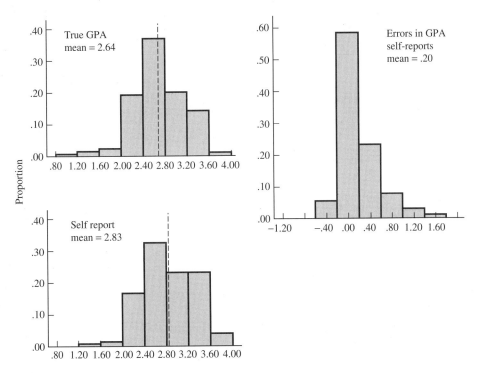

FIGURE 6.6
Distributions of true GPA, self-reported GPA, and errors in self-reports, for 160 students

test procedures described earlier in this chapter work equally well when our variable is a difference score. The term **paired-difference *t* test** refers to an ordinary one-sample *t* test, applied to a variable that happens to be a difference score.

Confidence interval for a mean difference

Let *d* represent a difference score variable, $d = y - x$; *s* is the sample standard deviation of *d*, and δ (delta) stands for the mean difference in the population.
    To form a **confidence interval for a mean difference**, assuming we have either

1. a reasonably large sample, *or*
2. a normally distributed variable *d*

find

$$\bar{d} \pm \frac{ts}{\sqrt{n}}$$

(6.13)

choosing *t* from the *t* distribution (see Table A.4) with $df = n - 1$ to obtain the desired degree of confidence.

Paired-difference *t* test for a mean

If the null hypothesis

$$H_0: \delta = \delta_0$$

is true, and if either

1. the sample is reasonably large, *or*
2. difference score *d* follows a normal distribution

then the test statistic

$$t = \frac{\bar{d} - \delta_0}{s/\sqrt{n}}$$

(6.14)

follows approximately a *t* distribution with $df = n - 1$.
    Typically, our null hypothesis asserts a mean difference of zero:

$$H_0: \delta = 0$$

(*continued*)

so equation (6.14) simplifies to

$$t = \frac{\bar{d} - 0}{s/\sqrt{n}}$$

$$= \frac{\bar{d}}{s/\sqrt{n}} \tag{6.14a}$$

A large t value (and a correspondingly low t tail probability) leads to rejection of the null hypothesis that, in the population, the mean difference equals 0.

The mean GPA error is $\bar{d} = .20$, with a standard deviation of $s = .38$. In this context the null hypothesis

$$H_0: \delta = 0$$

implies that, in the population (all sociology students at this university), the mean difference between true and self-reported GPA equals zero or, equivalently, true and self-reported GPAs have identical means. We test this hypothesis applying equation (6.14a):

$$t = \frac{.20}{.38/\sqrt{160}}$$

$$= 6.66$$

The sample mean difference, $\bar{d} = .20$, lies 6.66 estimated standard errors from the hypothesized population mean difference, $\delta = 0$. This distance appears too great to plausibly be due to chance. A t value of 6.66, with 120 degrees of freedom, falls off the right-hand side of Table A.4, indicating that

$$P < .001$$

We can comfortably reject the null hypothesis, and conclude that students' self-reported GPAs do differ significantly from their true GPAs.

Hypothesis tests tell us whether a significant difference exists, but do not suggest how large this difference might be. Confidence intervals are more informative in this regard. For a 95% confidence interval with roughly 120 degrees of freedom, we need $t = 1.98$. Applying equation (6.13) to form a 95% confidence interval for the mean of GPA errors:

$$.20 \pm 1.98 \times \frac{.38}{\sqrt{160}}$$

$$.20 \pm .06$$

so we are 95% confident, based on this sample, that the population mean difference δ lies somewhere between $.20 - .06 = .14$ and $.20 + .06 = .26$:

$$.14 < \delta < .26$$

If we are 95% confident that the parameter δ lies within the interval .14 to .26, we must be at least 95% confident that δ does not equal 0. This duplicates our earlier hypothesis-test conclusion. In general, we can reject a hypothesis (with a given level of confidence) if the hypothesized parameter value lies outside of the confidence interval. We fail to reject the hypothesis if the hypothesized value lies within our confidence interval. Confidence intervals can be used in this fashion to substitute for hypothesis tests. They provide the same guidance about accepting or rejecting H_0 as a formal two-tailed hypothesis test. They also provide new information that hypothesis tests do not: an interval estimate of the population parameter.

EXERCISES

6.7.1   Many elementary schoolteachers believe that teaching young children to write their own programs in the Logo computer language fosters thinking and problem-solving skills. A study involving 60 children found that their scores on a 10-point cognitive test improved by an average of $\bar{y} = 1.5$ points ($s = 3.0$) after instruction and experience with Logo programming. Test at $\alpha = .01$ whether this increase differs significantly from 0 (no change).

6.7.2   Interpret the t value obtained in Exercise 6.7.1 as a *distance*.

6.7.3   The study described in Exercise 6.7.1 also investigated the effects of more conventional computer instruction that did not include Logo programming. Among 40 children receiving conventional computer instruction, they observed an improvement of $\bar{y} = .9$ point ($s = 2.9$). Test at $\alpha = .01$ whether this differs significantly from 0.

6.7.4   Construct and interpret 95% confidence intervals for the mean differences described in Exercises 6.7.1 and 6.7.3.

6.8 One-Sample Sign Tests for Medians

The theoretical justification for t tests and t-based confidence intervals assumes that our variable follows a normal distribution. This "normality assumption" becomes less important in large samples such as the $n = 160$ examples above. The Central Limit Theorem assures us that with large samples, a mean's sampling distribution becomes approximately normal regardless of variable distributions. Nonnormal distributions cause more trouble in small samples, however, particularly if they involve severe outliers. There is no simple cutoff for deciding when a sample is too small and a variable too nonnormal for t tests to produce valid results. When in doubt, researchers often turn to a family of methods called **nonparametric tests**. Nonparametric tests do not assume that the variables follow normal or other specific probability distributions. The t and F methods described earlier, by contrast, belong to the family of **parametric tests**.

The **sign test for a median** provides a nonparametric alternative to the one-sample t test for a mean; t tests have greater *power* (see Table 6.2) than sign tests, when the t test's more stringent assumptions are met. Sign tests, on the other hand, remain valid under a wider range of circumstances, such as small samples with markedly non-normal distributions.

Sign test for a median

Let Md_0 represent the hypothesized population median of any continuous variable x. If the null hypothesis

$$H_0: Md = Md_0$$

is true, then by definition half of the population values of x lie above Md_0, and the other half lie below Md_0.

To test H_0 using sample data, count the number of "positive signs" (x values above Md_0), "negative signs" (for $x < Md_0$), and "zeroes" (for $x = Md_0$). Let c represent the count of positive signs or the count of negative signs, whichever is larger, and n_0 the number of zeroes. Use the binomial equation (5.1) to find, for samples of size $(n - n_0)$ given $p = .5$, the probability of counts greater than or equal to c:

$$P(f \geq c)$$

This furnishes a one-tailed test. For a two-tailed test, multiply this P-value by 2.

Sign tests, like their parametric counterpart, the one-sample t test, are often applied to paired-difference data. In paired-difference applications we usually test the null hypothesis that the median difference equals 0:

$$H_0: Md = 0$$

The terms "positive signs" and "negative signs" now have literal meaning: the actual signs of the difference-score values.

The distribution of GPA errors (Figure 6.7, page 200) appears distinctly nonnormal: positively skewed, with a heavier-than-normal right tail and a sharp peak of near-zero errors. Although the sample is fairly large, a cautious analyst might distrust our earlier paired-difference t test results, and choose instead a sign test that does not assume normality.

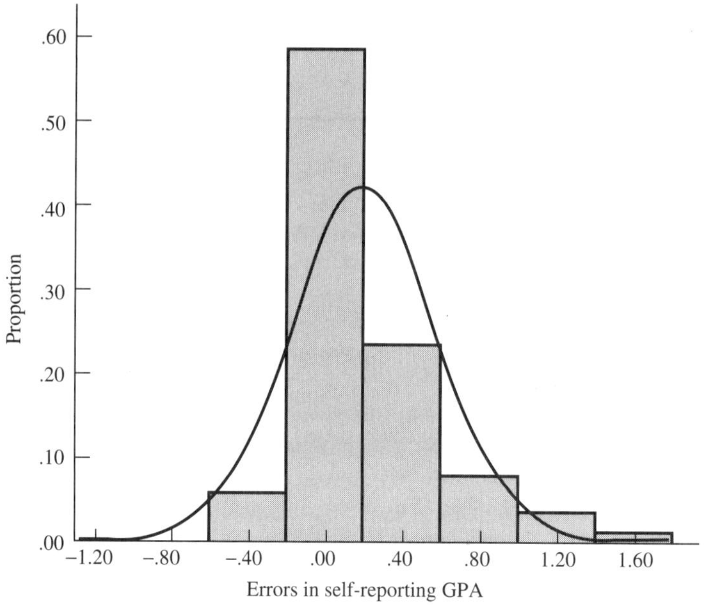

FIGURE 6.7
Distribution of errors in self-reported GPA

Almost two-thirds of the students made positive errors, and only two students reported their GPA "exactly" accurately:

105	positive (self-reports higher than true GPA)
53	negative (self-reports lower than true GPA)
2	zero (self-reports equal to true GPA)
160	cases

We therefore need to find the binomial probability $P(f \geq 105)$, given $n - n_0 = 160 - 2 = 158$, and $p = .5$. A statistical computer program supplies the estimate

$$P(f \geq 105) = .000021$$

Doubling this for a two-tailed test yields

$$2 \times P(f \geq 105) = .000042$$

This very low P-value presents strong evidence against the null hypothesis. We can reject

$$H_0: Md = 0$$

and agree instead with the alternative hypothesis that the population's median GPA error differs significantly from 0:

$$H_1: Md \neq 0$$

Except with tiny samples, the binomial equation (5.1) produces numbers too large for direct evaluation on a hand calculator. Computers can work around this difficulty. Alternatively, someone analyzing samples of $n \geq 50$ "by hand" might substitute the normal approximation for binomial probabilities. Unfortunately, this approximation performs poorly in samples of $n < 50$, which may still be too large to find binomial probabilities by hand.

Normal approximation of the sign test for a median (if $n \geq 50$)

To approximately test a hypothesis

$$H_0: Md = Md_0$$

regarding the population median of any continuous variable x, count the number of positives ($x > Md_0$), negatives ($x < Md_0$), and zeroes ($x = Md_0$). Let c represent the count of positives or of negatives, whichever is larger, and n_0 the number of zeroes. If $n - n_0 > 50$ then under a true H_0, the test statistic

$$z = \frac{c - .5(n - n_0)}{.5\sqrt{(n - n_0)}} \qquad (6.15)$$

follows approximately a standard normal distribution.

Applying equation (6.15) to the GPA error data, we have

$$z = \frac{105 - (.5 \times 158)}{.5\sqrt{158}}$$

$$= \frac{26}{6.28}$$

$$= 4.14$$

Table A.2 indicates the improbability of such a large z value, if $H_0: Md = 0$ were true: $P < .0001$ for absolute z values greater than 3.89. A computer obtains the more precise probability:

$$P(|z| > 4.14) = .000035$$

similar to the .000042 value we obtained earlier from the binomial sign test. Thus the normal approximation leads to the same conclusion (reject H_0) as the binomial sign test.

In any symmetrical population, median and mean are the same, so hypothesis test conclusions regarding medians apply equally well to means. A sign test that rejects

$$H_0: Md = 0$$

for example, tells us that we may also reject:

$$H_0: \mu = 0$$

With skewed distributions, on the other hand, median does not equal mean. Therefore the outcome of a sign test (regarding the median) does not necessarily imply any conclusion regarding the mean.

EXERCISES

6.8.1   Both t test (Section 6.6) and sign test (Section 6.7) indicate that students' self-reported GPAs differ significantly from their true values. Do similar patterns of exaggeration affect other self-reports? The same study collected information on SAT scores. Differences between true and self-reported math SAT scores were as follows:

68	positive (self-reports higher than true MSAT)
41	negative (self-reports lower than true MSAT)
51	zero (self-reports equal to true MSAT)
160	cases

   a.   Use the normal approximation [equation (6.15)] to perform a sign test of the null hypothesis that the median error equals 0. State your conclusion.
   b.   Use a computer's binomial probability function to calculate an exact P-value for this sign test. Does your conclusion from part **a** still stand?

6.8.2   Repeat the steps of Exercise 6.8.1 to test whether the median error in self-reporting verbal SAT equals 0, given

80	positive (self-reports higher than true VSAT)
35	negative (self-reports lower than true VSAT)
45	zero (self-reports equal to true VSAT)
160	cases

*6.8.3   Perform a sign test [calculating exact binomial probabilities either from equation (5.1) or with the aid of a computer] of the null hypothesis that the median difference between x and y equals 0, given the following small dataset:

x	y
4	5
5	5
6	7
7	10
8	12
9	9

*6.9 — How Large a Sample Do We Need?

Larger samples permit more precise estimates of unknown population parameters. In theory, a larger sample is always better, but in practice a larger sample is also more expensive, time-consuming, and difficult to collect. Furthermore, even with a huge sample, there would remain some uncertainty in our estimate of the parameter; our confidence interval would still not have zero width. This raises a practical question: Suppose we consider a certain confidence interval width, plus or minus w, to be "good enough" for our purposes. Then how large a sample do we need?

The algebraic relation between confidence intervals and sample size helps to answer this question. Equation (6.16) gives the minimum sample size needed to estimate a population mean with a precision of $\pm w$. Note that this equation requires us to supply a value for the population standard deviation σ, however. Our estimate of σ might come from knowledge of the population, previous research, or be simply an educated guess. The accuracy of sample size calculations depends on the accuracy of the σ estimate they incorporate.

Sample size needed to estimate a population mean

We want to estimate the population mean μ, with a confidence interval no wider than $\pm w$. The minimum sample size needed, n, is

$$n = \frac{z^2 \sigma^2}{w^2} \tag{6.16}$$

where σ^2 represents the population variance, or standard deviation squared. We choose z from a standard normal distribution to obtain the desired degree of confidence. For example, 95% confidence intervals ($z = 1.96$) require samples of size:

$$n = \frac{1.96^2 \sigma^2}{w^2} \tag{6.16a}$$

As an illustration, consider an achievement test that has a population mean among all high school students of 500, and a standard deviation of 75. We wish to draw samples of students from public, parochial, and independent private high schools, and estimate the mean achievement test scores of students at each type of school. In order to estimate these means within ± 4 points (and 95% confidence), how large must our samples be? Applying equation (6.16a), and assuming that for all three types of school, $\sigma = 75$, we find

$$n = \frac{1.96^2 \times 75^2}{4^2}$$

$$= 1,350.56$$

That is, we need more than 1,350 students selected randomly from each type of school, in order to estimate their respective means within ± 4 points. Suppose we wanted more precise estimates, within ± 2 points?

$$n = \frac{1.96^2 \times 75^2}{2^2}$$

$$= 5,402.25$$

We then need more than 5,402 students from each type of school. Thus to double our precision, from ± 4 to ± 2, requires 4 times as much data. Doubling precision again, from ± 2 to ± 1, would require 4 times more: about $4 \times 5,402.25 = 21,609$ cases.

A similar formula describes the sample size needed to estimate a population proportion [equation (6.17)]. Since any proportion π has variance $\sigma^2 = \pi(1 - \pi)$, the latter term rather than σ^2 appears in equation (6.17).

Sample size needed to estimate a population proportion

We want to estimate the population proportion π, with a confidence interval no wider than $\pm w$. The minimum sample size needed is

$$n = \frac{z^2 \pi(1 - \pi)}{w^2} \qquad \text{(6.17)}$$

We choose z from a standard normal distribution to obtain the desired degree of confidence. For example, 95% confidence intervals ($z = 1.96$) require samples of size

$$n = \frac{1.96^2 \pi(1 - \pi)}{w^2} \qquad \text{(6.17a)}$$

We do not know π, but the sample size required is largest if $\pi = .5$, in which case $\pi(1 - \pi) = .25$. Therefore the minimum sample size needed to estimate any unknown π with 95% confidence within $\pm w$, is no more than

$$n = \frac{.9604}{w^2} \qquad \text{(6.17b)}$$

Equation (6.17) suggests that to obtain any particular confidence level and precision, the sample size required is largest when the population proportion π equals .5. We

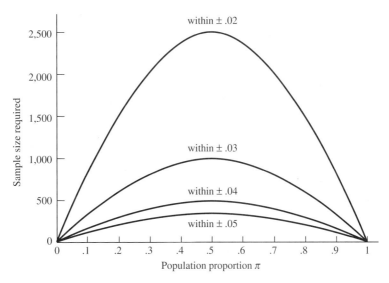

FIGURE 6.8
Minimum sample sizes required to estimate a proportion with 95%
confidence within plus or minus .05, .04, .03, or .02

need fewer cases when π is closer to 0 or 1. (As π gets very close to 0 or 1, however, the normal-distribution approximation used here becomes less trustworthy.) Figure 6.8 displays this relation graphically, by showing the sample sizes needed, at 95% confidence, to estimate proportions within $\pm .05$, .04, .03, or .02. The highest curve shows that to estimate π within $\pm .02$, at the 95% confidence level, would require $n = 2{,}401$ if $\pi = .5$ and lower n for π closer to 0 or 1. The second highest curve shows that to estimate π within $\pm .04$, the minimum sample size needed is no greater than 600.

Researchers do not know what π equals; their uncertainty is the whole point of a confidence interval. Furthermore, surveys generally aim to estimate many different proportions: the proportion favoring candidate Smith, the proportion opposing an assault rifle ban, and so forth. It therefore makes sense to conservatively choose n based on $\pi = .5$, yielding these recommended minimum sample sizes for 95% confidence intervals:

To estimate π within	n of cases required
$\pm .01$	9,604
$\pm .02$	2,401
$\pm .03$	1,067
$\pm .04$	600
$\pm .05$	384
$\pm .06$	267
$\pm .08$	150
$\pm .10$	96

Many public-opinion surveys, figuring that $\pm .04$ (plus or minus four percentage points) accuracy is adequate for their purposes, choose samples on the order of 600 cases. As national elections approach, and clients demand more precision, pollsters spend more money to obtain larger samples.

EXERCISES

6.9.1 Referring back to the achievement test example in this section (for which $\sigma = 75$), how large a sample would we need to obtain:

    a.   a 99% confidence interval of width no more than ± 5 points

    b.   a 95% confidence interval of width no more than ± 5 points

    c.   a 90% confidence interval of width no more than ± 5 points

    d.   a 95% confidence interval of width no more than $\pm .5$ point

6.9.2 Briefly summarize any patterns you see in your answers to Exercise 6.9.1.

Summary

A single statistic such as a sample mean provides a **point estimate** of the corresponding population parameter, but this estimate is unlikely to be exactly correct. We have a better chance of being correct if we propose **interval estimates**, which estimate that the population parameter lies within a certain range. The wider our intervals, the better chance we have of constructing one that does include the true value. Confidence interval procedures provide theoretical guidance on how wide we need to make the interval to obtain 90%, 95%, or some other specified degree of confidence.

Being "95% confident" does not imply a .95 probability that the parameter actually falls within our *particular* interval, as inexperienced analysts sometimes assume. Rather, the "95% confident" statement stands for a more abstract statistical idea:

> If we drew many random samples, and calculated 95% confidence intervals in this manner from each one, over the long run about 95% of those intervals should contain the true population parameter.

One particular interval either does or does not contain the parameter, though we do not know which. Figure 6.5 illustrated this key aspect of confidence intervals, using data from a computer experiment.

Hypothesis tests likewise depend on theories of how statistics would behave during repeated sampling. A null hypothesis specifies one value or range of values for the unknown population parameter. We then look at our sample and ask, over the long run, how often should we expect to see samples this divergent from the null hypothesis, if we sampled repeatedly from a population where that null hypothesis were true? A low probability (P-value) gives reason to disbelieve or reject the null hypothesis.

Small-sample tests for proportions employ the binomial distribution, described in Section 5.1. With larger samples the binomial distribution becomes approximately normal, which simplifies calculation of large-sample tests and confidence intervals for proportions.

Unless we know the population variance σ, tests or confidence intervals for means employ the t distribution. With many degrees of freedom (that is, large samples) t distributions too become approximately normal. A general formula for large-sample confidence intervals (proportions or means) might be written:

$$\text{sample statistic} \pm (t \text{ or } z) \times \text{estimated standard error} \qquad \textbf{(6.18)}$$

Equations (6.4) and (6.8) represent special cases of equation (6.18). Likewise, a general formula for large-sample hypothesis tests might be written:

$$t \text{ or } z = \frac{\text{sample statistic} - \text{hypothesized parameter value}}{\text{estimated standard error}} \qquad \textbf{(6.19)}$$

Equations (6.6) and (6.12) represent special cases of equation (6.19). Later chapters introduce other special cases of equations (6.18) and (6.19).

We usually employ the t distribution in confidence intervals and tests involving means, whether our sample is small or large. The z distribution should be used instead if we know the true population standard deviation, but that is less often the case. Confidence intervals and tests involving proportions employ either the binomial distribution (small samples) or the z distribution (large samples).

An assumption that our variable follows a normal distribution underlies the one-sample t test. With large enough samples, it may not matter a great deal whether this assumption is true; the test produces reasonable results anyway. With smaller samples, however, nonnormal distributions might cause a t test to reach incorrect conclusions. A nonparametric method called the sign test provides an alternative that does not assume normality or even symmetry in our variable's distribution.

Data analysts often apply both tests, using the nonparametric test to double-check conclusions from the more powerful, but less trustworthy, parametric test. Later chapters give further examples of this dual approach.

What We Learn from One-Sample Tests

Based on the evidence from this sample (and assuming the sample is random), can we confidently reject what the null hypothesis asserts about the population proportion, mean, or median? A statistically significant (e.g., $P < .05$) test result indicates that the answer is yes, we can reject or disbelieve H_0. If the test result is nonsignificant, on the other hand, we lack persuasive evidence that the null hypothesis is false.

In the case of **paired-difference tests**, the mean or median in question measures *change*, and we test null hypotheses such as "the population mean change is less than or equal to 0."

We can also construct a confidence interval to indicate our best guess about the true population proportion, mean, or median.

PROBLEMS

6.1   A 1985 Gallup poll of 1,021 American adults found that 63% believed America's involvement in the Vietnam War was a mistake.

  a.   Construct and interpret a 95% confidence interval for the population proportion with this belief.

  b.   A confidence interval's width is its upper limit minus its lower limit. What would be the width of your interval for part **a** if the poll had surveyed only 50 people, instead of 1,021?

  c.   What would be the width if 50,000 people had been surveyed?

  d.   What generalization does this demonstrate about the relationship between sample size and the width of a confidence interval?

6.2   Health inspectors in a northeastern state, examining a sample of 1,557 shellfish being sold for human consumption, found that 14.5% contained unsafe levels of contamination.

  a.   Assuming that these 1,557 shellfish were a random sample of those currently being sold in the state, construct a 99% confidence interval for the proportion of shellfish that are contaminated. Interpret this interval in terms of the problem.

  b.   Based on your answer to part **a**, what can you say about the following hypothesis: In the population of all shellfish being sold in this state, only 10% have been contaminated. Explain your decision to reject or not reject this hypothesis.

6.3   Researchers studying the spread of acquired immune deficiency syndrome (AIDS) collected data from a volunteer sample of 4,955 homosexual men in Baltimore, Chicago, Los Angeles, and Pittsburgh (Chmeil et al., 1987). Of these 4,955 men, 38% tested positive for HIV, the virus that causes AIDS.

  a.   Construct a 99.9% confidence interval for the percentage infected with HIV. Interpret the interval *as if* these 4,955 men were a random sample of adult male homosexuals.

  b.   Since the men in the sample volunteered, rather than being chosen at random, this is clearly not a random sample. How does that affect the interpretation of our confidence interval in part **a**?

6.4   Parts **a–c** refer to a sample of 122 homicides, selected randomly from Federal Bureau of Investigation records on all known U.S. homicides during 1984.

   a.   Forty-four of the 122 homicides involved a handgun. Find and interpret a 95% confidence interval for the population proportion involving handguns.

   b.   Eighty-six of the 122 homicide victims were male. Use a z test to evaluate the hypothesis that in the population of all 1984 homicides, half the victims were male. State your conclusion.

   c.   One hundred three of the 122 homicide offenders were male. Use a 99% confidence interval to test the hypothesis that half of the offenders were male. Explain your conclusion.

6.5   In a study of 180 female psychiatric patients suffering from recurrent depression, the mean age at the onset of their first depression episode was found to be 26 years, with a standard deviation of 11.2 years (Frank, Carpenter, and Kupfer, 1988). Assuming that these 180 cases constitute a random sample, find and interpret a 95% confidence interval for the population mean age of onset.

6.6   The mean duration of the most recent depression episode of the 180 patients (Problem 6.5) is 22.1 weeks, with a standard deviation of 17.4 weeks. Find and interpret a 95% confidence interval for the population mean length of most recent episode.

6.7   A 1985 study (Keane, Ducette, and Adler) investigated the extent of "burnout" among nurses in a variety of hospital settings. Nurses' levels of burnout-type feelings, such as "I often think about finding a new job," or "I frequently get angry with my patients," were measured using a questionnaire-based Staff Burnout Scale for Health Professionals. The study focused on whether burnout levels for Intensive Care Unit (ICU) nurses differed from those for other hospital nurses. For all nurses in the large hospital studied, the burnout scale had a mean of 52.1. Among a sample of 25 ICU nurses the mean was 49.9, with a standard deviation of 14.3. Assuming that the burnout scale has an approximately normal distribution, test the hypothesis that the mean burnout level of ICU nurses is different from that for this hospital's nurse population as a whole. Include these steps:

   a.   Formally state the null and alternative hypotheses, and explain whether a one- or a two-tailed test is appropriate.

   b.   Calculate the degrees of freedom. What critical value of t is required to reject H_0 at $\alpha = .05$?

   c.   Calculate the t statistic.

   d.   Summarize your conclusions in terms of the problem.

6.8   Burt and Neiman (1985) studied opinions about energy conservation policies among decision-makers in city government. They constructed an index to measure approval of a variety of conservation policies. The index ranged from 0 (opposed all conservation policies) to 7 (favored all conservation policies). In a sample of 32 decision-makers, the mean conservation-index score was 3.03, with a standard deviation of 1.66. Among the general public, their research found a mean conservation-index score of 3.91. Use this information to perform a t test ($\alpha = .01$) of the hypothesis that decision-makers' opinions about conservation policy differ significantly from those of the general public.

6.9   A study examined whether wearing rings affects health care workers' ability to wash their hands clean (Jacobsen et al., 1985). The subjects were 32 college microbiology students. Bacteria counts were made for each student's hands after a careful washing, once when the student was wearing rings and then on a different occasion when the student wore no rings. Difference scores equal each student's bacteria count with rings minus the same student's bacteria count without rings. The mean difference was $\overline{d} = 842$ bacteria per milliliter of rinse solution ($s = 4{,}215$); this positive mean difference indicates more bacteria, on average, when the students wore rings. (A negative mean difference would have indicated more bacteria without rings.) Are there *significantly* more bacteria when rings are worn? Apply a one-tailed t test using $\alpha = .05$.

6.10   Study of the historical distribution of water flow helps in predicting the frequency of floods or droughts, which occur with unusually high or low flows. Below are data on the average annual water flow of the White River near Nora, Wisconsin, 1960–1971 (from Wright, Houck, Diamond, and Randall, 1986). Construct and interpret a 95% confidence interval for the mean, assuming these 12 years represent a random sample of White River annual flow.

Year	Average flow in cubic feet/second
1960	845
1961	1,109
1962	1,027
1963	751
1964	1,066
1965	833
1966	441
1967	1,059
1968	1,167
1969	1,139
1970	1,117
1971	770

6.11   A survey attempted to measure the extent of drug and alcohol use among a sample of 497 high school students in River City. Eleven percent of these students said they regularly used cocaine. Other studies suggested that nationwide, about 6% of U.S. high school students regularly used cocaine. Are River City students significantly different from their peers elsewhere in the nation? Use a two-tailed z test to evaluate the hypothesis H_0: $\pi = .06$.

6.12   The 497-student survey mentioned in Problem 6.11 also asked about other drugs. For each of the following, test whether the River City proportion differs significantly from the national proportion:

a. occasional use of beer and wine: River City: .86; national: .76
b. occasional use of marijuana: River City: .45; national: .25
c. occasional use of liquor: River City: .79; national: .61
d. use of illegal stimulants: River City: .23; national: .27

6.13 Write a paragraph summarizing your conclusions after the tests of Problems 6.11–6.12.

Table 6.3 (file *hospital*) contains data on a sample of 19 hospitals, which were among a group of hospitals claimed to be "underfunded" and in need of $120 million in state assistance. Opponents of this expenditure questioned whether these hospitals really were much worse off than others in the state, which would lose money if an aid bill passed. The table reports 1986 occupancy rates, operating margins, and operating margin gains or losses. Problems 6.14–6.20 refer to these data.

Table 6.3
Financial data on 19 "underfunded" hospitals

Hospital	1986 Occupancy rate	1986 Operating margin %	Operating margin % gain or loss 1983–1986
1	70.0	6.99	353.0
2	73.4	1.02	24.0
3	78.6	1.78	242.9
4	52.3	− .94	− 93.8
5	65.9	3.23	411.3
6	73.1	.59	− 27.0
7	65.1	3.31	631.9
8	59.6	.79	132.8
9	54.0	.26	120.2
10	58.9	4.99	338.1
11	62.7	4.57	2,857.1
12	47.5	1.24	− 9.2
13	69.9	2.34	278.2
14	63.9	− 14.70	− 1,042.5
15	62.4	1.17	− 5.6
16	59.5	− .43	93.1
17	54.6	.76	131.8
18	53.5	5.51	76.2
19	50.7	2.13	22.0

Source: Adapted from Knox (1987).
File: *hospital*

6.14   Use boxplots and histograms to explore the three variables in Table 6.3. Briefly describe their distributions.

6.15   The mean occupancy rate among all hospitals in the state at this time was 65.6. Apply a one-tailed t test to the data of Table 6.3 to determine whether the mean occupancy rate among "underfunded" hospitals is significantly below the statewide mean.

6.16   A claim that hospitals are "underfunded" implies that their operating margins (excess of income over expenditures) are low. Among hospitals statewide at this time, the mean operating margin was 1.59. Apply a t test to judge whether "underfunded" hospitals have significantly lower mean operating margins.

6.17   The mean operating margin gain or loss among all hospitals in the state was $+115.8\%$. Test whether mean gain or loss among "underfunded" hospitals was significantly below this statewide mean.

6.18   Which of your conclusions in Problems 6.15–6.17 seem untrustworthy, in view of your graphical findings regarding these distributions (Problem 6.14)? By experimentally deleting the outliers, describe how they affected your sample means, standard deviations, standard errors, and t tests.

6.19   Outliers have little effect on nonparametric procedures such as the sign test. Use the data of Table 6.3 to perform one-tailed sign tests of the following null hypotheses, which state that the "underfunded" hospitals have medians at least as high as other hospitals in the state.
   a.   occupancy rates: $H_0: Md \geq 69$
   b.   operating margins: $H_0: Md \geq 1.6$
   c.   gain/loss: $H_0: Md \geq 50$

6.20   Summarize your conclusions from Problems 6.14–6.19.

Table 6.4 (file *precip*) lists data on changes in the chemistry of rain and snowfall at 13 rural U.S. sites. These data compare measurements taken between 1975 and 1978 with measurements taken between 1979 and 1982, and may provide evidence regarding the effectiveness of air pollution reduction efforts during these years. Sulfate and nitrate concentrations were measured in milligrams per liter; a positive change indicates that these pollutants increased. pH (potential of Hydrogen) measures acidity; a positive change indicates that acidity ("acid rain") *decreased*. For purposes of Problems 6.21–6.24, consider these measurements as a random sample of precipitation in nonmetropolitan areas of the United States.

6.21   Graph the change in pH, and describe this distribution. Using the $\alpha = .10$ significance level (in view of the small sample size), perform a t test of the hypothesis that mean change in pH equals 0, and a sign test of the hypothesis that median change in pH equals 0.

6.22   Graph the change in sulfate, and describe this distribution. Using the $\alpha = .10$ significance level, perform a t test of the hypothesis that mean change in sulfate equals

Table 6.4
Precipitation chemistry changes monitored at 13 rural U.S. sites

Monitoring site	Change in pH	Change in sulfate	Change in nitrate
Alamosa, Colorado	−1.10	−2.30	.05
Atlantic City, New Jersey	−.30	−1.10	−.08
Caribou, Maine	−.10	−.55	−.03
Huron, South Dakota	−.40	−.05	−.10
Macon County, North Carolina	−.20	−.15	.06
Mauna Loa, Hawaii	.60	−.42	−.12
Meridian, Mississippi	.00	.00	.04
Pendleton, Oregon	.10	−.20	.35
Raleigh, North Carolina	.30	−.07	−.09
Salem, Illinois	−.30	−.40	−.02
San Angelo, Texas	.60	.88	.16
Tahlequah, Oklahoma	.10	−.33	.05
Victoria County, Texas	−.30	.40	−.03

Source: Adapted from Council on Environmental Quality (1987).
File: *precip*

0, and a sign test of the hypothesis that median change in sulfate equals 0. Which test should we believe here, and why?

6.23 Graph the change in nitrate, and describe this distribution. Using $\alpha = .10$, carry out t and sign tests.

6.24 In what ways, if any, did precipitation chemistry change over this period? Summarize your findings from Problems 6.21–6.23.

Table 6.5 (page 214 file *matown*) contains data from a survey conducted in a Massachusetts town where wastes from a large chemical plant had contaminated the water supply. The variables include

lived   years respondent had lived in this community
standard   whether the town's water quality standards ought to be kept the same or made more strict, or made less strict (allowing more pollution)
bottle   whether respondent drinks bottled water always, occasionally, or never
pubmeet   whether respondent attended public meetings concerning the water contamination crisis
health   Is studying possible health effects from the contamination a high or low priority?
chemtrus   How much does the respondent trust announcements from the chemical company that caused the contamination?

Problems 6.25–6.31 refer to these data.

Table 6.5
Survey responses from a random sample of adult residents in one Massachusetts community with chemically contaminated water supplies

ID	lived	standard	bottle	pubmeet	health	chemtrus
1	2	same	occasion	no	low	low
2	31	same	never	no	high	low
3	3	same	never	no	high	low
4	4	more	never	yes	high	low
5	12	more	always	yes	high	no trust
6	13	same	never	no	low	moderate
7	12	same	never	yes	low	low
8	19	same	always	yes	low	no trust
9	22	more	occasion	yes	high	no trust
10	6	same	always	yes	low	low
11	7	more	always	no	high	no trust
12	13	more	often	yes	high	no trust
13	36	less	never	no	low	low
14	1	same	always	no	low	low
15	1	same	always	no	high	low
16	17	same	never	no	low	no trust
17	25	same	never	yes	low	no trust
18	1	more	never	no	high	low
19	2	same	occasion	no	low	low
20	20	same	occasion	no	low	low
21	2	same	occasion	no	high	low
22	17	more	often	yes	high	moderate
23	54	more	never	no	high	no trust
24	16	same	never	yes	low	no trust
25	6	more	never	yes	high	no trust
26	12	more	never	yes	low	low
27	25	same	always	no	high	no trust
28	8	more	never	no	low	no trust
29	10	same	occasion	yes	low	no trust
30	19	more	always	no	high	no trust
31	10	more	always	yes	high	no trust
32	5	same	occasion	yes	low	no trust
33	4	same	occasion	no	low	moderate
34	40	same	never	no	high	low
35	8	same	occasion	yes	low	no trust

Table 6.5 (*Continued*)

ID	lived	standard	bottle	pubmeet	health	chemtrus
36	5	same	occasion	no	high	low
37	28	same	never	no	low	no trust
38	19	same	occasion	yes	low	low
39	10	more	never	no	low	moderate
40	36	more	occasion	no	low	no trust
41	23	same	occasion	no	low	low
42	10	same	occasion	no	low	no trust
43	6	same	occasion	no	high	low
44	6	more	often	no	low	no trust
45	18	more	never	no	high	low
46	8	more	always	no	high	no trust
47	12	more	always	no	high	no trust
48	1	same	always	no	low	no trust
49	25	same	never	no	low	no trust
50	20	more	always	yes	high	no trust

Source: Hamilton (1985b).
File: *matown*

6.25 Use graphs and summary statistics to describe the distribution of years lived in the town.

6.26 Construct and interpret a 95% confidence interval for mean years lived in the town. (Although *lived* does not appear to follow a normal distribution, our sample is sufficiently large for this purpose.) Based on this interval, should we reject the hypothesis that "the average resident has lived here 20 years"?

6.27 Find the percentage expressing no trust in the chemical company. Calculate and interpret a 95% confidence interval for the population percentage, after applying the rule of thumb to confirm that this sample is large enough to justify equation (6.4).

6.28 Use equation (6.5) to calculate "margins of error" for the percentages of people who did and did not attend public meetings concerning the water crisis. Briefly report on your findings.

6.29 Assign these values to *standard*:

0 = water quality standards should be more strict

1 = water quality standards should be kept the same

2 = water quality standards should be less strict

    a. Use a t test to evaluate the null hypothesis H_0: $\mu = 1$.

    b. Use a sign test to evaluate the null hypothesis H_0: $Md = 1$. Does this test's general conclusion agree with part **a**?

6.30 Construct 95% confidence intervals for the percentage of people who never, occasionally, often, or always drink bottled water.

    a. Construct approximate intervals using the normal approximation [equation (6.4) or (6.8)].

    b. Construct exact intervals using a computer's "binomial confidence interval" function.

    c. Compare your results from parts **a** and **b**. For which percentage does the approximate interval most resemble the exact interval? For which percentage does the approximate interval least resemble the exact interval?

6.31 Carry out a test to evaluate the research hypothesis that a majority of residents view a health study as low priority. Show and explain the steps in your test, and interpret your final conclusions.

*6.32 Apply equation (6.17) to estimate the minimum random sample size needed in order to estimate, within plus or minus seven percentage points, the percentage of students at your school that voted in the most recent election. Calculate sample sizes for 90%, 95%, and 99% confidence intervals.

7

Cross-Tabulation and Chi-Square Tests

T he most interesting analytical questions involve relations between variables. How, if at all, does the distribution of *y* change with changing values of a second variable, *x*? Might *x* therefore be a cause of *y*, or are both caused by something else? Earlier chapters introduced some informal methods for exploring relations between pairs of variables: cross-tabulation (two categorical variables); mean or median comparisons and boxplots (one categorical, one measurement variable); and scatterplots (two measurement variables). Now we turn to more formal methods for analyzing intervariable relations. This chapter focuses on relations among categorical variables.

We begin with a simple two-variable example: skiing ability and injury. Our starting point is a **cross-tabulation**, similar to those seen earlier in Tables 1.6 and 4.3–4.5. Cross-tabulations tabulate the number of times each possible *combination* of two variables' values occur in a sample: how many uninjured beginners, injured beginners, uninjured experts, and so forth. Percentages help us see and describe patterns in these tables: What percentage of the beginners were hurt? What percentage of the experts?

To draw conclusions beyond the sample at hand, researchers often employ a significance test based on the theoretical **chi-square** (χ^2) distribution. The **chi-square test of independence** uses this theoretical distribution to evaluate a null hypothesis that, in the population, our categorical variables are independent of each other—for example, that in the population of young skiers, the probability of getting injured remains the same at all levels of ability.

7.1 Percentages in Cross-Tabulation

Child skiers seem more likely than adults to experience skiing injuries. The ski industry, naturally concerned about this pattern, has supported research aimed at learning what factors contribute to young skiers' higher accident rates. Table 7.1 cross-tabulates

Table 7.1.
Cross-tabulation of injury group by skiing ability, among 214 child skiers

Injury group	Skiing ability level			Total
	Beginner	Intermediate	Advanced	
No injury	60	84	39	183
Injured	20	9	2	31
Total	80	93	41	214

Source: Ungerholm and Gustavsson (1985).
File: tab7_1

data from one such study of 214 children. The two categorical variables shown are skiing ability (classified here into beginner, intermediate, and advanced categories) and whether the child was injured. Skiing ability forms the **column variable** because it defines the vertical columns of Table 7.1. Similarly, the **row variable**, injury group, defines the horizontal rows. Two rows and three columns produce six **cells**, which contain the **cell frequencies** or counts of cases in that combination of categories. The cell frequency for uninjured beginners equals 60; the cell frequency for injured intermediates equals 9, and so forth.

Marginal frequencies appear along the right and bottom margins of Table 7.1. **Row marginals** show the total number of cases in each row: 183 uninjured and 31 injured skiers. **Column marginals** indicate the total number of cases in each column: 80 beginner, 93 intermediate, and 41 advanced skiers. Either row or column marginals sum to the sample size ($n = 214$), at lower right.

Table 7.1 contains information on how skiing ability relates to injury, but it requires careful reading. Most of the skiers at each ability level were not injured. More beginners than experts got hurt, but more beginners than experts remained unhurt, too. Expressing cell frequencies as percentages brings out the patterns in this table. We need to carefully choose the appropriate type of percentage, however.

Table 7.2 repeats the cross-tabulation of Table 7.1, but with three types of percentage added to each cell:

row percentage   cell frequency as a percentage of cases in that row
column percentage   cell frequency as a percentage of cases in that column
total percentage   cell frequency as a percentage of cases in the table

Table 7.2
Cross-tabulation of injury group by skiing ability,
showing row, column, and total percentages

Injury group	Skiing ability level			Total
	Beginner	Intermediate	Advanced	
No injury	60	84	39	183
row %	33%	46%	21%	100%
column %	75%	90%	95%	
total %	28%	39%	18%	
Injured	20	9	2	31
row %	65%	29%	6%	100%
column %	25%	10%	5%	
total %	9%	4%	1%	
Total	80%	93	41	214
column %	100%	100%	100%	100%
total %				100%

Note that row percentages add to 100% across each row; column percentages add to 100% down each column; and total percentages add to 100% over the table as a whole.

In the beginner/no injury cell for example, we have the following three percentages:

33% of the uninjured skiers are beginners. To calculate a row percentage, divide cell frequency by row marginal, then multiply by 100: $^{60}\!/_{183} \times 100 = 33\%$.

75% of the beginners are uninjured. To calculate a column percentage, divide cell frequency by column marginal, then multiply by 100: $^{60}\!/_{80} \times 100 = 75\%$.

28% of the skiers in this table are uninjured beginners. To calculate a total percentage, divide cell frequency by sample size, then multiply by 100: $^{60}\!/_{214} \times 100 = 28\%$.

All three percentages legitimately describe the same 60 skiers, but not all will prove equally useful for understanding the relation between skiing ability and injury.

With Table 7.1 or 7.2, we would like to answer the question "How (if at all) does the probability of injury depend on skiing ability?" This question views ability as the suspected "cause," and injury as its "effect." Researchers often refer to an "independent" and "dependent" variable:

independent variable   suspected cause

dependent variable   suspected effect

Where possible, *use percentages based on the independent or "cause" variable*—row percentages if the independent variable defines the rows, column percentages if the independent variable defines the columns.

Independent variables appear as column variables in the cross-tabulations of this book, making column percentages the correct ones to use. This also gives cross-tabulation a structure similar to that of scatterplots: independent-variable values form the left-to-right scale, and dependent-variable values form the vertical scale. Other authors may not follow this convention with cross-tabulations, however, so you should not assume that it always applies. Furthermore, some tables have no obvious independent or dependent variables; in such cases, the choice of row or column percentages becomes less clear-cut.

For the skiers example, we need only the column percentages given in Table 7.3. Tables of column percentages, such as Table 7.3, often also list column marginal frequencies so that readers can see what numbers these percentages are based on. For the same reason, tables of row percentages often include row marginal frequencies.

Table 7.3 provides a clearer look at how the likelihood of injury depends on ability. Fully 25% of the beginning skiers were injured, as compared with only 10% of the intermediates, and 5% of the advanced skiers. In other words, among beginning skiers, the percentage injured was 5 times greater than among advanced skiers. Since these are column percentages, they already adjust for the unequal number of skiers in each column—that is, for the fact that there are more beginners than advanced skiers overall.

Table 7.3
Cross-tabulation of injury group by skiing ability, with column percentages

Injury group	Skiing ability level			Total
	Beginner	Intermediate	Advanced	
No injury	60 75%	84 90%	39 95%	183
Injured	20 25%	9 10%	2 5%	31
Total	80 100%	93 100%	41 100%	214

Figure 7.1 shows the percent injured, from Table 7.3, in bar chart form. Such bar charts can help readers to visualize the patterns in a percentage table, so they often appear in reports. We immediately see the way injury rates decline as skiing ability increases.

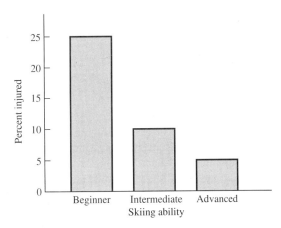

FIGURE 7.1
Bar chart showing the percentages of beginning, intermediate, and advanced skiers who were injured

EXERCISES

Table 7.4 (page 222; file *famtab*) cross-tabulates data from a survey of 969 married adults who were living with at least one child. People reported their type of family and whether they had experienced (as victim or aggressor) any violent acts of spousal abuse within the past year. In "reconstituted" families, one or both parents brought into the present family their children from an earlier marriage. All children in "remarried" families come from the current marriage only. Exercises 7.1.1–7.1.3 refer to this table.

Table 7.4

Cross-tabulation of spousal abuse by family type

| Spousal | Present family type | | |
abuse	intact	remarried	reconstituted
no abuse	743	92	78
abuse	36	9	11

Source: Kalmuss and Seltzer (1986).
File: *famtab*

7.1.1 Find marginal frequencies and row, column, and total percentages for Table 7.4.

7.1.2 The row percentage in the intact/no abuse cell equals 81%. We could put this into a sentence: "Eighty-one percent of the people reporting no spousal abuse lived in intact families." Write out similar sentences for each of the following:

    a.   the row percentage for the remarried/abuse cell

    b.   the column percentage for the intact/no abuse cell

    c.   the total percentage for the intact/no abuse cell

7.1.3 Which type of percentage (row, column, or total) best clarifies the relation between family type and spousal abuse? Write a short paragraph using the appropriate percentages to describe the relation you see in Table 7.4.

7.2 Independence and Expected Frequencies

Once we have a good understanding of the relation between two variables in our sample, the next question is, What generalizations does this sample suggest regarding the larger population? For example, assuming that they represent a random sample, what do the data on 214 children in Tables 7.1–7.3 tell us about the thousands of other young skiers who hit the slopes every winter? Can we reasonably conclude that an ability–injury relation exists in that larger, unanalyzed population too?

Answering this question calls for a test of the following null and alternative hypotheses:

H_0: In the population of all child skiers, ability and injury are unrelated (**independent** of each other).

H_1: In the population of all child skiers, ability and injury are related (not independent of each other).

Chapter 4 gave a *multiplication rule* [equation (4.1a)] for finding probabilities that two independent events both occur. If null hypothesis H_0 is true, then this multiplication rule should apply. For example, the probability that a randomly selected young skier is both a beginner and uninjured should (according to H_0) equal the probability of being a beginner, times the probability of being uninjured.

Let N represent the event "randomly selected skier is not injured," and B the event "randomly selected skier is beginner." Then under the null hypothesis of independence, the probability that a randomly selected skier is both not injured and a beginner should be:

$$P(N \text{ and } B) = P(N) \times P(B)$$

$$= \frac{183}{214} \times \frac{80}{214}$$

$$= .3197$$

If $P(N \text{ and } B) = .3197$, then out of $n = 214$ skiers we might expect about

$$P(N \text{ and } B) \times n = .3197 \times 214$$

$$= 68.4$$

uninjured beginners. Such **expected frequencies** indicate what we should expect to see in our cross-tabulation, *if* the null hypothesis of independence were true.

Expected frequency

If the null hypothesis of independence were true, then according to the multiplication rule the **expected frequency (E)** for any given cell in a cross-tabulation should be

$$E = \frac{r}{n} \times \frac{c}{n} \times n$$

$$= \frac{rc}{n} \tag{7.1}$$

where r stands for the number of cases in that cell's row, c for the number of cases in that cell's column, and n the number of cases in the table as a whole.

Table 7.5 (page 224) repeats the skiing ability and injury cross-tabulation, with both observed (O) and expected (E) frequencies shown in each cell. If the null hypothesis were true, we should expect 68.4 uninjured beginners; the study actually observed only 60. By similar reasoning, applying equation (7.1) we should expect

$$E = \frac{31 \times 80}{214}$$

$$= 11.6$$

injured beginners. The study observed more: $O = 20$. Notice that both expected and observed cell frequencies in Table 7.5 add up to exactly the same marginal frequencies. This will always be true for expected frequencies calculated under the independence hypothesis.

Table 7.5
Cross-tabulation of skiing ability by injury group, observed frequencies (O) with expected frequencies (E) in parentheses

Injury group	Skiing ability level			
	Beginner	Intermediate	Advanced	Total
No injury	60 (68.4)	84 (79.5)	39 (35.1)	183 (183)
Injured	20 (11.6)	9 (13.5)	2 (5.9)	31 (31)
Total	80 (80)	93 (93)	41 (41)	214 (214)

An informal comparison of observed and expected frequencies supports our earlier observation about the percentages. There are more injured beginners, and fewer injured intermediate or advanced skiers, than one might expect if ability and injury really were independent of each other. Are the differences between expected and observed frequencies so large that we should reject the independence hypothesis? The next section introduces a method for answering such questions.

EXERCISES

7.2.1   Show how equation (7.1) yields the expected frequencies for the remaining four cells of Table 7.5.

7.2.2   Construct a cross-tabulation showing observed and expected frequencies based on the family type and spousal abuse data in Table 7.4. Confirm that your expected frequencies add up to the same marginals as observed frequencies do.

7.2.3   Write a brief comparison describing the differences between expected and observed frequencies in Exercise 7.2.2.

7.3   Chi-Square Test of Independence

By squaring one or more independent standard normal variables, then adding them together, we obtain a new type of theoretical distribution called a **chi-square** (χ^2) distribution. Section 5.5 presented the theoretical rationale for this distribution. If the null hypothesis described earlier is true, then $(O - E)^2/E$ values in a cross-tabulation should resemble squared standard normal variables, and the sum of these $(O - E)^2/E$ values approximately follows a theoretical chi-square distribution. This reasoning underlies one of the most widely used statistical tests, the **chi-square test of independence**.

Chi-square test of independence

Hypotheses:

> H_0:   The row and column variables have no relation to each other (that is, they are independent) in the population.
> H_1:   The row and column variables are related in the population.

Assumption:

Cases are randomly and independently sampled from the population.

Rule of thumb:

No expected frequencies should be less than 5.

Test Statistic:

$$X^2 = \sum \frac{(O - E)^2}{E} \tag{7.2}$$

where O represents observed frequencies in a cross-tabulation, and

$$E = \frac{rc}{n}$$

are the frequencies expected under the null hypothesis H_0. If this null hypothesis is true then the X^2 statistic follows approximately a chi-square (χ^2) distribution with degrees of freedom

$$df = (\text{number of rows} - 1) \times (\text{number of columns} - 1) \tag{7.3}$$

Large values of X^2, corresponding to low chi-square tail probabilities, give us reason to reject H_0, and to conclude instead that the variables are related.

Chapter 6 introduced the terms **parametric** and **nonparametric tests**. Nonparametric tests, also called **distribution-free tests**, do not assume that variables follow a specific theoretical distribution such as the normal distribution. The chi-square test of independence, like the sign test in Chapter 6, is a nonparametric test. It assumes only that cases are randomly and independently sampled from the population, and that expected frequencies are large enough for the X^2 statistic to have an approximately chi-square distribution.

When expected frequencies are too low, this test can produce misleading results. The box notes a common rule of thumb: No expected frequencies should be less than 5. Some statisticians argue that the "none under 5" rule is too conservative, and we can reasonably apply chi-square tests so long as only a few expected frequencies are below 5, and none below 1. In an introductory text such as this one, however, the more conservative (safer) rule seems appropriate. Section 7.5 examines this problem more closely.

Table 7.6 lists O, E, and $(O - E)^2/E$ values for the skiers' cross-tabulation. In the beginner/no injury cell, for example, we observe 60 skiers, but expected 68.4, so

$$\frac{(O - E)^2}{E} = \frac{(60 - 68.4)^2}{68.4}$$

$$= 1.03$$

This and other $(O - E)^2/E$ values appear in each cell of Table 7.6. Below the cross-tabulation are calculations for the X^2 statistic ($X^2 = 11.87$) and its degrees of freedom ($df = 2$). The chi-square distribution table (Table A.3 in the Appendix) indicates that chi-square values larger than 11.87, given 2 degrees of freedom, occur with probability between .001 and .005:

$$.001 < P < .005$$

Computer calculation furnished the more precise estimate shown in Table 7.6:

$$P = .0026$$

Table 7.6
Cross-tabulation of injury group by skiing ability, showing observed frequencies (O), expected frequencies (E), $(O - E)^2/E$ values, and chi-square test statistic

Injury group	Skiing ability level			
	Beginner	Intermediate	Advanced	Total
No injury $(O - E)^2/E$	60 (68.4) 1.03	84 (79.5) .25	39 (35.1) .43	183 (183)
Injured $(O - E)^2/E$	20 (11.6) 6.08	9 (13.5) 1.50	2 (5.9) 2.58	31 (31)
Total	80 (80)	93 (93)	41 (41)	214 (214)

$$X^2 = \sum \frac{(O - E)^2}{E} = 1.03 + .25 + .43 + 6.08 + 1.50 + 2.58$$

$$= 11.87$$

df = (number of rows $-$ 1) $\times$ (number of columns $-$ 1) = (2 $-$ 1) $\times$ (3 $-$ 1) = 2

$P(\chi^2[2] > 11.87) = .0026$

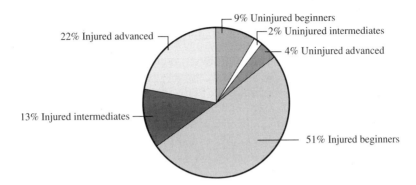

FIGURE 7.2
Pie chart showing the percentage contribution to the overall χ^2 statistic from each cell of Table 7.6

Obtained either way, this probability is very low—certainly low enough to justify rejecting the null hypothesis of independence at the usual $\alpha = .05$ significance level. By rejecting

H_0:   In the population of all child skiers, ability and injury are unrelated (**independent** of each other).

we conclude in favor of the alternative hypothesis

H_1:   In the population of all child skiers, ability and injury are related (not independent of each other).

In other words, we find *a statistically significant relation* between skiing ability and injury.

We reject the null hypothesis because the discrepancies between observed and expected frequencies are too large, as measured by X^2, to plausibly be due to chance. More than half of the size of the X^2 statistic itself (11.87) comes from the $(O - E)^2/E$ value of a single cell, the injured beginners (6.08). Thus the unexpectedly high number of injured beginners provides the strongest evidence against H_0 in this table. Figure 7.2 shows how much each cell in the table contributed to the overall X^2, and hence to rejecting the null hypothesis.

EXERCISES

7.3.1   Use Table A.3 or a computer to estimate the following chi-square distribution tail probabilities. For each one, state whether it would lead to rejection of H_0 at the $\alpha = .05$ significance level.
   a. $P(\chi^2[1] > 4)$
   b. $P(\chi^2[5] > 1)$
   c. $P(\chi^2[27] > 105)$
   d. $P(\chi^2[2] > .56)$

    e. $P(X^2 > 50)$, in a 6-row by 3-column cross-tabulation

    f. $P(X^2 > 13.49)$, in a 2-row by 10-column cross-tabulation

7.3.2 Is the relation between spousal abuse and family type statistically significant at $\alpha = .05$? Perform a chi-square test on the data of Table 7.4 (file *famtab*), and summarize your conclusion.

7.3.3 Perform chi-square tests of the following cross-tabulations, and summarize your conclusions from each:

    a. political-party preference by gender (Table 1.7, file *stats*)

    b. number of heterosexual partners this year by gender (Table 4.3, file *sextab*)

    c. number of heterosexual partners in lifetime by gender (Table 4.5, file *sextab*)

7.4   Comparing Two Proportions

The simplest cross-tabulation is a 2×2 table, like Table 7.7. This example, in which the cases are 30 college classes, cross-tabulates the class size (large or small) by whether the instructor has tenure. Untenured faculty taught 64% of the large classes, but only 44% of the small ones. A chi-square test indicates that this difference is not statistically significant; however, we cannot reject the null hypothesis that, in a larger population of classes, untenured faculty teach the same proportion of large and small classes.

Table 7.7
Cross-tabulation of faculty status by college class size,
with column percentages and chi-square test

Faculty status	Class size		Total
	Large	*Small*	
Untenured	9 64%	7 44%	16
Tenured	5 36%	9 56%	14
Total	14 100%	16 100%	30

$X^2 = 1.265$

df = (number of rows − 1) × (number of columns − 1)
    = (2 − 1) × (2 − 1) = 1

$P(\chi^2[1] > 1.265) = .261$

Chapter 8 will introduce methods for testing whether two means are significantly different. *A chi-square test applied to a 2 × 2 cross-tabulation performs a test for whether two proportions are significantly different.* In Table 7.7, we tested whether the proportions of large and small classes taught by untenured faculty significantly differ or, equivalently, whether the proportions of large and small classes taught by the complementary category, tenured faculty, significantly differ.

Another way to test for a difference between two proportions is described in the following box [equation (7.4)]. This z-test method yields results identical to the chi-square approach just shown, but it is simpler to calculate by hand. A related formula, equation (7.5) (page 230), gives confidence intervals for a difference between two proportions. To perform tests or calculate confidence intervals for differences between two percentages, recall that percentages are simply proportions multiplied by 100.

Large-sample test for a difference between two proportions

Hypotheses:

H_0:   A category occurs with equal proportions in populations 1 and 2.
H_1:   The category occurs with different proportions in populations 1 and 2.

Assumption:

Cases are randomly and independently sampled from the population.

Rule of thumb:

None of the following is less than 5: pn_1, pn_2, $n_1 - pn_1$, or $n_2 - pn_2$.

Test Statistic:

$$z = \frac{p_1 - p_2}{\sqrt{p(1 - p)(1/n_1 + 1/n_2)}}$$ (7.4)

where p_1 and p_2 represent the observed proportions, and n_1 and n_2 the sample sizes, in groups 1 and 2, respectively; p represents the proportion in the whole sample. If H_0 is true then the z statistic follows approximately a standard normal distribution. Large values of z, corresponding to low normal-distribution tail probabilities, give us reason to reject H_0, and conclude instead that the population proportions are different.

If we apply equation (7.4) to the data of Table 7.7, where the precise proportions are

$p_1 = 9/14 = .6428571$ (proportion of large classes taught by untenured faculty)

$p_2 = 7/16 = .4375$ (proportion of small classes taught by untenured faculty)

$p = 16/30 = .53333$ (proportion of all classes taught by untenured faculty)

we obtain

$$z = \frac{.6428571 - .4375}{\sqrt{.53333(1 - .53333)(1/14 + 1/16)}}$$

$$= \frac{.2053571}{\sqrt{.0333333}}$$

$$= 1.1247867$$

The probability of standard normal (z) values greater than ± 1.1247867 equals roughly .261—the same probability obtained through a chi-square test in Table 7.7. In fact, the X^2 statistic from any 2×2 table, including Table 7.7, equals the square of a z statistic calculated by equation (7.4):

$$z^2 = \chi^2[1]$$

Section 5.5 described the connection between z and theoretical χ^2 distributions in greater detail.

Large-sample confidence interval for a difference between two proportions

Under the same assumption and rule of thumb mentioned for equation (7.4), we calculate confidence intervals for the difference between two proportions as follows:

$$(p_1 - p_2) \pm z \sqrt{\frac{p_1(1 - p_1)}{n_1} + \frac{p_2(1 - p_2)}{n_2}} \qquad (7.5)$$

where z is chosen from a standard normal distribution to obtain the desired degree of confidence. For example, to construct confidence intervals that should contain the true population difference 95% of the time, use $z = 1.96$.

The sample percentages in Table 7.7, 64% and 44%, certainly look different. We failed to reject the null hypothesis of no population difference here, in part because the sample was small. The next two sections look more closely at the role of sample size in hypothesis testing.

EXERCISES

7.4.1   Show how to calculate expected frequencies, $(O - E)^2/E$ values, and the X^2 statistic for Table 7.7. What probability do we obtain if, instead of using a computer, we looked this X^2 value up in Table A.3?

7.4.2   Use equation (7.4) to test whether the proportion of large classes taught by tenured faculty differs from the proportion of small classes taught by tenured faculty. How does this result compare with that obtained earlier regarding untenured faculty?

7.4.3   Find a 95% confidence interval for the difference between percentages of large and small classes taught by tenured faculty.

7.5   Thin Cells

Cells that contain few observed or expected cases are called **thin cells**. Thin cells appear often in cross-tabulations based on small samples, and may arise in larger samples when the categories are many or have unequal marginal distributions. For example, even a sample of 10,000 cases could have many thin cells if we tried to cross-tabulate a rare category, such as childhood leukemia, with neighborhood and family background characteristics. Thin cells reflect the problem of not enough information. If only a few cases of childhood leukemia occur in a sample of 10,000, then we have little information on which to base conclusions about whether this illness occurs more often in houses near high-voltage power lines.

Thin cells can disproportionately influence the outcome of chi-square tests. The chi-square test of independence [equation (7.2)] becomes less trustworthy in the presence of thin cells. One widely used rule of thumb is: *Do not use the test if any of the expected frequencies are less than 5*. We will follow the "no E less than 5" rule in this text, although some authors have argued that it is too conservative, and the chi-square test remains usable even if one of the expected frequencies is as low as 1. In the presence of thin cells, the X^2 test statistic tends increasingly to depart from a theoretical chi-square distribution.

Chapter 6 introduced survey data from a Massachusetts community where public water supplies became contaminated by toxic wastes (Table 6.5). Table 7.8 (page 232) cross-tabulates two variables from this survey: whether respondents thought the town's water purity standards should be made more strict, less strict, or remain the same; and how often the respondent drank bottled water. We might hypothesize that people who drink bottled water would be more concerned about water quality, and hence also want stricter (cleaner) public water-supply standards.

Observed frequencies in Table 7.8 seem to support this hypothesis. The one person who said water quality standards should be less strict (that is, should allow more pollution) also said that he or she never drinks bottled water. Among those who never or occasionally drink bottled water, a majority favor keeping the same water-quality standards. Among those who often or always drink bottled water, a majority favor stricter standards.

Table 7.8
Cross-tabulation of water-quality standards opinion
by bottled-water drinking (data listed in Table 6.6)

| Water standards should be | How often do you drink bottled water? | | | | |
	never	occasionally	often	always	Total
more strict	8	2	3	7	20
kept same	10	13	0	6	29
less strict	1	0	0	0	1
Total	19	15	3	13	50

Source: Hamilton (1985b).
File: *matown*

Table 7.9 shows this cross-tabulation with expected frequencies and a chi-square test. The test yields $P = .064$, just above the usual .05 cutoff level. Thus we cannot reject the null hypothesis of independence; the relation between water-standards opinion and bottled-water drinking falls short of statistical significance. Table 7.9 contains many thin cells, however: Expected frequencies for six of the 12 cells fall below 5. Consequently the chi-square test here may be invalid. As the following example shows, a different and more exact test should be used instead.

Table 7.9
Cross-tabulation of water-quality standards opinion by bottled-water
drinking frequency, with expected frequencies and chi-square test

| Water standards should be | How often do you drink bottled water? | | | | |
	never	occasionally	often	always	Total
more strict	8 (7.6)	2 (6)	3 (1.2)	7 (5.2)	20
kept same	10 (11)	13 (8.7)	0 (1.7)	6 (7.5)	29
less strict	1 (.4)	0 (.3)	0 (.1)	0 (.3)	1
Total	19	15	3	13	50

$X^2 = 11.92$ $P(\chi^2[6] > 11.92) = .064$

An alternative to chi-square tests, when the data contain thin cells, is **Fisher's exact test**. As its name implies, this test calculates exact probabilities instead of relying on the chi-square approximation. The Fisher test calculations themselves are somewhat tedious, however, and will not be presented here. Some texts [for example, Everitt (1977), Upton (1978)] illustrate these calculations for the simplest situation, a small sample in a 2 × 2 table. Larger samples or tables require much more calculation, which is best done by a fast computer.

With a fast enough computer, we can obtain exact tests for any cross-tabulation where thin cells exist. If chi-square and exact test results appear much different, then we should believe the exact test results. (In the case of 2 × 2 tables, exact tests can find either one- or two-tail probabilities. The usual chi-square tests are two-tailed.) Fisher's exact test, applied to Table 7.8, yields $P = .02$. Contradicting the less accurate chi-square test, this exact test tells us that we do have a statistically significant relation between water-standards opinion and bottled-water drinking.

EXERCISES

7.5.1   Find column percentages for Table 7.8 (file *matown*), and use them to describe the relation between water-standards opinion and bottled-water drinking in this sample.

7.5.2   Perform Fisher's exact test on each of the following cross-tabulations, and compare the resulting two-tail probabilities with those from a chi-square test.
   a.   skiing ability by injury group (Table 7.1, file *skitab*)
   b.   spousal abuse by family type (Table 7.4, file *famtab*)
   c.   gender by political-party preference (Table 1.7, file *stats*)

7.6   Sample Size and Significance Tests

Statistical significance and practical importance are not the same thing. Consider Table 7.10 (page 234), from a survey in which college students were asked whether there were any areas around campus where they were afraid to walk alone at night. Most of the men said "no" (69.2%), and most of the women said "yes" (63.6%). These percentages reflect an unquestionably real and important social problem. A chi-square test applied to these data, however, finds insufficient evidence to reject the null hypothesis that (in the population) men and women are equally afraid of walking alone. Based on common sense we know that the gender difference is *real and important*; but based on the data in Table 7.10, we could only say that it is *not statistically significant*. In public debates, such apparent contradictions between statistics and common sense convince some people that scientists are heartless fools, or worse.

Table 7.10
Is there any area around campus where
you are afraid to walk alone at night?

Afraid to walk alone?	Gender		Total
	men	*women*	*Total*
no	9	4	13
	69.2%	36.4%	54.2%
yes	4	7	11
	30.8%	63.6%	45.8%
Total	13	11	24
	100.0%	100.0%	100.0%

$X^2 = 2.59$ $P(\chi^2[1] > 2.59) = .11$

File: *afraid*

This kind of misunderstanding arises because, to scientists, "statistical significance" has a special meaning whereas, to nonscientists, "significant" and "important" mean roughly the same thing. Significance tests evaluate whether *the data at hand provide convincing evidence against the null hypothesis.* Men's and women's percentages in Table 7.10 appear quite different, but they depend on just 13 men and 11 women. Common sense tells us that the percentages in this table reflect true gender differences in the population. But percentages this different theoretically could often arise by chance, if we repeatedly drew 24-student samples from a population in which no gender difference exists. Therefore, Table 7.10 *by itself* does not contain enough evidence to conclude that a gender difference exists. We know a difference really does exist because daily life has supplied us with much other information besides Table 7.10.

The large percentage differences seen in Table 7.10 are not statistically significant because the sample is small. Figure 7.3 illustrates the connection between sample size and statistical significance. For simplicity, we consider just a 2 × 2 cross-tabulation with equal numbers of cases in each row and each column. Under the null hypothesis, column (or row) percentages in each of the table's four cells should equal 50%. But we actually observe 60%–40% differences within each column. Are 60%–40% differences large enough to reject the no-difference (50%–50%) null hypothesis? The curved line shows how the chi-square test probability, for the same 60%–40% differences, declines as sample size increases. A 60%–40% difference becomes statistically significant ($P <$ .05) only in samples of about $n = 100$ or more. That is, only with these larger samples would we be confident that an observed 60%–40% sample difference reflects some real population difference, and not just random sampling error.

Figures 7.4 and 7.5 (page 236) carry this idea further. Suppose we observed only 55%–45% differences. These differences become statistically significant when sample size exceeds about 400 cases (Figure 7.4). And even very small differences are statisti-

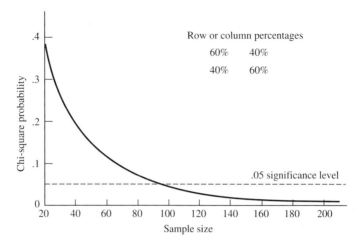

FIGURE 7.3
We could reject the null hypothesis based on the sample
percentages at upper right only if $n \geq 100$.

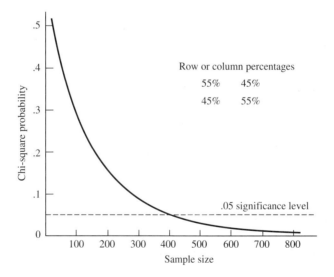

FIGURE 7.4
We could reject the null hypothesis based on the sample
percentages at upper right only if $n \geq 400$.

cally significant in large enough samples. Figure 7.5 shows that 51%–49% differences
become significant in samples of $n > 10,000$.

In summary, statistical significance does and does not tell us the following:

Statistically significant—the sample provides convincing evidence against the
null hypothesis (no relation). We therefore conclude in favor of our research

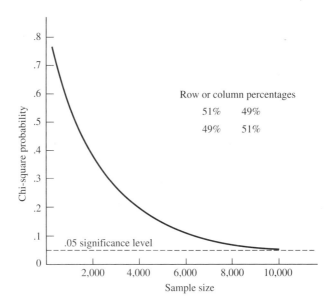

FIGURE 7.5
We could reject the null hypothesis based on the sample
percentages at upper right only if $n \geq 10,000$.

hypothesis (some relation). This "some relation" conclusion does not necessarily mean that the relation is strong, or has practical importance. In large samples, even a weak relation possessing no practical importance could be statistically significant.

Not statistically significant—the sample lacks convincing evidence against the null hypothesis. This conclusion does not *disprove* the research hypothesis; however, we find insufficient support for it in our sample. In small samples, even strong or important relations may not be statistically significant (as happened in Table 7.10).

These interpretations apply not only to the chi-square tests described in this chapter, but also to the other bivariate and multivariate tests of Chapters 8–10.

EXERCISES

7.6.1 The gender/fear relation in Table 7.10 (file *afraid*) is not statistically significant, despite the substantial difference between men and women, because this sample is so small. Suppose we had a table with exactly the same column percentages, but based on 240 students instead of 24. Would the gender/fear relation then be statistically significant? Manufacture such a table by multiplying each cell frequency in Table 7.10 by 10, then carrying out a chi-square test. How does your new X^2 value compare with that in Table 7.10?

7.6.2 Below are three 2 × 2 tables of "observed frequencies." Like the examples graphed in Figures 7.3–7.5, each table below has equal row and column marginals, and the same row or column percentage structure. They differ only in sample size.

$n = 20$:		$n = 40$:		$n = 60$:	
7	3	14	6	21	9
3	7	6	14	9	21

   a. Construct cross-tabulations with marginal frequencies and column percentages from each of the three ($n = 20$, 40, and 60) examples above. Carry out a chi-square test on each.

   b. Draw a graph in the manner of Figures 7.3–7.5 to display the relation between chi-square probability and sample size, based on your results from part **a**. Briefly describe what it shows.

*7.7 Three or More Variables: Multiway Cross-Tabulation

Although examples in this chapter have so far involved only two variables, we could also cross-tabulate three, four, or more categorical variables. Modern statistical methods permit detailed analysis of such multiway cross-tabulations, but most such methods lie beyond the scope of an introductory course. This section employs a three-variable example to introduce a few basic ideas of **multivariate** (three or more variable) analysis.

Table 7.11 (page 238) cross-tabulates data from a survey of residents in a small Vermont town where toxic waste contamination had been detected, at low levels, in two public schools near an industrial site. Some residents viewed the news with alarm, and argued that the schools should be closed to protect children until it could be proven that the schools were safe. Other residents reacted less strongly, and opposed the costly step of immediately closing the town's schools. They argued instead that until a clear danger was proven, the schools should stay open.

In Table 7.11 we see a significant relation between school closing opinion and whether the respondent had children under 19 years of age living in the town. The chi-square test results in $X^2 = 5.67$ with 1 degree of freedom, giving a probability ($P = .017$) below the usual .05 cutoff level. About half of the parents (51%), but less than one-third of the nonparents (32%), said that the schools should be closed until proven safe. Figure 7.6 (page 238) shows these percentage differences graphically. A graph is hardly worthwhile to convey only two numbers, but it is included here for later comparison.

Table 7.11

Cross-tabulation of school closing opinion by parenthood,
for 153 residents of a small Vermont town
(frequencies and column percentages shown)

| School closing opinion | Have children under 19 in town? | | Total |
	no	yes	
open	43 68%	44 49%	87
close	20 32%	46 51%	66
Total	63 100%	90 100%	153

$X^2 = 5.67$ $P(\chi^2[1] > 5.67) = .017$

Source: Hamilton (1985b).
File: *vttown*

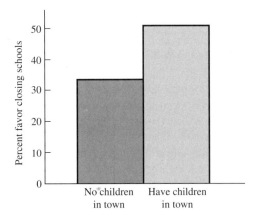

FIGURE 7.6
Percentage of nonparents and
parents who favor closing the
town's contaminated schools until
they can be proven safe

Table 7.12 constructs two separate subtables from the same data. The upper sub-table includes only the 60 survey respondents who are male. The lower subtable includes only the 93 female respondents. Each subtable cross-tabulates school closing opinion by whether the respondent had children younger than 19 living in the town. Table 7.12 thus constitutes a three-way cross-tabulation: school closing opinion by parenthood by gender.

Table 7.12
Three-way cross-tabulation of school closing opinion by
parenthood by gender, with column percentages

School closing opinion	Males: Have children under 19 in town?		Total
	no	yes	
open	85%	53%	67%
close	15%	47%	33%
Total	100%	100%	100%
	(26)	(34)	(60)

$X^2 = 6.65$ $P(\chi^2[1] > 6.65) = .010$

School closing opinion	Females: Have children under 19 in town?		Total
	no	yes	
open	57%	46%	51%
close	43%	54%	49%
Total	100%	100%	100%
	(37)	(56)	(93)

$X^2 = .95$ $P(\chi^2[1] > .95) = .33$

Each subtable in Table 7.12 depicts the relation between school opinion and parenthood, holding gender constant. Chi-square tests evaluate the opinion–parenthood relation within each subtable. (More elaborate tests, beyond the scope of this book, could simultaneously evaluate the net effects of parenthood, gender, and parenthood–gender combination.) Among both men and women, parents more often favored closing the schools. The contrast between parent and nonparent women, however, is not strong enough to achieve statistical significance in this relatively small sample. About 54% of the women with children under 19 favored school closing, as did 43% of the women without such children ($P = .33$).

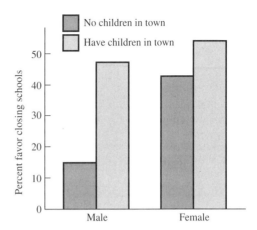

FIGURE 7.7
Percentage of nonparents and
parents who favor closing the
schools, by gender

The contrast between parent and nonparent men is more dramatic. Male parents were more than 3 times as likely to favor school closing as male nonparents (47% versus 15%, $P = .010$). Nonparent men emerge from this analysis as the oddest group: Unlike the other three groups, they overwhelmingly thought the schools should stay open unless proven dangerous.

Table 7.12 thus elaborates on the earlier results in Table 7.11. Whereas Table 7.11 simply showed that parents favored school closing more often than nonparents did, Table 7.12 permits a number of further comparisons:

1. Female parents favored school closing somewhat (and not significantly) more often than female nonparents.

2. Male parents favored school closing much (and significantly) more often than male nonparents.

3. Female parents favored school closing more often than male parents, and female nonparents favored school closing more often than male nonparents (this relation was not tested for significance, however).

4. Male nonparents least resemble the other three groups in their opinions about school closing.

Figure 7.7 allows visual comparison of percentages from Table 7.12.

EXERCISES

*7.7.1   Why do Tables 7.11 and 7.12 display column rather than row percentages?

*7.7.2   Of the 60 men in the first subtable of Table 7.12, 67% favored keeping the schools open. To convert any percentage to a frequency, express the percentage as a proportion, multiply that proportion by the base frequency, and round the result to the nearest integer:

$$.67 \times 60 = 40.2 \approx 40$$

Thus 40 men favored keeping the schools open.

   a.   Calculate the other observed frequencies of the first subtable of Table 7.12 by this method and reconstruct the original cross-tabulation. Next find the expected frequencies, and show steps in performing the chi-square test.
   b.   Calculate the observed frequencies of the second subtable in Table 7.12 by this method, and confirm the chi-square test calculations.

*7.7.3   Analyze the Massachusetts town survey data listed in Table 6.5 (file *matown*):
   a.   Cross-tabulate opinions regarding water-quality standards (*standard*) by opinions regarding a health study (*health*), with *health* as the column variable. Find column percentages and use these to describe the relation in this sample between *health* and *standard*.
   b.   Construct a three-way cross-tabulation of public meeting attendance (*pubmeet*) by *health* by *standard*. To do this, first separate the sample into people who did and did not attend public meetings. Within each of these two subsamples, construct new *standard* by *health* cross-tabulations, with *health* as the column variable. Find column percentages. Does the relation between *health* and *standard* appear equally strong among those who did and did not attend meetings?

*7.8   Experiments, Multivariate Analysis, and Causality

When we introduce a third or fourth variable into a cross-tabulation, it often changes our understanding of the relation between the original two variables. This becomes particularly important if we are interested in questions of causality.

In a laboratory experiment, researchers can physically control key variables. To ascertain whether the act of running mazes makes mouse brains grow more wrinkly, for instance, experimenters might randomly assign genetically similar mice to environments that were identical (same food, temperature, space, and so forth) except for maze-running. Then, if they found a significant difference in wrinkliness of their two mouse groups, they could reasonably conclude that maze-running had *caused* this difference. What else could it be?

Nonexperimental researchers, on the other hand, have little physical control over the circumstances that give rise to their data. This makes it much harder for them to determine cause and effect. If two wild populations of mice exhibit brain differences, that might be due to one living in a more challenging environment, but it could also be due to differences in diet, weather, crowding, or something else. Multivariate analysis, including (at the simplest level) three-way cross-tabulations, attempts to adjust or "control" statistically for the effects of other variables. When we include these other variables (call them x_2, x_3, . . .) in our analysis, we can learn whether the relation between y and x_1 remains the same even holding x_2, x_3, . . . constant.

In principle, multivariate analysis provides nonexperimental researchers with tools analogous to the experimenters' random assignment and physical control. We need such tools, because so many interesting research questions lie outside the realm of laboratory experiments. Alas, in practice a statistical analysis can never include "all possible" x variables, since infinitely many exist. The best we can try for is including at least the most important x variables, and even that will be difficult. Multivariate analysis of nonexperimental data, therefore, almost inevitably yields less conclusive evidence about causality than a well-designed experiment does.

Summary

Cross-tabulation extends the basic idea of one-variable frequency tables to encompass joint frequency distributions of two or more categorical variables. Percentages based on row or column marginals (whichever is the suspected "cause" variable, if one can be identified) help us see and describe whatever patterns exist in a cross-tabulation. Bar charts display these percentages visually; they are not needed for analysis, but may help the analyst present his or her findings to other people. Cross-tabulations with percentages, chi-square tests, and bar charts provide basic tools that are widely used by researchers working with survey data.

The usual null hypothesis for bivariate analysis is that our sample came from a population in which the two variables had no relation. In a two-variable cross-tabulation, "no relation" means that the row and column variables are independent as defined in Chapter 4. The multiplication rule allows us to calculate what frequencies we would expect to see if row and column variables really were independent. Chi-square tests systematically compare observed with expected frequencies; if these frequencies appear too different, then we can reject the null hypothesis of independence.

The X^2 statistic has an approximately chi-square distribution only for tables without thin cells, defined here as expected frequencies less than 5. If thin cells exist, then Fisher's exact test should be used instead. Computers ease the burden of exact-test calculations, but when faced with large samples or complex tables, even a computer may find these calculations difficult.

It is easy enough to cross-tabulate three or more categorical variables, and use percentages to describe what we see. The chi-square methods introduced in this chapter are too simple to fully analyze multiway cross-tabulations, however. The three-way example of Table 7.9, for instance, shows tests of the gender–school relation within categories of parenthood. But we would need further analyses to test the parenthood–school, parenthood–gender, or parenthood–gender–school relations for significance. New techniques for analyzing multiple categorical variables have proliferated over the past 20 years. They now comprise an important topic in advanced statistics courses, particularly in survey-oriented disciplines such as sociology and political science.

The chapter included an important note on "statistical significance" versus "practical importance." One does not necessarily imply the other, a source of confusion to people untrained in statistics. Chi-square tests readily illustrate the connection between significance and sample size, which exists with other types of hypothesis tests as well.

What We Learn from Chi-Square Tests of Independence

Describing Sample Data

How strong is the relation between our two categorical variables, in this sample? We calculate row or column percentages based on the independent (row or column) variable. For example, if each column represents a category of the independent variable ("cause" or "predictor"), find column percentages and compare these percentages between rows. The greater the differences between corresponding percentages in each row, the stronger the relation between variables.

Inferences about Population

Based on the evidence from this sample (and assuming the sample is random), can we reject the hypothesis that in the population our two categorical variables have no relation at all? A statistically significant (e.g., $P < .05$) chi-square test result indicates that the answer is yes. We thereby indirectly conclude that some relation does exist in the population. On the other hand, if the chi-square result is nonsignificant, we lack persuasive evidence that a relation exists between these variables in the population.

PROBLEMS

7.1   Table 7.13 (page 244; file *vactab*) gives results from a test of two vaccines intended to prevent typhoid fever. A total of 6,907 people in Nepal received either Vi capsular polysaccharide (Vi) or pneumococcus polysaccharide (Pneumo) vaccine. Of these 6,907 people, 71 later developed symptoms of typhoid fever.

Table 7.13
Cross-tabulation of typhoid fever incidence by type of vaccine

Outcome	Type of vaccine		Total
	Vi	Pneumo	
no typhoid	3,443	3,393	6,836
typhoid	14	57	71
Total	3,457	3,450	6,907

Source: Acharya et al. (1987).
File: vactab

a. Conduct a chi-square test to determine whether one vaccine was significantly more effective than the other.
b. Find the appropriate (row or column) percentages, and use them to summarize your conclusions comparing the vaccines' effectiveness.

7.2 Table 7.14 (file *nuketab*) contains a cross-tabulation of opinions, by gender, regarding whether a controversial nuclear power plant should be licensed to begin operations. The data reflect a telephone survey of 400 residents from communities near the plant. Use percentages to compare the opinions of men and women. Are the differences in this sample statistically significant?

Table 7.14
Cross-tabulation of opinions about
nuclear power plant by gender

Allow plant to operate?	Gender		Total
	male	female	
yes	84	56	140
no	74	138	212
don't know	21	27	48
Total	179	221	400

File: nuketab

7.3 Figure 2.12 in Chapter 2 graphed the unhappy history of Newfoundland's cod fishing industry, which collapsed due to overfishing in the early 1990s. Prior to this collapse, Newfoundland's economy had depended largely on fishing. As the population grew and fishing declined, many Newfoundlanders sought economic alternatives such as developing offshore oil resources. Tables 7.15–7.24 show results from a survey regarding the plans and hopes of high school students in 13 Newfoundland towns and villages. The survey was conducted in 1990, shortly after a $5-billion oil construction project began near some of these communities (Seyfrit, 1993; Hamilton and Seyfrit, 1994).

Because of the lack of industries other than fishing, many Newfoundlanders leave to seek jobs elsewhere. Advocates of oil development hope that providing new job opportunities will reduce young people's outmigration. To examine whether living near the oil project affects high school students' migration plans, Table 7.15 cross-tabulates community (whether in the oil-development impact area, or in a comparison area farther from the oil project) by whether students believed they were likely to leave Newfoundland permanently after graduation. Use percentages and a chi-square test to analyze this table, and summarize your conclusions.

Table 7.15
Cross-tabulation of whether respondent expects to leave
Newfoundland permanently by whether he or she
lives in oil impact or comparison area

| Likely to leave Newfoundland | Oil impact or comparison area? | | Total |
	comparison	*impact*	
no	505	645	1,150
yes	159	191	350
Total	664	836	1,500

Source: Seyfrit (1993).
File: *tab7_15*

7.4 Table 7.15 (file *tab7_15*) has many cases (observed or expected) in each cell, so the chi-square test's approximation should be reasonably accurate. Check this by calculating Fisher's exact test, and compare its two-tail probability with that obtained for chi-square. Are the two probabilities close?

7.5 Table 7.16 (page 246; file *tab7_16*) cross-tabulates the students' year in high school by whether they expect to attend a university after graduation. Use percentages and a chi-square test to analyze this table, and describe what you find. Suggest a possible explanation for this pattern.

Table 7.16
Cross-tabulation of whether respondent expects
to attend a university by year in high school

Expect to attend university?	What year of school now?			Total
	10	11	12	
no	210	260	274	744
yes	224	235	178	637
Total	434	495	452	1,381

Source: Seyfrit (1993).
File: tab7_16

7.6 Newfoundland's offshore oilfields lie under stormy North Atlantic waters over 100 miles from land. Like any megaproject, this oil development has been controversial. The students split over whether people in their area would be better off in the long run as a result of oil development. Are university-bound students significantly different from others in their view of this development? Analyze the data in Table 7.17 (file *tab7_17*) using column percentages and cross-tabulation.

Table 7.17
Cross-tabulation of agreement that "The people of this area will be better off if oil is developed" by whether respondent expects to attend a university

Area better off if oil developed	Expect to attend university?		Total
	no	yes	
strongly disagree	19	8	27
disagree	43	26	69
undecided	243	208	451
agree	358	316	674
strongly agree	123	97	220
Total	786	655	1,441

Source: Seyfrit (1993).
File: tab7_17

7.7 High-tech modern resource industries employ many skilled and unskilled laborers, but their top jobs generally require university educations. Does the oil industry appeal to Newfoundland high school students who expect to attend a university? Analyze Table 7.18 (file *tab7_18*) using column percentages and a chi-square test.

Table 7.18
Cross-tabulation of whether respondent expects to work in Newfoundland's oil industry by whether respondent expects to attend a university

Expect job in oil industry?	Expect to attend university?		Total
	no	yes	
no	725	635	1,360
yes	99	33	132
Total	824	668	1,492

Source: Seyfrit (1993).
File: *tab7_18*

7.8   The Newfoundland survey also asked students questions regarding how they felt about life in their small communities. Some interesting differences emerged between the responses of high school boys and girls. For example, one question stated "People give you a bad name here if you are different." Students chose among responses from "strongly disagree" to "strongly agree." Use percentages to describe the gender difference that you see in Table 7.19 (file *tab7_19*), and a chi-square test to determine whether this difference is statistically significant.

Table 7.19
Cross-tabulation of agreement that "People give you a bad name here if you are different" by respondent gender

Bad name if different	Gender		Total
	male	female	
strongly disagree	60	31	91
disagree	210	164	374
undecided	149	137	286
agree	196	280	476
strongly agree	107	155	262
Total	722	767	1,489

Source: Seyfrit (1993)
File: *tab7_19*

7.9 Do male and female students differ in their educational goals? Analyze Table 7.20 (file *tab7_20*) and summarize your conclusions. What consequences might these different goals have for people in small villages where there are few jobs for college graduates?

Table 7.20
Cross-tabulation of whether respondents expect
to attend a university by gender

Expect to attend university?	Gender		Total
	male	female	
no	461	363	824
yes	263	405	668
Total	724	768	1,492

Source: Seyfrit (1993).
File: *tab7_20*

7.10 Table 7.21 (file *tab7_21*) further investigates gender differences in the aspirations of Newfoundland high school students. Are these differences significant? How do your conclusions from Table 7.21 fit with those from Tables 7.19 and 7.20?

Table 7.21
Cross-tabulation of where respondents expect to spend
most of the rest of their lives by gender

Likely to live most of life	Gender		Total
	male	female	
don't know	211	181	392
same area	177	135	312
elsewhere in Newfoundland	178	261	439
elsewhere in Canada	128	154	282
outside of Canada	25	24	49
Total	719	755	1,474

Source: Seyfrit (1993).
File: *tab7_21*

7.11   Relatively few of these rural high school students expected to find jobs in the new oil industry. Are those who do expect jobs significantly more likely to agree that "People who object to Newfoundland oil development should move away?" Analyze Table 7.22 (file *tab7_22*).

Table 7.22
Cross-tabulation of agreement that "People who object to Newfoundland oil development should move away" by whether respondent expects to find work in the oil industry

Who objects to oil should move	Expect job in oil industry?		Total
	no	*yes*	
strongly disagree	158	13	171
disagree	410	25	435
undecided	466	25	491
agree	212	36	248
strongly agree	86	28	114
Total	1,332	127	1,459

Source: Seyfrit (1993).
File: *tab7_22*

7.12   Do students in the impact area, near the huge oil platform construction site, more often expect oil jobs? Analyze Table 7.23 (file *tab7_23*).

Table 7.23
Cross-tabulation of whether respondent lives in comparison or oil-construction impact area by whether respondent expects to find work in the oil industry

Expect job in oil industry?	Oil impact or comparison area?		Total
	comparison	*impact*	
no	613	747	1,360
yes	45	87	132
Total	658	834	1,492

Source: Seyfrit (1993).
File: *tab7_23*

*7.13 Table 7.24 (file *tab7_24*) shows a three-way cross-tabulation, set up to investigate whether the area/job relation seen in Table 7.23 is the same for both males and females. Find column percentages and chi-square probabilities for each of the two subtables in Table 7.24, and write up your conclusions.

Table 7.24
Three-way cross-tabulation of whether respondent expects
a job in the oil industry by whether respondent lives in
comparison or oil-construction impact area by gender

| Expect job in oil industry? | Males: Oil impact or comparison area? | | Total |
	compare	impact	
no	270	331	601
yes	38	85	123
Total	308	416	724

| Expect job in oil industry? | Females: Oil impact or comparison area? | | Total |
	compare	impact	
no	343	416	759
yes	7	2	9
Total	350	418	768

Source: Seyfrit (1993).
File: tab7_24

7.14 Despite the large sample, Table 7.24 contains several thin cells because so few high school girls (only 9 out of 768) expect jobs in the oil industry. Consequently, your chi-square test results appear questionable. Evaluate the area/jobs relation within each subtable again using Fisher's exact test. Do two-tail probabilities from these tests support the same general conclusion as your earlier chi-square tests?

7.15 Tables 7.11 and 7.12 introduced results from a survey of 153 residents in a small Vermont town. Many of these people were alarmed by the discovery that hazardous wastes from a local business had contaminated soil, groundwater, and two schools. Table 7.25 lists raw data from the survey, showing seven variables:

gender	Respondent's gender
lived	Years respondent has lived in this town
kids	Does respondent have children under 19 years of age in town?
educ	Highest year of schooling completed
active	Respondent attended two or more activist meetings
contam	Respondent's own property or water contaminated
school	The schools should close until proven safe

Problems 7.15–7.20 refer to these data.

Some concerned residents formed an activist group that pushed for immediate cleanup and precautionary measures such as closing the schools. Was participation in this group influenced by whether respondents thought their own property or water had been contaminated? Cross-tabulate *active* by *contam*, calculate percentages appropriate for this research question, and perform a chi-square test. Briefly summarize your findings.

Table 7.25
Survey of adult residents in a Vermont town
affected by toxic waste contamination

gender	lived	kids	educ	active	contam	school
female	32	no	13	no	yes	close
male	10	no	8	no	yes	open
female	18	no	16	no	no	open
male	19	no	16	yes	no	open
female	35	no	12	no	no	open
male	81	no	6	no	no	open
female	14	no	16	no	no	open
female	35	no	15	yes	no	open
female	28	no	14	no	no	open
male	21	no	12	yes	yes	close
male	24	no	12	no	no	open
female	1	no	15	no	no	open
male	65	no	9	no	yes	open
male	35	no	8	no	no	open
male	39	no	14	no	no	open
male	26	no	12	no	no	open
male	4	no	12	no	no	open
female	10	no	12	yes	yes	close
female	12	no	12	yes	no	close

(*continued*)

Table 7.25 (*Continued*)

gender	lived	kids	educ	active	contam	school
female	49	no	16	no	yes	open
female	51	no	8	no	yes	close
female	30	no	12	no	no	open
female	15	no	12	no	no	close
female	24	no	12	no	no	open
female	45	no	13	no	no	open
female	19	no	12	no	no	open
female	12	no	18	no	no	open
male	3	no	17	yes	yes	close
female	29	no	12	yes	yes	close
male	20	no	12	no	no	open
female	20	no	12	no	no	open
female	41	no	12	no	no	open
female	36	no	12	no	yes	open
female	40	no	12	no	yes	close
male	31	no	13	no	no	open
female	68	no	12	no	no	close
female	2	no	15	no	no	open
female	10	no	12	no	no	close
male	34	no	12	no	no	open
male	21	no	12	no	no	open
female	21	no	12	yes	yes	close
male	65	no	9	no	no	open
male	7	no	20	no	no	open
female	3	no	20	no	no	open
male	56	no	14	yes	yes	open
female	13	no	14	no	no	close
female	30	no	13	no	no	close
female	30	no	9	no	no	close
female	1	no	15	no	yes	close
female	22	no	12	yes	yes	close
female	4	no	12	no	no	open
male	24	no	12	no	no	open
female	2	no	13	no	yes	close
male	36	no	13	no	no	open
male	9	no	8	no	yes	close
male	54	no	12	no	no	open
female	38	no	12	no	no	open
male	50	no	8	no	no	open
male	6	no	16	no	no	open

Table 7.25

gender	lived	kids	educ	active	contam	school
male	65	no	12	no	no	open
male	29	no	10	yes	no	close
female	28	no	12	no	no	open
female	27	no	12	no	no	open
female	13	yes	12	no	no	open
female	4	yes	12	no	no	open
male	12	yes	16	no	no	open
female	1	yes	12	no	yes	open
female	6	yes	12	yes	no	close
female	5	yes	12	yes	no	close
male	8	yes	16	no	yes	open
female	5	yes	16	no	no	close
female	22	yes	12	no	no	close
female	17	yes	12	no	no	open
female	1	yes	12	yes	no	close
male	6	yes	18	yes	no	open
female	36	yes	9	no	no	open
female	21	yes	12	no	no	open
male	5	yes	16	no	no	open
male	35	yes	12	yes	yes	close
female	3	yes	12	yes	no	close
female	4	yes	14	no	no	close
male	5	yes	14	no	no	close
female	5	yes	16	yes	no	close
female	1	yes	16	yes	no	close
female	1	yes	12	yes	yes	open
female	13	yes	15	no	no	open
female	9	yes	12	no	no	open
female	6	yes	16	yes	no	open
female	6	yes	14	no	yes	close
female	4	yes	16	no	no	close
female	8	yes	15	no	yes	open
female	22	yes	16	no	no	open
male	5	yes	14	no	no	close
female	13	yes	12	yes	no	close
female	15	yes	16	no	yes	close
male	13	yes	12	yes	yes	close
male	12	yes	18	no	no	open
male	9	yes	12	yes	yes	close
female	5	yes	12	no	no	open

(*continued*)

Table 7.25 (*Continued*)

gender	lived	kids	educ	active	contam	school
male	20	yes	16	no	no	open
male	6	yes	13	yes	yes	close
female	11	yes	16	no	yes	open
male	18	yes	15	no	no	open
female	3	yes	13	yes	yes	close
female	9	yes	12	yes	yes	close
female	2	yes	12	no	no	open
male	4	yes	12	no	no	open
female	7	yes	12	yes	no	close
male	15	yes	12	no	no	close
male	20	yes	8	no	no	open
female	16	yes	16	no	no	open
female	37	yes	12	no	no	open
male	18	yes	14	no	no	close
female	3	yes	12	yes	yes	close
male	30	yes	12	yes	no	open
female	6	yes	7	no	no	open
male	5	yes	14	yes	no	close
male	55	yes	12	yes	no	open
female	5	yes	12	no	no	open
male	27	yes	12	yes	yes	close
male	10	yes	12	yes	yes	close
male	10	yes	12	no	no	open
male	2	yes	14	yes	no	close
female	3	yes	18	yes	no	close
male	15	yes	14	no	yes	close
female	15	yes	15	no	yes	close
male	1	yes	16	no	no	close
female	24	yes	12	no	no	open
male	42	yes	12	no	no	open
female	21	yes	9	no	no	close
female	20	yes	12	no	no	close
male	30	yes	10	yes	no	close
female	3	yes	16	yes	no	close
female	40	yes	12	yes	yes	open
female	6	yes	12	no	no	open
male	5	yes	16	no	no	open
female	15	yes	13	yes	no	close
female	4	yes	16	no	no	open

Table 7.25 (*Continued*)

gender	lived	kids	educ	active	contam	school
female	4	yes	12	yes	yes	close
male	50	yes	12	no	no	open
female	13	yes	17	no	yes	open
female	3	yes	13	yes	yes	close
male	20	yes	12	no	no	open
male	2	yes	12	no	yes	open
male	5	yes	16	yes	no	close
female	10	yes	12	yes	yes	close
female	17	yes	12	no	no	open
female	7	yes	10	yes	yes	close
male	55	yes	12	no	no	open
female	11	yes	12	no	no	close
female	25	yes	14	yes	yes	close
female	5	yes	12	yes	no	close
female	53	yes	12	no	no	open

Source: Hamilton (1985b).
File: *vttown*

7.16   Earlier in this chapter we saw evidence suggesting that gender and parenthood affected the town residents' opinions about school closing. Are these demographic variables also related to activist meeting attendance?
    a.   Analyze the cross-tabulation of *active* by *gender.*
    b.   Analyze the cross-tabulation of *active* by *kids.*

*7.17   Form a three-way cross-tabulation with separate *active* × *kids* subtables for males and for females. Find percentages and perform chi-square tests within each subtable. How do your findings here elaborate your conclusions from Problem 7.16a and 7.16b?

7.18   (*Review*)   The data in Table 7.25 include two measurement variables, years lived in town (*lived*) and years of education (*educ*). Do activists and nonactivists differ substantially with respect to the number of years they had lived in this town? Find the mean of *lived* for people who did and did not attend two or more activist meetings. Construct graphs to compare the distributions of *lived* for the two groups. Do the differences seem large enough to have any real-world importance?

7.19   (*Review*)   Do activists and nonactivists differ noticeably with respect to their years of education (*educ*)? Construct graphs, and find the mean education of people who did and did not attend two or more activist meetings. Does this difference seem large enough to have importance?

7.20 Pull your findings from Problems 7.15–7.19 together to write a paragraph summarizing ways in which the people attending activist meetings differed or did not differ from other residents of this Vermont town.

7.21 Apply a chi-square test to the cross-tabulation of political ambition by gender in Table 4.8 of Chapter 4 (file *ambition*). Calculate appropriate percentages, and use these together with the chi-square test results to summarize your conclusions.

7.22 Apply a chi-square test to the cross-tabulation of election success by family income for *male candidates* in Table 4.9 of Chapter 4 (file *success*). Use test results and the appropriate percentages to summarize your conclusions.

7.23 Apply a chi-square test to the cross-tabulation of election success by family income for *female candidates* in Table 4.9 of Chapter 4 (file *success*). Summarize your conclusions.

7.24 Table 7.26 derives from surveys commissioned by the U.S. Department of Interior's Minerals Management Service in Alaska. The survey's purpose was to provide baseline data for judging how oil and gas development might affect Alaska's traditional peoples and rural life. Responses from 227 adult residents of two rural regions appear in these tables. Table 7.26 cross-tabulates the percentage of the meat and fish respondents ate last year that reflected their own family's hunting and fishing efforts ("country foods"), by years of formal education.

  Apply a chi-square test and appropriate percentages to Table 7.26, to analyze the relation between reliance on country foods and education.

Table 7.26
Cross-tabulation of percent country foods in respondent's
meat/fish diet by years of formal education

% country meat/fish last year	Years of education			Total
	≤ 8 yrs	9–12 yrs	college	
< 50%	22	38	35	95
51–75%	15	25	9	49
over 75%	36	38	9	83
Total	73	101	53	227

Source: Minerals Management Service; described in Jorgensen (1991).
File: *cfoods*

7.25 About 85% of the survey respondents in Table 7.26 are Alaskan Natives, primarily Eskimos, whose ancestors survived for thousands of years by hunting and fishing. The remaining 15% consist of non-Natives, the majority of them college-educated professionals. Table 7.27 presents a three-way cross-tabulation of education by country foods by race. Analyze the subtables for Natives and non-Natives separately, to determine whether the apparent relation between education and foods, seen in Problem 7.24, remains significant when we hold race constant; or is that apparent relation spurious? Carefully explain your conclusions.

Table 7.27
Three-way cross-tabulation of race (Alaskan Native/non-Native) by education by percent country foods

| % country meat/fish last year | Alaskan Natives: Years of education | | | Total |
	≤8 yrs	9–12 yrs	college	
<50%	22	31	15	68
51–75%	15	22	7	44
over 75%	36	37	8	81
Total	73	90	30	193

| % country meat/fish last year | Non-Natives: Years of education | | Total |
	9–12 yrs	college	
<50%	7	20	27
51–75%	3	2	5
over 75%	1	1	2
Total	11	23	34

Source: Minerals Management Service; described in Jorgensen (1991).
File: *cfoods*

7.26 The non-Native subtable of Table 7.27 contains thin cells that may invalidate the usual chi-square test. Apply Fisher's exact test to this subtable, and compare its results with the results of the chi-square test.

7.27 The 1989 oil spill from the tanker *Exxon Valdez* contaminated hundreds of miles of Alaskan coastline, including many prime fishing grounds. Legal, scientific, and economic arguments continue about how severe and long-lasting the oil spill's effects will be. The Minerals Management survey discussed earlier asked respondents living near the oil spill area whether they believed that fish abundance had changed since the spill. Table 7.28 gives Native and non-Native responses.

Table 7.28
Cross-tabulation of race by whether respondent thinks
fish abundance has decreased, stayed the same,
or increased since the *Exxon Valdez* oil spill

Fishing since Exxon Valdez	Respondent's race		Total
	Native	*other*	*Total*
decrease	20	5	25
same	6	5	11
increase	1	1	2
Total	27	11	38

Source: Minerals Management Service; described in Jorgensen (1991).
File: *exxfish*

    a. Do Natives and non-Natives have significantly different views on this topic?
    b. Explain how this example illustrates the connection between sample size and statistical significance.

7.28   Table 7.29 cross-tabulates data from a study by Daly and Wilson (1982), entitled "Whom are newborn babies said to resemble?" The authors investigated patterns in whether mothers, fathers, and their relatives perceived a resemblance between newborn babies and the mother's or father's side of the family. Does the infant's birth order (first or later born) affect whether a paternal (father's side) or other resemblance is claimed?

Table 7.29
Cross-tabulation of alleged resemblance
by infant's birth order

Paternal resemblance claimed?	Baby's birth order	
	First	*Later*
other	80	80
paternal	132	71

Source: Daly and Wilson (1982).
File: *baby*

7.29   Presenting further results from the Daly and Wilson study, Table 7.30 investigates whether mothers, fathers, and their relatives have different perceptions about whom the baby resembles. Analyze this table and summarize your findings.

Table 7.30
Cross-tabulation of alleged resemblance by respondent identity

Paternal resemblance claimed?	Respondent identity			
	Father's relative	Father	Mother's relative	Mother
other	26	50	33	51
paternal	26	61	45	71

Source: Daly and Wilson (1982).
File: *baby*

8

ANOVA and Other Comparison Methods

This chapter looks at methods for analyzing the relation between one measurement and one (or more) categorical variable. The diverse methods share a common goal: to determine whether the distribution of the measurement variable appears similar across categories. For example, is mean family size the same among Americans belonging to Protestant, Catholic, Jewish, or other religions? Is median income the same among Democrats and Republicans? Boxplots (like Figure 3.8) allow quick visual comparisons of several distributions' medians, and also of their spread, skew, and outliers. The methods introduced in this chapter complement such visual displays by formally testing for differences between distributions.

The simplest comparison problems involve two distributions; that is, the categorical variable has only two categories. This chapter begins with such "two-sample" problems before moving on to "*K*-sample" problems, where we seek to compare distributions across three or more categories of the second variable. Finally, the chapter concludes with a look at three-variable methods, which compare means of one measurement variable across levels of two categorical variables.

8.1 — Two-Sample *t* Test

Table 8.1 contains data on 30 high school students in rural Alaska. The variables, which will serve to illustrate statistical comparison methods, are as follows:

gender	Student's gender
region	Northwest Arctic or Bristol Bay region, two large but sparsely populated areas in western Alaska
lived	Student has lived fewer than 14 years in this region (a "newcomer") or 14 years or more (a "long-term" resident)
size	Student currently attends school in a village (populations from 80 to 600) or a larger town (populations from 2,000 to 3,000)
where	Whether student expects to live most of his or her life in the same region, elsewhere in Alaska (typically, the cities of Anchorage or Fairbanks), or outside of Alaska
bonds	Scale measuring the strength of social and family bonds the student feels toward his or her present community

These six variables and 30 cases were drawn from a larger dataset on students and graduates in 15 towns and villages.

Table 8.1
Survey data from 30 rural Alaskan high school students

gender	region	lived	size	where	bonds
male	Arctic	long-term	village	same	96.8
male	Arctic	long-term	town	out AK	58.0
female	Arctic	newcomer	village	else AK	51.0
female	Arctic	long-term	town	else AK	17.3
female	Arctic	newcomer	town	out AK	36.3
female	Arctic	long-term	town	else AK	8.2
female	Bristol	long-term	village	same	88.9
male	Bristol	newcomer	town	out AK	18.3
female	Arctic	long-term	village	same	72.7
female	Arctic	newcomer	town	else AK	30.0
male	Arctic	long-term	village	else AK	61.2
male	Arctic	newcomer	town	else AK	24.6
female	Bristol	newcomer	town	out AK	58.5
female	Arctic	newcomer	village	same	23.4
male	Arctic	newcomer	town	else AK	49.8
male	Arctic	long-term	village	else AK	65.5
female	Bristol	newcomer	village	else AK	85.5
female	Arctic	long-term	town	else AK	43.1
female	Arctic	newcomer	town	out AK	47.5
male	Arctic	long-term	village	same	61.1
male	Arctic	long-term	village	else AK	71.5
male	Arctic	newcomer	village	same	74.2
female	Bristol	long-term	town	else AK	44.6
female	Bristol	long-term	village	same	85.3
female	Bristol	long-term	village	out AK	54.4
male	Arctic	newcomer	town	else AK	64.1
male	Arctic	long-term	town	same	43.8
male	Arctic	newcomer	town	out AK	14.0
male	Bristol	newcomer	town	out AK	12.3
male	Arctic	long-term	village	same	57.9

Source: Hamilton and Seyfrit (1993).
File: *akteens*

Most of the students in this study are Inupiat or Yupik Eskimo. Compared with communities in the lower 48 U.S. states, their Alaskan homes are isolated and remote. Since few roads exist, even basketball games against another high school often require trips in a single-engine plane. Their communities lack recreation or job opportunities, and more than half of these students say that they plan to move away after graduation.

Recent history suggests, however, that many who do leave will find themselves return-ing. One reason for not moving away, or for later returning, is the strong bonds people feel to their culture, families, and home communities. The variable *bonds* in Table 8.1 measures such bonds on a scale constructed from students' responses to 12 question-naire statements such as "I feel like I belong here" or "A person should be willing to sacrifice everything for his or her family." Higher values indicate stronger positive bonds to community and family.

Fourteen of the 30 students live in small villages of 80–600 people. The remain-der live in larger towns (Kotzebue or Dillingham) of 2,000–3,000 people, which consti-tute the regions' transportation, economic, and administrative centers. Social bonds to the community appear generally stronger among the village students (Table 8.2 and Figure 8.1).

Table 8.2
Summary statistics for *bonds*, by community size (village or town)

| Community size | Social bonds to community | | | |
	mean	standard deviation	median	frequency
village	$\bar{y}_1 = 67.81$	$s_1 = 18.83$	$Md_1 = 68.5$	$n_1 = 14$
town	$\bar{y}_2 = 35.65$	$s_2 = 18.14$	$Md_2 = 39.7$	$n_2 = 16$
all	$\bar{y} = 50.66$	$s = 24.40$	$Md = 52.7$	$n = 30$

The mean of *bonds* among the 14 village students ($\bar{y}_1 = 67.81$) is much higher than the mean among the 16 town students ($\bar{y}_2 = 35.65$). These 30 students were ran-domly selected from a larger study encompassing most of the high school students in

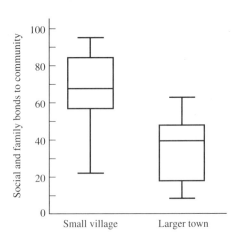

FIGURE 8.1
Boxplots of bonds to community among 30 rural Alaskan high school students, by whether student lives in a small village (population 600 or less) or a larger town (population 2,000–3,000)

their respective regions, so we can reasonably view Table 8.1 as a random sample. But is the evidence in this small sample sufficient to conclude that a mean difference exists among that larger population of students? The **two-sample *t* test** provides a formal test of the null hypothesis that two populations have identical means.

Two-sample *t* test for a difference of means

We wish to compare the mean of *y* in two independent groups of cases, termed sample 1 and sample 2. The subscript "1" denotes statistics from sample 1:

$\bar{y}_1$:   mean of *y* in sample 1
n_1:   number of cases in sample 1
s_1:   standard deviation of *y* in sample 1

Similarly, $\bar{y}_2$, n_2, s_2, denote statistics from sample 2.

Hypotheses:

H_0:   *y* has identical means in populations 1 and 2.
H_1:   *y* has different means in populations 1 and 2.

Assumptions:

1.   Cases are randomly and independently sampled from two populations.
2. $\bar{y}$ is normally distributed within populations 1 and 2.
3.   The variance (or standard deviation) of *y* is identical in both populations. (Variations of the usual *t* test exist that do not require this equal-variances assumption.)

Test statistic:

$$t = \frac{\bar{y}_1 - \bar{y}_2}{s_{\bar{y}_1 - \bar{y}_2}} \qquad (8.1)$$

The denominator in equation (8.1) is the estimated standard error of the difference between means:

$$s_{\bar{y}_1 - \bar{y}_2} = s_p \sqrt{\frac{1}{n_1} + \frac{1}{n_2}} \qquad (8.2)$$

where s_p is the pooled standard deviation of *y*:

$$s_p = \sqrt{\frac{(n_1 - 1)s_1^2 + (n_2 - 1)s_2^2}{n_1 + n_2 - 2}} \qquad (8.3)$$

The pooled standard deviation represents our best estimate of *y*'s standard deviation within each group, assuming that the standard deviation in each group is the same. (*continued*)

> Compare the ***t* statistic** from equation (8.1) to a theoretical *t* distribution with degrees of freedom:
>
> $$df = n_1 + n_2 - 2 \qquad\qquad (8.4)$$
>
> A low *t*-distribution probability indicates that we can reject H_0, and conclude instead that the two population means are different.
>
> Formally, this *t* statistic measures how many estimated standard errors separate the observed mean difference $(\bar{y}_1 - \bar{y}_2)$ from the null-hypothesis mean difference $(\mu_1 - \mu_2 = 0)$.

Table 8.2 and Figure 8.1 offer reassurance about assuming normality and equal variances. There are no outliers or obvious skew in Figure 8.1, and the two samples' standard deviations are nearly the same (Table 8.2), so we can reasonably apply a two-sample *t* test. Based on the summary statistics from Table 8.2, we first calculate a pooled standard deviation according to equation (8.3):

$$s_p = \sqrt{\frac{(14 - 1)18.83^2 + (16 - 1)18.14^2}{14 + 16 - 2}}$$

$$= 18.46$$

Next find the estimated standard error according to equation (8.2):

$$s_{\bar{y}_1 - \bar{y}_2} = 18.46\sqrt{\frac{1}{14} + \frac{1}{16}}$$

$$= 6.76$$

Finally, we obtain the test statistic using equation (8.1):

$$t = \frac{67.81 - 35.65}{6.76}$$

$$= 4.76$$

Comparing 4.76 to a theoretical *t* distribution (Table A.4) with $df = 14 + 16 - 2 = 28$, we obtain the following probability:

$$P(|t| > 4.76) < .001$$

Thus our test leads to rejecting the null hypothesis that town and village students have equally strong bonds to community. We find their means significantly different.

An alternative way to analyze differences between means is to construct confidence intervals [equation (8.5)]. If the 95% confidence interval does not include 0, then we know that a two-tailed *t* test would also reject the null hypothesis of equal means (that is, zero difference between means) at the $\alpha = .05$ significance level.

> **Confidence interval for a difference between two means**
>
> Under the same assumptions mentioned for equation (8.1), we calculate confidence intervals for the difference between two means as follows:
>
> $$(\bar{y}_1 - \bar{y}_2) \pm t s_{\bar{y}_1 - \bar{y}_2} \qquad\qquad \textbf{(8.5)}$$
>
> where $s_{\bar{y}_1 - \bar{y}_2}$, the estimated standard error of the difference between means, is defined as in equations (8.2) and (8.3), and t is chosen from a t distribution with $n_1 + n_2 - 2$ degrees of freedom to obtain the desired degree of confidence.

Exploratory graphs like the boxplots of Figure 8.1 can play an important role with *t* tests and confidence intervals, as they do with other measurement-variable inferences. Graphs alert researchers to potential problems such as outliers, nonnormality, or nonconstant variance. The Figure 8.1 plots are "all clear" in this respect. If our graphs or other analyses do cast doubt on the *t*-test assumptions, however, we could employ a nonparametric test instead. This chapter describes two nonparametric alternatives, the Mann–Whitney test and Kruskal–Wallis test.

What We Learn from Two-Sample *t* Tests

Describing Sample Data

What is the relation between a measurement variable and the categorical variable that defines the two samples? We describe this relation simply by contrasting the two sample means. The more different they are, the stronger the relation between our variables.

Inferences about Population

Based on this sample (assuming it is a random sample), can we reject the hypothesis that the two population means are equal? A statistically significant (e.g., $P < .05$) *t*-test result indicates that the answer is yes. We thereby indirectly conclude that the population means are unequal; hence the two variables are related. If the *t*-test result is nonsignificant, on the other hand, we lack persuasive evidence that a relation exists between these variables in the population.

We can also construct a confidence interval to indicate our best guess about the magnitude of the difference between these means in the population.

EXERCISES

8.1.1 Return to the Alaskan high schoolers data of Table 8.1 (file *akteens*). Compare the bonds to community expressed by male and female students.
  a. Construct boxplots comparing male and female *bonds*. Do these boxplots reveal outlier problems, or substantial differences in variability (as indicated by IQR or box height)?
  b. Construct a table similar to Table 8.2, showing means, standard deviations, and numbers of cases.
  c. Apply a two-sample *t* test (two-tailed) to determine whether the mean *bonds* of male students differs significantly from that of females.

8.1.2 Alaska's Northwest Arctic is a region with harsh climate and little economic development apart from Red Dog Mine, the world's second-largest zinc mine. Its people are predominantly Inupiat Eskimo. The Bristol Bay region of southwest Alaska, in contrast, has a milder climate and an economy based on commercial fishing. The Yupik Eskimo of Bristol Bay differ culturally and linguistically from the Northwest Arctic's Inupiat. Do students from the two regions differ in their bonds to community?
  a. Construct boxplots comparing Arctic and Bristol Bay *bonds*. Describe what they show.
  b. Construct a table showing means, standard deviations, and numbers of cases.
  c. Apply a *t* test (two-tailed), and summarize your findings.

8.1.3 It seems reasonable to hypothesize that students who have lived in a community for most of their lives (*lived* = "long-term") might feel stronger bonds to that place. Do the data of Table 8.1 support this idea? Since our research hypothesis specifies direction (*bonds* higher among long-term residents), unlike the hypotheses of 8.1.1 or 8.1.2, a one-tailed test is appropriate here. Graphically compare the distributions of *bonds* by *lived*, run a *t* test, and summarize your findings.

8.2 Mann–Whitney Test (Wilcoxon Rank Sum Test)

Two-sample *t* tests assume that *y* follows a normal distribution with the same variance in both populations. Often these assumptions are unrealistic. Particularly when distributions contain higher-than-normal proportions of outliers, the usual *t* test performs poorly. The **Mann–Whitney test**, also called the **Wilcoxon rank sum test**, provides an alternative two-sample procedure that focuses on ranks rather than actual measurements. Like other rank-based methods, the Mann–Whitney test is resistant to the effects of outliers.

The Mann–Whitney test belongs to the family called **nonparametric** or **distribution-free** tests, as do the sign and chi-square tests introduced in Chapters 6 and 7. "Distribution-free" indicates that such tests do not assume that variables follow any particular theoretical distribution such as the normal. The Mann–Whitney test, for instance, requires only that the population distribution of y be **continuous**—that is, within any given range, y theoretically could have infinitely many different values. Since it does not assume either normality or equal variances, the Mann–Whitney test remains valid under a wider range of conditions than the t test.

Mann–Whitney Test (Wilcoxon Rank Sum Test) for equality of two distributions

Hypotheses:

H_0: y has identical rank distributions in populations 1 and 2.
H_1: y does not have identical rank distributions in populations 1 and 2; for example, the medians may differ.

Assumptions:

1.   Cases are randomly and independently sampled from two populations.
2. y distributions are continuous, but not necessarily normal, in both populations.
3.   Ten or more cases in each sample (for the version given below)

Test statistic:

We have two independent samples or groups of sizes n_1 and n_2, with $n_1 \le n_2$. Combine these two groups into one large sample of n cases and sort from lowest to highest value on variable y. Assign ranks (1 = lowest, 2 = second lowest, etc.); tied cases receive the average of ranks they would get if not tied. Within group 1 find the sum of ranks T_1.

Statistical theory tells us that, *if H_0 were true*, T_1 would have an expected value of

$$E(T_1) = \frac{n_1(n + 1)}{2} \tag{8.6}$$

and variance

$$\mathrm{Var}(T_1) = \frac{n_1 n_2 s^2}{n} \tag{8.7}$$

where s is the standard deviation of the combined ranks for both groups. Theory further establishes that, when H_0 is true, the quantity

$$z = \frac{T_1 - E(T_1)}{\sqrt{\mathrm{Var}(T_1)}} \tag{8.8}$$

(*continued*)

approximately follows a standard normal sampling distribution. Low standard
normal probabilities suggest that we should reject H_0.

A more precise small-sample version of this test should be used when n for
either group is less than 10, but that version is not covered here [see, for example, Neave and Worthington (1988)].

The Alaskan community bonds example of the previous section does not demand
a nonparametric test, since the t test assumptions seemed plausible. For purposes of
illustration, however, we can perform one anyway. Table 8.3 shows the first step, order-
ing the y values from lowest to highest and assigning them ranks (1 = person with
lowest value of *bonds*, 2 = person with second-lowest value, and so on). No two cases
have identical y values, but if several were tied, we could give them all ranks equal to
the average of ranks they would have if not tied. For instance, if the first three students
all had *bonds* = 8.2, we would award all three a rank of 2:

$$rank = \frac{1 + 2 + 3}{3}$$

$$= 2$$

Table 8.3
Community size, social bonds scale, and ranks assigned
to social bonds scale values for 30 Alaskan students

size	bonds	rank	size	bonds	rank
town	8.2	1	village	54.4	16
town	12.3	2	village	57.9	17
town	14.0	3	town	58.0	18
town	17.3	4	town	58.5	19
town	18.3	5	village	61.1	20
village	23.4	6	village	61.2	21
town	24.6	7	town	64.1	22
town	30.0	8	village	65.5	23
town	36.3	9	village	71.5	24
town	43.1	10	village	72.7	25
town	43.8	11	village	74.2	26
town	44.6	12	village	85.3	27
town	47.5	13	village	85.5	28
town	49.8	14	village	88.9	29
village	51.0	15	village	96.8	30

Source: Hamilton and Seyfrit (1993).
File: *akteens*

To perform a Mann–Whitney test we need the sum of ranks in the smaller group (T_1). Table 8.4 lists the sums, frequencies, and standard deviations of ranks in these data.

Table 8.4
Sums of ranks for *bonds* (from Table 8.3),
by community size

Community size	Social bonds to community		
	sum of ranks	*frequency*	*s.d. of ranks*
village	$T_1 = 307$	$n_1 = 14$	$s_1 = 6.65$
town	$T_2 = 158$	$n_2 = 16$	$s_2 = 6.26$
all		$n = 30$	$s = 8.80$

If the null hypothesis were true then the expected sum of ranks among village students (the smaller group) can be obtained by equation (8.6):

$$E(T_1) = \frac{14(30 + 1)}{2}$$

$$= 217$$

Equation (8.7) estimates the variance of T_1:

$$\text{Var}(T_1) = \frac{14 \times 16 \times 8.80^2}{30}$$

$$= 578$$

Using these values for $E(T_1)$ and $\text{Var}(T_1)$, and $T_1 = 307$ from Table 8.4, we obtain the Mann–Whitney test statistic by applying equation (8.8):

$$z = \frac{307 - 217}{\sqrt{578}}$$

$$= 3.74$$

Standard normal (z) values as large as 3.74 are improbable. If the null hypothesis were true, according to Table A.2 we would encounter z values more than 3.48 standard deviations from 0 about 5 times in every 10,000 samples:

$$P(|z| > 3.48) = .0005$$

The actual z value, 3.74, is farther from 0, so its probability must be even lower:

$$P(|z| > 3.74) < .0005$$

Thus a Mann–Whitney test, like our earlier *t* test, leads to rejection of the null hypothesis. We have now rejected both the null hypothesis of equal population means (*t* test) and the null hypothesis of identical population rank distributions (Mann–Whitney test). The students from small Alaskan villages exhibit significantly higher levels of social bonds to community than do their counterparts from larger towns.

Applied to normally distributed variables, the Mann–Whitney test is almost as powerful as the two-sample *t* test. With nonnormal, heavy-tailed distributions, the Mann–Whitney test is superior. When unsure about making the *t* test assumptions, try both tests on your data. If they agree, report either one. If they substantially disagree, examine your distributions and consider whether the Mann–Whitney results might be more valid.

EXERCISE

8.2.1   Apply Mann–Whitney tests to the data of Table 8.1 (file *akteens*) in order to answer the following. Compare each result with your earlier *t* test for Exercise 8.1.1, 8.1.2, or 8.1.3.

a.   Does the distribution of *bonds* of male students in Table 8.1 differ significantly from that of females?

b.   Do students from the Northwest Arctic and Bristol Bay regions differ in their bonds to community?

c.   Do students who have lived in a community for most of their lives feel significantly stronger bonds to that community (one-tailed test)?

8.3 One-Way Analysis of Variance

Analysis of variance, or **ANOVA**, refers to a flexible set of methods for testing hypotheses about means. The two-sample *t* test described earlier compares two means. The simplest form of ANOVA, called **one-way ANOVA**, can compare *two or more* means. That is, one-way ANOVA analyzes the relation between a measurement variable *y* and a categorical variable *x* that has two or more categories. When *x* has just two categories, ANOVA reaches exactly the same conclusion as a *t* test. Because ANOVA can do anything a two-sample *t* test does, and a great deal more besides, we say that ANOVA is the *more general* method or, alternatively, that the *t* test is a *special case* of ANOVA.

"Analysis of variance" may seem a confusing name for a method that tests hypotheses about means. This name arises because ANOVA calculates the ratio of two variances: the variance of mean *y* values $\bar{y}_1, \bar{y}_2, \ldots$, where $\bar{y}_1, \bar{y}_2$, etc. are the means of *y* within the different categories of *x*, and the variance of individual *y* values within each *x* category. These variances derive from quantities called the **between-** and **within-**

groups sums of squares. The ratio of between- to within-groups variances follows approximately an F distribution. Section 5.7 described the theory behind F distributions; their critical values are tabulated in Table A.5 of Appendix II.

ANOVA sums of squares

To describe the variation of y across K samples or groups ($K \geq 2$), we employ several **sums of squares**, each with its own degrees of freedom. In the equations below (as elsewhere in this book), Σ indicates that we sum values for every case in the data.

Total sum of squares:

$$SS_T = \Sigma(y_i - \bar{y})^2 \tag{8.9}$$

The total sum of squares measures variation of individual y_i values around $\bar{y}$, the overall mean of y. It has degrees of freedom equal to the total sample size minus 1:

$$df_T = n - 1 \tag{8.10}$$

Within-groups sum of squares:

$$SS_W = \Sigma(y_i - \bar{y}_k)^2 \tag{8.11}$$

The within-groups sum of squares measures variation of individual y_i values around their respective group means ($\bar{y}_k$ represents the mean of y within the kth group). It has degrees of freedom equal to total sample size minus K, the number of groups:

$$df_W = n - K \tag{8.12}$$

Between-groups sum of squares:

$$SS_B = \Sigma(\bar{y}_k - \bar{y})^2 \tag{8.13}$$

The between-groups sum of squares measures variation of the group means ($\bar{y}_k$) around the overall mean. It has degrees of freedom equal to the number of groups minus 1:

$$df_B = K - 1 \tag{8.14}$$

Figures 8.2 and 8.3 (page 274) illustrate what the within-groups and between-groups sums of squares measure. In Figure 8.2, the variation between the three groups is large compared with the variation within each group. The opposite occurs in Figure 8.3: Variation between the groups is small relative to the variation within each one.

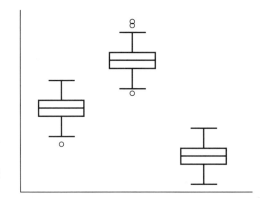

FIGURE 8.2
Three distributions for which the between-groups variation is large relative to the variation within each group

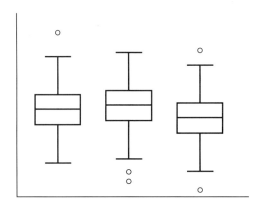

FIGURE 8.3
Three distributions for which the between-groups variation is small relative to the variation within each group

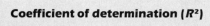

Coefficient of determination (R^2)

The total sum of squares equals the within-groups sum of squares plus the between-groups sum of squares:

$$SS_T = SS_W + SS_B \qquad\qquad (8.15)$$

Essentially, SS_W and SS_B divide y's total variation into two parts:

SS_B variation explained by x

SS_W variation not explained by x

A statistic called the **coefficient of determination** or R^2 measures the proportion of y's variance that is explained by x:

$$R^2 = \frac{SS_B}{SS_T} \qquad\qquad (8.16)$$

R^2 can range from 0 (none of y's variance explained) to 1 (100% of y's variance explained by x).

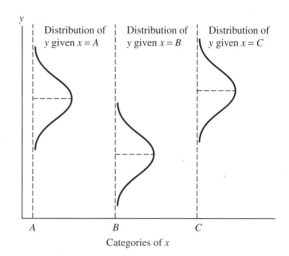

FIGURE 8.4
ANOVA and *t* tests assume that *y*
follows normal, independent and
identical distributions within every
category of *x*.

ANOVA is a parametric method like the two-sample *t* test described earlier, and it
requires similar assumptions: that cases are randomly and independently sampled, and
that *y* has an identical normal distribution at every category of *x*. Figure 8.4 illustrates
this assumption of identical, normal distributions. The differences in means are the only
differences among the three *y* distributions shown. If that assumption is true, then
ANOVA is the best analytical method.

F test for one-way analysis of variance (ANOVA)

Hypotheses:

H_0:   *y* has identical means in all *K* populations.
H_1:   At least one of the *K* populations has a different mean.

Assumptions:

1.   Cases are randomly and independently sampled from *K* populations.
2.   *y* follows normal distributions within each of the *K* populations.
3.   The variance or standard deviation of *y* is identical in each of the *K* popu-
     lations.

Test statistic:

$$F[df_B,\ df_W] = \frac{\Sigma(\bar{y}_k - \bar{y})^2/(K - 1)}{\Sigma(y_i - \bar{y}_k)^2/(n - K)}$$

$$= \frac{SS_B/df_B}{SS_W/df_W}$$

                                                                    (8.17)
                                                                    (*continued*)

> Compare this **F ratio** to a theoretical F distribution with df_B (numerator) and df_W (denominator) degrees of freedom. A low probability provides reason to reject H_0, and to decide instead in favor of H_1: The population means of the K groups are not all equal.

The survey data in Table 8.1 include one variable, *where*, based on a question that asked the students where they expected to spend most of the rest of their lives. This categorical variable has three responses: in the same rural region they presently live; elsewhere in Alaska; or outside of Alaska. Table 8.5 gives summary statistics for *bonds* within each of these three groups of students. Nine of the 30 students said they expect to stay in the same region, and eight said they expect to leave the state.

Table 8.5
Summary statistics for *bonds*, by where students
expect to live most of the rest of their lives

Expect to live most of life	Social bonds to community			
	mean	*standard deviation*	*median*	*frequency*
same region	67.12	23.30	72.7	9
elsewhere AK	47.42	22.62	49.8	13
outside AK	37.41	20.01	41.9	8
all	50.66	24.40	52.7	30

Both means and medians agree that in this sample, students expecting to stay in the same region tend to have strong social bonds, whereas students expecting to leave the state tend to have weaker bonds. To test whether this sample difference implies different population means, we proceed with an analysis of variance.

Research articles and computer programs commonly present ANOVA results in a form like Table 8.6. The body of such ANOVA tables lists sums of squares, degrees of freedom, and an F statistic. To help guide you through ANOVA tables, Table 8.6 adds footnotes defining each element.

Table 8.6 culminates in an F statistic equal to 4.04. Comparing this to the theoretical F distribution in Table A.5, given 2 and 27 (approximately 30) degrees of freedom, we obtain the probability $P < .05$. A computer program more precisely estimates the probability of an $F[2, 27]$ greater than 4.04:

$$P(F[2, 27] > 4.04) = .0291$$

By either reckoning, the obtained *P*-value is low enough to reject the null hypothesis that mean *bonds* are the same regardless of where the student expects to live. We conclude that the three means in Table 8.5 are significantly different.

Table 8.6
An example one-way ANOVA table with footnotes,
testing the null hypothesis that population means of *bonds*
are the same for all values of *where* (see Tables 8.1, 8.5)

Source	SS[a]	*df*[e]	MS[i]	*F*[m]	Prob > *F*[o]
		Analysis of Variance			
between groups	3,979.9[b]	2[f]	1,989.9[i]	4.04[n]	.0291[p]
within groups	13,287.4[c]	27[g]	492.1[k]		
Total	17,267.2[d]	29[h]	595.4[l]		

[a]Sum of squares
[c]Within-groups sum of squares; $SS_w = \Sigma(y_i - \bar{y}_k)^2$
[e]Degrees of freedom
[g]Degrees of freedom within groups; $df_w = n - K$
[i]Mean squares
[k]Within-groups mean square; $MS_w = SS_w/df_w$
[m]*F* statistic
[o]"The probability of a greater *F* statistic"

[b]Between-groups sum of squares; $SS_B = \Sigma(\bar{y}_k - \bar{y})^2$
[d]Total sum of squares; $SS_T = \Sigma(y_i - \bar{y})^2$
[f]Degrees of freedom between groups; $df_B = K - 1$
[h]Total degrees of freedom; $df_T = n - 1$
[i]Between-groups mean square; $MS_B = SS_B/df_B$
[l]Total mean square; $MS_T = SS_T/df_T = $ variance of *y*
[n]$F = MS_B/MS_w$
[p]$P(F[2, 27] > 4.04) = .0291$

As noted earlier, ANOVA assumes that *y* follows normal distributions with equal population variances within each category or group of *x*. Boxplots in Figure 8.5 appear

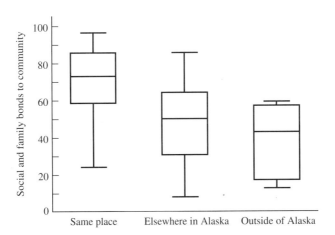

FIGURE 8.5
Boxplots of bonds to community, by where student expects to
live most of his or her life

consistent with these assumptions. If we did see serious problems such as outliers or grossly unequal variation, however, our ANOVA conclusions would be suspect. Then the nonparametric **Kruskal–Wallis test** (next section) would be more appropriate.

What We Learn from One-Way Analysis of Variance (ANOVA)

Describing Sample Data

What is the relation between a measurement variable and the categorical variable that defines the K samples? We describe this relation by contrasting the K sample means. The more unequal they are, the stronger the relation between these variables in our sample.

Inferences about Population

Based on this sample (assuming it is a random sample), can we reject the hypothesis that the K population means are all equal? A statistically significant (e.g., $P < .05$) F test result indicates that the answer is yes. We thereby indirectly conclude that the population means are unequal; hence our two variables are related. On the other hand, if the F test result is nonsignificant, we lack persuasive evidence that any relation exists between these variables in the population.

EXERCISES

8.3.1   Section 8.2 applied a t test to determine whether town and village students had significantly different mean *bonds*. In principle, when the number of groups equals 2, both ANOVA and t test should reach identical conclusions. Find out whether they do by applying ANOVA to this example, and by checking the following points:

   a.   The F statistic from ANOVA should equal the square of the two-sample t statistic.

   b.   Both tests should obtain exactly the same P-value.

8.3.2   Return to the Vermont data of Problems 7.18 and 7.19 in Chapter 7. Use one-way ANOVA to test whether

   a.   activists and nonactivists differ significantly in their mean years lived in the town (*lived*)

   b.   activists and nonactivists differ significantly in their mean years of education (*educ*)

Kruskal–Wallis Test

8.4

The **Kruskal–Wallis test** is a K-sample generalization of the two-sample Mann–Whitney test. It provides a nonparametric alternative to one-way ANOVA, useful when the ANOVA assumptions of normality or equal variances appear doubtful. Like a Mann–Whitney test, a Kruskal–Wallis test works with ranks rather than measurements, and makes no assumptions about the particular underlying distributions.

Kruskal–Wallis test for equality of *K* distributions

Hypotheses:

> H_0: y has identical distributions in all K populations.
> H_1: y does not have identical distributions in all K populations; for example, some may have different medians.

Assumptions:

1. Cases are randomly and independently sampled from K populations.

2. y distributions are continuous, but not necessarily normal, in all K populations.

3. At least three samples, with six or more cases in each sample. (For two samples, use the Mann–Whitney test instead.)

Test statistic:

Combine the data into one large sample of n cases and sort from lowest to highest value on variable y. Assign ranks (1 = lowest y, 2 = second lowest, etc.); tied cases receive the average of ranks they would get if not tied. Within each group find the sum of ranks T_k. Then calculate the test statistic:

$$X^2 = \frac{12}{n(n + 1)} \Sigma_k \frac{T_k^2}{n_k} - 3(n + 1) \tag{8.18}$$

Σ_k indicates summation over the K groups. Statistical theory establishes that, *if H_0 is true*, then X^2 approximately follows a chi-square sampling distribution with $K - 1$ degrees of freedom.

For comparison purposes we will perform a Kruskal–Wallis test using the same Alaskan example (social bonds and where young people expect to spend their lives) analyzed in Tables 8.5 and 8.6 of the previous section. Kruskal–Wallis calculations begin by ranking the 30 students from lowest to highest on *bonds*, as was already done in Table 8.3 for the earlier Mann–Whitney test example. For this Kruskal–Wallis test, we add up the ranks for each value of *where*, obtaining the three sums of ranks given in Table 8.7. For example, the ranks assigned to the nine students expecting to live in the same region add up to 191.

Table 8.7
Sums of ranks for *bonds* by where students
expect to spend most of the rest of their lives

Expect to live most of life	Social bonds to community	
	sum of ranks	*frequency*
same region	$T_1 = 191$	$n_1 = 9$
elsewhere AK	$T_2 = 189$	$n_2 = 13$
outside AK	$T_3 = 85$	$n_3 = 8$
all		$n = 30$

The sums in Table 8.7 allow us to calculate the Kruskal–Wallis test statistic, using equation (8.18):

$$X^2 = \frac{12}{30(30 + 1)} \times \left(\frac{191^2}{9} + \frac{189^2}{13} + \frac{85^2}{8} \right) - 3(30 + 1)$$

$$= .012903 \times 7{,}704.3387 - 93$$

$$= 6.41$$

Since there are $K = 3$ groups, we have $K - 1 = 2$ degrees of freedom for this test. Comparing our test statistic, 6.41, with a chi-square distribution (Table A.3) yields the approximate probability $P < .05$ (or by computer, $P = .0405$). Thus a Kruskal–Wallis test leads to rejecting the null hypothesis of identical rank distributions, just as our earlier one-way ANOVA led to rejecting the hypothesis of identical means. Among students expecting to move away, *bonds* are significantly lower.

EXERCISES

8.4.1   Table 6.5 (file *matown*) in Chapter 6 lists data from a survey conducted in a Massachusetts town contaminated by chemical wastes. Is respondents' trust in a local chemical factory (widely blamed for the contamination) related to how long they have lived in town?

    a.   Use boxplots to visually compare the distributions of *lived* at different levels of *chemtrus*. Describe what you see.

    b.   Perform one-way ANOVA and state your conclusions.

    c.   Perform a Kruskal–Wallis test and state your conclusions. Although both tests generally agree here, why is the Kruskal–Wallis more appropriate?

8.4.2   In the Massachusetts town data (file *matown*), are respondents' opinions on water quality standards related to how long they have lived in the community? Graph the distributions, carry out a Kruskal–Wallis test, and discuss your findings.

▲

What We Learn from Nonparametric Comparison Tests (Mann–Whitney or Kruskal–Wallis)

Based on this sample (assuming it is a random sample), can we reject the null hypothesis that in the population, our measurement variable has identical rank distributions across all categories of the categorical variable? A statistically significant (e.g., $P < .05$) test result indicates that the answer is yes. We thereby indirectly conclude that the population distributions differ; hence the variables are related. On the other hand, if the test result is nonsignificant, we lack persuasive evidence that any relation exists between these variables in the population.

▲

*8.5   Error-Bar Plots

Exercise 8.1.3 asked whether Alaskan students who had lived most of their lives in their present region felt stronger bonds to community and family. The answer is yes: A one-tailed *t* test confirms a significant difference between the means in Table 8.8 (page 282). Figure 8.6 displays the means visually as an **error-bar plot**. The diagonal line connects the two group means, 42.11 and 58.14; a horizontal line indicates the overall mean (50.66) for comparison. Bars indicate ranges of plus and minus one standard error around each mean.

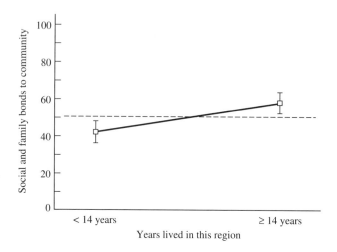

FIGURE 8.6
Error-bar plot showing mean *bonds* (plus or minus 1 standard error) by how long the student lived in this region of Alaska

Table 8.8
Summary statistics for *bonds*, whether respondent is newcomer (less than 14 years in region) or a long-term resident

| Years lived in region | Social bonds to community | | |
	mean	standard deviation	frequency
newcomer	42.11	23.06	14
long-term	58.14	23.71	16
all	50.66	24.40	30

pooled standard deviation: 23.41

Estimated standard errors of group means in *t* tests or ANOVA

The usual formula for estimating a mean's standard error is

$$s_{\bar{y}} = \frac{s}{\sqrt{n}} \qquad\qquad (6.7)$$

(*continued*)

where s denotes the standard deviation of y, and n the sample size. In two-sample t tests and ANOVA we have two or more subsamples of different means and perhaps different sizes, but we assume that within each group y has the same standard deviation. Our best estimate of that common standard deviation is either

1. (t test) the pooled standard deviation s_p [equation (8.3)], or
2. (ANOVA) the square root of the within-groups sum of squares divided by its degrees of freedom, $\sqrt{SS_w/df_w}$ [see equations (8.11) and (8.12)]. The quantity $\sqrt{SS_w/df_w}$ is sometimes termed the **root mean squared error** or **root MSE**.

Thus by extension of equation (6.7), we estimate the standard error of the kth mean, $\bar{y}_k$, as either

$$s_{\bar{y}_k} = \frac{s_p}{\sqrt{n_k}} \tag{8.19a}$$

or

$$s_{\bar{y}_k} = \frac{\sqrt{SS_w/df_w}}{\sqrt{n_k}} \tag{8.19b}$$

$$= \frac{\sqrt{MS_w}}{\sqrt{n_k}}$$

Equations (8.19a) and (8.19b) produce identical results when the number of groups equals 2.

Table 8.8 gives the pooled standard deviation as $s_p = 23.41$. Consequently, applying equation (8.19a), the standard error for mean *bonds* based on the 14 long-term residents is

$$s_{\bar{y}_1} = \frac{23.41}{\sqrt{14}}$$

$$= 6.26$$

The left-hand error bars in Figure 8.6 range from one standard error above the mean, $42.11 + 6.26 = 48.37$, to one standard error below the mean, $42.11 - 6.26 = 35.85$. The standard error for mean *bonds* among long-term residents is slightly smaller, because we have a slightly larger sample ($n_2 = 16$, compared with $n_1 = 14$):

$$s_{\bar{y}_2} = \frac{23.41}{\sqrt{16}}$$

$$= 5.85$$

The right-hand error bars in Figure 8.6 therefore range from $58.14 + 5.85 = 63.99$ to $58.14 - 5.85 = 52.29$.

Error-bar plots are sometimes drawn with the bars to ± 2 standard errors, or to ± 1 or ± 2 standard deviations, or some other distance. Read the accompanying caption carefully to understand what any particular plot shows.

Error-bar plots display the locations of sample means, and also give some indication of our uncertainty about the location of corresponding population means. With only two groups as in Figure 8.6, an error-bar plot is hardly necessary. With more complex analyses, however, error-bar plots help us to understand and communicate the results. The next section presents an example.

EXERCISE

8.5.1   Construct error-bar plots for the following:
   a.   mean *bonds* by community size, based on Table 8.2
   b.   mean *bonds* by where students expect to live, based on Tables 8.5 and 8.6
   c.   mean lead concentration by traffic density, based on Table 3.3 (file *trees*)

*8.6 Two-Way ANOVA

Two-way or **two-factor ANOVA** refers to analysis of variance with one measurement variable (y) and two categorical variables (x_1 and x_2). Table 8.9 illustrates the basic layout of two-way ANOVA, again using the Alaska survey. This table resembles a two-way cross-tabulation of x_1 by x_2 (here, community size by years lived in region), but with each cell containing a mean y (social bonds) value instead of a frequency. The margins contain means by community size (right column) and by years lived in region (bottom row), seen earlier in Tables 8.2 and 8.8, respectively. Figure 8.7 graphs these four means as an error-bar plot.

Table 8.9
Mean social bonds by community size (town or village)
and years respondent has lived in this region

Community size	Years lived in region		
	newcomer	*long-term*	*all*
village	58.52	71.53	67.81
town	35.54	35.83	35.65
all	42.11	58.14	50.66

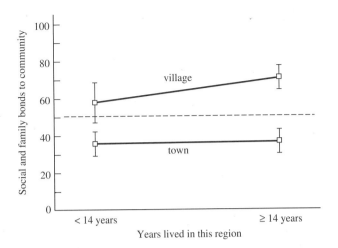

FIGURE 8.7
Error-bar plot showing mean *bonds* by years lived in this
region, separately for town and village students

Two-way ANOVA permits several different *F*-statistic significance tests:

1. A test of the **overall model**:   Can we reject the null hypothesis that the population
    mean of *y* is the same at every level of x_1 and x_2?

2. A test of the **main effect** of x_1:   Can we reject the null hypothesis that, holding x_2
    constant, the population mean of *y* is the same for each value of x_1?

3. A test of the main effect of x_2:   Can we reject the null hypothesis that, holding x_1
    constant, the population mean of *y* is the same for each value of x_2?

4. (*Optional*)   A test of the **interaction effect** of x_1 and x_2: Can we reject the null
    hypothesis that cell-to-cell variations in the population means of *y* reflect something
    particular about the *combination* of *x* and *y*, and not merely the sum of whatever x_1
    and x_2 main effects exist?

The various sums of squares used in calculating these *F* tests are more complicated than those found in one-way ANOVA, and will not be presented here. Introductory
texts sometimes describe the simplest version, for data where each cell contains the
same number of cases (a **balanced design**). However, such balanced designs rarely occur with nonexperimental data. Hinkle, Wiersma, and Jurs (1979) provide one illustration of the calculations for two-factor ANOVA with nonexperimental (unbalanced) data
such as in Table 8.9.

Previously, separate *t*-test analyses rejected the hypothesis that mean *bonds* is the
same in communities of different sizes (Section 8.1), or that it is the same among newcomers and long-term residents (Exercise 8.1.3). Two-way ANOVA can bring both of
these ideas together, and test whether the *bonds-size* relation remains significant after
we adjust for the effects of *lived,* or likewise for the *bonds-lived* relation adjusting for
the effects of *size*.

Table 8.9 and Figure 8.7 give some hints about the answers. Overall, the mean of social bonds is about 32 points higher (67.81 versus 35.65) among village students than among town students. Town-village differences in *bonds* remain large when we hold *lived* constant:

> 23 points higher among village than town students (58.52 versus 35.54), looking only at newcomers; 36 points higher among village than town students (71.53 versus 35.83), looking only at long-term residents.

Years lived in region exerts a weaker, though still significant, effect on *bonds*. Overall we see a mean difference of 16 points (42.11 versus 58.14) between newcomers and long-term residents. But this difference shrinks when we hold *size* constant. Mean *bonds* are

> 13 points lower among newcomers than long-term residents (58.52 versus 71.53), looking only at students in villages; less than 1 point lower among newcomers than long-term residents (35.54 versus 35.83), looking only at students in towns.

Figure 8.7 dramatizes the fact that *lived* affects *bonds* weakly among village students, and not at all among town students. However, a large gap separates town from village students regardless of the value of *lived*.

Table 8.10 contains a two-factor ANOVA table testing the significance of these effects. We see that *size* has a significant partial effect ($P = .0003$) controlling for *lived*, but *lived* does not have a significant partial effect ($P = .4301$) controlling for *size*. At upper right, the R^2 statistic indicates that *size* and *lived* together explain about 46% ($R^2 = .4602$) of the variance of *bonds*. In multivariable analysis, researchers often prefer to focus on **adjusted R^2**, which takes into account the complexity of the model (reflected in the model degrees of freedom, df_M) relative to the complexity of the data (the residual degrees of freedom, df_R). Adjusted for degrees of freedom, *size* and *lived* together explain about 42% of the variance in *bonds* ($R_a^2 = .4202$). Footnotes document these and other elements of Table 8.10.

Adjusted coefficient of determination (R_a^2)

R_a^2 gives the proportion of the variance of *y* explained by all *x* variables in the analysis, adjusting for model and data complexity:

$$R_a^2 = R^2 - \left(\frac{df_M}{df_R}\right)(1 - R^2) \qquad \text{(8.20)}$$

where df_M is the **model degrees of freedom**:

$$df_M = \text{number of categories among all } x \text{ variables} \qquad \text{(8.21)}$$
$$- \text{ number of } x \text{ variables}$$

(*continued*)

df_R is the **residual degrees of freedom**:

$$df_R = n - df_M - 1 \tag{8.22}$$

and R^2 is the unadjusted coefficient of determination [equation (8.16)].

The model degrees of freedom, equation (8.21), generalizes the concept of between-groups degrees of freedom, equation (8.14). Similarly the residual degrees of freedom, equation (8.22), is a multivariable generalization of the within-groups degrees of freedom, equation (8.12).

Table 8.10

Two-way ANOVA of *bonds* by community size and years lived in the region

	Number of obs = 30[a] Root MSE = 18.5803[b]		R-square = .4602[c] Adj. R-square = .4202[d]		
Source	**Partial SS**	**df**	**MS**	**F**	**Prob > F**
Model	7,946.0944[e]	2[j]	3,973.0472[o]	11.51[t]	.0002[w]
size	6,025.8710[f]	1[k]	6,025.8710[p]	17.45[u]	.0003[x]
lived	221.51923[g]	1[l]	221.51923[q]	.64[v]	.4301[y]
Residual	9,321.1580[h]	27[m]	345.22808[r]		
total	17,267.253[i]	29[n]	595.422[s]		

[a] Overall sample size, n

[b] Square root of residual mean square, root MSE = $\sqrt{SS_R/df_R}$

[c] Proportion of variance explained by model, $R^2 = SS_M/SS_T$

[d] Adjusted R^2, $R_a^2 = R^2 - (df_M/df_R)(1 - R^2)$; adjusting for degrees of freedom *size* and *lived* together explain about 42% of the variance in *bonds*

[e] Model sum of squares (similar to one-way ANOVA's between-groups sum of squares), $SS_M = \Sigma(\bar{y}_k - \bar{y})^2$

[f] Partial sum of squares due to *size*, SS_{size}

[g] Partial sum of squares due to *lived*, SS_{lived}

[h] Residual sum of squares (similar to one-way ANOVA's within-groups sum of squares), $SS_R = \Sigma(y_i - \bar{y}_k)^2$

[i] Total sum of squares, $SS_T = \Sigma(y_i - \bar{y})^2$

[j] Model degrees of freedom, $df_M = df_{size} + df_{lived}$

[k] *size* degrees of freedom, df_{size} = number of categories of *size* − 1

[l] *lived* degrees of freedom, df_{lived} = number of categories of *lived* − 1

[m] Residual degrees of freedom, $df_R = n - df_M - 1$

[n] Total degrees of freedom, $df_T = n - 1$

[o] Model mean square, $MS_M = SS_M/df_M$

[p] *size* mean square, $MS_{size} = SS_{size}/df_{size}$

[q] *lived* mean square, $MS_{lived} = SS_{lived}/df_{lived}$

[r] Residual mean square, $MS_R = SS_R/df_R$

[s] Total mean square, $MS_T = SS_T/df_T$

[t] Overall F statistic, $F = MS_M/MS_R$

[u] F statistic testing the partial effect of *size*, $F = MS_{size}/MS_R$

[v] F statistic testing the partial effect of *lived*, $F = MS_{lived}/MS_R$

[w] $P(F[2, 27] > 11.51) = .0002$

[x] $P(F[1, 27] > 17.45) = .0003$; *size* has a statistically significant effect on *bonds*, controlling for *lived*

[y] $P(F[1, 27] > .64) = .4301$; *lived* does not have a statistically significant effect on *bonds*, controlling for *size*

Three *F* statistics appear in Table 8.10:

1. The overall *F* statistic (footnote t) tests the null hypothesis that mean *bonds* are the same across all categories of *size* and *lived*. We can reject this null hypothesis ($P = .0002$); mean *bonds* are not the same.

2. Another *F* statistic (footnote u) tests the null hypothesis that mean *bonds* are the same for *size* = "town" and *size* = "village" students, if we hold *lived* constant. This hypothesis may also be rejected ($P = .0003$). Community size significantly affects social bonds, even when we hold constant how long people lived in the region.

3. The third *F* statistic in Table 8.10 (footnote v) tests the null hypothesis that mean *bonds* are the same for *lived* = "long-term" and *lived* = "newcomer" residents, if we hold *size* constant. We fail to reject this null hypothesis ($P = .4301$). Years resident does not significantly affect social bonds, once we hold constant the community size.

This two-way ANOVA modifies our understanding of how social bonds depend on community size and years lived in the region. Once we control for community size, the relation between *lived* and *bonds* (Figure 8.6) weakens to the point of statistical nonsignificance (Figure 8.7). Village students are more likely to be long-term residents of their Alaskan region, and they also are more likely to feel strong social bonds. This situation creates an apparent relation between *lived* and *bonds*, but the relation vanishes entirely if we look only at town students and falls from a 16-point mean difference to a 13-point difference if we look only at village students. Relations like that between *lived* and *bonds*, which appear significant in two-variable analysis but weaken or vanish when we control for some third variable, are called **spurious**. Detecting spurious relations is a major goal of multivariate methods such as two-way ANOVA or three-way cross-tabulation (Chapter 7).

Figure 8.7 suggests an interesting possibility: The relation between *lived* and *bonds* might be different among town and village students. A statistical relation that changes depending on the values of some third variable is called an **interaction**. ANOVA can test for the significance of such interaction effects, as illustrated in Table 8.11. [A more detailed explanation of interaction effects appears in Hamilton (1992).]

Table 8.11 indicates that the *size*lived* interaction effect does not significantly differ from 0. This interaction complicates our model without much improving its fit to the data, so adjusted R^2 actually declines slightly comparing Table 8.11 with the simpler Table 8.10. We may conclude that the relation between *bonds* and *size* is not significantly different for newcomers and long-term residents.

What might a significant interaction look like? Four made-up examples appear in Figure 8.8. Each error-bar plot depicts the relation between mean *y* and category of x_1, with separate lines for two different categories of another variable, x_2. At lower right in Figure 8.8, the relation between *y* and x_1 is the same for both categories of x_2. The remaining three plots show interactions: The relation between *y* and x_1 looks considerably different when we compare the two lines representing first and second categories of x_2. In contrast, the real-data interaction in Figure 8.7 was not statistically significant

Table 8.11
Two-way ANOVA of *bonds* by community size and years lived in the region, with *size∗lived* interaction effect

	Number of obs. = 30	R-square = .4754			
	Root MSE = 18.6662	Adj. R-square = .4148[a]			

Source	Partial SS	df	MS	F	Prob > F
model	8,208.12664	3	2,736.04221	7.85	.0007
size	5,584.11586	1	5,584.11586	16.03	.0005
lived	286.776808	1	286.776808	.82	.3726
size∗lived	262.032196	1	262.032196	.75[b]	.3938[c]
residual	9,059.12585	26	348.427917		
Total	17,267.2525	29	595.4225		

[a] Adjusting for degrees of freedom, *size, lived*, and the *size∗lived* interaction explain about 41.5% of the variance in *bonds*.
[b] F statistic testing the interaction effect of *size* and *lived* on *bonds*
[c] $P(F[1, 26] > .75) = .3938$; the *size∗lived* interaction is not statistically significant.

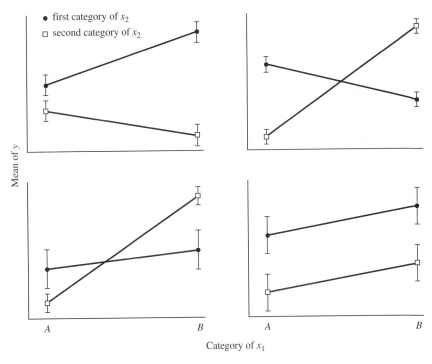

FIGURE 8.8
Three error-bar plots showing interaction effects, and one (lower right) showing no interaction

because those two relations (between *bonds* and years *lived* in region, at different categories of community *size*) are not different enough.

More complicated ANOVAs can test main effects and interactions involving three or more categorical *x* variables. A related method called **analysis of covariance (ANCOVA)** handles any number of categorical and measurement *x* variables. Such extensions make ANOVA a popular and broadly useful technique. ANOVA is particularly well suited to the analysis of data from experiments, where the categorical *x* variables might be treatments controlled by the researcher.

What We Learn from Two-Way Analysis of Variance (ANOVA)

Describing Sample Data

What is the relation between a measurement variable (y) and two categorical variables (x_1 and x_2)? We describe this relation by contrasting the sample means of y across combinations of categories of x_1 and x_2. The pattern of mean differences indicates the nature of relations (if any) among the three variables. We can summarize the strength of these relations with R_a^2: the proportion of y's sample variance that is explained by x_1 and x_2 together.

Inferences about Population

Two-way ANOVA provides three or four separate F tests. These tell us whether, based on this sample (and assuming it is random), we can reject the hypotheses that:

1. The population mean of y remains the same at all levels of x_1 and x_2.
2. The population mean of y remains the same at all levels of x_1, holding x_2 constant.
3. The population mean of y remains the same at all levels of x_2, holding x_1 constant.
4. (*Optional*) The population mean of y depends on the level of x_1 and the level of x_2, but does not depend in any nonadditive way on the *combination* of x_1 and x_2. Put another way, x_1 has the same effect on mean y, regardless of the level of x_2.

A statistically significant (e.g., $P < .05$) F-test result for any of these suggests that the null hypothesis may be rejected. We thereby indirectly conclude that the relation in question does exist in the population. On the other hand, if an F-test result is nonsignificant, we lack persuasive evidence that the relation exists.

We can show sample means of y within each combination of x categories, and the associated confidence intervals, graphically with an error-bar plot.

EXERCISES

*8.6.1 Use cross-tabulation, percentages, and a chi-square test to analyze the relation between *size* and *lived*, the two *x* variables of Table 8.10 (file *akteens*).

*8.6.2   We earlier saw a significant relation between *bonds* and *where* (where students expect to spend the rest of their lives). Does this relation remain significant when we control for community size? Perform and interpret a two-way ANOVA of *bonds* by *where* and *size*.

*8.6.3   Perform and interpret a two-way ANOVA that tests the effects of *gender*, *region*, and *gender*region* on *bonds*.

Summary

This chapter illustrated two parallel approaches to analyzing the relation between a measurement variable and a categorical variable: mean-based methods and rank-based methods. The mean-based methods (*t* test and analysis of variance) belong to a family called *parametric*. Two-sample *t* tests test whether two populations have identical means. One-way ANOVA tests whether K populations ($K \geq 2$) have identical means. (When $K = 2$, ANOVA and *t* tests are equivalent.) Two-way ANOVA extends this idea to test for identical means across categories of two *x* variables. Further extensions to three or more *x* variables are readily accomplished using the same computer programs that do one- or two-way ANOVA.

Parametric methods offer theoretical advantages and simplicity. Their drawbacks include a lack of resistance to outliers, and dependence on the sometimes unrealistic assumptions of normal and identical-variance population distributions. In contrast, *nonparametric* rank-based methods (Mann–Whitney and Kruskal–Wallis) do not require normality or equal-variance assumptions and have good resistance to outliers. Mann–Whitney tests, the nonparametric counterpart to two-sample *t* tests, test whether two populations have identical rank distributions. Kruskal–Wallis tests, the counterpart to one-way ANOVA, test whether K populations have identical rank distributions.

A third alternative approach, not illustrated in this chapter, offers a compromise that shares some advantages of both parametric and nonparametric tests. Simply transform your measurement variable to ranks, then apply parametric (*t* or ANOVA) tests to these ranks rather than to the original data. Such **nonparametric approximation** tests tend to be less disturbed by nonnormality or nonconstant variance than parametric tests are, but at the same time often appear statistically more powerful than nonparametric tests.

The tedium of hand calculation once discouraged analysts from routinely performing multiple tests. Older textbooks were designed to help readers choose a single test that was "most appropriate" for their data. Modern data analysis takes a different approach, supported by the computer's ability to produce quickly a variety of graphs and tests. Graphs allow a visual check on distribution shape, spread, and outliers. Conducting both a parametric and a nonparametric (or nonparametric approximation) test now takes scarcely more effort than any one test alone, so we have little excuse for not verifying that they reach similar substantive conclusions. If they do, we can state that conclusion with greater confidence. If they disagree, we should analyze further until we understand what is going on in the data. Perhaps there exist outlier problems, or differences in shape or spread, which should themselves be important parts of our discussion of how the populations compare.

PROBLEMS

8.1   Table 3.3 (file *trees*) in Chapter 3 lists data on lead concentrations of tree leaves in one Nigerian city where, unlike in the United States, most vehicles run on leaded gasoline. The *sample* lead concentrations show obvious differences between low-to-medium- and high-traffic areas, but this sample includes only 12 cases. Does the evidence in Table 3.3 justify concluding that the *population* (of all sites in the city) lead concentrations vary with traffic density?

    a.   Perform a two-sample t test for a significant difference between means ($\alpha = .05$).

    b.   Perform a Mann–Whitney test for a significant difference between distributions ($\alpha = .05$).

    c.   Compare the results you obtained in parts **a** and **b**, and summarize your general conclusion.

8.2   Data on former Colleges of Advanced Technology (CAT) and other British universities appear in Table 3.4 (file *britu*). Are there significant differences between ex-CATs and other schools? Compare the two types of schools with respect to the following measurement variables, each time using both a parametric and a nonparametric test:

    a.   graduate unemployment   b.   exam scores

    c.   cost index   d.   male/female ratio

8.3   Table 4.7 (file *teva180*) contains data on 118 college classes. Test whether classes taught by regular faculty members differ significantly from classes taught by teaching assistants (T.A.'s) with respect to the following variables:

class size

percent A and B grades given

percent high teaching evaluations received

In each analysis:

    a.   Compare the distributions graphically using boxplots or histograms.

    b.   Conduct a two-sample t test (or, equivalently, a one-way ANOVA).

    c.   Conduct a Mann–Whitney test.

    d.   Summarize your conclusions.

8.4   Table 3.5 (file *smoke*) in Chapter 3 introduced data on nicotine concentrations in airliner cabins. Researchers bought seats for their air-monitoring equipment on 75 flights of three different types of planes—Boeing 727-200, 737-200, and 737-300. Does nicotine concentration depend on the type of plane?

    a.   Construct histograms showing the distribution of nicotine concentration for each type of plane, and describe how they appear to differ (or not differ) in this sample.

    b.   Find sample means for each plane type, and test (one-way ANOVA) for significant differences using $\alpha = .05$. Does your graphical analysis of part **a** suggest reasons to distrust these ANOVA results?

    c.   Apply a Kruskal–Wallis test to determine whether the distributions of nicotine concentration are the same on all three airliner types. Why is this nonparametric test more appropriate here than ANOVA? Summarize your conclusions from parts **a–c**.

8.5   Referring again to the airliner smoking data of Table 3.5, analyze the relation between seating section and nicotine concentration.

    a.   Construct boxplots of nicotine concentrations within each category of seating. Describe these distributions, and note any potential problems that might affect ANOVA.

    b.   Do mean nicotine concentrations of the three seating sections significantly differ ($\alpha = .05$)? Test using one-way ANOVA.

    c.   Apply a nonparametric Kruskal–Wallis test (again, $\alpha = .05$). Does this Kruskal–Wallis test lead to the same general conclusion as ANOVA? Which test should we trust here, and why?

8.6 (*Review*)   Cross-tabulations can display relations between two categorical variables. Boxplots or histogram comparisons display relations between one measurement and one categorical variable. To display relations between two measurement variables, we use scatterplots. Construct a scatterplot from the airliner data of Table 3.5, showing the relation between number of cigarettes smoked (on the vertical or y-axis) and number of smokers (horizontal or x-axis). What general pattern does this plot show? Why should number of cigarettes form our plot's y-axis, rather than x?

8.7 (*Review*)   It seems reasonable to expect that airliner nicotine concentrations would increase as more cigarettes are smoked. Does a scatterplot support this expectation? Explain your choice of y and x variables, and describe what the plot shows.

8.8 (*Review*)   Does nicotine concentration increase with the number of smokers? Construct another scatterplot, explain your choice of y and x variables, and describe what you learn from this plot.

8.9. (*Review*)   Cross-tabulate, find appropriate percentages, perform a chi-square test, and summarize your conclusions regarding each of the following pairs of categorical variables from Table 8.1 (file *akteens*).

    a.   *lived* and *where*

    b.   *size* and *where*

    c.   *gender* and *where*

Table 8.12 (file *reading*) contains data from IQ tests given to 60 elementary-school boys. Half of these boys had previously been classified as poor or very poor readers, at least 2 years below their grade levels. The table lists the boys' full test IQ score, and also their scores on several of the specific subtests that make up IQ. Variables are as follows:

reading	reading ability, classified as very poor, poor, or normal
IQ	full WISC-R IQ score
vocab	vocabulary subtest
digits	digit span subtest
object	object assembly subtest

Problems 8.10–8.18 refer to these data.

Table 8.12
IQ scores and selected subtests for 60 elementary-school boys

reading	IQ	vocab	digits	object
1. very poor	90	5	4	17
2. very poor	84	4	4	13
3. very poor	86	5	4	11
4. very poor	85	6	3	13
5. very poor	84	7	8	1
6. very poor	95	6	6	9
7. very poor	81	5	5	8
8. very poor	83	8	5	10
9. very poor	88	7	4	10
10. very poor	87	7	5	7
11. very poor	93	5	4	11
12. poor	90	11	6	9
13. poor	103	13	7	14
14. poor	110	11	8	12
15. poor	105	9	5	11
16. poor	105	9	2	15
17. poor	101	10	8	9
18. poor	96	9	5	12
19. poor	111	10	8	16
20. poor	105	9	4	11
21. poor	105	11	7	9
22. poor	111	15	5	13
23. poor	102	12	5	9
24. poor	100	9	6	11

Table 8.12 (*Continued*)

reading	IQ	vocab	digits	object
25. poor	106	8	6	8
26. poor	115	13	6	13
27. poor	99	11	8	12
28. poor	106	11	7	11
29. poor	103	14	7	12
30. poor	93	9	5	12
31. normal	95	11	12	9
32. normal	102	8	9	12
33. normal	97	10	10	12
34. normal	92	9	8	11
35. normal	107	9	11	10
36. normal	92	8	12	9
37. normal	103	11	13	12
38. normal	106	9	11	12
39. normal	109	11	10	10
40. normal	105	13	9	7
41. normal	104	9	9	11
42. normal	98	8	12	8
43. normal	110	12	12	10
44. normal	94	11	12	10
45. normal	103	11	11	11
46. normal	102	10	12	11
47. normal	102	10	10	8
48. normal	98	10	11	7
49. normal	109	14	13	11
50. normal	96	8	12	9
51. normal	95	14	9	10
52. normal	101	10	10	9
53. normal	109	14	8	11
54. normal	112	9	10	12
55. normal	96	10	12	7
56. normal	93	9	15	10
57. normal	111	12	10	12
58. normal	96	12	10	10
59. normal	105	13	11	10
60. normal	105	11	9	13

Source: Treacy (1985).
File: *reading*

8.10 Do significant differences appear among the mean IQ scores of these very poor, poor, and normal readers? Test using one-way ANOVA (by design, IQ scores tend to have approximately normal distributions).

8.11 Construct an error-bar plot for the analysis of Problem 8.10, showing bars extending plus and minus 1 standard error from each group mean.

8.12 We might expect to find that reading ability is related to performance on the vocabulary subtest. Do the data of Table 8.12 support this expectation? Use one-way ANOVA to test for significant differences in mean vocabulary score among very poor, poor, and normal readers.

8.13 Construct an error-bar plot to go with your analysis of Problem 8.12.

8.14 Digit span, or the number of random digits a person can remember, is often employed to measure short-term memory. Is digit span related to reading ability? Apply one-way ANOVA.

8.15 Construct an error-bar plot for Problem 8.14.

8.16 The object assembly subtest measures spatial skills, rather than verbal or memorization skills. Use ANOVA to decide whether object assembly scores are significantly related to reading ability.

8.17 Construct an error-bar plot for Problem 8.16.

8.18 Summarize your findings from Problems 8.10–8.17 regarding differences among very poor, poor, and normal readers.

Problems 8.19–8.23 refer to a study of college students described in Ward and Ault (1990). Its purpose was to investigate aspects of student behavior that might have a bearing on the problem of "acquaintance rape," or sexual assault within a dating context. The 243 students surveyed were selected randomly from the enrollment at one university. The variables include the following:

gender	Gender
year	Year in college
gpa	Cumulative grade-point average
greek	Belong to fraternity or sorority
athlete	Are you a varsity athlete?
employed	Are you employed?
drink	College drinking scale
aggress	Aggressive behavior scale

8.19 Table 8.13 gives means of *drink* (college drinking scale) by gender and year in college, and an analysis of variance table. Use this information to write a report about the relation between drinking, gender, and year in college. Include discussion of the partial F tests of *gender* and *year* effects, the adjusted R^2, and the patterns exhibited by the sample means.

Table 8.13
Means of college drinking scale (0–33 points, high values indicate heavier drinking), by student gender and year in college

Gender	Year in college				Total
	Freshman	*Sophomore*	*Junior*	*Senior*	
Female	18.67	18.27	18.00	14.92	17.31
Male	19.44	24.16	21.03	19.28	21.31
Total	18.97	21.17	19.45	16.65	19.11

Number of obs. = 243   *R*-square = .14
Root MSE = 6.29   Adj. *R*-square = .12

Source	Partial SS	df	MS	F	Prob > F
Model	1,517.95	4	379.49	9.59	.0001
gender	851.75	1	851.75	21.53	.0001
year	556.96	3	185.65	4.69	.0033
Residual	9,417.27	238	39.57		
Total	10,935.22	242	45.19		

Data source: Ward and Ault (1990).

8.20 Do the means in Table 8.13 give any indication that there might exist an interaction—that is, that year in college might affect drinking differently for men and women? Formally test this possibility by repeating the ANOVA of Problem 8.19 with a *gender*∗*year* interaction. Describe your findings.

8.21 Table 8.14 (page 298) gives means of *gpa* (cumulative grade-point average) by whether students are employed or are varsity athletes. Use this information to write a report about the relation between grades, employment, and athletics. Include discussion of the partial F tests of *employed* and *athlete* effects, the adjusted R^2, and the patterns shown by the sample means.

Table 8.14

Means of cumulative grade-point average (0–4 scale),
by student employment and varsity athlete status

Are you employed?	Are you a varsity athlete?		Total
	no	*yes*	
no	2.75	2.57	2.73
yes	2.88	2.34	2.87
Total	2.83	2.51	2.81

Number of obs. = 215   R-square = .0401
Root MSE = .45   Adj. R-square = .0310

Source	Partial SS	df	MS	F	Prob > F
Model	1.796	2	.898	4.43	.0131
employed	.649	1	.649	3.20	.0751
athlete	.856	1	.856	4.22	.0412
Residual	42.985	212	.203		
Total	44.781	214	.209		

Data source: Ward and Ault (1990).

8.22   Table 8.15 contains means and ANOVA tables similar to Tables 8.13 and 8.14, but most of the ANOVA output is missing. Fill in the 24 blanks of this table, using the information given and formulas from Table 8.10. Write a report on the relation between aggressive behavior, gender, and fraternity/sorority membership, based on your reconstructed ANOVA table.

Table 8.15
Means of aggressive behavior scale (0–7 points,
high values indicate more aggressive acts such as fighting,
vandalism), by gender and fraternity/sorority membership

	Belong to fraternity or sorority		
Gender	no	yes	Total
Female	.724	1.056	.769
Male	2.125	2.448	2.211
Total	1.296	1.9156	1.416

Number of obs. = 243   R-square = _____
Root MSE = _____   Adj. R-square = _____

Source	**Partial SS**	*df*	**MS**	*F*	**Prob > F**
Model	128.98	——	———	———	———
gender	114.46	——	———	———	———
greek	3.94	——	———	———	———
Residual	536.04	——	———	———	———
Total	———	——	———	———	———

Data source: Ward and Ault (1990).

8.23   Construct the following error-bar plots, with bars indicating plus and minus 1 standard error:
   a.   Mean drinking scale by year in college, with separate lines plotted for men and women, based on Table 8.13.
   b.   Mean grade-point average by athlete status, with separate lines plotted for employed and nonemployed students, based on Table 8.14.
   c.   Mean aggressive behavior scale by gender, with separate lines plotted for fraternity/sorority members and nonmembers, based on Table 8.15.

8.24   Table 8.16 (page 300) lists means and incomplete output from a two-way AN-OVA. The data come from a survey about environmental issues in the city of Tulsa, Oklahoma (Blocker and Eckberg, 1989). The *y* variable in Table 8.16, called *local*, is a scale measuring respondents' concern about local environmental issues. The two *x* variables are *gender* and whether respondents have children living at their home (*kids*). Reconstruct the ANOVA table, and use these results to describe the relation between local environmental concern, gender, and parenthood.

Table 8.16
Means of local environmental concern scale
(higher values indicate stronger concern),
by gender and children living at home

Gender	Children living at home?		Total
	no kids	*has kids*	*Total*
male	44.876	47.923	46.001
female	51.952	54.385	53.190
Total	48.480	52.108	50.109

Number of obs. = 196   *R*-square = _____
Root MSE = _____   Adj. *R*-square = _____

Source	Partial SS	df	MS	F	Prob > F
Model	2,823.955	___	_____	_____	_____
gender	2,185.518	___	_____	_____	_____
kids	342.811	___	_____	_____	_____
Residual	_____	___	_____	_____	_____
Total	44,004.735	___	_____	_____	_____

Data source: Blocker and Eckberg (1989).

Table 8.17 (file *missile*) lists Cold War data compiled by Donald MacKenzie, for his book *Inventing Accuracy: A Historical Sociology of Nuclear Missile Guidance* (1990). The cases are 44 types of long-range nuclear missiles developed by the United States or Soviet Union between 1958 and 1990. Variables are as follows:

missile	missile name
country	United States (U.S.) or Soviet Union (USSR)

	era	historical period during which this missile went into service (Note that, as coded, this is a categorical rather than measurement variable.)
	type	land- or submarine-launched missile
	range	range in nautical miles
	CEP	circular error probable: the radius of a bull's-eye (in miles) within which 50% of the warheads are expected to land. The smaller the CEP, the more accurate the missile.

Problems 8.25–8.31 refer to these data.

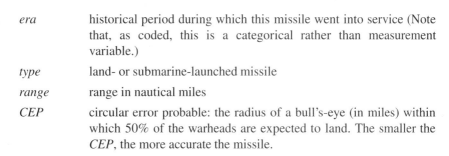

Table 8.17
Accuracy (*CEP*) and other characteristics of 44 U.S. and Soviet nuclear missiles

missile	country	era	type	range	CEP
1. Atlas D	U.S.	1958–65	land	.	1.80
2. Polaris A1	U.S.	1958–65	sub	1,200	2.00
3. Atlas E	U.S.	1958–65	land	.	1.00
4. Atlas F	U.S.	1958–65	land	.	1.00
5. Minuteman 1	U.S.	1958–65	land	.	1.10
6. Polaris A2	U.S.	1958–65	sub	1,500	2.00
7. Titan 1	U.S.	1958–65	land	.	.65
8. Titan 2	U.S.	1958–65	land	.	.65
9. Polaris A3	U.S.	1958–65	sub	2,500	.50
10. Minuteman 2	U.S.	1966–79	land	.	.26
11. Minuteman 3	U.S.	1966–79	land	.	.21
12. Poseidon C3	U.S.	1966–79	sub	2,500	.25
13. Minuteman 3i	U.S.	1966–79	land	.	.12
14. Trident C4	U.S.	1966–79	sub	4,000	.25
15. Trident C4i	U.S.	1980–90	sub	4,000	.12
16. MX	U.S.	1980–90	land	.	.06
17. Trident D5	U.S.	1980–90	sub	4,000	.06
18. SS-N-4	USSR	1958–65	sub	350	2.00
19. SS-6	USSR	1958–65	land	.	2.00
20. SS-7	USSR	1958–65	land	.	1.50
21. SS-N-5	USSR	1958–65	sub	700	1.50
22. SS-8	USSR	1958–65	land	.	1.00
23. SS-11 mod 1	USSR	1966–79	land	.	.75
24. SS-9	USSR	1966–79	land	.	.50
25. SS-N-6 mod 1	USSR	1966–79	sub	1,300	1.00

(*continued*)

Table 8.17 (*Continued*)

missile	country	era	type	range	CEP
26. SS-13 mod 1	USSR	1966–79	land	.	1.00
27. SS-11 mod 3	USSR	1966–79	land	.	.60
28. SS-N-6 mod 2	USSR	1966–79	sub	1,600	1.00
29. SS-N-8 mod 1	USSR	1966–79	sub	4,200	.84
30. SS-13 mod 2	USSR	1966–79	land	.	.81
31. SS-11 mod 2	USSR	1966–79	land	.	.60
32. SS-18 mod 1	USSR	1966–79	land	.	.23
33. SS-N-6 mod 3	USSR	1966–79	sub	1,600	1.00
34. SS-19 mod 1	USSR	1966–79	land	.	.25
35. SS-17 mod 1	USSR	1966–79	land	.	.24
36. SS-18 mod 3	USSR	1966–79	land	.	.19
37. SS-N-8 mod 2	USSR	1966–79	sub	4,900	.84
38. SS-18 mod 2	USSR	1966–79	land	.	.23
39. SS-19 mod 2	USSR	1966–79	land	.	.23
40. SS-N-18 mod 1&3	USSR	1966–79	sub	3,500	.76
41. SS-17 mod 2	USSR	1966–79	land	.	.23
42. SS-18 mod 4	USSR	1966–79	land	.	.14
43. SS-17 mod 3	USSR	1980–90	land	.	.20
44. SS-19 mod 3	USSR	1980–90	land	.	.21

Source: MacKenzie (1990).
File: *missile*

8.25   Do U.S. and Soviet missiles differ significantly in their accuracy? Examine sample means, perform a one-way ANOVA of *CEP* by *country*, and summarize your findings.

8.26   Are ANOVA's normality and equal-variances assumptions plausible with respect to your missile-accuracy analysis of Problem 8.25? Construct boxplots of *CEP* by country, and discuss what they show.

8.27   Carry out and interpret an appropriate nonparametric test of whether *CEP* differs by *country*. Do your results support or challenge the ANOVA results in Problem 8.25?

*8.28   (For purposes of Problems 8.28–8.31, accept the usual ANOVA assumptions as true.) Obtain a table of sample means and perform a two-way ANOVA of *CEP* by *country* and *era* (years the missile first went into service). Refer to the sample means and ANOVA to describe

    a.   the relation between mean accuracy and years the missile went into service in the United States, and in the Soviet Union.

b.   the relation between mean accuracy and country, holding constant the years the missile went into service

c.   why this two-way analysis finds a significant *country* effect, but your one-way analysis of Problems 8.25 and 8.27 did not

d.   how much of the variance of *CEP* is explained by *country* and *era* together, and how much by *country* alone (from Problem 8.25)

*8.29   Use two-way ANOVA to test for a significant *country*era* interaction effect on *CEP*.

*8.30   Analyze the relation between missile accuracy (*CEP*) and whether it is land or submarine launched (*type*), through the following steps. At each step, discuss the ANOVA results with reference to a corresponding table of sample means:

a.   perform and interpret a one-way ANOVA of *CEP* by *type*

b.   perform and interpret a two-way ANOVA of *CEP* by *type* and *country*

c.   perform and interpret a three-way ANOVA of *CEP* by *type, country*, and *era*

*8.31   Elaborate your three-way ANOVA of Problem 8.30c by including *type*country, type*era*, and *country*era* interactions. Which interactions, if any, reach statistical significance ($P < .05$)? How much does R^2 increase, comparing this more complicated model with that of Problem 8.30c? What happens to the adjusted R^2? Which model seems better?

Table 8.18 (file *caribou*) lists data from a study by Cameron et al. (1992) regarding how Alaska's North Slope oil development affected caribou living in the area. Caribou populations fluctuate naturally in the severe Arctic environment, but the study found evidence that industrial activity (increasing from 1978 to 1987) had reduced this area's capacity to sustain caribou reproduction. Variables include counts of the calves and adult caribou observed along transects within the study area, and also whether the spring snow melt of that season occurred relatively early or late. Late snow melt presents a hardship condition. Problems 8.32–8.33 refer to these data.

Table 8.18
Caribou observed and snow-melt status near
Milne Point road system in Arctic Alaska

Year	Total caribou	Number of calves	Snow-melt timing	Ratio of calves/ adults
1978	486	187	late	.63
1979	648	281	early	.77
1980	232	72	late	.45

(*continued*)

Table 8.18 (*Continued*)

Year	Total caribou	Number of calves	Snow-melt timing	Ratio of calves/ adults
1981	720	325	early	.82
1982	305	112	late	.58
1983	771	328	early	.74
1984	1,259	559	early	.80
1985	532	224	late	.73
1986	455	160	late	.54
1987	266	115	late	.76

Source: Cameron et al. (1992).
File: *caribou*

8.32   Carry out a suitable parametric test to determine whether the calf/adult ratio significantly depends on snow-melt timing. Viewing the data graphically, do you see any reason to doubt your test's assumptions?

8.33   Use a suitable nonparametric test to compare the calf/adult ratios of early and late snow-melt years. Does your conclusion following this test generally agree with that from Problem 8.32?

$\mathcal{9}$

Simple
Regression
Analysis

Regression analysis encompasses a broad class of statistical methods. Many elementary techniques presented earlier in this book can be viewed, mathematically, as special cases of regression. So too can many of the techniques covered in more advanced courses. This chapter concentrates on simple regression: finding the "best" straight line to summarize the trend of points in a scatterplot. Regression lines help us understand and describe relations between two measurement variables, complementing cross-tabulation/chi-square methods (for two categorical variables) or comparison methods (for one measurement and one categorical variable). More readily than other methods, however, regression also extends to analyses involving any number of categorical and measurement variables.

In either its simple or more advanced forms, regression serves a variety of analytical purposes:

1. Predicting future (or otherwise unknown) values of a variable, based on known values of one or more other variables

2. Describing simply the patterns in complicated data, for instance by summarizing thousands of data points with a single equation

3. Identifying particular cases that do not fit the general pattern of the data

4. Evaluating and refining theories about how changes in one variable cause change in another

Regression constitutes the core technique of data analysis in many research fields, including sociology and economics.

This chapter begins with an example of regression in the graphical context of a scatterplot. Subsequently, we will see regression through the same lens used by a working data analyst: the output tables of a typical computer program. Such tables have similar organization whether the regression is simple or complicated, as we will see in Chapter 10.

9.1   Scatterplot and Regression Line

Table 9.1 contains data on a random sample of 20 U.S. cities. The variables listed are population, percentage of families with incomes below the poverty line, and homicide victims per 100,000 people. Figure 9.1 (page 308) begins our analysis of relations among these measurement variables by graphing homicide rate (y) against percent families below poverty (x). We show homicide rate as the y variable because it is the variable to be predicted or explained here: the **dependent variable**. Poverty rate, the x variable, is a possible **predictor** of homicide rate. The graph shows data points drifting upward to the right. Dallas, at upper right, appears as an outlier due to its exceptionally high homicide rate. Dallas' poverty rate is not unusual, however.

Table 9.1
1980 Population in thousands, percent families below poverty,
and yearly homicides per 100,000 population (averaged
over 1980–84) in a random sample of 20 U.S. cities

City	State	Population (1,000s)	Percent poor	Homicide rate
1. Tulsa	OK	360.9	7.40	8.64
2. Columbus	GA	169.4	14.50	9.21
3. Dallas	TX	904.1	10.80	29.98
4. Virginia Beach	VA	262.2	7.70	3.81
5. Fullerton	CA	102.0	4.70	2.35
6. Berkeley	CA	103.3	11.70	8.52
7. Honolulu	HI	365.0	7.40	9.15
8. Portland	OR	366.4	8.50	8.62
9. Albuquerque	NM	331.8	9.30	6.39
10. Salt Lake	UT	163.0	10.50	6.01
11. Tempe	AZ	106.7	5.50	4.12
12. Concord	CA	103.3	4.60	3.10
13. Sunnyvale	CA	106.6	3.70	2.44
14. Rochester	NY	241.7	14.50	10.84
15. Allentown	PA	103.8	8.40	4.24
16. Erie	PA	119.1	10.20	4.70
17. Independence	MO	111.8	4.90	3.58
18. Peoria	IL	124.2	9.40	4.03
19. Milwaukee	WI	636.2	6.80	7.83
20. Sterling Heights	MI	109.0	3.10	.55

Source: Williams and Flewelling (1988).
File: *urban*

We might summarize this pattern of up-to-right drift by drawing a straight line onto the scatterplot, as done in Figure 9.2 (page 308). That is the basic idea of two-variable **regression analysis**: Find the straight line that best fits the data. *Such lines show how the mean of y changes, at changing levels of x.* In Figure 9.2 we see mean homicide rates rising from near 0 to over 10, as percent below poverty increases from about 3 to 15.

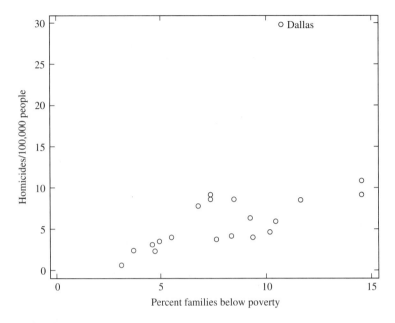

FIGURE 9.1
Scatterplot of homicide rate versus poverty rate, for a random sample of 20
U.S. cities

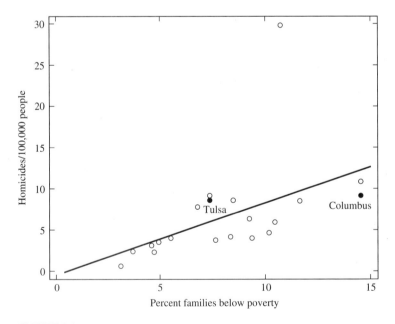

FIGURE 9.2
Scatterplot of homicide rate versus poverty rate, with regression line

Any regression line corresponds to an equation with the general form:

$$\hat{y} = a + bx$$

where $\hat{y}$ ("y-hat") denotes the **predicted value of y**, or the mean value of y for a given level of x; b represents the line's *slope*, or the change in $\hat{y}$ per 1-unit increase in x. Slopes can be

positive	tending up to right: $\hat{y}$ increases as x increases
negative	tending down to right: $\hat{y}$ decreases as x increases
zero	horizontal: $\hat{y}$ does not change as x increases

In a linear equation, a denotes the line's **y-intercept**, which is the value of $\hat{y}$ when x = 0. Graphically, y-intercept corresponds to the height of the line where it crosses the y (vertical) axis.

The line in Figure 9.2 has the equation

$$\hat{y} = -.815 + .944x$$

which is to say that $a = -.815$ and $b = .944$. Figure 9.3 shows the meaning of this y-intercept and slope graphically. Slope indicates steepness, or "rise over run." As x in

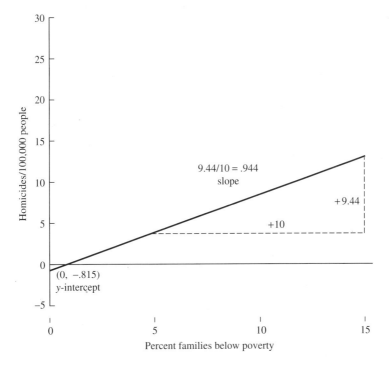

FIGURE 9.3
Graphical meanings of the y-intercept and slope of the regression line
$\hat{y}_i = -.815 + .944x_i$

Figure 9.3 increases 10 points, from 5 to 15, the regression line rises by 9.44. Therefore its slope is

$$b = \frac{\text{rise}}{\text{run}} = \frac{9.44}{10} = .944$$

This tells us that across these 20 cities, average homicide rates rise by .944 with each 1-point increase in the percentage of families below poverty.

Figure 9.3 shows the regression line crossing the y-axis at (x, y) coordinates $(0, -.815)$, so the y-intercept is

$$a = -.815$$

This implies that the average homicide rate should equal $-.815$, in cities with 0 percent below poverty. That interpretation makes no sense, and we have no cities without poverty anyway. Regression lines may yield unreasonable results when projected beyond the x range of the data. Researchers often ignore the intercept, and focus instead on the slope, if their data's x values do not extend down to 0. Although a y-intercept remains mathematically necessary, it need not have any substantive interpretation unless 0 is a realistic value for x.

Finding the best line to summarize a scatter of points amounts to selecting the best values for intercept and slope. Several techniques exist for doing this; "best fitting line" is an imprecise term with a variety of specific statistical definitions. One such technique, **ordinary least squares** or **OLS**, is described in the box. OLS is much more popular than other regression techniques, so the term "regression" by itself generally means "OLS regression."

Ordinary least squares (OLS) regression

Regression analysis finds the straight line that best describes the relation between two measurement variables y and x:

$$y_i = a + bx_i + e_i \qquad (9.1)$$

where b is the line's **slope**

$$b = \frac{\Sigma(x_i - \bar{x})(y_i - \bar{y})}{\Sigma(x_i - \bar{x})^2} \qquad (9.2)$$

and a is the line's **y-intercept**

$$a = \bar{y} - b\bar{x} \qquad (9.3)$$

The predicted value of y for the ith case, written $\hat{y}_i$, is

$$\hat{y}_i = a + bx_i \qquad (9.4)$$

Values of $\hat{y}_i$ lie on the regression line but, unless the line fits perfectly, actual y_i values will be scattered above and below this line. The ith-case **residual,** e_i, equals the prediction error or difference between actual y_i and predicted $\hat{y}_i$:

$$e_i = y_i - \hat{y}_i \tag{9.5}$$

Calculating slope and intercept values according to equations (9.2) and (9.3) ensures that the sum of squared residuals or prediction errors

$$SS_R = \Sigma e_i^2 \tag{9.6}$$

will be lower for this regression line than for any other line applied to the same data—hence the name **ordinary least squares**, or **OLS**.

In principle, we could apply equations (9.2) and (9.3) to calculate a regression slope and intercept by hand. In practice this is tedious, so analysts rely on computers, which produce output like that shown in Table 9.2. By typing or selecting from menus a command such as "**regress *homic poor***" and reading slope and intercept from the output table (they appear in bold at lower left), we quickly get our regression equation:

$$\hat{y} = -.815 + .944x$$

or, writing this equation in terms of the computer program's variable name abbreviations:

$$\text{predicted } homic = -.815 + .944poor$$

The output table contains much other information too.

Table 9.2
Regression output table showing the regression of homicide rate (*homic*) on percent families below poverty (*poor*), using the data of Table 9.1

Source	SS	df	MS	
				Number of obs. = 20
				$F(1, 18) = 6.14$
Model	181.37	1	181.37	Prob $> F = .023$
Residual	531.57	18	29.53	R-square = **.254**
				Adj. R-square = **.213**
Total	712.94	19	37.52	Root MSE = 5.434

homic	Coef.	Std. Err.	t	$P > \lvert t \rvert$	[95% Conf. Interval]	
poor	**.944**	.381	2.478	.023	.144	1.744
_cons	**-.815**	3.344	-.244	.810	-7.841	6.210

9.1.1   Construct a scatterplot with regression line showing the relation between homicide rate (as y variable) and population (x), using the cities data of Table 9.1 (file *urban*). Write out the regression equation, and interpret its intercept and slope. Does the intercept make real-world sense?

9.1.2   The relation between temperature in degrees Fahrenheit (F) and degrees Celsius (C) can be described by a linear equation with the form

$$F = a + bC$$

   a.   Water freezes at 0 degrees Celsius or 32 degrees Fahrenheit. It boils at 100 degrees Celsius or 212 degrees Fahrenheit. Use this information to determine the values of a and b, and write out this equation.
   b.   Draw this line graphically, indicating intercept and slope.
   c.   What is the temperature in degrees Fahrenheit, when a Celsius thermometer reads 500 degrees? When a Celsius thermometer reads -25 degrees?

9.2   Predicted Values and Residuals

Table 9.3 repeats the urban poverty and homicide rates from Table 9.1, also adding predicted homicide rate:

$$\hat{y}_i = -.815 + .944x_i$$

and prediction error or residual:

$$e_i = y_i - \hat{y}_i$$

For example, the city of Columbus reported a poverty rate of $x_2 = 14.5$, one of the highest in this sample. Our regression equation therefore predicts that Columbus' should also have a high homicide rate:

$$\hat{y}_2 = -.815 + .944 \times 14.5$$

$$= 12.87$$

Columbus' actual homicide rate was indeed high ($y_2 = 9.21$), but not so high as predicted ($\hat{y}_2 = 12.87$). The city's prediction error or residual equals:

$$e_2 = 9.21 - 12.87$$

$$= -3.66$$

A negative residual occurs when actual y is lower than predicted $\hat{y}$. Cases with negative residuals fall *below the regression line*, as Columbus does in Figure 9.2.

Table 9.3
Percent families below poverty (x), homicide rate (y), predicted homicide rate
($\hat{y}$), and prediction errors or residuals (e)

i	City	Percent poor x_i	Homicide rate y_i	Predicted homicide rate[a] $\hat{y}_i$	Prediction error[b] e_i
1	Tulsa	7.40	8.64	6.17	2.47
2	Columbus	14.50	9.21	12.87	−3.66
3	Dallas	10.80	29.98	9.38	20.60
4	Virginia Beach	7.70	3.81	6.46	−2.64
5	Fullerton	4.70	2.35	3.62	−1.27
6	Berkeley	11.70	8.52	10.23	−1.71
7	Honolulu	7.40	9.15	6.17	2.98
8	Portland	8.50	8.62	7.21	1.41
9	Albuquerque	9.30	6.39	7.96	−1.57
10	Salt Lake	10.50	6.01	9.10	−3.09
11	Tempe	5.50	4.12	4.38	−.26
12	Concord	4.60	3.10	3.53	−.43
13	Sunnyvale	3.70	2.44	2.68	−.24
14	Rochester	14.50	10.84	12.87	−2.03
15	Allentown	8.40	4.24	7.11	−2.87
16	Erie	10.20	4.70	8.81	−4.11
17	Independence	4.90	3.58	3.81	−.23
18	Peoria	9.40	4.03	8.06	−4.03
19	Milwaukee	6.80	7.83	5.60	2.23
20	Sterling Heights	3.10	.55	2.11	−1.56

[a]Predicted homicide rate: $\hat{y}_i = -.815 + .944x_i$
[b]Prediction error or residual: $e_i = y_i - \hat{y}_i$

Tulsa had less poverty ($x_1 = 7.4$) than Columbus, so the regression equation predicts a somewhat lower homicide rate:

$$\hat{y}_1 = -.815 + .944 \times 7.4$$

$$= 6.17$$

Tulsa's actual homicide rate ($y_1 = 8.64$) was higher than predicted ($\hat{y}_1 = 6.17$), resulting in a positive residual:

$$e_1 = 8.64 - 6.17$$

$$= 2.47$$

Cases with positive residuals fall above the regression line, as does Tulsa in Figure 9.2. The largest positive residual belongs to Dallas ($e_3 = 20.6$), which reported far more homicides than we might expect based on its poverty rate alone.

Ideally, a regression line summarizes all the patterns to be found in a scatterplot, so residuals show just random variations around this line. If some nonrandom pattern remains in the residuals, however, perhaps the initial regression analysis needs modification. Patterns among the residuals might show up in a **residuals versus predicted plot** (or **e versus ŷ** plot), like Figure 9.4, which displays the data of Table 9.3. Residuals (*e*) form the vertical dimension of such plots, and predicted values (ŷ) the horizontal dimension. Boxplots added to the margins of Figure 9.4 depict the univariate distributions of *e* (right margin) and ŷ (top margin). The shape of the residual distribution has particular importance in regression, as noted later.

With OLS regression, the mean residual always equals 0. Negative residuals (reflecting too-high predictions) fall below the horizontal $\bar{e} = 0$ line in Figure 9.4. The right-hand boxplot indicates that these residuals have a median lower than their mean, a symptom of positive skew. This boxplot also emphasizes that Dallas constitutes a severe outlier relative to the other cities' residuals. That is, our regression prediction is most dramatically wrong in the case of Dallas.

One pattern evident in Figure 9.4 is the fact that most cities had negative residuals;

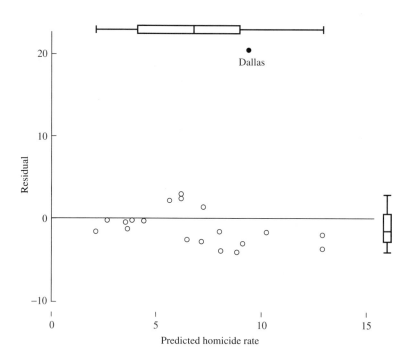

FIGURE 9.4
Residual versus predicted (*e* versus ŷ) plot for the regression of homicide rate on poverty rate

our predictions were too high in 15 out of 20 cases. Looking back at the original regression in Figure 9.2, we can see why this happened: Dallas' high homicide rate pulled the regression line up. OLS belongs to the same mathematical family as the arithmetic mean, and shares its sensitivity to outliers. Chapter 10 describes **robust regression**, a more complicated kind of regression that resists the pull of outliers. For now, however, we will continue with basic OLS.

EXERCISES

9.2.1   Table 9.4 (file *basket*) contains data on eight professional basketball players. Perform a regression analysis of the relation between player height and number of rebounds.

Table 9.4
Data on Eight Basketball Players, 1986–1987 Season

Player	Height in inches	Season rebounds	Season points	Minutes played
Willis	84	704	1,010	2,300
Bird	81	805	2,115	3,113
Walton	83	544	606	1,546
Leavell	73	67	583	1,190
Lee	82	351	431	1,197
Brewer	76	53	211	570
Sampson	88	781	1,597	2,467
Reid	80	301	986	2,157

File: *basket*

a.   Construct and label a scatterplot of rebounds (*y*) versus height (*x*). Draw a regression line, and describe what it shows.
b.   Write out the regression equation. Interpret its *y*-intercept and slope. Does the intercept make real-world sense?
c.   List the eight players' height, rebounds, $\hat{y}$, and *e* values. Show how $\hat{y}$ and *e* are calculated for Larry Bird and Bill Walton, and explain what these two residuals mean.
d.   Construct and label a residual versus predicted plot for this analysis.

9.2.2   Analyze the relation between points scored (as *y* variable) and minutes played (as *x*), among the eight basketball players of Table 9.4.
a.   Construct a scatterplot with regression line.
b.   Write out the regression equation, and interpret its *y*-intercept and slope.

    c.   Find predicted values and residuals. Which player has the largest negative residual, and why?

    d.   Construct and label a residual versus predicted plot for this analysis. Do you see any systematic trends among the residuals?

9.2.3   The regression of homicide on population (Exercise 9.1.1) involves two apparent outliers, Milwaukee and Dallas. How much did these two cities influence your conclusion that homicide rates increase with population? To explore this question, compare the graphs and equations from two regressions: one with all 20 cities, the other using only the 18 smaller cities. What does, and does not, change when we set aside the outliers?

9.3 Correlation and R^2

A correlation coefficient measures the strength of a relation between two variables. In a regression context, this amounts to asking "How well does the best-fitting line fit?" Pearson correlation, defined in the box, reflects the closeness of fit between OLS line and data. Just as OLS is the most common regression method, Pearson correlation is the most common correlation, so the word "correlation" by itself usually refers to Pearson correlation. Pearson correlations vary from -1 to $+1$, with -1 indicating a perfect negative relation (all data points lie on a line with negative slope) and $+1$ a perfect positive relation (all points lie on a line with positive slope). A correlation of 0 indicates no linear relation.

Pearson correlation between *y* and *x*

The Pearson correlation (r) between y and x measures how well an ordinary least squares regression line fits the data:

$$r = \frac{\Sigma(x_i - \bar{x})(y_i - \bar{y})}{\sqrt{\Sigma(x_i - \bar{x})^2}\,\sqrt{\Sigma(y_i - \bar{y})^2}} \qquad (9.7)$$

Values of r fall in the range $-1 \le r \le +1$.

    Figure 9.5 illustrates the meaning of correlation graphically, using nine scatterplots of artificial data. At upper left, all points lie on the regression line, so $r = +1$. As the data become more scattered around the regression line, r decreases toward 0. When there exists no linear relation between the two variables, $r = 0$ (center right plot in

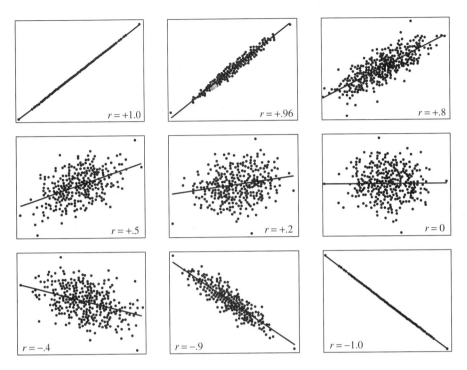

FIGURE 9.5
Nine scatterplots illustrating the meaning of Pearson correlation (artificial data)

Figure 9.5). The regression line is horizontal, with data scattered randomly above and below. A regresssion line sloping down to the right implies a negative correlation. The closer the scatter around a negative-slope line, the nearer this correlation comes to -1. Finally, if all data points lie on a line sloping down to the right, then $r = -1$ (bottom right).

Table 9.5 (page318) offers guidelines for talking about correlations. We might call a correlation of $r = .8$ or higher a "strong positive relation," and so on. Refer to Figure 9.5 to see visually what these adjectives "strong," "moderate," or "weak" imply. The correlation between homicide and poverty rates in Figure 9.2 is moderate and positive: $r = .5044$. Note that correlations refer only to linear (straight-line) relations.

Chapter 8 introduced the **coefficient of determination** or R^2 statistic, which tells what proportion of y's variance can be explained by x. The box (page 318) defines R^2 for regression analysis. In the simple case of two-variable (y and x) regression, R^2 equals the square of the Pearson correlation coefficient. Table 9.5 lists R^2 values at right; a correlation of $r = .8$ corresponds to $R^2 = r^2 = .8^2 = .64$, and so on. For the homicide-poverty regression, $R^2 = .5044^2 = .2544$. Thus about 25% of the variance in the 20 cities' homicide rates is explained by their poverty rates. The remaining 75% must be explained by variables other than poverty rates.

Table 9.5
Guidelines for interpreting Pearson correlation
and coefficient of determination

Correlation coefficient	Interpretation	Coefficient of determination
r		R^2
1.0	Perfect positive linear relation	1.00
.8	Strong positive linear relation	.64
.5	Moderate positive linear relation	.25
.2	Weak positive linear relation	.04
.0	No linear relation	.00
−.2	Weak negative linear relation	.04
−.5	Moderate negative linear relation	.25
−.8	Strong negative linear relation	.64
−1.0	Perfect negative linear relation	1.00

Coefficient of determination (R^2)

The coefficient of determination or R^2 statistic in regression is defined as the ratio of the model's explained variance (variance of $\hat{y}$) to the total variance of y:

$$R^2 = \frac{s_{\hat{y}}^2}{s_y^2} \tag{9.8a}$$

Values of R^2 fall in the range $0 \le R^2 \le 1$. Interpret R^2 as "the proportion of the variance of y explained by x."

Equivalently, we could define R^2 as the ratio of two sums of squares:

$$R^2 = \frac{SS_M}{SS_T} \tag{9.8b}$$

where SS_M represents the model sum of squares, or variation of predicted y around the mean y

$$SS_M = \Sigma(\hat{y}_i - \bar{y})^2 \tag{9.9}$$

and SS_T represents the total sum of squares, or variation of actual y values around the mean y,

$$SS_T = \Sigma(y_i - \bar{y})^2 \tag{9.10}$$

At right is the corresponding regression performed after we have transformed both variables to ranks. The right-hand plot depicts the relation summarized by the Spearman correlation $r_S = .7509$. Rank transformations eliminate outliers, so Dallas (vertically, the highest data point in both scatterplots) neither appears so exceptional, nor exerts so much influence on the regression, in the rank-based plot. With Dallas "pulled in" by the rank transformation, the data cluster more closely around the regression line. That is why the Spearman correlation reports a closer fit, $r_S = .7509$, compared with the Pearson correlation, $r = .5044$.

EXERCISES

9.3.1 Find Pearson correlations among the four basketball-player variables of Table 9.4 (file *basket*). Which pair of variables has the strongest linear relation? Which has the weakest? Can you explain why the second correlation is weaker, based on what you know about basketball?

9.3.2 All of the correlations in Exercise 9.3.1 happen to be positive.
   a. Suggest two additional variables, not in Table 9.4, that also describe attributes of professional basketball players and that might correlate negatively with the variables in Table 9.4. Explain your reasoning.
   b. Suggest two additional variables that might have near-zero correlations with the variables in Table 9.4. Explain your reasoning.

9.3.3 Calculate the Spearman rank correlation between basketball players' height and rebounds. Refer to a scatterplot to explain any difference you see between Pearson and Spearman correlation.

9.4 Confidence Intervals

A variety of confidence-interval and hypothesis-test procedures accompany regression analysis. The validity of these procedures depends on a set of assumptions, detailed in the box. Briefly, we assume that the scatter of data follows identical normal distributions, centered around the regression line, at every value of x. A shorthand term for this set of assumptions is "normal i.i.d. errors." We made essentially the same set of assumptions regarding the t tests and ANOVA of Chapter 8. Figure 9.7 (page 322) illustrates regression's normal i.i.d. errors assumptions graphically. The corresponding ANOVA assumptions appeared in Figure 8.4.

These are strong assumptions, seldom well justified in social research. To a greater or lesser degree, they are often false. To assess whether serious violations exist, the box (page 322) also suggests simple "plausibility checks" for each assumption. Serious violations of the assumption of normal i.i.d. errors render regression's usual confidence intervals and tests untrustworthy.

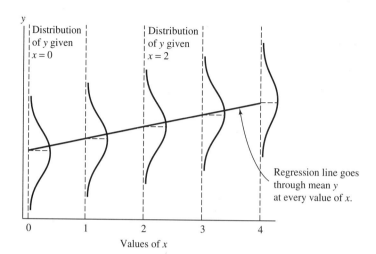

FIGURE 9.7
OLS regression assumes that errors, or variations around the regression line, follow normal, independent and identical distributions at every value of *x*.

Normal, independent, and identically distributed errors

The usual confidence-interval and hypothesis-test procedures for ordinary least squares regression assume that *errors follow normal, independent, and identical distributions* (abbreviated as **normal i.i.d.**). Taking this assumption one piece at a time:

Errors
Errors represent the combined influence of everything else, besides the *x* variable(s) in the regression equation, that causes variation in *y*. Sample residuals reflect these errors, so residual analysis plays a key role in checking the plausibility of our assumptions about errors.

Normal
The population distribution of *y* is normal and centered on the regression line, at every value of *x*. *A plausibility check:* Does the distribution of residuals look approximately normal?

Independent
Errors are independent of each other. This should be approximately true when cases are sampled randomly from a large population. It may not hold true for cases related in time or space, such as crime rates for a series of years or unemployment rates of neighboring states. *Plausibility check:* Does a graph of residuals versus case number (case 1, case 2, case 3, . . . , case *n*) show any clear trends

in positive and negative residuals, or do they appear randomly scattered as independence implies?

·   *Identical*   Error distributions have the same variance for every value of *x*. *Plausibility check*: Do residuals exhibit similar spread around the regression line at all values of *x*?

Regression texts provide fuller statements of these assumptions, their statistical consequences, and more elaborate plausibility tests [see, for example, Hamilton (1992); Hanushek and Jackson (1977)].

Standard errors estimate the amount of sample-to-sample variation in a statistic. Earlier chapters introduced standard errors for means and other elementary statistics. Regression analysis involves several different statistics—notably the *y*-intercept, slope, and predicted *y*. Each has its own standard error, used to form confidence intervals and perform certain tests. The box gives equations for estimating standard errors in two-variable regression.

Estimating standard errors for bivariate regression analysis

Standard deviation of the residuals, e:

$$s_e = \sqrt{\frac{SS_R}{df_R}} \qquad\qquad (9.14)$$

The standard deviation of the residuals measures spread around the regression line.

Standard error of the slope, b:

$$s_b = \frac{s_e}{\sqrt{\Sigma(x_i - \bar{x})^2}} \qquad\qquad (9.15)$$

The standard error of the slope estimates the degree of sample-to-sample variation, if regression slopes were calculated from many random samples of size *n*. A small standard error implies a higher likelihood that most of the sample slopes would be near the true population slope. Note that, according to equation (9.15), this sample-to-sample variation: (1) becomes larger when there is more variation around the regression line (s_e is large); and (2) becomes smaller when there is more variation in *x* [the sum of squared deviations around $\bar{x}$, $\Sigma(x_i - \bar{x})^2$, is large].

Standard error of the y-intercept, a:

$$s_a = s_e \sqrt{\frac{1}{n} + \frac{\bar{x}^2}{\Sigma(x_i - \bar{x})^2}} \qquad\qquad (9.16)$$

(*continued*)

Standard error of the prediction, ŷ:

$$S_\mu = S_e \sqrt{\frac{1}{n} + \frac{(x_0 - \bar{x})^2}{\Sigma(x_i - \bar{x})^2}}$$ (9.17)

More formally, equation (9.17) is the standard error for an estimated conditional mean of y, μ_0, given x equal to some specific value x_0. We use a different standard error for the less common purpose of individual-case (rather than conditional mean) prediction:

$$S_{\hat{y}_0} = S_e \sqrt{\frac{1}{n} + \frac{(x_0 - \bar{x})^2}{\Sigma(x_i - \bar{x})^2} + 1}$$ (9.18)

Confidence interval for a regression coefficient

Assuming normal i.i.d. errors, we form confidence intervals for an individual regression coefficient by

$$b \pm ts_b$$ (9.19)

where b is the sample regression coefficient, s_b is its estimated standard error [equation (9.15)], and we choose t from a theoretical t distribution with

$$df_R = n - \text{number of } x \text{ variables} - 1$$

degrees of freedom to obtain the desired degree of confidence.

We can form confidence intervals around a regression slope, intercept, or predicted y by using the theoretical t distribution and an appropriate standard error. For example, Table 9.2 lists the slope $b = .944$, and its standard error $s_b = .381$ (in the "Std. Error" column right of b). For 95% confidence interval with $20 - 2 = 18$ degrees of freedom, Table A.4 gives $t = 2.101$. Placing these numbers into equation (9.19) yields

$$.944 \pm 2.101(.381)$$

or

$$.944 \pm .800$$

In other words, based on this sample we have 95% confidence that the true population slope, which we denote by the Greek letter β (beta), lies within the interval

$$.144 < \beta < 1.744$$

The output in Table 9.2 shows this interval at far right, and below it a similarly constructed confidence interval around the population y-intercept, denoted by α (alpha):

$$-7.841 < \alpha < 6.210$$

Confidence intervals constructed in this fashion should, over the long run, contain the true population parameters about 95% of the time, *if* errors really are normal i.i.d.

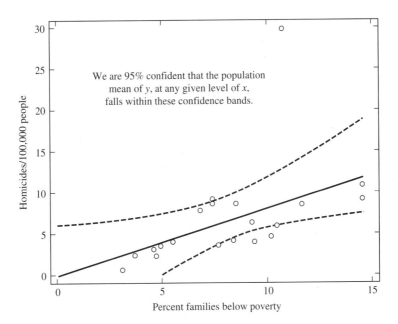

FIGURE 9.8
Regression of homicide rate on poverty rate, with 95% confidence bands
for the conditional mean homicide rate

Confidence intervals around $\hat{y}$ derive from a similar formula:

$$\hat{y} \pm ts_\mu$$

with s_μ obtained by equation (9.17). Such intervals do not appear in tables like Table 9.2 because the standard error s_μ, and hence also the intervals' width, depends on the specific value of x. Graphs of prediction confidence intervals exhibit an hourglass form, narrowest where $x = \bar{x}$. This shape reflects sample-to-sample variation in both a and b. Figure 9.8 illustrates with a 95% confidence interval for conditional mean homicide rates.

Based on this sample, we are 95% confident that the true conditional mean homicide rate, at any given level of poverty, lies within the bands shown. More formally, over repeated sampling about 95% of the bands constructed in this manner should contain the true conditional mean. Note that this does *not* imply 95% confidence for predicting that the homicide rate of any one particular city will fall within the bands. Confidence intervals for individual-case predictions must be wider [based on equation (9.18) instead of (9.17)].

EXERCISES

9.4.1   Write out and interpret 95% confidence intervals for the slopes in the following regressions:
  a.   urban homicide rates on population (Table 9.1, file *urban*)
  b.   basketball players' rebounds on height (Table 9.4, file *basket*)
  c.   basketball players' points on minutes (Table 9.4, file *basket*)

9.4.2 Construct scatterplots with regression lines and 95% confidence bands for the three regressions of Exercise 9.4.1.

9.4.3. Return to the airliner smoking data of Table 3.5 (file *smoke*), and regress the number of cigarettes smoked (y) on the number of people smoking (x).

    a. Write out the regression equation, interpreting values of a, b, and R^2.

    b. Write out and interpret the 95% confidence interval based on b.

    c. Draw a scatterplot with regression line and 95% confidence bands around predicted y.

    d. Which flight had the largest positive residual? Which flight had the largest negative residual? Illustrate the calculation of residual and predicted y for these two flights.

9.5   **Hypothesis Tests**

Regression tables typically print two types of hypothesis test:

    individual coefficient t tests, one for each individual regression coefficient (a or b)

    overall F tests, a single test covering all of the slope (b) coefficients in the model

When the model has only one x variable, and hence only one b coefficient, the overall F test and the t test of b are equivalent and yield identical probabilities. These tests, like the confidence-interval methods described earlier, rest on the assumption of normal i.i.d. errors.

---

t test for an individual regression coefficient

To test the null hypothesis that an individual population regression coefficient equals 0,

$$H_0: \beta = 0$$

obtain the t statistic

$$t = \frac{b}{s_b} \qquad\qquad\qquad (9.20)$$

where b is the sample regression coefficient and s_b its estimated standard error.

    Equation (9.20) measures how far the sample regression coefficient b is from the hypothesized population parameter (if H_0 were true, then $\beta = 0$), in estimated standard errors. Statistical theory shows that, *if H_0 is true* (and normal i.i.d. errors can be assumed), this t statistic follows a theoretical t distribution with df_R

(continued)

degrees of freedom. A large t value (large distance between b and 0) implies a low probability, allowing us to reject H_0: $\beta = 0$, and conclude instead that in the population β does not equal 0:

H_1: $\beta \neq 0$

Computer programs routinely print two-tail test results. One-tail tests are warranted instead if we began with a directional research hypothesis such as

H_1: $\beta > 0$

or

H_1: $\beta < 0$

To obtain a one-tail t test, divide a regression table's two-tail probability in half.

The homicide regression of Table 9.2 gives $b = .944$ and $s_b = .381$, so b's t statistic (listed to the right of the standard error) is

$$t = \frac{.944}{.381}$$

$$= 2.478$$

Looking this t value up in Table A.4, with $n - 2 = 18$ degrees of freedom, we obtain $P < .05$. The computer output lists a more precise value, $P = .023$. Either way, we can reject the null hypothesis that in the population of all U.S. cities, the slope relating poverty to homicide equals 0.

Earlier we considered the 95% confidence interval around b:

$$.144 < \beta < 1.744$$

This interval does not include 0. *If the 95% confidence interval around a regression coefficient does not include 0, then at the .05 significance level a two-tailed t test will reject the null hypothesis that the regression coefficient equals 0.* In this respect confidence intervals and t tests provide overlapping information, and we did not really need the t test.

Confidence intervals and t tests for y-intercepts follow formulas similar to those for slopes. We noted that y-intercepts often have no real-world interpretation, however. For this reason the y-intercept intervals and tests receive less attention in most research.

Overall F test for all coefficients in a regression analysis

To test the null hypothesis that all β (population slope) coefficients in a regression equation equal 0, obtain an F statistic:

$$F = \frac{SS_M/df_M}{SS_R/df_R}$$

(9.21)

(*continued*)

where SS_M and df_M are model sum of squares and degrees of freedom [equations (9.9) and (9.12)]; SS_R and df_R are residual sum of squares and degrees of freedom [equations (9.6) and (9.13)]. Assuming normal i.i.d. errors, under a true null hypothesis, this F statistic follows an F distribution with df_M and df_R degrees of freedom. A low enough P-value (for example, $P < .05$) indicates that we can reject the null hypothesis that all $\beta = 0$.

If the analysis involves only one x variable, then this overall F test is equivalent to a two-tailed t test [equation (9.20)] of that variable's coefficient.

Table 9.2 shows overall F test results among the statistics at upper right. This test, calculated from the sums of squares in the upper left subtable, yields exactly the same probability as the t test of b: $P = .023$. With one x variable, both tests evaluate the same null hypothesis. They become different in multiple regression, which includes more than one x variable.

Table 9.6 repeats the regression output of Table 9.2, this time with a full set of footnotes explaining the 27 numbers it contains. At bottom, Table 9.6 includes a brief summary interpreting the results from this regression analysis.

Table 9.6
An example regression output table with definitions, showing the regression of homicide rate (*homic*) on percent families below poverty (*poor*), using the data of Table 9.1

Source	SS	df	MS
Model	181.37[a]	1[d]	181.37[g]
Residual	531.57[b]	18[e]	29.53[h]
Total	712.94[c]	19[f]	37.52[i]

Number of obs. = 20[j]
$F(1, 18) = 6.14$[k]
Prob > F = .023[l]
R-square = .254[m]
Adj. R-square = .213[n]
Root MSE = 5.434[o]

homic	Coef.	Std. Err.	t	P > |t|	[95% Conf. Interval]	
poor	.944[p]	.381[r]	2.478[t]	.023[v]	.144[x]	1.744[z]
_cons	−.815[q]	3.344[s]	−.244[u]	.810[w]	−7.841[y]	6.210[aa]

[a] Model sum of squares, $SS_M = \Sigma(\hat{y}_i - \bar{y})^2$
[b] Residual sum of squares, $SS_R = \Sigma(y_i - \hat{y}_i)^2 = \Sigma e_i^2$
[c] Total sum of squares, $SS_T = \Sigma(y_i - \bar{y})^2$
[d] Model degrees of freedom, df_M = number of x variables
[e] Residual degrees of freedom, $df_R = n - df_M - 1$
[f] Total degrees of freedom, $df_T = n - 1$
[g] Model mean square, $MS_M = SS_M/df_M$
[h] Residual mean square, $MS_R = SS_R/df_R$
[i] Total mean square, $MS_T = SS_T/df_T$ = variance of y

[i]Number of observations or cases, n

[k]Overall F statistic testing null hypothesis that all slopes in the model equal 0, $F = MS_M/MS_R$

[l]Probability of a greater overall F statistic; in this example we can reject the hypothesis that all slopes equal 0 ($P = .0233$)

[m]Coefficient of determination, $R^2 = SS_M/SS_T$

[n]R^2 adjusted for degrees of freedom, $R_a^2 = R^2 - (df_M/df_R)(1 - R^2)$

[o]Residual standard deviation, $s_e = \sqrt{MS_R}$

[p]Slope or regression coefficient b; see equation (9.2)

[q]y-intercept or regression constant a; see equation (9.3)

[r]Estimated standard error of b, s_b; see equation (9.15)

[s]Estimated standard error of a, s_a; see equation (9.16)

[t]t statistic testing whether the slope b differs significantly from 0; $t = b/s_b$

[u]t statistic testing whether the y-intercept a differs significantly from 0; $t = a/s_a$

[v]This t statistic indicates that b significantly differs from 0 ($P = .023$)

[w]This t statistic indicates that a does not significantly differ from 0 ($P = .810$)

[x]Lower limit of a 95% confidence interval for the population slope

[y]Lower limit of a 95% confidence interval for the population y-intercept

[z]Upper limit of a 95% confidence interval for the population slope β; based on this sample we are 95% confident that $.144 < \beta < 1.744$

[aa]Upper limit of a 95% confidence interval for the population y-intercept α; based on this sample we are 95% confident that $-7.841 < \alpha < 6.210$

Interpretation: This table shows the regression of *homic* on *poor*. The regression equation is

predicted *homic* $= -.815 + .944poor$

The coefficient on *poor*, .944, is significant at the .05 level ($P = .023$); *poor* explains about 25.4% of the variance in homicide rates, or 21.3% adjusting for degrees of freedom. We are 95% confident that, with each 1-unit increase in *poor* (that is, with each percentage point increase in families below poverty), the mean homicide rate rises by .144 to 1.744 homicides per 100,000 people.

What We Learn from Simple (Bivariate) Regression

Describing Sample Data

The regression equation summarizes the linear relation in this sample between two measurement variables: x, called the independent, predictor, or cause variable; and y, called the dependent, predicted, or effect variable. Graphically, the regression equation corresponds to that line which best fits the two-variable scatterplot. We could use this equation to calculate the mean or predicted value of y ($\hat{y}$) at any particular value of x. Sample residuals ($e_i = y_i - \hat{y}_i$) indicate to what extent each case does or does not fit the general pattern of the data. The slope tells us how much the mean y changes—increasing if the slope is positive, decreasing if it is negative—with each 1-unit increase in x. R^2 indicates the proportion of y's variance that is explained by x. Correlation provides a standardized measure of how well our regression line fits (perfectly if $r = -1$ or $r = +1$).

Inferences about Population

Based on this sample (assuming it is a random sample), can we reject the hypothesis that in the population x and y have no linear relation at all? A statistically significant (e.g., $P < .05$) result from a t test on the regression slope indicates that the answer is yes. We thereby indirectly conclude that some linear relation does exist in the population. On the other hand, if the *t* test result is nonsignificant, we cannot draw this conclusion.

We can also construct confidence intervals to indicate our estimate of the population regression slope, or of the true population mean of *y* given a particular *x* value.

EXERCISES

9.5.1   Table 2.9 (file *islands*) in Chapter 2 introduced data on the relation between island land area and biodiversity. Table 9.7 displays results from regressing number of bird genera (*birds*) on area in square kilometers (*area*). Write an interpretation of these results, similar to the interpretation given at the bottom of Table 9.6.

Table 9.7
Regression of number of bird genera (*birds*) on island area in square kilometers (*area*), for eight Pacific island groups (based on data of Table 2.9)

Source	SS	df	MS	
				Number of obs. = 8
				$F(1, 6) = 162.96$
Model	9,669.83	1	9,669.83	Prob > F = .0000
Residual	356.04	6	59.34	R-square = .9645
				Adj. R-square = .9586
Total	10,025.87	7	1,432.27	Root MSE = 7.7033

birds	Coef.	Std. Err.	t	P > |t|	[95% Conf. Interval]	
area	.0027	.0002	12.8	.000	.0021	.0032
_cons	13.9717	3.7905	3.7	.010	4.6968	23.2466

Source: Cox (1993).
File: *islands*

9.5.2   Below is a regression in which the cases are 226 college faculty members. Variables are

pay   salary in thousands of dollars
rank   a three-point scale with 1 = "assistant professor," 2 = "associate professor," and 3 = "professor"

Fill in the blanks of this table, adding footnotes to explain your calculations.

Source	SS	df	MS	Number of obs. = 226
				$F(1, 224) = $ _____
Model	15,211.08	_____	_____	Prob > F = _____
Residual	6,089.40	_____	_____	R-square = _____
				Adj. R-square = _____
Total	_____	_____	_____	Root MSE = _____

pay	Coef.	Std. Err.	t	$P > \|t\|$	[95% Conf. Interval]
rank	11.222	.474	_____	_____	_____ _____
_cons	16.960	.996	_____	_____	_____ _____

9.5.3   Write an interpretation of the regression in Exercise 9.5.2 similar to the one given in Table 9.6.

9.6   Words of Caution

"A little knowledge can be a dangerous thing," commented one reviewer who saw an earlier draft of this book. He worried that students, having read a brief introduction to regression analysis, might proceed to use the technique without understanding its limitations. Of course this hazard exists with any statistical method, but regression's popularity for causal research—plus the difficulty of understanding intuitively just what the computer is doing—make it particularly liable to be abused. No first course in statistics can provide more than "a little knowledge," but to lessen the danger, here are a few words of caution.

1. **Simple regression assumes a straight-line relation**.   If a curve best describes the true relation between y and x, then straight-line regression is the wrong approach. Two errors could result: We might mistakenly believe that the true relation is linear; or we might mistakenly believe that no relation exists, just because we found no linear relation.

2. **Outliers can control regression results**.   It is easy to make up artificial datasets demonstrating how even a single outlier can produce huge changes in the regression equation, correlation, R^2, significance tests, and confidence intervals. Like other mean-based, least-squares methods, OLS regression lacks resistance to outliers.

3. **The regression equation summarizes how mean y changes over the range of x values in the data**.   Unless the equation represents some underlying causal law, we should not expect it to provide accurate predictions of y for x values much higher or lower than those in the data.

4. **The "normal i.i.d. errors" assumption could be wrong**. Unlike points 1 and 2, this problem would not detract from regression's usefulness in describing sample data. Normal i.i.d. errors are necessary only for the validity of standard errors, significance tests, and confidence intervals—that is, for our efforts to draw inferences about the population.

5. **Even if those assumptions about errors are true, any inferences we draw regarding a population assume that the sample was selected randomly from that population**. This obvious point often gets overlooked. It applies to all the significance-test and confidence-interval procedures described in this book. Admittedly, researchers often calculate tests and intervals based on nonrandom samples. But if they do, their tests and intervals cannot support generalizations about some real population.

6. **Regression alone cannot prove that *x* causes *y***. A significant regression relation between *x* and *y* is consistent with the idea that *x* causes *y*, but it is consistent with other possibilities as well: that *y* causes *x*, or that *x* and *y* appear related because *z* causes them both. We need further information from theory, research design, and analysis beyond simple regression to make progress in ruling out these other possibilities.

For classes that continue from this point, Chapter 10 addresses ways to work around some of these limitations. Otherwise, do not trust any regression without examining the scatterplot (points 1 and 2); treat "the usual" assumptions with skepticism (point 4); and be realistically modest in stating your wider conclusions (points 3, 4, 5, and 6).

Summary

Simple regression analyzes relations between pairs of measurement variables, by finding the best-fitting line for their scatterplot. The regression line indicates how mean *y* changes with each 1-unit increase in *x*. Other statistics summarize how well the line fits (correlation and R^2) or test whether the population slope might be 0 (*t* test).

Regression equations compactly summarize the data, and also permit calculating a predicted *y* value for any value of *x*. Such predictions are usually wrong to some degree; the magnitude of prediction error is measured by the residual *e*. Residuals show the extent to which any case does not fit the overall pattern of the data. Sometimes the "exceptions to the rule" (cases with large residuals) reveal more interesting things about the data than the rule (regression equation) itself does.

Ordinary least squares regression, like most statistical techniques, depends on assumptions that might not be true. Chapter 10 describes more about regression analysis, including how to incorporate more than two variables, how to diagnose statistical problems, and what else to try when the usual assumptions do not hold.

PROBLEMS

9.1 Table 3.7 (file *skijump*) in Chapter 3 lists distances achieved by 56 competitors in the 90-meter ski jump at the 1994 Winter Olympics. How well does a skier's first jump distance predict his second jump distance?

    a.   Find and interpret the Pearson correlation between first and second distances. Compare this with the Spearman correlation.

    b.   Construct a scatterplot with regression line, using second jump as the *y* variable. Write out the regression equation, and interpret its *y*-intercept and slope.

    c.   Calculate predicted values and residuals. Which skier's second jump was the most disappointing, based on what we might have predicted from his first? Which skier's second jump was most improved over what the regression line predicted?

    d.   Find and interpret the Pearson correlation between skier's place and the combined distance of his first plus second jumps. Why is this correlation negative?

The archaeological data in Table 9.8 describe 10 river valley regions in France, famous for their cave paintings. The authors of this study were interested in whether the prevalence of specific types of animals in the paintings was related to the frequency with which those animals were hunted or caught. They compared, for example, the percentage of mammoths in the caves' art with the percentage of mammoth bones in debris piles near the caves, the latter indicating hunting success. Problems 9.2 and 9.3 refer to these data.

Table 9.8
Paleolithic cave art and animal bone prevalence
in 10 French river valley regions

Region	Mammoth bones %	Mammoth art %	Reindeer bones %	Reindeer art %
1. N. Garonne	4	14	21	4
2. Dronne	2	4	30	0
3. Isle	0	0	42	18
4. Vezere	2	7	34	13
5. Dordogne	0	21	24	3
6. Lot	6	21	19	4
7. Aveyron	0	0	29	0
8. Gers	1	3	28	11

(continued)

Table 9.8 (*Continued*)

Region	Mammoth bones %	Mammoth art %	Reindeer bones %	Reindeer art %
9. S. Garonne	0	3	31	7
10. Ariege	0	0	31	10

Source: Rice and Paterson (1985).
File: *artbone*

9.2 Regress the mammoth art prevalence (*y*) on mammoth bone prevalence.
    a. Write the regression equation and interpret its intercept, slope, and R^2.
    b. Examine a scatterplot with regression line. Do you see any possible problems? What effect might this problem have?
    c. List predicted values and residuals, and show how they were calculated for the regions with the largest positive and largest negative residuals.

9.3 Regress reindeer art prevalence on reindeer bone prevalence, following the steps of Problem 9.2.

9.4 Patricia Rice and Ann Paterson, authors of the French cave art/bones study considered in Problems 9.2 and 9.3, subsequently went on to repeat their analysis using data from Spain. (Testing conclusions derived from one dataset by applying similar methods to a second dataset provides an important scientific "reality check" called **replication**.) Table 9.9 shows an incomplete regression table, with the regression of reindeer art prevalence on reindeer bone prevalence. The cases comprise four Spanish regions having prehistorically inhabited caves.
    a. Fill in the blanks in Table 9.9, adding footnotes to show the formulas you used.
    b. Write out and interpret the regression equation and R^2.
    c. Is the relation statistically significant? Explain how this conclusion illustrates the connection between sample size and statistical significance, described earlier in Section 7.5.

Table 9.9
Regression of reindeer art prevalence (*reinart*) on reindeer bone prevalence (*reinbon*), in four Spanish regions

Source	SS	df	MS	
Model	2.9958	_____	_____	Number of obs. = 4
Residual	5.1955	_____	_____	$F(1, 2)$ = _____
				Prob > F = _____
Total	_____	_____	_____	R-square = _____
				Adj. R-square = _____
				Root MSE = _____

Table 9.9 (*Continued*)

reinart	Coef.	Std. Err.	t	P > |t|	[95% Conf. Interval]	
reinbon	.31966	.298	———	———	———	———
_cons	.75649	1.184	———	———	———	———

Source: Rice and Paterson (1986).

9.5 Complete Table 9.10, by calculating predicted values and residuals using the regression equation of Problem 9.4.

Table 9.10
Reindeer bone prevalence and reindeer art prevalence in caves of two Spanish regions

Region	Reindeer bone prevalence	Reindeer art prevalence	Predicted art	Residual
East	7.26	3.61	———	———
Central	3.07	.67	———	———

Source: Rice and Paterson (1986).

9.6 Table 9.11 contains another incomplete regression table based on the Spanish cave data. This one involves ibex, a long-horned European mountain goat. Fill out and interpret Table 9.11 as you did earlier with Table 9.9.

Table 9.11
Regression of ibex art prevalence (*ibexart*) on ibex bone prevalence (*ibexbon*), in four Spanish regions

Source	SS	df	MS	
Model	2.1470	———	———	Number of obs. = 4
Residual	4.7046	———	———	$F(1, 2)$ = ———
				Prob > F = ———
				R-square = ———
Total	———	———	———	Adj. R-square = ———
				Root MSE = ———

(*continued*)

Table 9.11 (*Continued*)

ibexart	Coef.	Std. Err.	*t*	*P* > |*t*|	[95% Conf. Interval]	
ibexbon	.15598	.163	⎯⎯	⎯⎯	⎯⎯	⎯⎯
_cons	6.66438	3.623	⎯⎯	⎯⎯	⎯⎯	⎯⎯

Source: Rice and Paterson (1986).

9.7 Complete Table 9.12, by calculating predicted values and residuals using the regression equation of Problem 9.6.

Table 9.12
Ibex bone prevalence and ibex art prevalence in caves of two Spanish regions

Region	Ibex bone prevalence	Ibex art prevalence	Predicted art	Residual
West	24.73	11.11	⎯⎯	⎯⎯
Far West	25.25	11.54	⎯⎯	⎯⎯

Source: Rice and Paterson (1986).

Data from a newspaper story on lawsuits at 14 Massachusetts hospitals appear in Table 9.13 (file *suedoc*). These data, the topic of Problems 9.8–9.10, contain several missing values.

Table 9.13
Number of patient admissions (1984), number of beds
(1984), and number of doctors sued, disciplined,
or charged (1983–1986) at 14 Massachusetts hospitals

Hospital	Patient admissions	Number of beds	Number of doctors sued, etc.
1. Ludlow	2,041	.	10
2. Brookline	2,126	98	20
3. Amesbury	2,364	63	14

(*continued*)

Table 9.13 (*Continued*)

Hospital	Patient admissions	Number of beds	Number of doctors sued, etc.
4. North Shore Children's	2,398	50	11
5. Southwood	2,425	.	12
6. J. B. Thomas	2,857	99	16
7. Fairlawn	.	104	15
8. Sancta Maria	3,916	.	18
9. Anna Jacques	.	156	22
10. Milton	.	161	24
11. Cambridge	5,527	182	27
12. Choate Symmes	8,560	.	43
13. Mercy	.	311	49
14. Newton Wellesley	12,129	351	64

Source: *Boston Globe*, June 19, 1986.
File: *suedoc*

9.8 Regress the number of doctors sued, disciplined, or charged on the number of patient admissions.
   a. Write the equation, interpreting intercept, slope, and R^2.
   b. Newton Wellesley, the largest of these hospitals, unsurprisingly also had the most doctors in trouble. Which hospital had the largest positive residual—that is, more doctors in trouble than we predicted based on patient admissions? Which hospital had the largest negative residual?
   c. Show this regression in a scatterplot, and label the two hospitals identified in part **b**.

9.9 Regress the number of patient admissions on the number of beds. Use this equation to calculate predicted patient admissions for each hospital where actual patient admissions are missing. Create and list a new variable equal to actual patient admission or (if actual admission is missing) equal to predicted patient admission. This technique, called "missing value substitution," is another use for regression analysis.

9.10 Regress the number of doctors sued, disciplined, or charged on the new "patient admissions" variable you generated for Problem 9.9. Compare the results of this regression with those from Problem 9.8.

Table 9.14 (page 338; file *dolphin*) lists data on 13 free-ranging bottlenose dolphins. Researchers in Florida had observed these particular dolphins since birth, and so knew their actual ages. The study's purpose was to evaluate a method of estimating wild dolphins' ages from growth layers in their teeth (each dolphin in this study had to sacrifice one or two teeth, but they were otherwise unharmed). Estimated ages in Table 9.14 are based on tooth growth layers. Problems 9.11 and 9.12 refer to these data.

Table 9.14
Thirteen free-ranging bottlenose dolphins

Dolphin	Sex	Length in cm	Age in years	Estimated age in years
1	female	217	2.3	1.6
2	male	192	2.3	2.6
3	female	218	2.5	2.4
4	female	204	2.5	2.2
5	male	214	3.5	3.4
6	female	213	3.0	4.5
7	female	212	3.0	3.8
8	female	213	3.0	2.3
9	male	215	3.9	5.0
10	male	226	4.0	5.2
11	female	226	5.0	3.2
12	male	221	6.0	6.0
13	male	228	7.8	8.0

Source: Hohn et al. (1989).
File: *dolphin*

9.11 Can we predict dolphins' true ages reasonably well based on teeth? Regress age (y) on estimated age (x), and graph the results with a 95% confidence band. Use correlation and R^2 to describe the strength of this relation.

9.12 Analyze the relation between dolphins' lengths and ages.
   a. Obtain scatterplots and correlations for the interrelations among sex, length, age, and estimated age in Table 9.14. (*Optional*: A **scatterplot matrix** combines all six scatterplots into one compact display. Similarly, a **correlation matrix** is a table with all six correlations.) Do true age and estimated age have equally strong correlations with length?
   b. Regress length (y) on true age (x). Interpret the values of slope, y-intercept, and R^2.
   c. Is the slope from part **b** significantly different (at the .05 significance level) from 0? Write out and interpret a 95% confidence interval for this slope.
   d. Construct a scatterplot with regression line, and also a residual versus predicted plot. Do either of these graphs suggest problems with the linear regression model? How could this model be improved or made more realistic?

9.13 Table 9.15 (file *mskate*) lists times of 10 men who skated in both the 500- and 1,000-meter races of the 1994 Winter Olympics. The 500-meter race occurred first, and provided sportscasters with some grounds for speculating about who would do well in the 1,000-meter race. American speed skater Dan Jansen already held the world record at 500 meters and was expected to win that race, but he slipped and finished poorly. After this mishap, the 1,000-meter race presented Jansen's last opportunity to win an Olympic medal.

Table 9.15
Times of 10 speed skaters who completed 500-meter and 1,000-meter races in the 1994 Winter Olympics

Skater	Country	500-meter time in seconds	1,000-meter time in seconds
Sergei Klevchenya	Russia	36.39	72.85
Hongbo Liu	China	36.54	72.85
Junichi Inoue	Japan	36.63	73.75
Dan Jansen	United States	36.68	72.43
Sylvain Bouchard	Canada	37.01	73.56
Patrick Kelly	Canada	37.07	73.67
Peter Adeberg	Germany	37.35	74.15
Gerard Van Velde	Netherlands	37.45	73.81
Roland Brunner	Austria	37.47	74.08
Nico Van Der Vlies	Netherlands	37.94	74.29

File: *mskate*

  a. Regress 1,000-meter race time on 500-meter race time to obtain a prediction equation.
  b. Graph the resulting regression line on a scatterplot. Attach names of individual skaters to each point on this plot.
  c. Calculate predicted values and residuals. Identify the skaters with the largest positive and negative residuals. In this context, what does a large positive or a large negative residual tell us?

Education statistics provide a rich field for statistical analysis, as attested by many of the examples in this book. Table 9.16 (page 340; file *tpass*) lists another such example, which includes mean high school achievement tests (ACT) for students in six U.S. states. The second measurement variable comes from tests given not to students, but to teachers. Such tests reflect a movement to ensure that teachers meet minimum competency standards. Rudner (1987) writes about teacher examinations:

Given that the tests are not difficult and that the passing scores appear to be relatively low, one would expect virtually everyone to pass teacher examinations. Yet, this is not the case.

Problems 9.14–9.16 explore these data.

Table 9.16
Mean high school achievement tests (ACT) and percentage of teachers passing the national teacher examinations (NTE) in six U.S. states, 1986

State	Mean student ACT	Percentage of teachers passing NTE
Kansas	19.2	94
Kentucky	17.9	93
Louisiana	16.6	87
Mississippi	15.6	88
Montana	19.4	92
New Mexico	17.6	88

Source: NTE passing rates from Rudner (1987).
File: *tpass*

9.14   Regress mean student ACT score on percentage of teachers passing the NTE. Construct a scatterplot showing data and regression line, and interpret
   a.   correlation coefficient
   b.   regression equation
   c. R^2
   d.   *t* test of $H_0 : \beta = 0$ (Since $n = 6$ is a very small sample, use .10 instead of the usual .05 cutoff for deciding statistical significance.)

9.15   List predicted values and residuals from the regression of Problem 9.14. Interpret and show the calculation of these statistics for the two states that have the highest (positive) and lowest (negative) residuals. Construct a plot of residuals versus predicted values and label each state.

9.16   Write a brief essay discussing this question: Does the statistically significant relation seen in Problem 9.14 convince you that more competent teachers (as indicated by higher percentages passing the NTE) cause better student performance (as indicated by mean ACT scores)? Why or why not?

Academic researchers publish their work in scholarly journals. Each discipline offers many different journals, which vary widely in prestige and importance. Table 9.17 (file *journals*) contains data on 61 journals of interest to sociologists. Variables are the journal's prestige score (a subjective rating by other sociologists), and a more objective measure indicating how much impact the articles in that journal have. Impact scores equal the number of citations (mentions in other research) received by articles in a journal, divided by the number of citable articles that journal published. High-impact articles are those cited more often in other research articles. Some journals average less than one citation per 10 articles, suggesting that they have little impact on other researchers. Problems 9.17–9.20 examine these data.

Table 9.17
Prestige and impact of 61 journals in sociology

Journal	Prestige	Impact
Acta Sociologica	6.1	.174
Administrative Science Quarterly	6.7	2.293
American Anthropologist	7.7	1.815
American Behavioral Scientist	6.6	.483
American Economic R.	7.1	1.552
American J. of Economics & Sociology	5.3	.237
American J. of Sociology	9.6	2.034
American Political Science R.	7.5	1.973
American Sociological R.	10.0	3.367
American Sociologist	6.2	.740
Annals Am. Academy Political & Social Science	7.2	.425
Behavioral Science	6.8	.587
British J. of Criminology	5.3	.394
British J. of Sociology	7.8	.535
Canadian R. of Sociology & Anthropology	6.4	.233
Crime & Delinquency	5.2	.831
Current Sociology	6.4	.095
Daedalus	6.5	.958
Demography	7.4	1.133
European J. of Sociology	6.9	.435
Federal Probation	3.8	.326
Gerontologist	5.3	.877
Harvard Educational R.	6.4	2.816
Human Organization	6.7	.436
Human Relations	6.5	.519
International J. of Comparative Sociology	6.7	.171
International Social Science J.	6.3	.230
J. of Conflict Resolution	6.2	.638

(*continued*)

Table 9.17 (*Continued*)

Journal	Prestige	Impact
J. of Crime Law, Criminology & Police Science	5.1	1.921
J. of Gerontology	5.4	1.316
J. of Health & Social Research	6.2	1.602
J. of Marriage & the Family	6.2	.988
J. of Negro Education	4.5	.076
J. of Personality & Social Psychology	7.1	2.390
J. of Research in Crime & Delinquency	5.4	.735
J. of Social Issues	6.6	1.031
J. of Social Psychology	6.7	.283
Jewish J. of Sociology	4.9	.288
Law & Society R.	5.7	1.760
Milbank Memorial Fund Quarterly	6.7	1.192
New Society	4.5	.065
Phylon	5.0	.098
Population Studies	6.5	1.017
Public Opinion Quarterly	7.1	.851
Rural Sociology	6.7	.798
Science & Society	5.2	.309
Social Biology	5.0	.571
Social Forces	8.1	.971
Social Problems	7.6	1.041
Social Psychology Quarterly	7.8	.944
Social Research	6.6	.395
Social Science Quarterly	6.0	.479
Society	5.7	.198
Sociological Analysis	5.7	.197
Sociological Inquiry	5.8	.187
Sociological Perspectives	5.7	.222
Sociological Quarterly	6.1	.221
Sociological R.	6.3	.244
Sociology	5.9	.694
Sociology & Social Research	5.9	.103
Sociology of Education	6.1	.403

Source: Christenson and Sigelman (1985).
File: *journals*

9.17 Obtain histograms and detailed univariate statistics (means, medians, standard deviations, skewness, etc.) of each of the two variables, prestige and impact, in Table 9.17. Describe these distributions.

9.18   Christenson and Sigelman, who assembled the data in Table 9.17, were interested
in how closely the prestige of social science journals matched the actual impact or importance of their articles. Find out for yourself by regressing prestige (y) on impact (x).
Write out the regression equation, and draw a scatterplot with regression line and confidence bands. What proportion of the variance in prestige can be explained by actual
impact? What proportion is apparently explained by other factors?

9.19   Construct a plot of residual versus predicted values for the regression of journal
prestige on impact. Use this plot and your scatterplot from Problem 9.18 to identify
some journals that appear to be particularly "underrated": Their subjective prestige is
lower than we might expect, given their actual impact. Similarly, identify some journals
that appear "overrated": Their subjective prestige is higher than predicted, given their
actual impact.

9.20   Obtain the Pearson correlation between journal prestige and impact. What does
this correlation tell us? Since the impact distribution is obviously nonnormal, we might
also consult the rank-based Spearman correlation, which is less sensitive to outliers.
Does the Spearman correlation lead to the same general conclusion about the strength
of relation between prestige and impact?

9.21   Construct your own artificial dataset consisting of 10 cases, and four variables w,
x, y, and z, such that:
- a.   the Pearson correlation between w and x equals 0 (obtain computer output
  showing the actual correlation to demonstrate that this is true)
- b.   the correlation between w and y equals 1, and the regression equation is
  $\hat{y} = 10 + 2w$ (demonstrate)
- c.   the correlation between w and z equals -1 (demonstrate)

9.22   If one variable derives from another by some linear law, as in physics or taxation,
regression can help us learn what that law is. For example, property taxes may be a
linear function of how much the property is worth. Below are property values and
amount of tax owed by five property owners in the town of Newmarket, New Hampshire.
Use the regression of taxes on value to find out what Newmarket's tax rate is, and state
this as . . . dollars per $1,000 worth of property. How much of the variance in taxes does
property value explain?

Owner	Value in $	Taxes in $
1	600	1.54
2	27,200	70.04
3	230,400	593.28
4	68,800	177.16
5	113,500	292.26

Table 9.18 (page 344; file *realtor*) contains data from a study of ethnicity and real
estate practices in 27 neighborhoods around Denver, Colorado. For each neighborhood,
the author, Risa Palm (1986), collected data on the percentage of Anglo (white,

non-Hispanic) real estate agents who list properties in that neighborhood, and the percentage of the neighborhood's residents who are Anglo themselves. Similarly, we know the percentage of black real estate agents with listings in that area, and the percentage of black residents. Do real estate agents tend to concentrate their business in neighborhoods dominated by their own ethnic groups? Problems 9.23–9.27 investigate this question.

Table 9.18
Ethnicity and real estate listings in 27 Denver-area neighborhoods

Neighborhood	% Anglo agents listing	% Anglo residents	% Black agents listing	% Black residents
Aurora	36	88.1	51.1	6.9
Arvada	34	82.0	4.4	0
Barnum	24	55.5	0	1.2
Cherry Creek	12	98.6	6.7	1.3
City Park	10	47.2	46.7	49.9
College	12	62.1	8.9	2.6
Commerce	12	72.6	0	.1
Curtis	6	19.5	13.3	39.5
Englewood	26	93.5	0	0
Federal	10	91.7	4.4	0
Greenwood	18	98.9	0	0
Hampden	12	91.3	2.2	5.5
Highland	10	37.5	0	.7
Lakewood	36	94.1	6.7	0
Littleton	28	95.8	4.4	3.8
Montbello	8	40.1	60.0	46.1
Montclair	6	94.4	20.0	5.1
Northglen	22	87.9	13.3	0
Park Hill	4	26.8	64.4	71.8
Sheridan	12	83.1	2.2	0
South Glen	16	96.9	2.2	0
Swansea	4	7.8	8.9	41.6
Thornton	20	85.6	11.1	1.2
University	18	95.5	8.9	1.6
Valverde	10	48.6	2.2	1.1
Westminster	22	86.3	2.2	1.0
Wheat Ridge	34	95.5	2.2	0

Source: Palm (1986).
File: *realtor*

9.23 Obtain correlations and scatterplots showing interrelations between the four measurement variables in Table 9.18. Write a brief essay describing what these reveal about neighborhoods, ethnicity, and realtors in Denver.

9.24 Regress the percentage of Anglo agents listing a neighborhood on the percentage of residents who are Anglo. Graph your results (with confidence bands) and write an interpretation.

9.25 Obtain a residual versus predicted plot from the Anglo realtors/Anglo residents regression of Problem 9.24. This graph shows a strong pattern in the residuals: They fan out, becoming more dispersed around the regression line, from left to right. Such patterns indicate a violation of the "identically distributed" part of the "normal i.i.d. errors" assumption. If this assumption is untrue, how does that affect your interpretation given earlier in Problem 9.24?

9.26 Regress the percentage of black agents listing a neighborhood on the percentage of residents who are black. Graph (with confidence bands) and interpret your results. Compare them with those for Anglo realtors in Problem 9.24.

9.27 Construct a residual versus predicted plot for the black realtor/black residents regression of Problem 9.26. If the "normal i.i.d. errors" assumption were true, we should see no pattern but a random, normally distributed scatter of dots around the regression line. Describe the pattern visible in this particular e versus $\hat{y}$ plot. In what respects is it similar to or different from that in Problem 9.25?

Data on a randomly selected sample of 10 countries appear in Table 9.19 (file *fertile*). The variables are

mschool	percentage of school-age males enrolled in secondary schools
fschool	percentage of school-age females enrolled in secondary schools
fertile	total fertility rate: lifetime number of children expected per female
birth	crude birth rate: live births per 1,000 people per year

Problems 9.28–9.32 refer to these data.

Table 9.19
Secondary school enrollment and crude birth rate
in a sample of 10 countries, 1985

Country	*mschool*	*fschool*	*fertile*	*birth*
Singapore	70	73	1.7	17
New Zealand	84	86	2.1	16
Czechoslovakia	31	54	2.1	15
Austria	73	79	2.1	12

(*continued*)

Table 9.19 (*Continued*)

Country	mschool	fschool	fertile	birth
Zambia	22	12	6.8	49
Chile	63	69	2.5	22
Cameroon	29	18	6.8	47
Saudi Arabia	47	29	7.1	42
Bhutan	6	1	6.2	43
Tanzania	4	2	7.0	50

Source: World Bank (1987).
File: *fertile*

9.28   Obtain histograms, correlations, and scatterplots for the four measurement variables in Table 9.19. Describe what these show.

9.29   Regress birth rate on the percentage of school-age males enrolled in secondary school. Graph the regression with 95% confidence bands for the prediction. Interpret
   a.   the 95% confidence interval for the slope
   b.   the 95% confidence interval for the *y*-intercept
   c.   the 95% confidence bands (graphed) for the prediction

9.30   Regress *birth* on *fschool*. How do results from this regression compare with those in Problem 9.29?

9.31   Regress fertility rate on birth rate, and fully interpret the numerical and graphical results.

9.32   Construct a residuals versus predicted plot for the fertility/birth regression of Problem 9.31. What pattern, if any, do you see?

10

More about
Regression

C hapter 9 introduced regression in its simplest, "ideal" form. Research, however, often seeks answers to questions that are not simple. Furthermore, data may be messy and far from ideal, so the usual assumptions of regression (or other elementary techniques) look implausible. Regression remains a practical research tool nonetheless, because of extensions that allow it to cope with a wide variety of common problems. This chapter introduces a few of these extensions: troubleshooting, multiple regression, robust regression, and nonlinear transformations.

Regression troubleshooting is a diagnostic process through which we check for certain things that go wrong with regression analysis. Section 9.4 noted regression's usual assumptions, abbreviated as *normal i.i.d. errors*. Can we believe each of these assumptions? Statisticians have devoted much thought to techniques for answering that question. Most such techniques lie beyond the scope of this book, but a few are straightforward.

Multiple regression broadens the regression model to include any number of x variables. For example, Chapter 9 examined the relation between urban homicide and poverty rates. In the present chapter we elaborate on that analysis by considering both poverty rate and city population as predictors of homicide. Multiple regression can include any number (theoretically, up to $n - 1$) of x variables. These x variables could include not only measurement variables, but also categorical information in a special form called **dummy variables**.

Chapters 6 and 8 presented mean-based methods (such as t tests or ANOVA), then suggested nonparametric alternatives (such as sign tests or Kruskal–Wallis) for when outliers or other problems render the mean-based methods untrustworthy. Ordinary least squares (OLS) regression is also a mean-based method, and it shares that family's lack of resistance to outliers. Nonparametric methods, however, do not easily extend to complicated research questions like those addressed by multiple regression. For an outlier-resistant alternative to OLS regression, researchers turn to **robust regression** techniques.

Finally, our discussion to this point assumes that the analyst wants to fit a linear model to the data. Linear models are easy but not always realistic. **Nonlinear transformations** provide a way to fit curvilinear models, within the familiar framework of either OLS or robust regression. Transformations also help work around several other statistical problems, making them an indispensable part of the analyst's toolkit.

*10.1   Regression Troubleshooting

F igure 10.1 depicts two "ideal" regressions, in which no patterns exist except those summarized by the regression lines themselves. The random errors around these lines

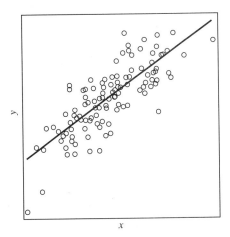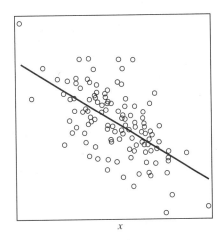

FIGURE 10.1
Two "ideal" regressions with normal i.i.d. errors (artificial data)

truly follow normal, independent, and identical distributions. We can be certain of this because the data are artificial, created to match the usual regression assumptions.

Real-data scatterplots frequently appear less ideal. Outliers, skew, and other problems are common. Data analysts use graphs to watch out for such problems, and to evaluate different ways of coping with them. Figure 10.2 (page 350) illustrates four kinds of problems that occur frequently in research.

Influential cases result from unusual combinations of x and y values. Regression lines may "track" the influential case, in much the same way means track high or low outliers. Most of the data points in the top left graph of Figure 10.2 exhibit a clear positive relation: Higher y goes with higher x. But one influential case combines the sample's highest x value with its lowest y value. This case pulls the regression line down, so it no longer fits the pattern seen in most of the data. To find out how much influence a case has, try repeating the regression without that case. Possible coping strategies include the following:

1. Leave the influential case out of the analysis. This step is justifiable only if we have some reason (besides influence) to discredit the case—evidence that it reflects measurement error or belongs to a different population, for instance. To maintain the integrity of your research, if you leave out any data, be certain that you also inform readers about your reasons for doing so, and exactly how this omission has affected your results. To show the effects of influential cases and give readers enough information to draw their own conclusions, some researchers present their analysis both ways: with and without the influential cases included.

2. Use **robust regression**, which is designed to have greater resistance to influential cases, although it is not wholly immune to them.

3. Seek other variables that explain why the influential case is so unusual, and include those variables in a **multiple regression** (ordinary or robust).

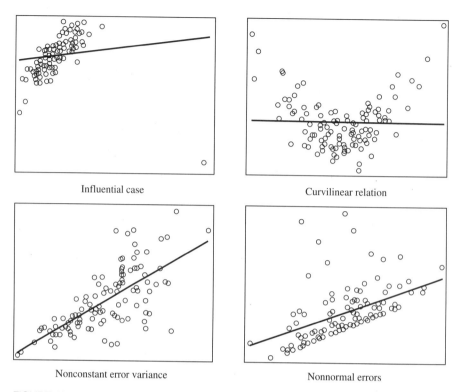

Influential case

Curvilinear relation

Nonconstant error variance

Nonnormal errors

FIGURE 10.2

Four problems that often complicate regression: Situations where the normal i.i.d.-errors assumption is untrue (artificial data)

4. **Nonlinear transformations** such as logarithms often work wonders in reducing outlier and influence problems.

Curvilinear relations imply that our efforts to fit a linear regression model are basically misguided; we should try fitting a curve instead. In scatterplots or residual versus predicted plots, curvilinearity may appear as a run of cases mostly below the regression line, followed by a run of cases mostly above the line, then a final run below the line again (or the reverse). We can accommodate curvilinearity in the following ways:

1. Nonlinear transformations allow fitting certain curves while still using ordinary linear regression methods. Perform regression as usual but with transformed variables such as logarithms of population.

2. Specialized **nonlinear regression** methods exist for fitting many other nonlinear models, or for letting the data suggest what model to fit (for examples, see Hamilton 1993a).

Nonconstant error variance suggests that errors are not "identically distributed"; their variance changes systematically with *x*. If so, our estimated standard errors, confidence intervals, and hypothesis tests become untrustworthy. The right-opening megaphone pattern at lower left in Figure 10.2 represents one common form of nonconstant variance. Nonlinear transformations might correct this problem.

Nonnormal errors, like nonconstant error variance, represent a departure from the "normal i.i.d. errors" assumption. Boxplots or histograms of sample residuals may provide evidence regarding the normality of errors. At lower right in Figure 10.2, nonnormality is manifest in the asymmetrical scatter of points above and below the regression line. Nonnormality reduces the validity of confidence intervals and hypothesis tests, particularly with small samples. Again, nonlinear transformations provide one possible cure, because they can "normalize" some skewed distributions. A second alternative is robust regression, which does not assume normality.

EXERCISES

*10.1.1 Table 10.1 (file *trouble*) contains six variables and 30 cases of artificial data, hiding a variety of statistical problems. Use scatterplots, residual boxplots, and residual versus predicted plots to identify any potential problem(s) in each regression. Also note possible consequences and cures.

    a.   regress y_1 on x_1 b.   regress y_2 on x_2
    c.   regress y_3 on x_3 d.   regress x_2 on x_3

Table 10.1
Troublesome regression data

case	x_1	y_1	x_2	y_2	x_3	y_3
1	20	3	1.3	−3.8	.5	−1.0
2	20	4	1.8	−3.4	−.2	1.0
3	40	28	−.5	.5	1.9	−1.7
4	0	1	−1.1	−31.3	.6	−1.7
5	12	2	−.5	−7.9	−1.9	3.2
6	10	2	2.9	−3.0	1.2	−2.9
7	18	2	1.3	−1.4	−.1	0
8	20	6	−.3	.1	.4	−1.6
9	26	7	−.5	−4.0	−.4	0
10	9	2	.2	−1.1	.1	0
11	25	8	.5	−1.3	.4	−.2
12	6	3	−.9	−3.7	.5	−1.3

(*continued*)

Table 10.1 (*Continued*)

case	x_1	y_1	x_2	y_2	x_3	y_3
13	14	3	1.2	-5.0	2.0	-2.8
14	19	3	-.5	-.9	.8	.4
15	13	1	-1.6	-10.8	-1.2	1.9
16	34	15	-1.1	-4.5	-.3	.9
17	12	3	1.9	-1.9	.1	.6
18	8	1	-.3	.2	-.8	1.1
19	20	3	-2.0	1.8	.2	-.4
20	24	7	-.4	-3.3	.7	-1.6
21	30	11	-2.4	2.4	1.3	-2.0
22	8	1	.3	-.3	.8	-2.0
23	2	2	-3.1	2.8	-1.3	-4.0
24	34	16	-.4	-4.1	-.7	.3
25	17	3	0	-.2	1.6	-3.5
26	9	3	-1.2	-17.2	.1	-.9
27	14	2	2.4	-2.4	1.9	4.0
28	17	4	-1.0	-.7	.7	0
29	22	6	-.2	-1.8	.5	.6
30	26	7	.8	-5.9	-.2	.3

File: *trouble*

*10.1.2   Construct your own artificial two-variable dataset illustrating a serious statistical problem (other than outliers). Explain what this problem is, show how an analyst might discover it, and explain what might be done to cope with it.

*10.2 Multiple Regression in Theory

Multiple regression extends regression analysis to encompass two or more x (predictor or "cause") variables. This capability helps analysts to

1.   Better predict y values, by explaining a larger fraction of y's variance
2.   Study the relation between y and one x while adjusting or controlling for the effects of other x variables

The second capability makes multiple regression especially attractive if we are interested in cause and effect.

Regression (or any other statistical method) is not enough, by itself, to prove that x causes y. A statistically significant relation between x and y might arise because

x causes y

y causes x

some other variable(s) causes both x and y

or any combination of these three. For example, consider children's shoe size and reading ability. In a U.S. elementary school these two variables may exhibit a significant positive relation, but not because shoe size causes reading ability. Nor does reading ability cause shoe size; rather, they both tend to increase with age. Age thus constitutes the "other variable" that explains the correlation between shoe size and reading ability.

Nonexperimental researchers depend chiefly on theory or knowledge about their subject to reach conclusions regarding causal order (whether x causes y or vice versa) and other-variable explanations. In addition, multiple regression can assist in checking out at least a few of the possible other-variable explanations. It does so by allowing researchers to include some other variables in the analysis. If the relation between y and x vanishes when we adjust for these other variables—as the reading ability–shoe size relation would vanish after we adjust for children's age—then our analysis suggests that x does not cause y. On the other hand, if the relation between y and x does not vanish, we have not proved causality, but the results are at least consistent with causality.

Instead of fitting a simple one-x model

$$\hat{y} = a + bx \tag{10.1}$$

multiple regression fits a model with two x variables

$$\hat{y} = a + b_1x_1 + b_2x_2 \tag{10.2}$$

or with three x variables

$$\hat{y} = a + b_1x_1 + b_2x_2 + b_3x_3 \tag{10.3}$$

and so on. Geometrically, equation (10.1) describes a line fit to two-dimensional data. Equation (10.2) describes a plane fit to three-dimensional data. Although we can no longer visualize it, equation (10.3) describes a three-dimensional hyperplane fit to four-dimensional data. Each variable comprises one dimension.

The y-intercept (a) terms in equations (10.1)–(10.3) share a common meaning: They represent the predicted value of y when all x variables in the equation equal 0. The b coefficients represent the effect of each x variable, statistically adjusted for whatever other x variables appear in the model. For example, b_1 in equation (10.3) indicates *the amount by which $\hat{y}$ changes, per 1-unit increase in x_1, if x_2 and x_3 remain the same.*

We find the regression equation (that is, the values of a, b_1, etc.) that best fits the data. Equations (10.4)–(10.7) (page 354) describe in general terms the ordinary least-squares criterion for "best fitting." Equations (10.9)–(10.11) give the specific formulas for regression with two x variables. Regression with more than two x variables requires formulas that are most conveniently expressed through a notation called **matrix algebra**.

Ordinary least squares (OLS) multiple regression

We seek values for the a and b coefficients in a linear model with J predictor (x) variables ($0 \leq J \leq n - 1$):

$$y_i = a + b_1 x_{1i} + b_2 x_{2i} + \cdots + b_J x_{Ji} + e_i \qquad (10.4)$$

where a is the **y-intercept** or **constant**, b_1 is the **partial regression coefficient on x_1**, b_2 is the partial regression coefficient on x_2, and so forth. A partial regression coefficient indicates the change in predicted y, per 1-unit increase in a particular x variable, if the other x variables do not change.

Predicted values are

$$\hat{y}_i = a + b_1 x_{1i} + b_2 x_{2i} + \cdots + b_J x_{Ji} \qquad (10.5)$$

and residuals or predictions errors are

$$e_i = y_i - \hat{y}_i \qquad (10.6)$$

Ordinary least squares (OLS) regression finds a and b values for equation (10.5) such that the sum of squared residuals or prediction errors

$$SS_R = \Sigma e_i^2 \qquad (10.7)$$

will be the lowest possible.

OLS multiple regression: The two-x case

Var[y], Var[x_1], and Var[x_2] represent the variances of y, x_1, and x_2, respectively. For example,

$$\mathrm{Var}[y] = s_y^2$$

$$= \frac{\Sigma(y_i - \bar{y})^2}{n - 1}$$

Cov[y, x_1] represents the **covariance of y and x_1**:

$$\mathrm{Cov}[y, x_1] = \frac{\Sigma(y_i - \bar{y})(x_{1i} - \bar{x}_1)}{n - 1} \qquad (10.8)$$

Similarly Cov[y, x_2] is the covariance of y and x_2, and Cov(x_1, x_2) is the covariance of x_1 and x_2. Covariance measures the extent to which two variables vary

(*continued*)

together. Pearson correlation, introduced earlier, is a covariance standardized to range from -1 to $+1$.

In the **multiple regression of y on x_1 and x_2**, we obtain ordinary least squares (OLS) estimates of the a and b coefficients for the model

$$\hat{y}_i = a + b_1 x_{1i} + b_2 x_{2i}$$

as follows:

$$b_1 = \frac{Var[x_2]Cov[y,\ x_1]\ -\ Cov[x_1,\ x_2]Cov[y,\ x_2]}{Var[x_1]Var[x_2]\ -\ Cov[x_1,\ x_2]^2} \tag{10.9}$$

$$b_2 = \frac{Var[x_1]Cov[y,\ x_2]\ -\ Cov[x_1,\ x_2]Cov[y,\ x_1]}{Var[x_1]Var[x_2]\ -\ Cov[x_1,\ x_2]^2} \tag{10.10}$$

$$a = \bar{y} - b_1\bar{x}_1 - b_2\bar{x}_2 \tag{10.11}$$

Equations (10.9) and (10.10) find the effect of each x variable, statistically adjusting for the effect of the other x variable. Using calculus (taking partial derivatives of the residual sum of squares), one can derive equations (10.9)–(10.11) from equations (10.5)—(10.7).

In the special case that x_1 and x_2 are completely uncorrelated, meaning that their covariance equals 0,

$$Cov[x_1,\ x_2] = 0$$

equation (10.9) reduces to

$$b_1 = \frac{Cov[y,\ x_1]}{Var[x_1]} \tag{10.9a}$$

which is identical to the regression coefficient we would obtain through the simple regression of y on x_1 only [equation (9.2)]. Similarly, equation (10.10) would reduce to the same coefficient obtained by regressing y on x_2 only:

$$b_2 = \frac{Cov[y,\ x_2]}{Var[x_2]} \tag{10.10a}$$

Thus, when the x variables are uncorrelated, their multiple regression coefficients are no different from the corresponding simple regression coefficients.

EXERCISES

*10.2.1 Describe an example involving two variables that are correlated with each other because both are, or might be, caused by the same third variable.

*10.2.2 Variance might be described as the "covariance of one variable with itself." Refer to the definitions of variance and covariance [equation (10.8)] to explain why this description makes sense.

*10.2.3 Write out the equation [along the lines of equation (10.3)] of a regression model with three *x* variables. What is the general meaning of each *a* and *b* coefficient?

▪ ▪ ▪ ▪ ▪ ▪ ▪ ▪ ▪ ▪ ▪ ▪ ▪ ▪

*10.3 **Multiple Regression in Practice**

Multiple regression output tables follow the same format as simple regression. To make this clear, let us return to the urban homicide rate data of Chapter 9. Table 9.2 showed the simple regression of homicide rate on poverty rate. Table 10.2 now shows the multiple regression of urban homicide rates on two *x* variables: percent below poverty, and total population in thousands. Apart from new numbers and an added line for the second *x* variable *pop*, Table 10.2 is no different from Table 9.2.

Table 10.2

Multiple regression of homicide rate (*homic*) on percent families below poverty (*poor*) and city population in thousands (*pop*)

Source	SS	df	MS	
Model	577.67	2	288.83	Number of obs. = 20
Residual	135.28	17	7.96	$F(2, 17) = 36.300$
				Prob > F = 0
				R-square = .810
Total	712.94	19	37.52	Adj. R-square = .788
				Root MSE = 2.821

homic	Coef.	Std. Err.	t	P > |t|	[95% Conf. Interval]	
poor	.6562	.2019	3.251	.005	.2304	1.0821
pop	.0222	.0032	7.057	.000	.0156	.0289
_cons	−3.8990	1.7900	−2.178	.044	−7.6756	−.1224

File: *urban*

The coefficients at lower left in Table 10.2 imply this multiple regression equation:

$$\text{predicted } homic = -3.899 + .6562 poor + .0222 pop \qquad \textbf{(10.12)}$$

The *y*-intercept, which predicts −3.899 homicides per 100,000 people in cities with no poverty and no population, makes mathematical but not substantive sense here. The coefficients on *poor* and *pop*, however, do permit substantive interpretation:

1. Predicted homicide rate increases by .656 with each 1-point increase in the percentage of families below poverty, if city population remains the same. Poverty's effect is statistically significant ($b_1 = .656$, $t = 3.251$, $P = .005$).

2. Predicted homicide rate increases by .022 with each 1,000 increase in city population, if the percentage of families below poverty remains the same. Population's effect is statistically significant ($b_2 = .022$, $t = 7.057$, $P = .000$)

The R^2 in Table 10.2 indicates that poverty and population together explain about 81% (or 78.8%, adjusted for complexity) of the variance in homicide rates.

We saw earlier that the simple regression model

$$\text{predicted } homic = -.815 + .944poor \tag{10.13}$$

explains only about 25% of the variance in homicide rates. Including a second predictor, population, thus greatly improved the fit between model and data. The coefficient on *poor* decreases when we statistically adjust for city population by including *pop* in the regression: from .944 in equation (10.13) to .6562 in equation (10.12). Thus part of the effect that equation (10.13) attributes to poverty can actually be explained by the fact that poverty and homicide rates are both higher in large cities.

This example illustrates two motivations given earlier for multivariate analysis in general, and multiple regression in particular:

1. In social science most phenomena have more than one cause. Multiple regression can incorporate (with certain limitations) a large number of x variables, thus allowing models that better fit the data and our understanding of the real world.

2. A relation between two variables, x_1 and y, does not by itself imply causality. We need to consider alternative explanations: perhaps the relation between x_1 and y partly or wholly results from a third variable x_2, which affects both x_1 and y. With multiple regression we can find out whether the relation between x_1 and y shrinks, vanishes, or even grows stronger after we statistically adjust for the effects of other variables.

Table 10.3 (page 358) lists predicted homicide rates and residuals from this multiple regression. Predicted homicide rates were obtained by substituting each city's poverty rate and population into equation (10.12). For example, Columbus' homicide rate is predicted from its poverty rate (14.5) and its population (169.4) as follows:

$$\text{predicted } homic_1 = -3.899 + .6562(14.5) + .0222(169.4)$$

$$= 9.38$$

Residuals, as usual, equal the difference between actual and predicted y. For Columbus

$$e_1 = 9.21 - 9.38$$

$$= -.17$$

Note that Columbus' residual or prediction error, and most of the others in Table 10.3, are much smaller than residuals from the simple regression (Table 9.3)—another indication that equation (10.12) fits the data better than equation (10.13).

Table 10.3
Percent families below poverty (x_1), city population (x_2), homicide rate (y), homicide rate predicted from equation (10.12) ($\hat{y}$), and residuals (e)

i	City	Percent poor x_1	Population x_2	Homicide rate y	$\hat{y}$	e
1	Tulsa	7.40	360.9	8.64	8.98	−.34
2	Columbus	14.50	169.4	9.21	9.38	−.17
3	Dallas	10.80	904.1	29.98	23.29	6.69
4	Virginia Beach	7.70	262.2	3.81	6.98	−3.17
5	Fullerton	4.70	102.0	2.35	1.45	.90
6	Berkeley	11.70	103.3	8.52	6.08	2.44
7	Honolulu	7.40	365.0	9.15	9.07	.08
8	Portland	8.50	366.4	8.62	9.83	−1.21
9	Albuquerque	9.30	331.8	6.39	9.58	−3.19
10	Salt Lake	10.50	163.0	6.01	6.62	−.61
11	Tempe	5.50	106.7	4.12	2.08	2.04
12	Concord	4.60	103.3	3.10	1.42	1.68
13	Sunnyvale	3.70	106.6	2.44	.90	1.54
14	Rochester	14.50	241.7	10.84	10.99	−.15
15	Allentown	8.40	103.8	4.24	3.92	.32
16	Erie	10.20	119.1	4.70	5.44	−.74
17	Independence	4.90	111.8	3.58	1.80	1.78
18	Peoria	9.40	124.2	4.03	5.03	−1.00
19	Milwaukee	6.80	636.2	7.83	14.71	−6.88
20	Sterling Hts.	3.10	109.0	.55	.56	−.09

Multiple regression makes the same (normal i.i.d. errors) assumptions described in Section 9.4, so residual analysis remains important as a way to check on their plausibility. Figure 10.3 shows a residual versus predicted plot of the data of Table 10.3. This graph is not reassuring. Dallas appears as an obvious outlier at upper right. Among the other 19 cities, residuals tend to be positive (implying too-low predictions) at low $\hat{y}$, then negative (too-high predictions) at mid-range $\hat{y}$. Such patterns could result from one influential case, curvilinearity, nonconstant variance, and/or nonnormal errors. Whatever the true problem, Figure 10.3 makes clear that we should not accept the multiple regression in Table 10.2 as final. It rests on dubious assumptions.

Problems that arise in multiple regression can often be understood by returning to simpler, two-variable analyses. Research reports commonly print a **correlation matrix**, tabulating the Pearson correlations among all variables. Table 10.4 gives an example. Note that the correlation of any variable with itself is perfect, $r = 1.0$. Correlations above the diagonal are left out because they would be the same as those below the diagonal. The correlation of *poor* with *homic* equals the correlation of *homic* with *poor* (.5044), for instance.

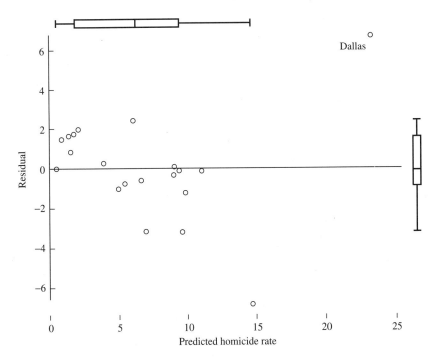

FIGURE 10.3
Residual versus predicted plot for the regression homicide rate on poverty rate and city population

Table 10.4
Correlation matrix with poverty rate (*poor*),
city population (*pop*), and homicide rate (*homic*)

	poor	*pop*	*homic*
poor	1.0000		
pop	.2019	1.0000	
homic	.5044	.8320	1.0000

Individual scatterplots or, more conveniently, a **scatterplot matrix** should be viewed alongside any correlation matrix. Figure 10.4 (page 360) gives a scatterplot matrix corresponding to the correlation matrix in Table 10.4. Scatterplot matrices are graphical counterparts to correlation matrices, and have a similar overall structure: They contain small scatterplots of each variable against each of the others. For instance, the middle-left plot in Figure 10.4 graphs the population in thousands (*pop*, on the y-axis) versus the percent families below poverty (*poor*, on the x-axis). The lower left plot, *homic* versus *poor*, corresponds to Figure 9.1.

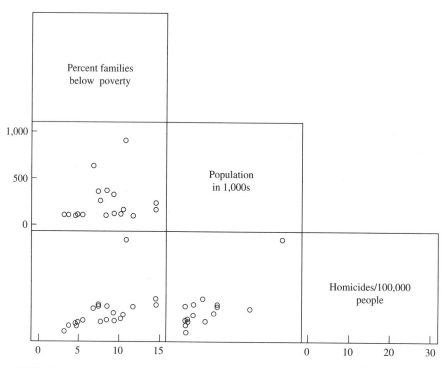

FIGURE 10.4
Scatterplot matrix corresponding to Table 10.4

The bottom center plot in Figure 10.4, *homic* versus *pop*, reveals that Dallas is a severe outlier in both its homicide rate and population. This one city produces a strong correlation between *homic* and *pop*: $r = .832$, but drops to $r = .5652$ if we set Dallas aside. Dallas may also influence the multiple-regression results in Table 10.2. Later sections of this chapter describe two possible ways to cope with influential data and other regression problems. We will return to the urban homicide data in Exercises 10.6.1 and 10.6.2.

What We Learn from Multiple Regression

Describing Sample Data

The regression equation summarizes the linear relation between two or more measurement (or {0, 1}) independent variables, x_1, x_2, etc., and one measurement dependent variable, y, in this sample. We could use this equation to calculate the mean or predicted value of y at any particular combination of x_1, x_2, . . . , values. The regression coefficient on variable x_k tells us how much the mean y changes—increasing if the coefficient is positive, decreasing if it is negative—with each 1-unit increase in x_k, if the other x variables do not change. R^2 indicates the proportion of y's variance that is explained by all of the x variables together. Adjusted R^2 takes into account the degrees of freedom, or difference in complexity between model and data.

Inferences about Population

Based on this sample (assuming it is a random sample), can we reject the hypothesis that, in the population, x_k and y have no relation at all, after we adjust for the effects of other x variables? A statistically significant (e.g., $P < .05$) result from a t test on the regression coefficient b_k indicates that the answer is yes. We thereby indirectly conclude that some relation does exist in the population. On the other hand, if the t test result is nonsignificant, we lack persuasive evidence that a relation exists between these variables in the population.

We can also construct confidence intervals to indicate our estimates of the population regression coefficients, or of the true population mean of y given a particular set of x-variable values.

EXERCISES

*10.3.1   Table 1.9 (file *urban*) in Chapter 1 contains other data on the same sample of 20 U.S. cities: divorce rate, median years of education, inequality, and population change rate. Sociologists often view divorce rates (along with rates of suicide, crime, and alcoholism) as an indicator of social disorganization. How does divorce rate relate to other urban characteristics? Regress *divorce* on *educ, inequal*, and *change*. Write out the regression equation, interpret all four coefficients, state which are statistically significant at the .05 level, and interpret R^2 and R_a^2.

*10.3.2   From your regression of Exercise 10.3.1, explain the calculation of residual and predicted values for two cities: Albuquerque and Honolulu. Plot residuals versus predicted values.

*10.3.3   Following up on your analysis of Exercises 10.3.1 and 10.3.2, obtain a correlation matrix and scatterplot matrix of these four variables. Describe any statistical problems you see in the scatterplot matrix or in the residual versus predicted values plot of Exercise 10.3.2.

*10.4 Standardized Regression Coefficients (Beta Weights)

To interpret a regression coefficient, researchers must think about it in terms of the variables' units—"the homicide rate increases by .65 victim per 100,000 people, with each percentage point increase in the families below poverty," for instance. The various units involved make it difficult to compare regression coefficients for different variables. Furthermore, many variables, such as indexes measuring self-esteem or socioeconomic status, have no natural units to begin with. Both of these reasons lead some social scientists to prefer **standardized regression coefficients** rather than the natural-units regression coefficients we have used up to this point. Standardized regression coefficients simplify interpretation and comparisons by re-expressing all regression coefficients in the same units: standard deviations. A standardized regression coefficient answers the question:

By how many *standard deviations* does predicted *y* change, with each *1-standard-deviation* increase in *x*?

Standardized regression coefficients or "beta weights"

If b_1 is the usual coefficient obtained by regressing y on x_1, then the corresponding **standardized regression coefficient**, written b_1^*, is

$$b_1^* = b_1 \left(\frac{s_1}{s_y} \right) \tag{10.14a}$$

where s_1 represents the standard deviation of x_1, and s_y the standard deviation of y. Similarly, if b_2 is the regression coefficient of y on x_2, and s_2 the standard deviation of x_2, then the corresponding standardized regression coefficient b_2^* is

$$b_2^* = b_2 \left(\frac{s_2}{s_y} \right) \tag{10.14b}$$

Equations along the lines of equations (10.14a) and (10.14b) work the same way in bivariate regression or in multiple regression with any number of x variables.

Standardized regression coefficients usually fall within the range from $+1$ to -1, with values toward either extreme indicating a stronger relation. In this respect they resemble correlation coefficients. Indeed *for simple (one x and one y) OLS regression*, the standardized regression coefficient equals the Pearson correlation. For multiple regression, however, the standardized regression coefficient does not equal the correlation.

In computer output and in journal articles, standardized regression coefficients are sometimes called "beta weights." Unfortunately, that name invites confusion with *un*standardized population regression coefficients, which statisticians traditionally write as the Greek letter β, or beta. Another completely unrelated use of this Greek letter occurs in the context of statistical power (see Table 6.2). Although the term "standardized regression coefficient" is more awkward than "beta weight," it seems less likely to cause confusion.

Standardized regression coefficients are obtained from a regression in which we had first transformed y and all x variables to standard score form, as defined in equation (5.7a). The standard score transformation

$$y^* = \frac{y - \bar{y}}{s}$$

creates a new variable y^*, which has a mean of 0 and a standard deviation of 1. Similarly, each x variable can be transformed to a standard score

$$x_1^* = \frac{x_1 - \bar{x}_1}{s_1}$$

or

$$x_2^* = \frac{x_2 - \bar{x}_2}{s_2}$$

and so forth. A **standardized regression equation** includes all variables as standard scores, accompanied by standardized regression coefficients. For example, a three-variable standardized regression equation has the general form

$$\hat{y}^* = b_1^* x_1^* + b_2^* x_2^* \qquad \textbf{(10.15)}$$

No intercept appears in equation (10.15), because in standardized regression equations the y-intercept always equals 0.

Table 10.5 (page 364) repeats the homicide-rate regression of Table 10.1, but this time displaying standardized coefficients in the column labeled "Beta" at lower right. The standardized regression equation is

$$\text{predicted } homic^* = .3507 poor^* + .7612 pop^* \qquad \textbf{(10.16)}$$

where $homic^*$, $poor^*$, and pop^* denote these variables in standard-score form. Equation (10.16) tells us that

1. Predicted homicide rate increases by .3507 standard deviation with each 1-standard-deviation increase in the percentage of families below poverty, if city population remains the same.

2. Predicted homicide rate increases by .7612 standard deviation with each 1-standard-deviation increase in city population, if the percentage of families below poverty remains the same.

Note that in R^2, significance test results, and every other aspect, the standardized regression results of Table 10.5 are no different from the unstandardized results of Table 10.2. We are fitting exactly the same model, but presenting it in a different way. Equation (10.16) is equivalent to equation (10.12).

A 1-standard-deviation increase in pop produces a larger change $(+.7612)$ in the dependent variable than does a 1-standard-deviation increase in $poor$ $(+.3507)$. From this result, one might argue that "pop has a stronger effect on homicide rates than $poor$ does." Such straightforward comparisons of the strengths of different x variables' effects are a principal reason for the popularity of standardized coefficients in sociology and psychology.

Table 10.5

Multiple regression of homicide rate (*homic*) on percent families below poverty (*poor*) and city population in thousands (*pop*) with standardized regression coefficients or "beta weights" at lower right

Source	SS	df	MS	
Model	577.67	2	288.83	
Residual	135.28	17	7.96	
Total	712.94	19	37.52	

Number of obs. = 20
$F(2, 17) = 36.300$
Prob > $F = 0$
R-square = .810
Adj. R-square = .788
Root MSE = 2.821

homic	Coef.	Std. Err.	t	P > |t|	Beta
poor	.6562	.2019	3.251	.005	.3507
pop	.0222	.0032	7.057	.000	.7612
_cons	−3.8990	1.7900	−2.178	.044	.

This popularity persists despite cautionary writing from statisticians, however, who point out that comparisons such as the one quoted in the previous paragraph depend on a narrow, unintuitive definition of "strength" [for example, see criticisms in Bring (1994), and the studies he cites]. Furthermore, standardized coefficients can be misleading if used for comparisons across subsamples or across different *y* variables (Specht and Warren, 1975). Researchers in fields such as economics and biology, where the key variables do have natural units (dollars, years, grams, and so on), tend to avoid standardized coefficients. From a data analysis perspective, too, the statistical properties of unstandardized coefficients make them preferable even though they require extra thought in interpretation.

EXERCISES

*10.4.1 Return to the regression of Exercise 10.3.1. Regress *divorce* on *educ, inequal*, and *change*. This time, write out and interpret the standardized regression equation.

*10.4.2 Generate a new variable representing *divorce* as a standard score: Subtract the mean *divorce*, and then divide by its standard deviation. Similarly, create standard score versions of *educ, inequal*, and *change*. Confirm that the following are approximately (within three decimal places) true:

a. The standard score variables all have means of 0 and standard deviations of 1.

b.   The regression of standardized *divorce* on standardized *educ, inequal*, and *change* produces regression coefficients similar to the standardized coefficients of Exercise 10.4.1, and a *y*-intercept close to 0.

*10.5 — Dummy Variables

Up to this point, we have considered only measurement variables. Regression readily incorporates categorical information too, in the special form of **dummy variables**. Dummy variables have only two categories, coded 0 and 1. Examples from a survey of college students might include voting (0 = did not vote in last election, 1 = did vote), gender (0 = male, 1 = female), or official residence (0 = in state, 1 = out of state). Such dummy variables can then be included among the predictor or *x* variables in a regression.

Table 10.6 lists data from Taylor (1984), seen in Chapter 3, on unemployment rates among graduates of 44 British universities. Ten of these schools were formerly Colleges of Advanced Technology (CATs). Table 10.6 indicates former CAT status with a dummy variable (0 = other university, 1 = former CAT). It also gives the average A-level examination score achieved by entering students, a measure (somewhat like average SAT scores) that reflects the school's selectivity.

Table 10.6
Data on 44 British universities

University	Type	Dummy variable *CAT*	Percent graduates unemployed	Average exam scores
Bath	CAT	1	8.8	10.5
Brunel	CAT	1	8.3	7.1
Loughborough	CAT	1	10.4	9.1
Aston	CAT	1	6.8	7.2
Bradford	CAT	1	13.0	7.9
Strathclyde	CAT	1	10.1	7.7
City	CAT	1	8.5	8.4
Heriot-Watt	CAT	1	10.6	8.7
Surrey	CAT	1	11.7	8.2
Salford	CAT	1	9.1	6.8

(*continued*)

Table 10.6 (*Continued*)

University	Type	Dummy variable *CAT*	Percent graduates unemployed	Average exam scores
Warwick	other	0	18.4	9.0
Kent	other	0	19.9	7.9
East Anglia	other	0	23.6	7.3
London	other	0	14.4	9.7
Ulster	other	0	28.8	9.7
Sussex	other	0	23.4	9.4
Hull	other	0	16.8	7.9
Aberdeen	other	0	11.4	8.5
Cambridge	other	0	9.1	13.6
Dundee	other	0	9.2	8.2
Bristol	other	0	14.0	12.1
Sheffield	other	0	12.9	10.0
Edinburgh	other	0	15.1	10.7
Leicester	other	0	16.5	9.2
Durham	other	0	12.9	11.8
St. Andrews	other	0	16.9	10.5
Stirling	other	0	21.0	7.8
Nottingham	other	0	15.3	10.3
Leeds	other	0	13.6	9.7
Wales	other	0	16.1	7.8
Southampton	other	0	11.5	10.8
Liverpool	other	0	10.7	9.5
Oxford	other	0	10.4	13.1
Lancaster	other	0	20.4	8.1
Birmingham	other	0	9.8	10.3
Exeter	other	0·	13.5	9.6
Newcastle	other	0	11.4	8.6
York	other	0	18.4	10.2
Keele	other	0	21.0	7.0
Essex	other	0	18.1	6.3
Reading	other	0	16.4	9.8
Glasgow	other	0	8.7	9.2
Queens	other	0	11.5	9.7
Manchester	other	0	13.0	10.4

Source: Taylor (1984).
File: *britu*

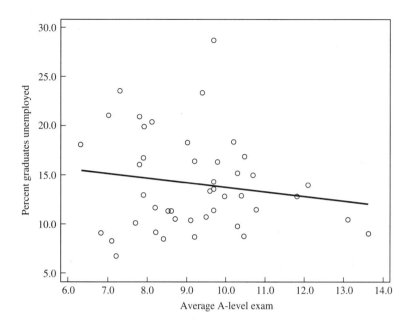

FIGURE 10.5
Regression of British universities' graduate unemployment rates on
average A-level examination score of students

Are unemployment rates lower among graduates of more selective schools?
Table 10.7 and Figure 10.5 depict the regression of unemployment rate on average exam
score:

$$\text{predicted } unemp = 18.36 - .46exam \tag{10.17}$$

This relation is negative, as expected: Graduates of higher-scoring schools tend to have
lower unemployment. It is extremely weak, however, with an adjusted R^2 near 0. The
scatter of points in Figure 10.5 shows little evidence of a linear trend.

Table 10.7
Regression of British-university-graduate unemployment rates
on average exam score

Source	SS	df	MS	
Model	23.82	1	23.82	Number of obs. = 44
Residual	998.24	42	23.77	$F(1, 42) = 1.00$
				Prob > F = .3225
				R-square = .0233
				Adj. R-square = .0001
Total	1,022.06	43	23.77	Root MSE = 4.8752

(continued)

Table 10.7 (*Continued*)

unemp	Coef.	Std. Err.	t	P> |t|	[95% Conf. Interval]	
exam	− .4605	.4600	− 1.001	.323	− 1.389	.4678
_cons	18.3643	4.3001	4.271	.000	9.686	27.0422

Analyses in earlier chapters established that unemployment rates tend to be lower among former-CAT graduates. We might therefore include the dummy variable for CAT status as a second *x* variable in our regression, as done in Table 10.8.

Table 10.8
Dummy variable regression: Regressing graduate unemployment rate
on average exam score and a dummy variable indicating former
Colleges of Advanced Technology (CATs)

Source	SS	df	MS	
				Number of obs. = 44
				$F(2, 41) = 11.96$
Model	376.52	2	188.26	Prob > F = .0001
Residual	645.54	41	15.75	R-square = .3684
				Adj. R-square = .3376
Total	1,022.06	43	23.77	Root MSE = 3.968

unemp	Coef.	Std. Err.	t	P> |t|	[95% Conf. Interval]	
exam	− 1.1373	.4007	− 2.838	.007	− 1.947	− .3280
CAT	− 7.2321	1.5280	− 4.733	0	− 10.318	− 4.1462
_cons	26.2423	3.8755	6.771	0	18.415	34.0691

Table 10.8 yields the multiple regression equation

$$\text{predicted } unemp = 26.24 - 1.14exam - 7.23CAT \qquad \textbf{(10.18)}$$

Notice that including *CAT* in the model causes the coefficient on *exam* to more than double, from − .46 [equation (10.17)] to − 1.14 [equation (10.18)]. Furthermore, adjusted R^2 jumps from near 0 (Table 10.7) to about 34% ($R_a^2 = .3376$ in Table 10.8). Plainly, the multiple regression model predicts unemployment rates more successfully than our earlier simple regression does.

To interpret dummy variable regressions, it helps to write out the regression equation substituting first 0, then 1 for the dummy variable. Among non-CAT schools (*CAT* = 0), equation (10.18) becomes

$$\text{predicted } unemp = 26.24 - 1.14 exam - 7.23 \times 0 \qquad \textbf{(10.18a)}$$
$$= 26.24 - 1.14 exam$$

Among CAT schools ($CAT = 1$), however, equation (10.18) becomes

$$\text{predicted } unemp = 26.24 - 1.14 exam - 7.23 \times 1$$
$$= 26.24 - 1.14 exam - 7.23 \qquad \textbf{(10.18b)}$$
$$= 19.01 - 1.14 exam$$

Thus the equations for CAT and non-CAT schools differ only in their y-intercepts. Since equation (10.18b) has a lower intercept, it tells us that, at any given value of *exam*, CAT schools tend to have a lower predicted unemployment rate than non-CAT schools. How much lower? The amount of difference equals the coefficient on the dummy variable *CAT*, which is $b_2 = -7.23$ points.

Figure 10.6 shows this dummy variable regression graphically. CAT and non-CAT schools appear as squares and circles, respectively, in this scatterplot. Among both types of colleges, unemployment tends to fall as exam scores increase. But the CAT unemployment rates stay consistently below those of non-CAT schools with similar exam scores. The lower line in Figure 10.6 depicts the relation between unemployment and

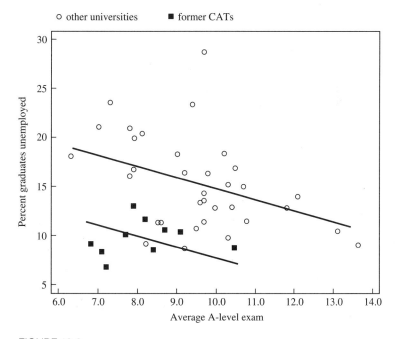

FIGURE 10.6
Regression of graduate unemployment rates on average exam scores and a dummy variable representing CAT status

exam scores among CAT schools; the upper line depicts this relation among non-CAT schools. We now see why the coefficient on *exam* became stronger after we included *CAT* in the model: The *unemp-exam* relation is most apparent within categories of *CAT*, and gets masked when we mix both CAT and non-CAT schools together as in Figure 10.5.

A dummy variable regression such as Table 10.8 thus fits two separate regression lines, having identical slopes but intercepts that differ by an amount equal to the dummy variable's coefficient (see Figure 10.7). We could actually include more than one dummy variable. To think through the meaning of any dummy variable regression, write out the equations with 0 and 1 substitution as done in equations (10.18a) and (10.18b).

Categorical variables with more than two categories can be coded as a series of dummy variables. For example, religion (1 = Protestant, 2 = Catholic, 3 = Jewish, 4 = other) could be expressed as three dummy variables:

Protestant   (0 = not Protestant, 1 = Protestant)

Catholic   (0 = not Catholic, 1 = Catholic)

Jewish   (0 = not Jewish, 1 = Jewish)

We do not need a fourth category; anyone who is 0 on *Protestant, Catholic*, and *Jewish* must fall in the omitted category of "other." Table 10.9 shows how this works.

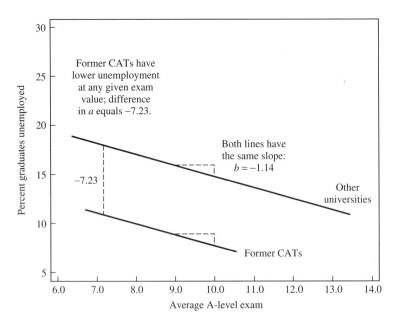

FIGURE 10.7

Graphical interpretation of a dummy variable regression: Two lines with identical slopes, but different intercepts

Table 10.9
Coding a four-category *religion* variable
as three dummy variables

If a person's religion is	His or her dummy variable values are		
	Protestant	**Catholic**	**Jewish**
Protestant	1	0	0
Catholic	0	1	0
Jewish	0	0	1
other	0	0	0

In general, $K - 1$ dummy variables completely capture the information of any K-category variable. We do not need a Kth dummy variable. In fact, for technical reasons (called **multicollinearity**) we *cannot* enter K dummy variables for a K-category variable in the same regression; if we try, computer programs will print an error message, and perhaps arbitrarily drop one dummy variable.

OLS regression readily incorporates dummy variables as predictors (x variables), but does not work well with dummy dependent (y) variables. To analyze dummy (or other categorical) y variables requires more advanced techniques such as **logit regression** [for example, see Hosmer and Lemeshow (1989)].

EXERCISES

*10.5.1   The urban dataset in Table 3.4 includes the categorical variable *region*, coded as follows:

   region   {1 = South, 2 = West, 3 = Northeast, 4 = Midwest}

We can re-express all the information of this four-category variable by creating three dummy variables. For example:

   south   {1 if South, 0 otherwise}

   west   {1 if West, 0 otherwise}

   midwest   {1 if Midwest, 0 otherwise}

A city that equals 0 on all three dummy variables must belong to the omitted category, the Northeast.

   Regress *divorce* on *change* and the dummy variable *south*. Write out and interpret the resulting regression equation.

*10.5.2   Construct a scatterplot showing the two regression lines (one for *south* = 0 cities, the second for *south* = 1) implied by your analysis in Exercise 10.5.1.

*10.5.3   Regress *divorce* on three measurement-variable predictors: *educ, inequal*, and *change*. Next regress *divorce* on six predictors, the three measurement variables plus the three dummy variables defined in Exercise 10.5.1.

  a. Write out and interpret the resulting regression equation. The dummy variable coefficients should be interpreted with reference to the omitted region, the Northeast.

  b. Compare the changes in R^2 and R_a^2 between these two regressions. Why did the former show a greater increase?

*10.6 — Robust Regression

Ordinary least squares regression lacks resistance to outliers, and works best when errors follow normal distributions. Unfortunately, researchers often encounter outliers and nonnormality; in many kinds of data such features are the rule rather than the exception. Consequently they need **robust** techniques that not only retain regression's analytical power, but also resist outliers and do not require normality. The theories behind robust regression are relatively advanced, but the techniques themselves, executed by a computer, provide easily used diagnostic tools to confirm OLS results and warn when they may be misleading.

  One common form of robust regression assigns **weights** (w_i) to each case in the data:

$$0 \le w_i \le 1$$

Outliers get lower weights than other cases, and so have less influence over the regression results. Typically, robust regression proceeds in a series of steps or **iterations**. On each iteration, the computer performs a regression, calculates residuals, and then assigns weights using a formula based on each case's residuals; larger residuals lead to lower weights, perhaps as low as 0, and $w_i = 0$ effectively drops the outlier from the analysis. Cases with small residuals, on the other hand, receive weights closer to 1. Ordinary least squares regression corresponds to a weighted regression in which all cases have $w_i = 1$.

  Table 10.10 lists data relevant to debates over whether high-spending schools have better-performing students. The cases comprise 24 public school districts. Table 10.11 (page 374) and Figure 10.8 depict the OLS regression of districts' average Scholastic Aptitude Test scores on their per-pupil educational expenditures. We see a weak ($R^2 = .05$) and statistically nonsignificant ($P = .294$) relation. The wide confidence bands in Figure 10.8 include the possibility that the coefficient on expenditure is 0, or even negative. Since expenditures do not significantly predict SAT scores, these results seem to argue against spending more money on education.

Table 10.10
Per-pupil expenditures (*expend*) and average composite
Scholastic Aptitude Test scores (*CSAT*) in 24
Massachusetts school districts, with OLS
predicted values and residuals

District	*expend*	*CSAT*	Predicted *CSAT*	Residual
1. Boston	4,087	762	929.4	−167.4
2. Cambridge	4,681	831	945.8	−114.8
3. Waltham	3,472	860	912.3	−52.3
4. Quincy	2,979	814	898.6	−84.6
5. Watertown	3,481	877	912.5	−35.5
6. Milton	3,183	874	904.3	−30.3
7. Arlington	3,714	936	919.0	17.0
8. Somerville	2,625	834	888.8	−54.8
9. Chelsea	2,290	808	879.5	−71.5
10. Salem	2,617	851	888.6	−37.6
11. Brookline	3,903	985	924.3	60.7
12. Braintree	2,945	892	897.7	−5.7
13. Burlington	3,215	922	905.2	16.8
14. Peabody	2,321	836	880.4	−44.4
15. Marblehead	3,140	927	903.1	23.9
16. Lynn English	2,460	860	884.2	−24.2
17. Manchester	3,420	960	910.9	49.1
18. Wellesley	4,036	1022	927.9	94.1
19. Newton	3,606	987	916.0	71.0
20. Needham	3,204	975	904.9	70.1
21. Winchester	3,491	1004	912.8	91.2
22. Belmont	3,160	989	903.6	85.4
23. Swampscott	2,775	956	893.0	63.0
24. Canton	2,971	979	898.4	80.6

Source: *Boston Globe*, October 24, 1986.
File: *boschool*

Table 10.11
Ordinary least squares regression of composite SAT scores (*CSAT*)
on per-pupil expenditures (*expend*) of 24 school districts

Source	SS	df	MS	
Model	6,173.03	1	6,173.03	Number of obs. = 24
Residual	117,511.59	22	5,341.44	$F(1, 22) = 1.16$
				Prob > F = .294
				R-square = .050
Total	123,684.62	23	5,377.59	Adj. R-square = .007
				Root MSE = 73.085

CSAT	Coef.	Std. Err.	t	P > |t|	[95% Conf. Interval]	
expend	.028	.026	1.075	.294	−.026	.081
_cons	815.968	84.952	9.605	.000	639.788	992.148

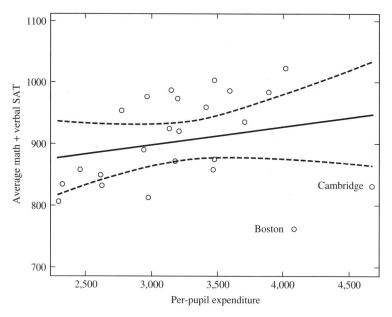

FIGURE 10.8
OLS regression of average composite SAT score on per-pupil expenditure,
with 95% confidence bands, in 24 school districts

Two high-spending but low-SAT districts, Boston and Cambridge, might be pulling down the regression line and widening the confidence band in Figure 10.8. Their large residuals indicate that these two cases contradict the general pattern among other school districts, where SAT scores do appear to drift upward with expenditures.

Table 10.12 (page 376) and Figure 10.9 show a robust regression using these same data. Unlike OLS, robust regression is not one particular method, but rather a broad category of methods. Different computer programs will produce essentially identical results when performing OLS, but they may produce quite different results when performing "robust regression"—because they use different specific methods. Technically speaking, Table 10.12 and Figure 10.9 show results from a robust regression based on the Tukey biweight function with a tuning constant of 6 [see Hamilton (1992, pp. 190–203)].

In contrast to the OLS results seen earlier, this robust regression finds a significant positive relation between expenditures and SAT scores. Due to their large residuals, Boston and Cambridge received weights of 0 (see Table 10.13). After downweighting these two outliers, robust regression provides a more reasonable summary of the pattern followed by the other 22 cases. Robust regression generally exhibits less sample-to-sample variation than OLS when applied to outlier-prone data. The smaller standard errors of Table 10.12 and the narrower confidence band of Figure 10.9 reflect this stability.

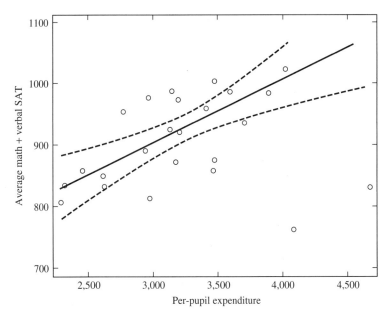

FIGURE 10.9

Robust regression of average composite SAT score on per-pupil expenditure, with 95% confidence bands; less affected by Boston and Cambridge (lower right), the line is steeper and has narrower confidence bands than the OLS line in Figure 10.8.

Table 10.12
Robust regression of composite SAT scores (*CSAT*) on per-pupil expenditures (*expend*) of 24 school districts

Robust regression estimates

Number of obs. = 24
$F(1, 22) = 21.55$
Prob > F = .000

CSAT	Coef.	Std. Err.	t	P > |t|	[95% Conf. Interval]	
expend	.100	.021	4.64	.000	.055	.144
_cons	603.477	70.827	8.52	.000	456.59	750.36

Table 10.13
Predicted values, residuals, and weights from the robust regression
of composite SAT scores (*CSAT*) on per-pupil expenditures
(*expend*) of 24 Massachusetts school districts

District	expend	CSAT	Predicted CSAT	Residual	Weight
1. Boston	4,087	762	1011.7	−249.7	0
2. Cambridge	4,681	831	1071.0	−240.0	0
3. Waltham	3,472	860	950.3	−90.3	.58
4. Quincy	2,979	814	901.0	−87.0	.60
5. Watertown	3,481	877	951.2	−74.2	.70
6. Milton	3,183	874	921.4	−47.4	.87
7. Arlington	3,714	936	974.4	−38.4	.92
8. Somerville	2,625	834	865.7	−31.7	.94
9. Chelsea	2,290	808	832.2	−24.2	.97
10. Salem	2,617	851	864.9	−13.9	.99
11. Brookline	3,903	985	993.3	−8.3	1.00
12. Braintree	2,945	892	897.6	−5.6	1.00
13. Burlington	3,215	922	924.6	−2.6	1.00
14. Peabody	2,321	836	835.3	.7	1.00
15. Marblehead	3,140	927	917.1	9.9	.99
16. Lynn English	2,460	860	849.2	10.8	.99
17. Manchester	3,420	960	945.1	14.9	.99
18. Wellesley	4,036	1022	1006.6	15.4	.99
19. Newton	3,606	987	963.7	23.3	.97
20. Needham	3,204	975	923.5	51.5	.85

(*continued*)

Table 10.13 (*Continued*)

District	*expend*	*CSAT*	Predicted CSAT	Residual	Weight
21. Winchester	3,491	1,004	952.2	51.8	.85
22. Belmont	3,160	989	919.1	69.9	.73
23. Swampscott	2,775	956	880.6	75.4	.69
24. Canton	2,971	979	900.2	78.8	.67

Figure 10.10, a graph of robust weights versus residuals from Table 10.13, outlines the mathematical **weight function**. Weights approach 1 for cases with near-zero residuals, but fall to 0 for cases with residuals beyond about ±175 SAT points. This particular weight function is called a **biweight** [see Hamilton (1992) for the equation and other details].

Robust regression offers a degree of protection against conclusions that depend too much on just a few unusual cases. It does not require us to know in advance whether unusual cases exist, which ones they are, or why. Unusual cases get downweighted in a smooth, nonarbitrary fashion, unlike the all-or-nothing tactic of dropping suspected outliers from the analysis "by hand." Despite its computational complexity, robust regression will often be safer than ordinary regression in the hands of inexperienced data analysts.

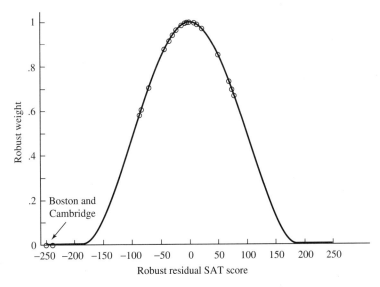

FIGURE 10.10
Robust weights versus residuals from the robust regression of Figure 10.9

In these data, Boston high schools include a larger proportion of poor and minority students than the other districts. Such population characteristics, which affect average SAT scores, may help explain why Boston and Cambridge are outliers. Armed with population data, we might use multiple regression (ordinary or robust) to develop a better equation for predicting SAT scores. Robust regression extends to multivariate analysis just as readily as OLS regression does.

What We Learn from Robust Regression

Describing Sample Data

Robust regression serves to summarize sample data in much the same manner as ordinary regression (simple or multiple). Since robust regression is designed to resist the effects of outliers, its coefficients and predicted values are less likely to be controlled by a few unusual data points.

Inferences about Population

Similar to ordinary regression, robust regression provides t tests of the null hypotheses that population (robust) regression coefficients equal 0. Robust regression also provides robust confidence intervals for coefficients or for predicted y. When the data often contain outliers, robust regression tends to exhibit milder sample-to-sample variation than ordinary regression. Consequently we can obtain more reliable estimates of population parameters. Furthermore, robust inferences do not require normally distributed errors.

EXERCISES

*10.6.1 (*Requires software that supports robust regression*) Perform a robust regression of homicide rate on poverty rate, using the data of Table 9.1 (file *urban*). Graph the results with 95% confidence bands. Compare this graph with Figure 9.8. Is the robust line steeper or less steep, and why? Are the robust confidence bands narrower or wider, and why?

*10.6.2 Perform a robust multiple regression of homicide rate on poverty and population, using the data of Table 9.1.
   a. Write out and interpret the robust regression equation. In what respects does it differ from equation (10.12)?
   b. Compare the standard errors (estimates of sample-to-sample variation in b coefficients) from your robust regression with the standard errors from the regression in Table 10.2.
   c. Construct a residual versus predicted plot. How does this plot look different from Figure 10.3?

*10.7   Regression with Transformed Variables

Nonlinear transformations such as logarithms, square roots, and powers change the shape of variable distributions. Used with ordinary or robust regression, transformations often help solve problems like those pictured in Figure 10.2: influential cases, curvilinear relations, nonconstant error variance, or nonnormal errors. Their versatility makes transformations a valuable tool. Although mathematically simpler than robust regression, they nonetheless require some interpretive effort. This section illustrates the basic ideas.

Table 10.14 (page 380) lists data on a sample of 19 nations. Life expectancies tend to be lower in poor countries. Figure 10.11 shows, however, that a straight-line regression model,

$$\text{predicted } life = 58.739 + 1.507 GNP \tag{10.19}$$

does not well describe the relation between life expectancy (*life*) and per-capita gross national product (*GNP*). A straight line unrealistically implies that life expectancy improves at a constant rate—by 1.507 years with each thousand dollars of *GNP*. The scatter of data in Figure 10.11 suggests instead that life expectancy rises more steeply than this going from very poor to mid-GNP countries, but then almost levels off going from mid-GNP to wealthy countries.

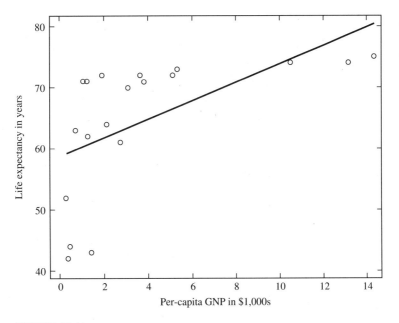

FIGURE 10.11
Linear regression of life expectancy on per-capita gross national product in 19 countries shows poor fit.

Table 10.14
**Per-capita gross national product in thousands of U.S. dollars (*GNP*),
life expectancy in years (*life*), adult literacy rates (*literacy*),
and births per 1,000 people (*birth*) in 19 countries, 1982–83**

Country	GNP	life	literacy	birth
1. United States	13.16	74	99	15.5
2. Barbados	3.84	71	98	19.9
3. Brazil	2.14	64	76	30.6
4. Costa Rica	1.08	71	93	30.5
5. Dominican Republic	1.26	62	74	33.1
6. El Salvador	.76	63	66	40.2
7. Haiti	.29	52	30	41.3
8. Jamaica	1.30	71	92	28.3
9. Belgium	10.54	74	99	11.9
10. Norway	14.30	75	100	12.3
11. Bulgaria	5.16	72	95	13.6
12. Spain	5.37	73	93	17.0
13. Yugoslavia	3.11	70	87	16.4
14. Cyprus	3.70	72	89	19.7
15. Fiji	1.95	72	82	27.2
16. Angola	1.41	43	28	47.3
17. Gambia	.36	42	20	48.4
18. Senegal	.48	44	23	47.7
19. South Africa	2.73	61	80	38.7

Source: World Bank (1987).
File: *gnp*

Computers easily calculate the **logarithms** (powers of 10) of a variable such as *GNP*. For example, the United States had a gross national product of $13.16 thousand per person when these data were collected. The logarithm (base 10) of 13.16 equals 1.119, because $10^{1.119} = 13.16$. Similarly, for Barbados

$$\log_{10}(GNP) = \log_{10}(3.84)$$

$$= .584$$

because $10^{.584} = 3.84$, and so on. We can transform each value of *GNP* by taking logarithms in this fashion.

If we now regress life expectancy on logarithms of *GNP*, instead of on *GNP* itself, we obtain a new equation:

$$\text{predicted } life = 58.746 + 17.108\log(GNP) \qquad \textbf{(10.20)}$$

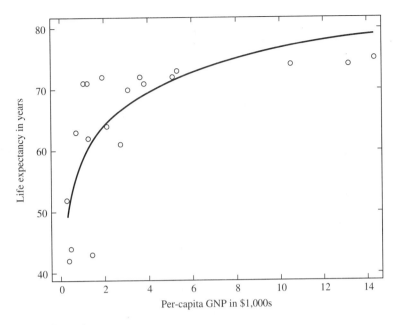

FIGURE 10.12
Curvilinear regression accomplished by regressing life expectancy on
logarithms of per-capita GNP

By performing linear regression with one or more transformed variables, we actually fit
a curve to the original data. Figure 10.12 shows that the curve implied by equation
(10.28) describes the data much better than does the straight line of equation (10.19).

Other common transformations include **natural logarithms** (powers of $e =$
$2.7182818\ldots$), squares (considering both x and x^2 as predictors of y, for instance), and
square roots. Deciding when to use transformations, which transformations to choose,
and how to interpret the results raise statistical issues beyond the scope of this book.
The Summary section suggests further readings on transformations and other topics
introduced in this chapter.

EXERCISES

*10.7.1 Return to the 19-country data of Table 10.14 (file *gnp*).
    a. Obtain a boxplot of *GNP*, and describe this distribution's shape.
    b. Create a new variable called *logGNP*, equal to base-10 logarithms (also
       called common logarithms) of *GNP*. Graph *logGNP* versus *GNP* in a
       scatterplot, and describe what the transformation has done.
    c. Obtain a boxplot of *logGNP*, and describe this new distribution's shape.

*10.7.2   Analyze the relation between literacy rate and per-capita GNP.
    a.   Regress *literacy* on *GNP*, and graph the result. What is wrong with this picture?
    b.   Regress *literacy* on *logGNP* and calculate predicted values. Graph *literacy* and predicted literacy against *GNP* to see the implied curve. What does this curve suggest about the relation between *literacy* and *GNP*?

*10.7.3   Analyze the relation between birth rate and per-capita GNP. First, perform a linear regression (*birth* on *GNP*) and discuss the resulting graph. Next, regress *birth* on *logGNP* and graph the implied curve, using the method described in Exercise 10.7.2. Discuss differences between your two *literacy–GNP* models.

Summary

Many ideas from simple regression carry over into multiple regression, which works with two or more *x* variables. Multiple regression coefficients indicate the average change in *y* per 1-unit increase in a given *x* variable, if the other *x* variables do not change. Models with multiple *x* variables provide more realistic descriptions of data, and help researchers evaluate competing causal explanations. More than half the articles in leading social science research journals use some form of multiple regression.

Although computers allow someone to use regression without ever looking at scatterplots, this is the statistical equivalent of flying blind. Many problems that can bedevil regression show up clearly in scatterplots. Once we recognize a problem we can consider how to deal with it. Robust regression and nonlinear transformations help solve several common types of problems. Nonlinear transformations require extra interpretive effort from the analyst. Robust regression requires the computer, but not necessarily the analyst, to work harder. Because robust regression is as easy for the analyst as ordinary regression, we can employ it routinely to check on whether ordinary regression results were unduly affected by outliers.

Where might we go from here? A companion book, *Regression with Graphics* (Hamilton, 1992) takes up where this text leaves off. It provides more detail, at the level of a second course in statistics, on topics including multiple regression, robustness, and transformations. To work with these methods you need computer software. Two book/software packages, *StataQuest* (Anagnoson and DeLeon, 1994) and *Statistics with Stata* (Hamilton, 1993a), present the statistical program behind all graphs and analyses in this book. *StataQuest* aims at an undergraduate audience, whereas *Statistics with Stata* aims at graduate students and practicing researchers.

Two excellent volumes edited by Hoaglin, Mosteller, and Tukey (1983, 1985) cover exploratory data analysis in greater depth. Other books recommended for non-mathematicians include those by Fox and Long (1990) and Velleman and Hoaglin, (1981). Several brief monographs published by Sage (Achen, 1982; Berry and Feldman, 1985; Schroeder, Sjoquist, and Stephan, 1986) help readers to start using multiple regression. Much more about the theory and practice of regression analysis appears in books by Hanushek and Jackson (1977) and Rawlings (1988), among many others.

PROBLEMS

Table 10.15 (file *states*) lists 1990–1991 data on the U.S. states. The variables are

income	Per-capita annual income, in dollars
metro	Percent of population living in metropolitan areas
density	People per square mile of land area
senate	Percentage of "pro-environment" votes cast by the state's senators in 1991
waste	Per-capita annual solid waste generation, in tons

Problems 10.1–10.7 refer to these data.

Table 10.15
Environmental data on 50 U.S. states

State	income	metro	density	senate	waste
1. Alabama	9,615	67.4	77.08	10	1.11
2. Alaska	13,263	41.1	.96	20	.91
3. Arizona	11,521	79.0	32.25	33	.79
4. Arkansas	9,061	40.1	45.15	37	.85
5. California	13,197	95.7	190.80	47	1.51
6. Colorado	12,271	81.5	31.76	58	.73
7. Connecticut	16,094	92.4	678.43	87	.88
8. Delaware	12,785	66.3	340.66	83	1.13
9. Florida	12,456	90.8	239.61	47	1.45
10. Georgia	11,406	65.0	111.85	50	.68
11. Hawaii	12,290	75.5	172.51	50	1.17
12. Idaho	9,159	20.4	12.17	14	.84
13. Illinois	12,437	82.7	205.62	70	1.28
14. Indiana	11,078	68.5	154.56	24	1.03
15. Iowa	11,198	44.0	49.70	53	.83
16. Kansas	11,520	53.8	30.28	27	.97
17. Kentucky	9,380	46.5	92.75	10	.95

(*continued*)

Table 10.15 (*Continued*)

State	income	metro	density	senate	waste
18. Louisiana	8,961	69.5	96.86	17	.83
19. Maine	10,478	35.9	39.79	87	.77
20. Maryland	14,697	92.8	489.10	90	1.07
21. Massachusetts	14,389	90.4	767.54	97	1.13
22. Michigan	11,973	80.1	163.62	70	1.26
23. Minnesota	12,281	67.7	54.95	77	1.01
24. Mississippi	8,088	30.1	54.85	14	.54
25. Missouri	11,203	66.2	74.27	20	1.47
26. Montana	9,322	23.9	5.49	47	.75
27. Nebraska	11,139	48.5	20.53	67	.82
28. Nevada	12,603	82.9	10.95	60	.83
29. New Hampshire	13,529	56.1	123.65	52	.99
30. New Jersey	15,028	100.0	1,041.92	94	.92
31. New Mexico	9,434	48.4	12.48	27	.99
32. New York	13,167	91.1	380.95	67	1.22
33. North Carolina	10,856	56.7	136.07	37	.91
34. North Dakota	9,641	40.3	9.26	54	.63
35. Ohio	11,323	79.0	264.86	83	1.45
36. Oklahoma	9,927	59.4	45.81	20	.95
37. Oregon	11,045	68.5	29.60	20	1.16
38. Pennsylvania	11,544	84.8	265.10	63	.80
39. Rhode Island	12,351	92.5	959.81	90	1.20
40. South Carolina	9,967	60.6	115.80	37	1.15
41. South Dakota	8,910	29.5	9.17	37	1.15
42. Tennessee	10,448	67.7	118.32	63	1.03
43. Texas	10,645	81.6	64.86	30	1.06
44. Utah	9,288	77.5	20.97	13	.70
45. Vermont	11,234	23.4	60.87	94	.69
46. Virginia	13,658	72.5	156.25	54	1.45
47. Washington	12,184	81.7	73.10	64	1.05
48. West Virginia	8,980	36.4	74.44	57	.95
49. Wisconsin	11,417	67.4	90.07	57	.70
50. Wyoming	9,826	29.6	4.68	10	.70

Source: World Resources Institute (1993).
File: *states*

*10.1 Obtain correlation and scatterplot matrices showing the five measurement variables of Table 10.15. Write a summary of what you see in the scatterplot matrix.

    a. For which variable pairs does linear OLS regression seem reasonable?

Among these pairs, which appear to have stronger relations, and which weak or near 0?
b. Which pairs exhibit signs of nonlinearity or serious outliers, so linear regression (and the correlation coefficients) may not be reasonable?
c. Which individual variable appears the most severely skewed?

*10.2 Regress per-capita waste generation on per-capita income. Interpret the regression equation and R^2. Is the slope significantly different from 0? Graph the regression line on a scatterplot.

*10.3 Regress *waste* on *metro*. Graph and summarize your findings.

*10.4 Perform a multiple regression of *waste* on both *income* and *metro*. Interpret the regression equation and R^2. How do these multiple regression results differ from your simple regressions in Problems 10.2 and 10.3?

*10.5 Regress *senate* on *density*. Graph the results, and discuss any problems you see. Which states appear as outliers?

*10.6 Regress *senate* on *density, metro*, and *income*.
a. Interpret the regression equation and R^2.
b. Which x variables have statistically significant effects?
c. Construct a residual versus predicted plot. Does this suggest any possible problems?

*10.7 Obtain base-10 logarithms of *density*. Regress *senate* on log (*density*), *metro*, and *income*. Compare the results with your findings from Problem 10.6. In what respects is this new regression an improvement?

Earlier chapters included two datasets from surveys in Vermont and Massachusetts communities where chemical wastes had contaminated drinking water supplies. Table 10.16 (page 386; file *nhtown*) lists data from another such survey, this one conducted in Milford, New Hampshire, in 1983. Variables are

water83   Household's summer 1983 water use, in cubic feet
income   Approximate household income in thousands of dollars
educ   Highest year of schooling completed by respondent (for example, 16 indicates college graduate)
retire   Household head retired? Dummy variable: 0 = not retired, 1 = retired
kids   Any children under 18 living in the household? Dummy variable: 0 = no, 1 = yes
gender   Respondent gender. Dummy variable: 0 = male, 1 = female
people   Number of people living in this household
drink   Respondent is willing to drink the water, despite reports of contamination (takes values 1, 2, 3, 4, 5, 6, 7, where 1 = strongly disagree, 7 = strongly agree)

Problems 10.8–10.14 work with the data of Table 10.16.

Table 10.16
Survey of 158 households in Milford, New Hampshire,
after reports of water contamination

Case	water83	income	educ	retire	kids	gender	people	drink
1	1,000	5	14	1	0	1	2	3
2	2,000	45	13	0	0	0	3	3
3	1,800	10	11	0	1	1	4	4
4	1,300	15	12	1	0	0	2	4
5	600	25	18	0	0	1	2	2
6	1,100	20	12	0	0	1	2	1
7	2,200	25	12	0	1	1	5	4
8	3,200	15	14	0	1	1	4	2
9	2,400	35	14	0	1	1	4	1
10	2,900	25	20	0	1	1	6	2
11	4,300	30	12	0	1	0	7	4
12	1,600	25	12	0	0	1	2	1
13	6,900	35	13	0	1	0	5	3
14	2,300	35	13	0	1	0	4	1
15	3,900	25	16	0	0	1	5	4
16	3,800	15	14	0	1	1	5	3
17	2,600	20	18	0	1	1	4	1
18	700	5	7	1	0	0	2	4
19	1,900	5	12	1	0	0	2	4
20	2,100	30	20	0	0	0	1	3
21	2,100	30	16	0	0	0	3	5
22	3,100	25	14	0	1	0	5	3
23	2,300	30	16	0	1	0	5	1
24	2,100	30	14	0	1	0	4	3
25	1,500	40	14	0	0	0	2	1
26	1,600	55	18	0	0	0	2	1
27	3,100	35	10	0	1	0	5	1
28	1,500	20	20	0	0	0	4	2
29	300	15	12	1	0	1	2	2
30	2,200	20	16	0	1	1	3	2
31	3,500	65	12	0	1	0	5	1
32	2,800	25	20	0	1	0	3	1
33	1,200	15	12	1	0	0	2	3
34	1,100	20	12	1	0	0	2	3
35	1,100	30	18	1	0	0	2	5
36	3,500	45	20	0	1	1	5	2
37	2,000	40	16	0	1	0	4	4

Table 10.16 (*Continued*)

Case	water83	income	educ	retire	kids	gender	people	drink
38	2,400	15	16	0	1	0	4	5
39	600	20	14	0	0	0	3	1
40	600	20	16	0	0	0	3	5
41	2,200	20	12	0	1	1	4	1
42	3,600	98	20	0	0	0	2	1
43	1,500	10	13	1	0	0	2	4
44	700	15	8	1	0	0	2	5
45	2,800	10	12	1	0	0	3	5
46	2,200	15	10	0	1	0	4	5
47	1,500	20	18	0	1	1	3	1
48	1,500	5	12	1	0	1	1	1
49	1,200	40	20	0	1	1	3	1
50	700	10	14	0	0	0	1	3
51	1,100	20	16	0	0	0	2	1
52	2,700	45	12	0	1	1	4	4
53	2,000	40	20	0	0	0	2	1
54	2,700	60	18	0	1	0	3	1
55	700	50	13	1	0	0	2	5
56	1,900	35	13	1	0	0	3	6
57	1,600	45	20	0	1	1	4	2
58	2,300	25	14	0	1	1	4	3
59	2,400	30	11	0	1	0	4	2
60	2,200	30	13	0	1	1	4	1
61	3,100	40	20	0	1	0	4	3
62	2,000	55	16	0	1	0	4	1
63	900	25	16	0	1	1	3	2
64	1,000	20	16	0	0	0	2	2
65	500	5	14	1	0	1	1	3
66	1,400	20	14	0	1	0	4	3
67	1,800	25	13	0	1	0	4	4
68	4,100	35	14	0	1	1	4	1
69	3,100	10	13	0	0	1	1	1
70	1,600	25	14	0	0	0	2	4
71	2,400	20	12	0	1	0	5	2
72	2,700	5	12	1	1	0	5	4
73	2,700	15	12	0	1	1	4	1
74	900	20	18	1	0	0	2	2
75	1,400	40	16	0	1	1	5	3

(*continued*)

Table 10.16 (*Continued*)

Case	water83	income	educ	retire	kids	gender	people	drink
76	1,800	40	18	0	0	1	2	7
77	1,500	20	14	1	0	0	2	5
78	700	10	12	1	0	0	2	4
79	1,800	45	20	0	1	0	4	1
80	3,100	20	12	0	1	0	5	3
81	700	5	16	1	0	1	2	4
82	1,500	50	18	0	1	1	3	1
83	1,300	25	13	1	0	1	2	4
84	2,000	35	16	0	1	1	5	5
85	3,300	15	12	0	1	1	4	4
86	2,600	45	12	0	1	1	5	1
87	1,700	30	12	0	1	1	3	5
88	1,800	25	14	0	0	0	2	5
89	4,200	45	14	0	1	0	6	5
90	700	5	14	1	0	1	1	2
91	900	25	13	1	0	0	3	5
92	1,700	10	12	0	1	1	3	4
93	1,500	35	13	0	0	1	2	3
94	1,300	20	16	0	0	0	2	5
95	1,900	25	14	0	1	0	3	2
96	400	15	16	1	0	0	2	5
97	1,400	10	12	1	0	1	2	3
98	800	15	12	1	0	1	1	3
99	900	5	16	1	0	0	2	7
100	1,400	50	12	0	1	1	3	1
101	500	10	20	1	0	1	1	1
102	4,200	30	20	1	1	0	5	2
103	2,700	35	12	0	1	1	4	1
104	400	20	12	0	0	0	2	2
105	1,800	15	13	0	1	1	4	1
106	1,100	30	12	1	0	0	2	5
107	500	5	13	1	0	1	1	1
108	3,500	45	14	0	0	1	5	1
109	2,100	40	14	0	0	0	3	4
110	2,300	20	12	0	1	1	6	3
111	800	15	13	1	0	0	2	6
112	2,600	20	10	1	0	0	2	1
113	2,100	35	14	0	1	0	4	1
114	2,600	45	12	0	0	0	2	1
115	2,400	25	13	0	1	0	4	2

Table 10.16 (*Continued*)

Case	water83	income	educ	retire	kids	gender	people	drink
116	600	5	12	1	0	1	1	3
117	2,100	30	12	0	1	0	4	3
118	300	5	10	1	0	1	1	2
119	1,400	0	8	1	0	1	2	4
120	1,900	15	12	1	0	1	2	4
121	1,000	5	12	1	0	0	2	3
122	2,300	30	14	0	1	0	5	4
123	1,300	15	9	1	0	0	2	4
124	2,100	53	13	0	1	0	4	2
125	900	10	16	0	0	1	2	2
126	1,000	30	16	0	0	0	2	1
127	3,000	15	16	0	1	1	4	1
128	800	0	12	1	0	1	2	4
129	4,100	35	14	0	1	1	7	3
130	1,700	20	16	0	1	0	3	5
131	2,200	52	14	0	1	0	3	3
132	500	0	8	1	0	1	1	3
133	2,200	30	12	0	1	0	5	2
134	2,000	20	12	0	0	0	4	1
135	1,900	20	13	0	1	1	4	2
136	600	5	18	0	1	1	2	4
137	3,300	25	13	0	1	0	4	1
138	600	10	8	1	0	0	2	1
139	4,200	40	12	0	1	0	4	3
140	1,400	10	12	0	0	1	1	4
141	1,500	5	12	1	0	0	2	3
142	2,100	20	16	0	1	0	4	5
143	1,100	10	12	0	1	1	3	3
144	2,300	45	14	0	1	0	4	3
145	2,100	20	14	0	1	1	3	4
146	300	5	11	1	0	1	1	4
147	1,600	20	14	0	0	0	2	4
148	700	40	13	0	0	1	2	1
149	1,400	30	16	0	0	1	2	1
150	200	5	13	1	0	0	2	4
151	5,000	25	12	0	1	0	5	1
152	3,800	25	14	0	1	0	5	4
153	600	0	16	1	0	1	1	4
154	4,600	30	8	0	0	1	5	4

(*continued*)

Table 10.16 (*Continued*)

Case	water83	income	educ	retire	kids	gender	people	drink
155	2,000	20	8	0	1	1	5	1
156	2,600	25	16	1	1	1	5	1
157	1,500	40	20	0	0	0	2	2
158	1,800	30	12	0	1	1	4	2

Source: Hamilton (1985a).
File: *nhtown*

*10.8   What sort of person was still willing to drink water from a well that was known to be contaminated by industrial wastes? Perform a multiple regression of *drink* on *income, education, retire,* and *gender*. Write out the multiple regression equation, state whether each coefficient is statistically significant ($P < .05$), and interpret those coefficients that are. What does R_a^2 indicate? Summarize your conclusions about how people willing to drink the water differ from other folks.

*10.9   Regress household water use on the dummy variable *kids*, and explain the resulting coefficient, t test, and R^2.

*10.10   Does *kids* still significantly predict water use, after we control for the number of people in a household? Carry out the multiple regression of *water83* on *kids* and *people*. Compare your results with those from Problem 10.9. Why does the conclusion regarding *kids* change?

*10.11   How does household *income* relate to other household or individual characteristics? Investigate through multiple regression of *income* on *educ, retire, gender, kids,* and *people*. Interpret and substantively explain each statistically significant coefficient.

*10.12   Income distributions often contain outliers, such as the $98,000 household in this survey. To check whether this or other high-income households unduly affected your analysis in Problem 10.11, repeat the *income* analysis using robust multiple regression. Compare OLS and robust results.

*10.13   What variables predict household water use? Begin by regressing *water83* on all seven other variables in this dataset. Then repeat the regression with only six x variables, dropping the one that had the lowest t value in your first regression. Continue in this manner, dropping one variable at a time until only those x variables that are statistically significant remain in the regression. (This follows a procedure called **backward stepwise regression**.)

    a.   Describe and explain how R^2 and R_a^2 changed with each simplification of the model. Judging by R_a^2, which model is the best?
    b.   Interpret the coefficients in your final model.
    c.   Graph residuals versus predicted water use. Does this graph reveal any potential problems with the regression?

*10.14   Repeat your final regression of Problem 10.13 using robust regression. Are the results much different?

Table 10.17 (file *akcounty*) contains census data on 25 Alaskan boroughs or census areas. These range from the urban concentrations of Anchorage, Fairbanks, and Juneau to large but sparsely populated areas of "bush Alaska." The state's non-Native population includes a relatively large proportion of young men who moved into the state for its job opportunities or lifestyles. For each of these 25 Alaskan regions, Table 10.17 lists the total 1990 population, and what percentage of the 20–39-year-old white population is female. A region's percent female has obvious implications for the marriage prospects of both men and women who live there. Problems 10.15–10.17 analyze these data.

Table 10.17
1990 Census data on 25 Alaskan boroughs or census areas

Borough or census area	Total 1990 population	% female among whites 20–39
1. Aleutians East borough	2,464	30.9
2. Aleutians West census area	9,478	30.4
3. Anchorage borough	226,338	48.0
4. Bethel census area	13,656	40.4
5. Bristol Bay borough	1,410	32.1
6. Dillingham census area	4,012	44.9
7. Fairbanks North Star borough	77,720	45.3
8. Haines borough	2,117	45.9
9. Juneau borough	26,751	50.5
10. Kenai Peninsula borough	40,802	48.0
11. Ketchikan Gateway borough	13,828	47.9
12. Kodiak Island borough	13,309	41.1
13. Lake and Peninsula borough	1,668	39.4
14. Matanuska-Susitna borough	39,683	49.8
15. Nome census area	8,288	41.1
16. North Slope borough	5,979	34.8
17. Northwest Arctic borough	6,113	37.1
18. Prince of Wales-Outer Ketchikan census area	6,278	41.3
19. Sitka borough	8,588	47.2
20. Skagway-Yakutat-Angoon census area	4,385	41.1
21. Southeast Fairbanks census area	5,913	46.3
22. Valdez-Cordova census area	9,952	44.2

(*continued*)

Table 10.17 (*Continued*)

Borough or census area	Total 1990 population	% female among whites 20–39
23. Wade Hampton census area	5,791	43.9
24. Wrangell-Petersburg census area	7,042	45.2
25. Yukon-Koyukuk census area	8,478	39.2

Source: 1990 Census
File: *akcounty*

*10.15   Regress percent female on population using the Alaskan data of Table 10.17.
 a.   Interpret the values of intercept, slope, and R^2.
 b.   Graph the results on a scatterplot, and discuss any possible problems you see.

*10.16   Create a new variable equal to base-10 logarithm of population, and regress percent female on log population.
 a.   Graph this regression line on a scatterplot (percent female versus log population).
 b.   Calculate predicted values from this regression. Graph these predicted values versus population (not log population) to see the curve implied by your transformed-variable regression. What does this curve indicate about the relation between percent female and population in Alaska?
 c.   Comparing the R^2 from this problem with that from Problem 10.15, does population or log population seem to be a stronger predictor of percent female?

*10.17   Check your conclusions of Problem 10.16 by performing a robust regression of percent female on log population. Graph the robust regression curve. Does this robust analysis reach the same basic conclusion about percent female and population?

Table 10.18 (file *teva194*) lists data from 44 classes taught by one university sociology department in the Spring of 1994. Variables include

evals	Mean overall student evaluation of the course, on a 1–5 scale where 5 indicates best
enroll	Number of students enrolled in the course
hours	Mean number of out-of-class hours per week students report spending on this course
grades	Mean grade students expect in the course, on a 0–4 scale where 4 indicates an "A"
ttrack	Dummy variable indicating whether the course was taught by non-tenure-track (0) or tenure-track (1) instructor

gender   Dummy variable indicating whether the course was taught by a male
            (0) or female (1) instructor

Problems 10.18–10.22 refer to these data.

Table 10.18
Mean student evaluations and other variables from 44 sociology classes

class	evals	enroll	hours	grades	ttrack	gender
1	4.26	88	4.42	3.1	1	1
2	4.37	74	4.29	3.29	0	0
3	4.05	92	3.88	3.47	0	0
4	4.7	45	2.95	3.19	0	1
5	4.84	57	4.05	3.78	0	0
6	4.33	10	5.38	3.33	1	0
7	4.63	67	4.6	3.37	1	0
8	4.12	36	3.24	3.44	0	1
9	4.3	48	4.09	3.16	0	0
10	3.91	55	3.16	3.2	0	0
11	4.14	63	4.68	3.02	0	0
12	4.62	13	3.77	3.46	1	0
13	4.36	96	4.09	2.96	1	0
14	4.48	79	5.25	2.86	1	0
15	3.3	57	4.06	2.94	0	1
16	3.67	80	3.41	3.15	1	1
17	3.7	59	5.1	3.08	1	0
18	4.06	69	3.33	3.14	0	0
19	4.63	28	4.08	3.48	0	1
20	4.32	54	3.88	3.12	0	0
21	4.56	44	2.97	3.06	0	1
22	4.03	45	4	2.97	0	1
23	2.65	52	2.7	2.96	1	0
24	4.8	9	5.6	3.4	1	0
25	4.82	27	4.73	3.18	0	1
26	4.2	21	4.93	3.4	0	1
27	4.31	46	3.85	3.21	0	0
28	4.25	38	4.14	3.25	0	0
29	3.91	43	4.43	3.06	1	0
30	2.79	39	3.42	3.11	1	1
31	3.82	13	3.55	2.58	1	0
32	4.59	46	4.41	3.49	0	1
33	4.71	39	3.9	3.66	1	0
34	3.8	5	4.6	3.4	1	1

(*continued*)

Table 10.18 (*Continued*)

class	evals	enroll	hours	grades	ttrack	gender
35	4.75	6	7.25	3.33	1	1
36	4.57	16	5.29	3.25	1	0
37	5	3	6	3	1	0
38	5	3	8.5	3.5	1	0
39	4.56	9	8	3	1	0
40	4.2	6	6.6	3.75	1	1
41	4.71	7	16	3.71	1	1
42	5	4	4	4	1	0
43	5	7	7.8	4	1	0
44	4.57	10	6.71	3.71	1	0

File: *teva194*

*10.18   Perform a multiple regression of mean teaching evaluation on the other five variables and interpret the results, with special attention to
  a.   adjusted R^2
  b.   which predictors do and do not have significant effects at the .10 statistical significance level
  c.   interpreting the coefficients of predictors that are significant at the .10 level

*10.19   Teaching evaluations often play a role in decisions about the hiring and promotion of faculty. Based on your analysis of Problem 10.18, what type of instructor would you expect (other things being equal) to have the highest mean teaching evaluations? How might studying the residuals from the regression in Problem 10.18 help us if we were asked for an opinion about the evaluations of a teacher being considered for promotion?

*10.20   Regress teaching evaluations on grades only, and graph the resulting line on a scatterplot. On your graph, identify the classes that had the two highest (positive) and two lowest (negative) residuals. Explain the meaning of predicted values and residuals for these four classes.

*10.21   Before making any policy recommendation from our analysis, we should make sure our conclusions are well founded. Graphically explore the data of Table 10.18, looking for potential statistical problems with such tools as
  a.   scatterplot matrix
  b.   boxplots of *evals* by each dummy variable
  c.   a residual versus predicted value plot

*10.22   Perform a robust regression of *evals* on the other five variables of Table 10.18. Which predictors remain statistically significant? Summarize how this robust regression and your graphical analysis of Problem 10.21 modify the conclusions you initially reached in Problem 10.18.

*10.23 Table 10.19 shows incomplete regression output from analysis with the following variables:

mathtop	percent of fourth graders in district who scored in the top quartile (top 25%) on a state math exam
income	median family income
diploma	percent of high school graduates among adults

The cases are 53 school districts. Fill in the blanks of this table, showing formulas in footnotes. Interpret the results, including regression equation, R^2, t tests, F test, and confidence intervals for the regression coefficients.

Table 10.19
Percent of fourth-grade students in district testing in top quartile on state math exam (*mathtop*) regressed on median family income (*income*) and percent of adults with high school diplomas (*diploma*), in 53 school districts

Source	SS	df	MS	
				Number of obs. = 53
				$F(2, 50)$ = _____
Model	3,650	_____	_____	Prob > F = _____
Residual	8,140	_____	_____	R-square = _____
				Adj. R-square = _____
Total	_____	_____	_____	Root MSE = _____

mathtop	Coef.	Std. Err.	t	P > |t|	[95% Conf. Interval]	
income	.00043	.00025	_____	_____	_____	_____
diploma	.49602	.19655	_____	_____	_____	_____
_cons	−31.82232	12.23552	_____	_____	_____	_____

Table 10.20 (page 396; file *aluminum*) lists measurements taken at eight ridgetop sites near an aluminum reduction plant in western Tennessee. For each site, we have

distance	distance from the aluminum plant, in kilometers
aluminum	aluminum concentration in forest litter (organic debris), measured in milligrams of aluminum per kilogram of debris
louse	the median percentage of woodlice, placed in this litter, that survived for 12 weeks—an indicator of how "healthy" the litter is for living things

These data permit analysis of how emissions from the aluminum plant affect the surrounding forest environment, in Problems 10.24–10.26.

Table 10.20
Woodlouse survival rate and aluminum
concentration in forest litter near an aluminum
reduction plant in Kentucky

Site	distance	aluminum	louse
1	1.2	6,100	17.5
2	1.4	4,400	47.5
3	3.6	2,800	65.0
4	4.4	2,700	72.5
5	4.5	2,600	60.0
6	8.8	2,800	60.0
7	32.0	2,500	67.5
8	33.0	2,700	55.0

Source: Beyer, Fleming, and Swineford (1987).
File: *aluminum*

*10.24   Regress aluminum concentration on distance from the plant, and draw the resulting regression line. What is wrong with this line?

*10.25   The scatterplot in Problem 10.24 shows *aluminum* decreasing as we get farther from the plant, but not in a linear fashion. Many physical phenomena that spread out over an area decrease approximately with the inverse square ($1/x^2$) of the distance from the source. Perhaps this will provide a better model for the aluminum pollution. To find out, follow these steps:
    a. Define a new variable equal to 1/*distance*^{2}.
    b. Regress aluminum on this new variable and graph the result. Judging from R^2, how does the fit of this curvilinear model compare with the linear model fit in Problem 10.24?
    c. Write out the new regression equation and use it to calculate predicted aluminum concentrations.
    d. On a scatterplot of *aluminum* versus *distance*, graph the predicted values from part **c** and connect them with line segments.
    e. Summarize what your graph indicates about how aluminum concentration changes with distance from the plant.

*10.26   Is forest litter with high aluminum concentrations any less healthy? Regress woodlouse survival rate on *aluminum*. Graph the result and summarize your findings. Does a linear model seem reasonable for this relation?

*10.27   Return to the 10-nation sample of Table 9.20 (file *fertile*). Perform three regressions:
    a. regress birth rate on percentage of school-age males enrolled in secondary school

b. regress birth rate on percentage of school-age females enrolled in secondary school
c. regress *birth* on both *mschool* and *fschool*
d. How does the effect of male enrollment on birth rate change, after we adjust for the percentage of females enrolled (part **c**)?

New England rivers such as the Connecticut once teemed with Atlantic salmon. Generations of damming and pollution almost eliminated the fish from these rivers, but in recent years sport fishers and environmentalists have sought to clean up the rivers and bring salmon back. Part of their efforts involved reducing the numbers of Atlantic salmon caught at sea by commercial fisheries off Newfoundland and Greenland.

Despite success in reducing pollution and ocean fishing, as of 1994 the Atlantic salmon were not returning. Some researchers blamed environmental factors, such as changes in ocean temperature, salinity, or winds. Others suggested that overfishing had affected the salmon stocks. Table 10.21 (file *salmon*) contains data that fisheries scientists employed to construct a regression model for predicting salmon abundance. Predictions from this model provided a basis for recommending how many fish could be caught by the ocean fisheries, without depleting the salmon population. The variables are

year	1974–1994
thermal	Thermal habitat index. Higher numbers indicate better (warmer) conditions for salmon. The values shown are in "scientific notation." For instance, $1.75e \pm 09$ means $1.75 \times 10^9 = 1,750,000,000$ (1.75 billion). Computer programs often employ scientific notation to display very large or very small numbers.
wind	wind speed index (meters per second), in an area south of Greenland in December
salmon	estimated abundance of salmon, before fishing

Problems 10.28–10.31 analyze these data.

Table 10.21
Data for model predicting salmon abundance

year	thermal	wind	salmon
1974	1.75e+09	9.68	688,402
1975	1.84e+09	9.98	794,855
1976	1.95e+09	11.38	706,625
1977	1.99e+09	13.10	566,473
1978	1.98e+09	12.10	321,118
1979	2.00e+09	12.56	706,360
1980	2.09e+09	11.68	619,446

(*continued*)

Table 10.21 (*Continued*)

year	thermal	wind	salmon
1981	1.80e+09	10.34	592,079
1982	1.77e+09	10.53	491,149
1983	1.63e+09	13.64	270,869
1984	1.37e+09	13.90	292,750
1985	1.47e+09	12.66	467,691
1986	1.70e+09	12.46	500,576
1987	1.52e+09	11.71	461,324
1988	1.73e+09	11.76	367,593
1989	1.64e+09	12.73	300,342
1990	1.57e+09	14.34	256,222
1991	1.48e+09	12.02	276,284
1992	1.37e+09	15.78	171,869
1993	1.33e+09	10.80	.
1994	1.39e+09	9.72	.

Source: North Atlantic Salmon Work Group (1994, unpublished).
File: *salmon*

*10.28   Construct time plots showing how the thermal index, wind speed, and salmon abundance changed over the years covered by these data. Describe any trends you see in these three time series.

*10.29   Use regression to evaluate possible models for predicting salmon abundance. Which of these seems best (has the highest adjusted R^2)?
    a.   regress *salmon* on *thermal*
    b.   regress *salmon* on *wind*
    c.   regress *salmon* on both *thermal* and *wind*

*10.30   Calculate predicted salmon abundance using your best regression model from Problem 10.29. Graph both the predicted values and the estimated salmon abundance together on one time plot. In what respects do the model's predictions fit the data? What does your model predict about salmon abundance during 1993 and 1994?

*10.31   Preliminary data from 1993 and 1994 suggest that salmon abundance actually declined further. These results do not agree with predictions of a thermal/wind speed model (Problems 10.29 and 10.30). For comparison, we might contrast the thermal/wind speed model with a simpler alternative: that salmon abundance declined steadily (due to overfishing or other factors) over the years 1974–92. To fit this "trend model," just regress *salmon* on *year*. How well does the trend model fit, compared with the more complicated thermal/wind speed model? What does it predict for 1993 and 1994?

References

Acharya, Iswar L., et al. (1987). "Prevention of typhoid fever in Nepal with the Vi capsular polysaccharide of Salmonella typhi." *New England Journal of Medicine* 317(18): 1101–1104.

Achen, Christopher H. (1982). *Interpreting and Using Regression*. Beverly Hills, CA: Sage.

Anagnoson, J. Theodore, and Richard E. DeLeon (1994). *StataQuest*. Belmont, CA: Duxbury.

Babbie, Earl (1995). *The Practice of Social Research*, 7th ed. Belmont, CA: Wadsworth.

Barron's Educational Series (1992). *Barron's Compact Guide to Colleges*, 8th ed. New York: Barron's Educational Series.

Berry, William D., and Stanley Feldman (1985). *Multiple Regression in Practice*. Newbury Park, CA: Sage.

Beyer, W. Nelson, W. James Fleming, and Douglas Swineford (1987). "Changes in litter near an aluminum reduction plant." *Journal of Environmental Quality* 16(3): 246–250.

Blocker, T. Jean, and Douglas Lee Eckberg (1989). "Environmental issues as women's issues: General concerns and local hazards." *Social Science Quarterly* 70(3): 586–593.

Bring, Johan (1994). "How to standardize regression coefficients." *The American Statistician* 48(3): 209–213.

Brown, Lester R., Hal Kane, and David Malin Roodman (1994). *Vital Signs 1994: The Trends That Are Shaping Our Future*. New York: W. W. Norton.

Burt, Barbara J. and Max Neiman (1985). "Urban legislative response to regulatory energy policy." *Policy Studies Review* 5(1): 81–88.

Cameron, Raymond D., Daniel J. Reed, James R. Dau, and Walter T. Smith (1992). "Redistribution of calving caribou in response to oil field development on the Arctic Slope of Alaska." *Arctic* 45(4): 338–342.

Chmeil, Joan S. et al. (1987). "Factors associated with prevalent immunodeficiency virus (HIV) infection in the Multicenter AIDS Cohort Study." *American Journal of Epidemiology* 126(4): 568–576.

Christenson, James A., and Lee Sigelman (1985). "Accrediting knowledge: Journal stature and citation impact in social science." *Social Science Quarterly* 66(4): 964–975.

Clarke, R. D. (1946). "An application of the Poisson distribution." *Journal of the Institute of Actuaries* 22:48.

Cleves, Mario A. (1995). "Robust tests for the equality of variances." *Stata Technical Bulletin* 25: 13–15.

Condon, Richard G. (1988). *Inuit Youth: Growth and Change in the Canadian Arctic*. New Brunswick, NJ: Rutgers University.

Council on Environmental Quality (1987). *Environmental Quality 1985*. Washington, D.C: Council on Environmental Quality.

Cox, C. Barry, and Peter D. Moore (1993). *Biogeography: An Ecological and Evolutionary Approach*. London: Blackwell.

Daly, Martin, and Margo I. Wilson (1982). "Whom are newborn babies said to resemble?" *Ethology and Sociobiology* 3:69–78.

Everitt, B. S. (1977). *The Analysis of Contingency Tables*. London: Chapman and Hall.

Fatoki, O. S. (1987). "Calorimetric determination of lead in tree leaves as indicators of atmospheric pollution." *Environment International* 13:369–373.

Fox, John, and J. Scott Long, Eds. (1990). *Modern Methods of Data Analysis*. Newbury Park, CA: Sage.

Frank, Ellen, Linda L. Carpenter, and David J. Kupfer (1988). "Sex differences in recurrent depression: Are there any that are significant?" *American Journal of Psychiatry* 145(1): 41–45.

Hamilton, Lawrence C. (1980). "Grades, class size, and faculty status predict teaching evaluations." *Teaching Sociology* 8:47–62.

Hamilton, Lawrence C. (1981). "Self-reports of academic performance: Response errors are not well behaved." *Sociological Methods and Research* 10:165–185.

Hamilton, Lawrence C. (1985a). "Who cares about water pollution? Opinions in a small-town crisis." *Sociological Inquiry* 55(2): 170–181.

Hamilton, Lawrence C. (1985b). "Concern about toxic wastes: Three demographic predictors." *Sociological Perspectives* 28(4): 463–486.

Hamilton, Lawrence C. (1992). *Regression with Graphics: A Second Course in Applied Statistics*. Pacific Grove, CA: Brooks/Cole.

Hamilton, Lawrence C. (1993a). *Statistics with Stata 3*. Belmont, CA: Duxbury.

Hamilton, Lawrence C. (1993b). "Overestimating mineral wealth: U.S.G.S. quantitative assessment methods." *American Statistical Association 1993 Proceedings of the Section on Statistics and the Environment,* 117–122.

Hamilton, Lawrence C., and Carole L. Seyfrit (1993). "Town-village contrasts in Alaskan youth aspirations." *Arctic* 46(3): 255–263.

Hamilton, Lawrence C., and Carole L. Seyfrit (1994). "Resources and hopes in Newfoundland." *Society and Natural Resources* 7(6): 561–578.

Hanushek, Eric A. and John E. Jackson (1977). *Statistical Methods for Social Scientists*. New York: Academic Press.

Hearst, N., and S. Hulley (1988). "Preventing the heterosexual spread of AIDS: Are we giving our patients the best advice?" *Journal of the American Medical Association* 259:2428–2432.

Herman, Wayne L., Jr., Michael Hawkins, and Charles Berryman (1985). "World place name location skills of elementary pre-service teachers." *Journal of Educational Research* 79(1): 33–35.

Hinkle, Dennis E., William Wiersma, and Stephen G. Jurs (1979). *Applied Statistics for the Behavioral Sciences*. Chicago: Rand McNally.

Hoaglin, David C., Frederick Mosteller, and John W. Tukey, Eds. (1983). *Understanding Robust and Exploratory Data Analysis*. New York: Wiley.

Hoaglin, David C., Frederick Mosteller, and John W. Tukey, Eds. (1985). *Exploring Data Tables, Trends, and Shapes*. New York: Wiley.

Hohn, Aleta A., Michael D. Scott, Randall S. Wells, Jay C. Sweeney, and A. Blair Irvine (1989). "Growth layers in teeth from known-age, free-ranging bottlenose dolphins." *Marine Mammal Science* 5(4): 315–342.

Hornbein, Thomas F. (1966). *Everest: The West Ridge*. San Francisco: Sierra Club.

Hornbein, Thomas F., Brenda D. Townes, Robert B. Schoene, John R. Sutton, and Charles S. Houston (1989). "The cost to the central nervous system of climbing to extremely high altitude." *New England Journal of Medicine* 321(25): 1714–1720.

Hosmer, David W., and Stanley Lemeshow (1989). *Applied Logistic Regression*. New York: Wiley.

Houghton, A., E. W. Munster, and M. V. Viola (1978). "Increased incidence of malignant melanoma after peaks of sunspot activity." *The Lancet*, 8 April, 759–760.

Jacobsen, Grace, Joan E. Thiele, Joan H. McCune, and Larry D. Farrell (1985). "Handwashing: Ring-wearing and number of microorganisms." *Nursing Research* 34(3): 186–188.

Johnson, Anne M., Jane Wadsworth, Kaye Wellings, Sally Bradshaw, and Julia Field (1992). "Sexual lifestyles and HIV risk." *Nature* 360 (3 December): 410–412.

Jorgensen, Joseph G. (1990). *Oil Age Eskimos*. Berkeley, CA: University of California Press.

Jorgensen, Joseph G. (1991). *Social Indicators Project II Research Methodology: Design, Sampling, Reliability, and Validity*. New Haven, CT: Human Relations Area Files.

Kalmuss, Debra, and Judith A. Seltzer (1986). "Continuity of marital behavior in remarriage:

The case of spouse abuse." *Journal of Marriage and the Family* 48:113–120.

Keane, Anne, Joseph Ducette, and Diane C. Adler (1985). "Stress in ICU and non-ICU nurses." *Nursing Research* 34(4): 231–236.

Knox, Richard A. (1987). "Empty beds in hospitals fuel health bill debate." *Boston Globe* 1 November: 1, 26.

League of Conservation Voters (1990). *The 1990 National Environmental Scorecard.* Washington, DC: League of Conservation Voters.

Lehman, Betsy A. (1988). "The water won't kill you, but . . ." *Boston Globe,* May 16, 1988: 45.

MacKenzie, Donald (1990). *Inventing Accuracy: A Historical Sociology of Nuclear Missile Guidance.* Cambridge, MA: MIT Press.

McGee, Glenn W. (1987). "Social context variables affecting the implementation of microcomputers." *Journal of Educational Computing Research* 3(1): 95–111.

Mendenhall, William (1987). *Introduction to Probability and Statistics.* Boston: Prindle, Weber & Schmidt.

Miller, Lawrence W. (1986). "Political recruitment and electoral success: A look at sex differences in municipal elections." *The Social Science Journal* 23(1): 75–90.

Mosteller, Frederick, and John W. Tukey (1977). *Data Analysis and Regression.* Reading, MA: Addison-Wesley.

Murray, M. L., D. B. Chambers, R. A. Knapp, and S. Kaplan (1987). "Estimation of long-term risk from Canadian uranium mill tailings." *Risk Analysis* 7(3): 287–295.

Mussala-Rauhamaa, H., S. S. Salmela, A. Leppänen, and H. Pyysalo (1986). "Cigarettes as a source of some trace and heavy metals and pesticides in man." *Archives of Environmental Health* 41(1): 49–55.

Neave, H. R., and P. L. Worthington (1988). *Distribution-Free Tests.* London: Unwin Hyman.

Oldaker, Guy B. III, and Fred C. Conrad, Jr. (1987): "Estimation of effect of environmental tobacco smoke on air quality within cabins of commercial aircraft." *Environmental Science and Technology* 21(10): 994–998.

Palm, Risa (1986). "Racial and ethnic influences in real estate practices." *The Social Science Journal* 23(1): 45–53.

Perrow, Charles (1984). *Normal Accidents: Living with High-Risk Technologies.* New York: Basic Books.

Pynchon, Thomas (1973). *Gravity's Rainbow.* New York: Viking.

Rand Corporation (1955). *A Million Random Digits with 100,000 Normal Deviates.* Glencoe, IL: Free Press.

Rawlings, John O. (1988). *Applied Regression Analysis: A Research Tool.* Pacific Grove, CA: Wadsworth and Brooks/Cole.

Rice, Patricia C., and Ann L. Paterson (1985). "Cave art and bones: Exploring the interrelationships." *American Anthropologist* 87:94–100.

Rice, Patricia C., and Ann L. Paterson (1986). "Validating the cave art-archeofaunal relationship in Cantabrian Spain." *American Anthropologist* 88:658–667.

Root, David H., W. David Menzie, and William A. Scott (1992). "Computer Monte Carlo simulation in quantitative resource estimation." *Nonrenewable Resources* 1(2): 125–138.

Rudner, Lawrence M. (1987). *What's Happening in Teacher Testing: An Analysis of State Teacher Testing Practices.* Washington, DC: U.S. Department of Education.

Schroeder, Larry D., David L. Sjoquist, and Paula E. Stephan (1986). *Understanding Regression Analysis: An Introductory Guide.* Newbury Park, CA: Sage.

Seyfrit, Carole L. (1993). *Hibernia's Generation: Social Impacts of Oil Development on Adolescents in Newfoundland. Offshore Oil Project Report.* St. John's: Institute of Social and Economic Research, Memorial University of Newfoundland.

Seyfrit, Carole L., and Lawrence C. Hamilton (1992). "Who will leave? Oil, migration, and Scottish island youth." *Society and Natural Resources* 5(3): 263–276.

Sivard, Ruth Leger (1985). *World Military and Social Expenditures 1985.* Washington, D.C.: World Priorities.

Smith, Peter K. and Kathryn Lewis (1985). "Rough-and-tumble play, fighting, and chasing in nursery school children." *Ethnology and Sociobiology* 6: 175–181.

Specht, David A., and Richard D. Warren (1975). "Comparing causal models," In *Sociological Methodology 1976,* edited by David R. Heise, 46–82. San Francisco: Jossey-Bass.

Spika, John S., Francois Dabis, Nancy Hargrett-Bean, Joachim Salcedo, Serge Veillard, and Paul A. Blake (1987). "Shigellosis at a Caribbean resort." *American Journal of Epidemiology* 126(6): 1173–1181.

Statistics Canada (1991). *Human Activity and the Environment.* Ottawa: Statistics Canada.

Taylor, Jim (1984). "The unemployment of university graduates." *Research in Education* 31(May): 11–24.

Treacy, Paul (1985). "WISC-R Profiles of Truly Reading-Disabled Boys." Ph.D. diss., Kensington University, California.

Tufte, Edward R. (1983). *The Visual Display of Quantitative Information.* Cheshire, CT: Graphics Press.

Tukey, John W. (1977). *Exploratory Data Analysis.* Reading, MA: Addison-Wesley.

Ubell, Earl (1989). "Is your job killing you?" *Parade* 8 January: 4–6.

Ungerholm, S., and J. Gustavsson (1985). "Skiing safety in children: A prospective study of downhill skiing injuries and their relation to the skier and his equipment." *International Journal of Sports Medicine* 6(6): 353–358.

United States National Park Service (1991). *1986 National Park Statistical Abstract.* Denver, CO: Department of Interior.

Upton, Graham J. G. (1978). *The Analysis of Cross-Tabulated Data.* New York: Wiley.

Velleman, Paul F., and David C. Hoaglin (1981). *Applications, Basics, and Computing of Exploratory Data Analysis.* Belmont, CA: Duxbury.

Velleman, Paul F., and Leland Wilkinson (1993). "Nominal, ordinal, interval and ratio typologies are misleading." *American Statistician* 47(1): 65–72.

Ward, Sally, and Susan Ault (1990). "AIDS knowledge, fear, and safe sex practices on campus." *Sociology and Social Research* 74(3): 158–161.

Williams, Kirk R., and Robert L. Flewelling (1988). "The social production of criminal homicide: A comparative case study of disaggregated rates in American cities." *American Sociological Review* 53(3): 421–431.

World Bank (1987). *World Development Report 1987.* New York: Oxford University Press.

World Resources Institute (1993). *The 1993 Information Please Environmental Almanac.* Boston: Houghton Mifflin.

Wright, Jeff R., Mark H. Houck, James T. Diamond, and Dean Randall (1986). "Drought contingency planning." *Civil Engineering Systems* 3 (December): 210–215.

Appendix I: Results for Selected Exercises

Chapter 1

1.3.1a.

Gender	Frequency	Percentage
male	12	27.91
female	31	72.09
Total	43	100.00

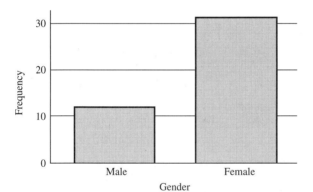

1.3.1b.

Age	Frequency	Percentage
17	1	2.33
18	6	13.95
19	4	9.30
20	17	39.53
21	6	13.95
22	3	6.98
23	1	2.33
24	2	4.65
25	1	2.33
30	1	2.33
43	1	2.33
Total	43	100.00

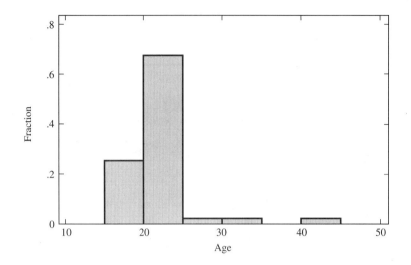

1.4.1a.

Percent male 1991	Frequency	Percentage
40–44	2	18.18
45–49	5	45.45
50–54	2	18.18
55–59	1	9.09
60–64	1	9.09
Total	11	100.00

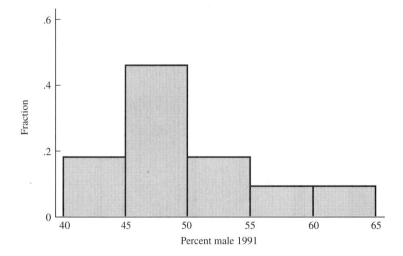

1.5.1.

Variable	n	average
enroll	11	2,971.9

1.6.1.

Expected grade in statistics	Gender male	female	Total
C	3 25.0%	3 9.7%	6 13.9%
B	6 50.0%	22 71.0%	28 65.1%
A	3 25.0%	6 19.3%	9 20.9%
Total	12 100.0%	31 100.0%	43 100.0%

1.6.2.

Expected grade in statistics	Summary of Mathematics SAT score average	n
C	475.00	6
B	524.09	22
A	557.50	8
Total	523.33	36

Chapter 2

2.1.1.

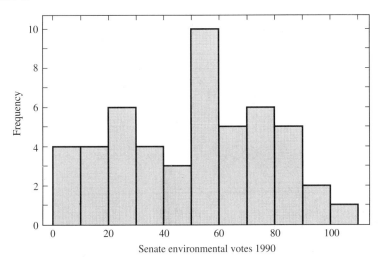

2.2.1.

Senate votes grouped	Freq.	Percent	Cum.
0–9	4	8.00	8.00
10–19	4	8.00	16.00
20–29	6	12.00	28.00
30–39	4	8.00	36.00
40–49	3	6.00	42.00
50–59	10	20.00	62.00
60–69	5	10.00	72.00
70–79	6	12.00	84.00
80–89	5	10.00	94.00
90–99	2	4.00	98.00
100–109	1	2.00	100.00
Total	50	100.00	

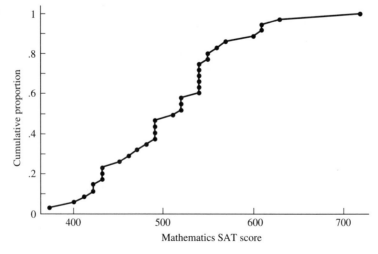

2.2.2.

2.3.1a. The distribution is positively skewed. Most of the students could name no more than one concept from the reading. A few were able to name more, up to seven concepts.

2.3.2a. The weights of Olympic marathon runners and sumo wrestlers should form a distribution with two distinct peaks: a group of lighter weights (the runners) and a group of heavier weights (the wrestlers).

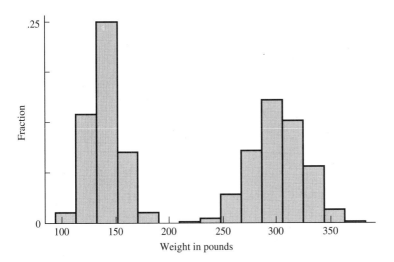

2.4.1. Stem-and-leaf display for Senate environmental voting: Stems digits are 10's, leaves are 1's; 9 | 2 means 92% of votes were cast in the direction recommended by environmentalists.

```
 0 | 0888
 1 | 3777
 2 | 155555
 3 | 3348
 4 | 226
 5 | 4444555899
 6 | 33377
 7 | 111559
 8 | 04448
 9 | 26
10 | 0
```

The distribution has a central peak in the 50's. Secondary peaks appear in the 20's and in the 70's, indicating subgroups of Senators with more strongly anti- or pro-environmentalist records.

2.6.1.

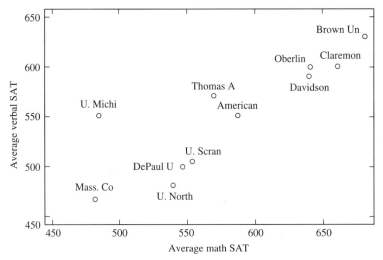

Chapter 3

3.1.1.

Gender	Mean episodes
girl	14.1
boy	21.5
Total	18.7

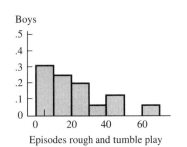

3.2.1.

Gender	Episodes of rough & tumble play		
	Mean	Std. Dev.	Freq.
girl	14.1	12.1	10
boy	21.5	16.7	16
Total	18.7	15.3	26

3.3.1a. $Md = 2{,}765$

3.3.2. $Md(\text{girls}) = 9.5$, $Md(\text{boys}) = 19$

3.4.1a. $Md = 520$, $\bar{y} = 523.33$

3.4.2a. $\bar{y}\,(\text{with }1{,}000) = 523.33$, $\bar{y}\,(\text{without }1{,}000) = 509.71$

3.5.1.   🖾 # episodes rough & tumble play

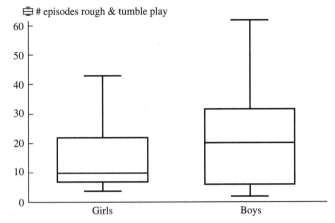

3.6.1.

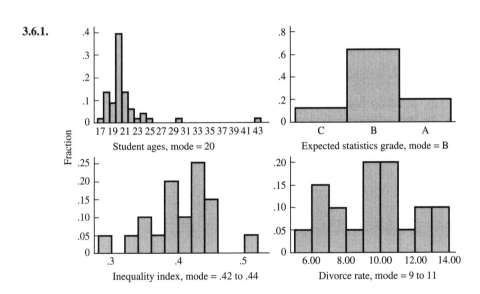

Chapter 4

4.1.2a.

```
                          ┌ girl   P(G2) = .49    P(G1 and G2) = .2401
         ┌ girl   P(G1) = .49 ┤
         │                └ boy    P(B2) = .51    P(G1 and B2) = .2499
         │
         │
         │                ┌ girl   P(G2) = .49    P(B1 and G2) = .2499
         └ boy    P(B1) = .51 ┤
                          └ boy    P(B2) = .51    P(B1 and B2) = .2601
```

We can use the simple addition rule, since the final outcomes are mutually exclusive events:

$$P\{(B1 \text{ and } G2) \text{ or } (G1 \text{ and } B2)\} = P(B1 \text{ and } G2) + P(G1 \text{ and } B2)$$
$$= .2499 + .2499$$
$$= .4998$$

4.2.2a. $P(Q) = 4/52 = .076923$

4.2.2b. $P(\text{not } Q) = 1 - .076923$

4.4.1.

Heterosexual partners in lifetime	Gender		Total
	male	female	
none	.03	.02	.03
one	.15	.31	.24
two	.09	.18	.14
three or more	.73	.49	.59
Total	1.00	1.00	1.00

4.4.2. Having three or more partners is not independent of gender; the conditional probability of three or more partners among males:

$P(\text{three or more} \mid \text{male}) = .73$

is higher than the unconditional probability of three or more partners:

$P(\text{three or more}) = .59.$

Correspondingly, the conditional probability of three or more partners among females:

$P(\text{three or more} \mid \text{female}) = .49$

is lower than the unconditional probability.

4.4.3a. Among both males and females, only a small proportion (2 or 3%) report having no heterosexual partners in their lifetimes.

4.5.1a. $P(3) \times P(3) \times P(3) \times P(3) \times P(3) = .1^5 = .00001$

Chapter 5

5.1.1. With eight trials ($n = 8$), and a constant probability $p = .5$ of heads on each trial, $P(f \geq 6) = .1445.$

5.1.2. With five trials ($n = 5$), and a constant probability $p = .47$ of scoring on each trial:

$P(f = 5) = .0229,$
$P(f \geq 4) = .1522,$
$P(f \geq 3) = .4439.$

5.2.2. $P(y \geq 4) = .3528$, $P(y \geq 8) = .0120$

5.3.3a. $z = (800 - 500)/75 = 4$

A score of 800 is 4 standard deviations above the mean.

5.4.1a. $P[(x < \mu - 3\sigma) \text{ or } (x > \mu + 3\sigma)] = 2 \times (.5 - .4987) = .0026$

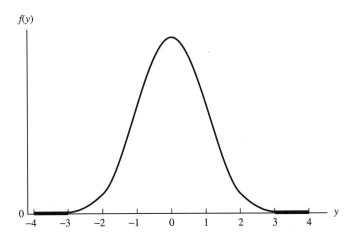

5.4.2b. $P(y < \mu + 1\sigma) = .8413$

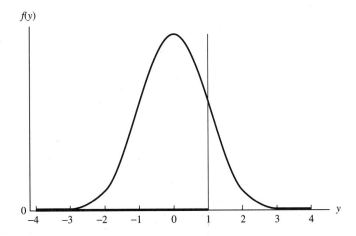

5.4.3a. The top 2.28% of students have grade point averages of 3.82 or higher.

5.4.3b. In a normal distribution, 2.28% of the values lie at least this far below the mean.

5.5.1a. $P(\chi^2[4] > 50) < .001$

5.5.1b. $P(\chi^2[2] > .5) > .500$

5.5.2a. $P(\chi^2[4] > 50) = 3.611 \times 10^{-10}$

5.5.2b. $P(\chi^2[2] > .5) = .7788$

5.6.1a. $P(t[5] > 2.015) = .05$

5.6.1c. $P(|t[13]| > 2.650) = .02$

5.6.2a. $.005 < P(t[3] > 5) < .01$

5.6.2c. $.05 < P(|t[\infty]| > 1.7) < .10$

5.6.3a. $P(t[3] > 5) = .0077$

5.6.3c. $P(|t[\infty]| > 1.7) = .0891$

5.7.1a. $P(F[4, 30] > 8.3) < .001$

5.7.2a. $\text{VR} = 9/4 = 2.25, P(F[20, 12] > 2.25) = .0756$

The two-tail probability is $.0756 + 1 - .9475 = .1281$, so we cannot reject the null hypothesis that population variances are equal.

Chapter 6

6.2.1. 90% confidence interval:

$$.6 \pm 1.645 \sqrt{\frac{.6(1 - .6)}{160}}$$

$$.6 \pm .064$$

Based on this one sample, we are 90% confident that the larger population of students is between 53.6% and 66.4% female.

6.3.1a. $H_0: \pi \geq .10, H_1: \pi < .10$

π represents the proportion defective, among all those parachutes we manufacture.

6.3.2a. Type I error: mistakenly concluding that less than 10% of our parachutes are defective, when the true proportion defective is higher. This error leads us to believe the parachutes are safer than they actually are.

Type II error: mistakenly not concluding that less than 10% of our parachutes are defective, when the true proportion defective is in fact below 10%. This error leads us to believe the parachutes are more dangerous than they actually are.

6.4.1. $z = \dfrac{.59 - .5}{\sqrt{.5(1 - .5)/160}} = 2.277$

$.02 < P(|z| > 2.277) < .05$

Since $P < .05$, we can reject the null hypothesis. The population proportion that would accurately report their GPA does not equal 50%.

6.4.2. $z = \dfrac{.88 - .95}{\sqrt{.95(1 - .95)/7,500}} = -27.82$

$P(z < -27.82) < .0000005$

Since $P < .05$, we easily reject the null hypothesis. The population proportion of smokers surviving to at least 55 is lower than 95%, the proportion surviving among nonsmokers.

6.5.1a. $s_{\bar{y}} = .4/\sqrt{44} = .06$

6.5.1b. Since $n = 44$, $df = 44 - 1 = 43$ (approximately 40). For an 80% confidence interval, according to Table A.4, we need $t = 1.303$. Therefore the interval is

$$1.4 \pm 1.303 \times .4/\sqrt{44}$$

Based on this sample, we are 80% confident that in the population of all cigarette brands, the mean cadmium content is between 1.32 and 1.48 micrograms/gram:

$$1.32 < \mu < 1.48$$

6.6.1. $t = (525 - 536)/(95/\sqrt{160})$
$= -1.46$

$.10 < P(|t[159]| > 1.46) < .20$

We cannot reject the null hypothesis. The sociology student mean may be no different from the mean for the college's undergraduates as a whole.

6.7.1. $t = (1.5 - 0)/(3/\sqrt{60})$
$= 3.87$

$P(|t[59]| > 3.87) < .001$

We can reject the null hypothesis. The children's mean scores changed significantly following the Logo programming experience.

6.8.1a. $z = \dfrac{68 - .5(160 - 51)}{.5\sqrt{160 - 51}} = 2.59$

$P(|z| > 2.59) < .01$ (by computer, $P = .0096$)

6.8.1b. For samples of size $n - n_0 = 109$ observations, given $p = .5$, the probability of counts greater than or equal to 68 is $P(f \geq 68) = .0062$. The two-tail probability is therefore .0124, slightly higher than that estimated through the normal approximation in 6.8.1a; both methods lead to rejecting the null hypothesis that the median difference equals zero.

6.8.3. 0 positive (x higher than y)
4 negative (x lower than y)
2 zero (x equal to y)

Given $n - n_0 = 4, f = 4, p = .5, 2 \times P(f \geq 4) = .1250$. Based on these data, we cannot reject the null hypothesis of 0 median difference.

6.9.1a. $n = \dfrac{2.576^2\ 75^2}{5^2} = 1{,}493$

Chapter 7

7.2.2.

Spouse abuse	Present family type			Total
	intact	remarried	reconstituted	
no abuse	743 (734)	92 (95.2)	78 (83.9)	913
abuse	36 (45)	9 (5.8)	11 (5.1)	56
	779	101	89	969

Apart from round-off error, the expected frequencies (in parentheses) add to the same row and column marginals as the observed frequencies do.

7.3.1a. $.025 < P(\chi^2[1] > 4) < .05$ (from Table A.3), $P(\chi^2[1] > 4) = .0455$ (from computer)

7.3.2. $P(\chi^2[2] > 10.81) = .004$. We reject the null hypothesis that in the population, spouse abuse and family type are independent. There does exist some relation between these two variables.

7.4.2. $z = \dfrac{5/14 - 9/16}{\sqrt{(14/30)(1 - 14/30)(1/14 + 1/16)}}$
$= -1.124787$

This z statistic is identical to that obtained earlier. It does not matter whether we test the proportions of large and small classes taught by untenured faculty, or by tenured faculty. Since the two faculty groups are complementary, these two tests are equivalent, and each leads to the same conclusion as the chi-square test of Table 7.7.

7.4.3. $(5/14 - 9/16) \pm 1.96 \sqrt{\dfrac{(5/14)(1 - 5/14)}{14} + \dfrac{(9/16)(1 - 9/16)}{16}}$
$-.2054 \pm .3494$

Thus we are 95% confident, based on this sample, that the population difference in proportions lies in the interval

$-.5548 < \pi < .1441$

Since this interval includes 0, we cannot rule out the null hypothesis that tenured faculty teach the same proportions of large and small classes.

Chapter 8

8.1.1b, c.

	Summary of social bonds to community		
Gender	Mean	Std. Dev.	Freq.
male	51.54	24.527676	15
female	49.78	25.10197	15
Total	50.66	24.401281	30

$$t[28] = .19, P(|t[28]| > .19) = .8474$$

We cannot reject the null hypothesis that in the population, mean male and female bonds are equal. The difference seen in this sample is slight, and not statistically significant.

8.2.1a. $z = .44$ $P(|z| > .44) = .6632$. The Mann–Whitney test reaches a conclusion similar to our earlier t test: no significant difference between males and females.

8.4.1a. The normality and equal-variances assumptions appear questionable. Two distributions are positively skewed, and a third exhibits less variation.

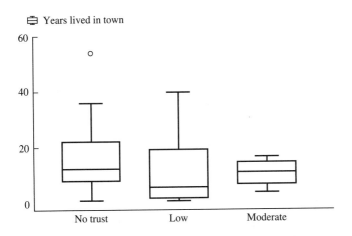

8.4.1b. ANOVA: $F = .85$, $P(F[2, 47] > .85) = .4321$. We cannot reject the null hypothesis of equal population means.

8.4.1c. Kruskal–Wallis test: $X^2 = 3.088$, $P(\chi^2[2] > 3.088) = .2135$. We cannot reject the null hypothesis that the population rank distributions are the same. Although they reach similar conclusions, Kruskal–Wallis is preferable to ANOVA here because of possible violations of the normality and equal-variance assumptions.

8.5.1a.

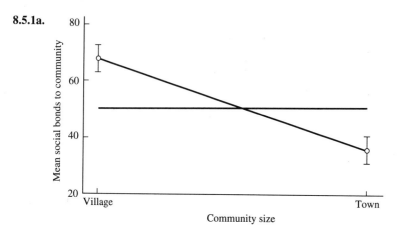

8.5.1b.

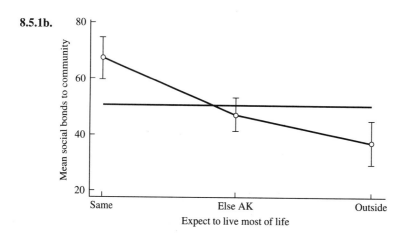

8.5.1c.

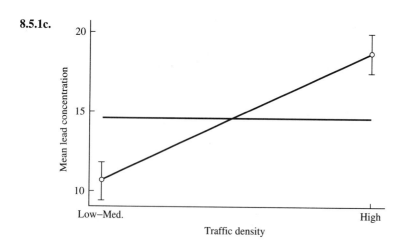

8.6.2. Means of Social bonds to community

Expect to live most of life	Town or village village	town	Total
same	70.0375	43.799999	67.122222
else AK	66.94	35.212499	47.415384
out AK	54.400002	34.985714	37.4125
Total	67.814286	35.649999	50.66

Number of obs = 30 R-squared = 0.4581
Root MSE = 18.9708 Adj R-squared = 0.3956

Source	Partial SS	df	MS	F	Prob > F
Model	7910.09132	3	2636.69711	7.33	0.0010
where	185.516107	2	92.7580535	0.26	0.7747
size	3930.22051	1	3930.22051	10.92	0.0028
Residual	9357.16116	26	359.890814		
Total	17267.2525	29	595.4225		

The relation between *where* and *bonds* becomes nonsignificant ($P = .7747$) once we control for *size*. The relation between *size* and *bonds* remains significant ($P = .0028$), controlling for *where*. Evidently, the bivariate relation we saw earlier between *bonds* and where students expect to live can be explained partly by the facts that both *bonds* and *where* are related to community size: Students in smaller villages express stronger bonds, and also are more likely to stay there.

8.6.3. Means of Social bonds to community

Gender	Arctic or Bristol Bay? Bristol	Arctic	Total
male	15.3	57.115384	51.54
female	69.533334	36.61111	49.78
Total	55.975001	48.727272	50.66

Number of obs = 30 R-squared = 0.4028
Root MSE = 19.9145 Adj R-squared = 0.3339

Source	Partial SS	df	MS	F	Prob > F
Model	6955.95323	3	2318.65108	5.85	0.0034
gender	1331.04992	1	1331.04992	3.36	0.0784
region	92.5333263	1	92.5333263	0.23	0.6331
gender * region	6535.28084	1	6535.28084	16.48	0.0004
Residual	10311.2993	26	396.588433		
Total	17267.2525	29	595.4225		

The *gender* ∗ *region* interaction is statistically significant, meaning that the relation between *gender* and *bonds* is different in the two regions. Among Bristol Bay respondents, females expressed stronger bonds than males; but among Northwest Arctic respondents, the opposite was true.

Chapter 9

9.1.1. predicted *homicide* = .9634 + .0243*pop*

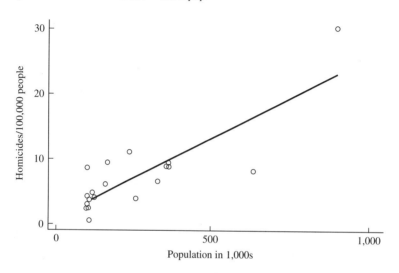

The *y*-intercept, .9634, predicts that a city with 0 population would have a .9634 homicide rate. This makes no substantive sense, since no large U.S. cities have 0 population. The slope, .0243, suggests that predicted homicide rate (homicide victims per 100,000 people) increases by .0243 with each one unit (1,000-person) increase in population, or by 24.3 with each 1-million increase in population.

9.2.1c.

player	height	rebounds	ŷ	e
1. Willis	84	704	621.7792	82.22077
2. Bird	81	805	457.5912	347.4088
3. Walton	83	544	567.0499	− 23.04988
4. Leavell	73	67	19.75634	47.24366
5. Lee	82	351	512.3205	− 161.3205
6. Brewer	76	53	183.9444	− 130.9444
7. Sampson	88	781	840.6967	− 59.69665
8. Reid	80	301	402.8618	− 101.8618

Larry Bird caught 347 more rebounds than we might predict, based on his comparatively modest 6′9″ height alone. Bill Walton, a taller player, caught 23 fewer rebounds than we might predict based on his height.

9.2.1d.

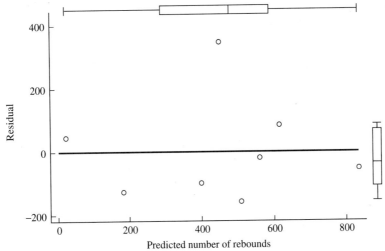

9.3.1.

	height	rebounds	points	minutes
height	1.0000			
rebounds	.8424	1.0000		
points	.4835	.8044	1.0000	
minutes	.5779	.8577	.9512	1.0000

9.3.3. Spearman rank correlation $r_s = .7381$, Pearson correlation $r = .8424$

9.4.1a. Based on this sample of cities, we are 95% confident that in the population consisting of all U.S. cities, the slope relating population to homicide rate lies in the interval

$$.0162781 < \beta < .0323234$$

9.4.2a.

*homic = .9633553 + .0243008 * pop*

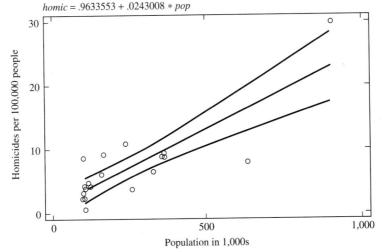

Chapter 10

10.1.1a.

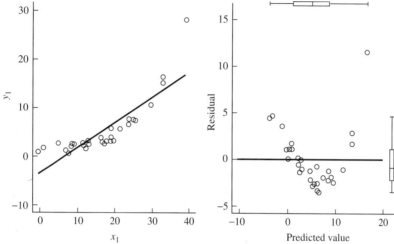

10.1.1b.

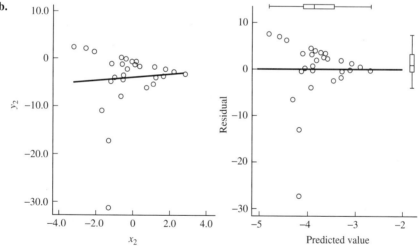

10.1.1c.

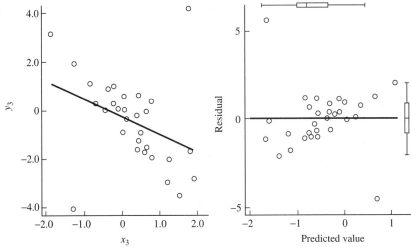

10.1.1d.

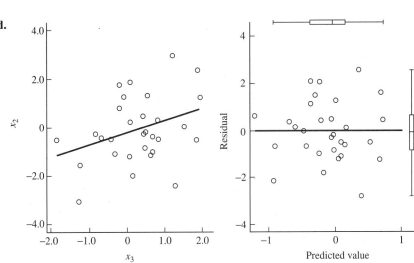

10.3.1.

Source	SS	df	MS
Model	32.6938081	3	10.897936
Residual	83.3510487	16	5.20944054
Total	116.044857	19	6.10762404

Number of obs = 20
$F(3, 16)$ = 2.09
Prob > F = 0.1416
R-squared = 0.2817
Adj R-squared = 0.1471
Root MSE = 2.2824

divorce	Coef.	Std. Err.	t	$P > |t|$	[95% Conf. Interval]	
educ	−.2745061	.7283994	−0.377	0.711	−1.818644	1.269632
inequal	32.17406	15.42536	2.086	0.053	−.5262254	64.87435
change	.0584221	.0268554	2.175	0.045	.0014912	.1153531
_cons	−.4275268	8.158205	−0.052	0.959	−17.72215	16.86709

predicted *divorce* = −.4275 − .2745*educ* + 32.17*inequal* + .0584*change*

The predicted divorce rate decreases by .2745 divorces per 1,000 people with each 1-year increase in median years of education, if inequality and population change are held constant.

Predicted divorce rate increases by 32.17 with each 1-unit increase in the inequality index, if education and population change are held constant.

Predicted divorce rate increases by .0584 with each 1-percent increase in the 1970–1980 population change, if education and inequality are held constant.

Population change rate is the only one among these predictors that has a statistically significant (distinguishable from 0) coefficient.

Together, *educ, inequal,* and *change* explain about 28% of the variance in divorce rates among these 20 cities. However, adjusting for the complexity of our model (3 coefficients plus a y intercept) relative to the complexity of the data (only 20 cases), $R_a^2 = .1471$.

10.3.2.

Albuquerque	
educ	12.9
inequal	.4
change	35.7
divorce	13.965
yhat	10.98664
e	2.978504

Honolulu	
educ	12.7
inequal	.44
change	12.4
divorce	8.109
yhat	10.96727
e	−2.858655

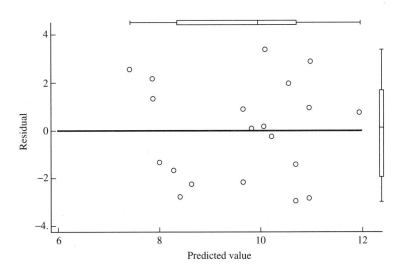

10.3.3.

	educ	inequal	change	divorce
educ	1.0000			
inequal	.3748	1.0000		
change	.0740	−.5964	1.0000	
divorce	.1946	.2373	.2342	1.0000

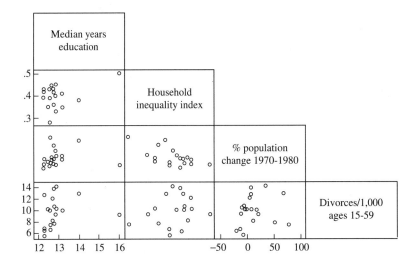

10.5.1.

Source	SS	df	MS
Model	20.6949468	2	10.3474734
Residual	95.34991	17	5.60881823
Total	116.044857	19	6.10762404

Number of obs = 20
$F(2, 17)$ = 1.84
Prob > F = 0.1883
R-squared = 0.1783
Adj R-squared = 0.0817
Root MSE = 2.3683

divorce	Coef.	Std. Err.	t	$P > \lvert t \rvert$	[95% Conf. Interval]	
change	.0176041	.0206722	0.852	0.406	−.0260103	.0612186
south	2.133816	1.334922	1.598	0.128	−.6826244	4.950256
_cons	8.99308	.6359214	14.142	0.000	7.651403	10.33476

predicted $divorce$ = 8.993 + .0176$change$ + 2.1338$south$

For non-south cities, this equation simplifies to

predicted $divorce$ = 8.993 + .0176$change$ + 2.1338×0
= 8.993 + .0176$change$

For southern cities, it becomes

predicted $divorce$ = 8.993 + .0176$change$ + 2.1338×1
= 11.1268 + .0176$change$

Predicted divorce rates go up as population change increases. At any given level of population change, divorce rates tend to be higher (by 2.1338) in southern cities than elsewhere.

10.5.2.

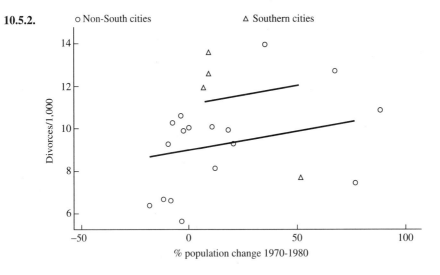

10.7.2a.

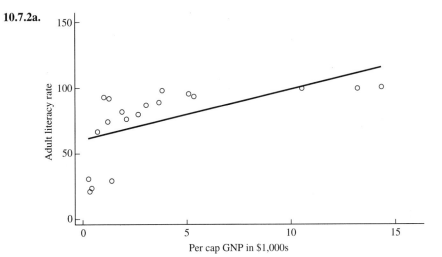

10.7.2b.

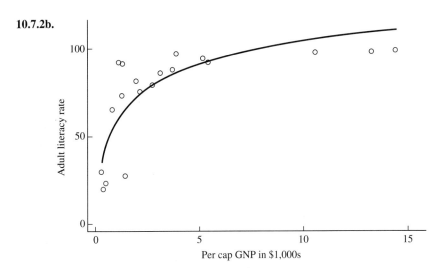

10.7.3a.

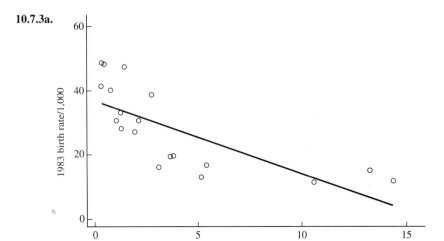

10.7.3b.

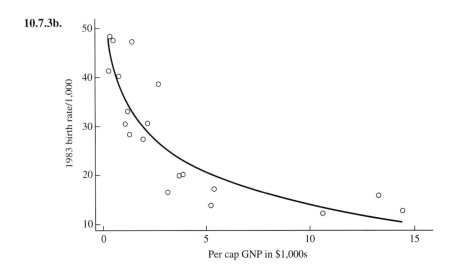

Appendix II: Statistical Tables

TABLE A.1 Probabilities for the Standard Normal Distribution

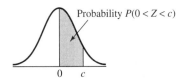

Probability $P(0 < Z < c)$

c	.00	.01	.02	.03	.04	.05	.06	.07	.08	.09
.0	.0000	.0040	.0080	.0120	.0160	.0199	.0239	.0279	.0319	.0359
.1	.0398	.0438	.0478	.0517	.0557	.0596	.0636	.0675	.0714	.0753
.2	.0793	.0832	.0871	.0910	.0948	.0987	.1026	.1064	.1103	.1141
.3	.1179	.1217	.1255	.1293	.1331	.1368	.1406	.1443	.1480	.1517
.4	.1554	.1591	.1628	.1664	.1700	.1736	.1772	.1808	.1844	.1879
.5	.1915	.1950	.1985	.2019	.2054	.2088	.2123	.2157	.2190	.2224
.6	.2257	.2291	.2324	.2357	.2389	.2422	.2454	.2486	.2517	.2549
.7	.2580	.2611	.2642	.2673	.2704	.2734	.2764	.2794	.2823	.2852
.8	.2881	.2910	.2939	.2967	.2995	.3023	.3051	.3078	.3106	.3133
.9	.3159	.3186	.3212	.3238	.3264	.3289	.3315	.3340	.3365	.3389
1.0	.3413	.3438	.3461	.3485	.3508	.3531	.3554	.3577	.3599	.3621
1.1	.3643	.3665	.3686	.3708	.3729	.3749	.3770	.3790	.3810	.3830
1.2	.3849	.3869	.3888	.3907	.3925	.3944	.3962	.3980	.3997	.4015
1.3	.4032	.4049	.4066	.4082	.4099	.4115	.4131	.4147	.4162	.4177
1.4	.4192	.4207	.4222	.4236	.4251	.4265	.4279	.4292	.4306	.4319
1.5	.4332	.4345	.4357	.4370	.4382	.4394	.4406	.4418	.4429	.4441
1.6	.4452	.4463	.4474	.4484	.4495	.4505	.4515	.4525	.4535	.4545
1.7	.4554	.4564	.4573	.4582	.4591	.4599	.4608	.4616	.4625	.4633
1.8	.4641	.4649	.4656	.4664	.4671	.4678	.4686	.4693	.4699	.4706
1.9	.4713	.4719	.4726	.4732	.4738	.4744	.4750	.4756	.4761	.4767
2.0	.4772	.4778	.4783	.4788	.4793	.4798	.4803	.4808	.4812	.4817
2.1	.4821	.4826	.4830	.4834	.4838	.4842	.4846	.4850	.4854	.4857
2.2	.4861	.4864	.4868	.4871	.4875	.4878	.4881	.4884	.4887	.4890
2.3	.4893	.4896	.4898	.4901	.4904	.4906	.4909	.4911	.4913	.4916
2.4	.4918	.4920	.4922	.4925	.4927	.4929	.4931	.4932	.4934	.4936
2.5	.4938	.4940	.4941	.4943	.4945	.4946	.4948	.4949	.4951	.4952
2.6	.4953	.4955	.4956	.4957	.4959	.4960	.4961	.4962	.4963	.4964
2.7	.4965	.4966	.4967	.4968	.4969	.4970	.4971	.4972	.4973	.4974
2.8	.4974	.4975	.4976	.4977	.4977	.4978	.4979	.4979	.4980	.4981
2.9	.4981	.4982	.4982	.4983	.4984	.4984	.4985	.4985	.4986	.4986
3.0	.4987	.4987	.4987	.4988	.4988	.4989	.4989	.4989	.4990	.4990
3.1	.4990	.4991	.4991	.4991	.4992	.4992	.4992	.4992	.4993	.4993
3.2	.4993	.4993	.4994	.4994	.4994	.4994	.4994	.4995	.4995	.4995
3.3	.4995	.4995	.4995	.4996	.4996	.4996	.4996	.4996	.4996	.4997
3.4	.4997	.4997	.4997	.4997	.4997	.4997	.4997	.4997	.4997	.4998

c	P	c	P	c	P
3.5	.49977	4.0	.499968	4.5	.4999960
3.6	.49984	4.1	.499979	4.6	.4999979
3.7	.49989	4.2	.499987	4.7	.4999987
3.8	.499928	4.3	.4999915	4.8	.4999992
3.9	.499952	4.4	.4999946	4.9	.4999995

TABLE A.2 Critical Values for the Standard Normal Distribution

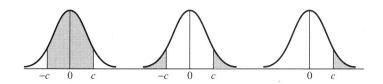

Confidence Intervals $P(\|Z\| \le c)$	Two-Tailed Tests $P(\|z\| \ge c)$	One-Tailed Tests $P(Z \ge c)$	Critical Value c
.10	.90	.45	.126
.20	.80	.40	.253
.30	.70	.35	.385
.40	.60	.30	.524
.50	.50	.25	.674
.60	.40	.20	.842
.70	.30	.15	1.036
.80	.20	.10	1.282
.90	.10	.05	1.645
.95	.05	.025	1.960
.98	.02	.01	2.326
.99	.01	.005	2.576
.995	.005	.0025	2.807
.999	.001	.0005	3.290
.9995	.0005	.00025	3.480
.9999	.0001	.00005	3.890
.99999	.00001	.000005	4.420
.999999	.000001	.0000005	4.900

Source: D. B. Owen and D. T. Monk (March 1957), *Tables of the Normal Probability Integral,* Sandia Corporation Technical Memo 64-57-51.

TABLE A.3   Critical Values for the Chi-Square (χ^2) Distribution

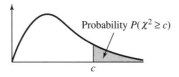

Probability $P(\chi^2 \geq c)$

df	Probability							
	.500	.250	.100	.050	.025	.010	.005	.001
1	.455	1.323	2.706	3.841	5.024	6.635	7.879	10.83
2	1.386	2.773	4.605	5.991	7.378	9.210	10.60	13.82
3	2.366	4.108	6.251	7.815	9.348	11.34	12.84	16.27
4	3.357	5.385	7.779	9.488	11.14	13.28	14.86	18.47
5	4.351	6.626	9.236	11.07	12.83	15.09	16.75	20.52
6	5.348	7.841	10.64	12.59	14.45	16.81	18.55	22.46
7	6.346	9.037	12.02	14.07	16.01	18.48	20.28	24.32
8	7.344	10.22	13.36	15.51	17.53	20.09	21.96	26.12
9	8.343	11.39	14.68	16.92	19.02	21.67	23.59	27.88
10	9.342	12.55	15.99	18.31	20.48	23.21	25.19	29.59
11	10.34	13.70	17.28	19.68	21.92	24.72	26.76	31.26
12	11.34	14.85	18.55	21.03	23.34	26.22	28.30	32.91
13	12.34	15.98	19.81	22.36	24.74	27.79	29.82	34.53
14	13.34	17.12	21.06	23.68	26.12	29.14	31.32	36.12
15	14.34	18.25	22.31	25.00	27.49	30.58	32.80	37.70
16	15.34	19.37	23.54	26.30	28.85	32.00	34.27	39.25
17	16.34	20.49	24.77	27.59	30.19	33.41	35.72	40.79
18	17.34	21.60	25.99	28.87	31.53	34.81	37.16	42.31
19	18.34	22.72	27.20	30.14	32.85	36.19	38.58	43.82
20	19.34	23.83	28.41	31.41	34.17	37.57	40.00	45.32
21	20.34	24.93	29.62	33.67	35.48	38.93	41.40	46.80
22	21.34	26.04	30.81	33.92	36.78	40.29	42.80	48.27
23	22.34	27.14	32.01	35.17	38.08	41.64	44.18	49.73
24	23.34	28.24	33.20	36.42	39.36	42.98	45.56	51.18
25	24.34	29.34	34.38	37.65	40.65	44.31	46.93	52.62
26	25.34	30.43	35.56	38.89	41.92	45.64	48.29	54.05
27	26.34	31.53	36.74	40.11	43.19	46.96	49.64	55.48
28	27.34	32.62	37.92	41.34	44.46	48.28	50.99	56.89
29	28.34	33.71	39.09	42.56	45.72	49.59	52.34	58.30
30	29.34	34.80	40.26	43.77	46.98	50.89	53.67	59.70
40	39.34	45.62	51.81	55.76	59.34	63.69	66.77	73.40
50	49.33	56.33	63.17	67.50	71.42	76.15	79.49	86.66
60	59.33	66.98	74.40	79.08	83.30	88.38	91.95	99.61
70	69.33	77.58	85.53	90.53	95.02	100.4	104.2	112.3
80	79.33	88.13	96.58	101.9	106.6	112.3	116.3	124.8
90	89.33	98.65	107.6	113.1	118.1	124.1	128.3	137.2
100	99.33	109.1	118.5	124.3	129.6	135.8	140.2	149.4

Source: Abridged from Table 8 of *Biometrika Tables for Statisticians,* Vol. 1, edited by E. S. Pearson and H. O. Hartley (1962), London: Cambridge University Press.

TABLE A.4   Critical Values for Student's *t* Distribution

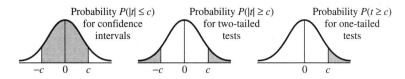

					Probability					
	.50	.80	.90	.95	.98	.99	.995	.998	.999	*Confidence Intervals*
	.50	.20	.10	.05	.02	.01	.005	.002	.001	*Two-Tailed Tests*
df	.25	.10	.05	.025	.01	.005	.0025	.001	.0005	*One-Tailed Tests*
1	1.000	3.078	6.314	12.706	31.821	63.637	127.32	318.32	636.62	
2	.816	1.886	2.920	4.303	6.965	9.925	14.089	22.326	31.598	
3	.765	1.638	2.353	3.182	4.541	5.841	7.453	10.213	12.924	
4	.741	1.533	2.132	2.776	3.747	4.604	5.598	7.173	8.610	
5	.727	1.476	2.015	2.571	3.365	4.032	4.773	5.893	6.869	
6	.718	1.440	1.943	2.447	3.143	3.707	4.317	5.208	5.959	
7	.711	1.415	1.895	2.365	2.998	3.499	4.020	4.785	5.408	
8	.706	1.397	1.860	2.306	2.896	3.355	3.833	4.501	5.041	
9	.703	1.383	1.833	2.262	2.821	3.250	3.690	4.297	4.781	
10	.700	1.372	1.812	2.228	2.764	3.169	3.581	4.144	4.537	
11	.697	1.363	1.796	2.201	2.718	3.106	3.497	4.025	4.437	
12	.695	1.356	1.782	2.179	2.681	3.055	3.428	3.930	4.318	
13	.694	1.350	1.771	2.160	2.650	3.012	3.372	3.852	4.221	
14	.692	1.345	1.761	2.145	2.624	2.977	3.326	3.787	4.140	
15	.691	1.341	1.753	2.131	2.602	2.947	3.286	3.733	4.073	
16	.690	1.337	1.746	2.120	2.583	2.921	3.252	3.686	4.015	
17	.689	1.333	1.740	2.110	2.567	2.898	3.222	3.646	3.965	
18	.688	1.330	1.734	2.101	2.552	2.878	3.197	3.610	3.922	
19	.688	1.328	1.729	2.093	2.539	2.861	3.174	3.579	3.883	
20	.687	1.325	1.725	2.086	2.528	2.845	3.153	3.552	3.850	
21	.686	1.323	1.721	2.080	2.518	2.831	3.135	3.527	3.819	
22	.686	1.321	1.717	2.074	2.508	2.819	3.119	3.505	3.792	
23	.685	1.319	1.714	2.069	2.500	2.807	3.104	3.485	3.767	
24	.685	1.318	1.711	2.064	2.492	2.797	3.091	3.467	3.745	
25	.684	1.316	1.708	2.060	2.485	2.787	3.078	3.450	3.725	
26	.684	1.315	1.706	2.056	2.479	2.779	3.067	3.435	3.707	
27	.684	1.314	1.703	2.052	2.473	2.771	3.057	3.421	3.690	
28	.683	1.313	1.701	2.048	2.467	2.763	3.047	3.408	3.674	
29	.683	1.311	1.699	2.045	2.462	2.756	3.038	3.396	3.659	
30	.683	1.310	1.697	2.042	2.457	2.750	3.030	3.385	3.646	
40	.681	1.303	1.684	2.021	2.423	2.704	2.971	3.307	3.551	
60	.679	1.296	1.671	2.000	2.390	2.660	2.915	3.232	3.460	
120	.677	1.289	1.658	1.980	2.358	2.617	2.860	3.160	3.373	
∞	.674	1.282	1.645	1.960	2.326	2.576	2.807	3.090	3.291	

Source: Abridged from Table 12 of *Biometrika Tables for Statisticians,* Vol. 1, edited by E. S. Pearson and H. O. Hartley (1962), London: Cambridge University Press.

TABLE A.5 Critical Values for the *F* Distribution

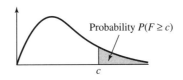

Probability $P(F \geq c)$

c

		Numerator Degrees of Freedom, df_1										
	P	1	2	3	4	5	6	8	10	20	40	∞
1	.25	5.83	7.50	8.21	8.58	8.82	8.98	9.19	9.32	9.58	9.71	9.85
	.10	39.86	49.50	53.59	55.83	57.24	58.20	59.44	60.19	61.74	62.53	63.33
	.05	161.4	199.5	215.7	224.6	230.2	234.0	238.9	241.9	248.0	251.1	254.3
2	.25	2.57	3.00	3.15	3.23	3.28	3.31	3.35	3.38	3.43	3.45	3.48
	.10	8.53	9.00	9.16	9.24	9.29	9.33	9.37	9.39	9.44	9.47	9.49
	.05	18.51	19.00	19.16	19.25	19.30	19.33	19.37	19.40	19.45	19.47	19.50
	.01	98.50	99.00	99.17	99.25	99.30	99.33	99.37	99.40	99.45	99.47	99.50
	.001	998.5	999.0	999.2	999.2	999.3	999.3	999.4	999.4	999.4	999.5	999.5
3	.25	2.02	2.28	2.36	2.39	2.41	2.42	2.44	2.44	2.46	2.47	2.47
	.10	5.54	5.46	5.39	5.34	5.31	5.28	5.25	5.23	5.18	5.16	5.13
	.05	10.13	9.55	9.28	9.12	9.01	8.94	8.85	8.79	8.66	8.59	8.53
	.01	34.12	30.82	29.46	28.71	28.24	27.91	27.49	27.23	26.69	26.41	26.13
	.001	167.0	148.5	141.1	137.1	134.6	132.8	130.6	129.2	126.4	125.0	123.5
4	.25	1.81	2.00	2.05	2.06	2.07	2.08	2.08	2.08	2.08	2.08	2.08
	.10	4.54	4.32	4.19	4.11	4.05	4.01	3.95	3.92	3.84	3.80	3.76
	.05	7.71	6.94	6.59	6.39	6.26	6.16	6.04	5.96	5.80	5.72	5.63
	.01	21.20	18.00	16.69	15.98	15.52	15.21	14.80	14.55	14.02	13.75	13.46
	.001	74.14	61.25	56.18	53.44	51.71	50.53	49.00	48.05	46.10	45.09	44.05
5	.25	1.69	1.85	1.88	1.89	1.89	1.89	1.89	1.89	1.88	1.88	1.87
	.10	4.06	3.78	3.62	3.52	3.45	3.40	3.34	3.30	3.21	3.16	3.10
	.05	6.61	5.79	5.41	5.19	5.05	4.95	4.82	4.74	4.56	4.46	4.36
	.01	16.26	13.27	12.06	11.39	10.97	10.67	10.29	10.05	9.55	9.29	9.02
	.001	47.18	37.12	33.20	31.09	29.75	28.84	27.64	26.92	25.39	24.60	23.79
6	.25	1.62	1.76	1.78	1.79	1.79	1.78	1.78	1.77	1.76	1.75	1.74
	.10	3.78	3.46	3.29	3.18	3.11	3.05	2.98	2.94	2.84	2.78	2.72
	.05	5.99	5.14	4.76	4.53	4.39	4.28	4.15	4.06	3.87	3.77	3.67
	.01	13.75	10.92	9.78	9.15	8.75	8.47	8.10	7.87	7.40	7.14	6.88
	.001	35.51	27.00	23.70	21.92	20.81	20.03	19.03	18.41	17.12	16.44	15.75
7	.25	1.57	1.70	1.72	1.72	1.71	1.71	1.70	1.69	1.67	1.66	1.65
	.10	3.59	3.26	3.07	2.96	2.88	2.83	2.75	2.70	2.59	2.54	2.47
	.05	5.59	4.74	4.35	4.12	3.97	3.87	3.73	3.64	3.44	3.34	3.23
	.01	12.25	9.55	8.45	7.85	7.46	7.19	6.84	6.62	6.16	5.91	5.65
	.001	29.25	21.69	18.77	17.19	16.21	15.52	14.63	14.08	12.93	12.33	11.70
8	.25	1.54	1.66	1.67	1.66	1.66	1.65	1.64	1.63	1.61	1.59	1.58
	.10	3.46	3.11	2.92	2.81	2.73	2.67	2.59	2.54	2.42	2.36	2.29
	.05	5.32	4.46	4.07	3.84	3.69	3.58	3.44	3.35	3.15	3.04	2.93
	.01	11.26	8.65	7.59	7.01	6.63	6.37	6.03	5.81	5.36	5.12	4.86
	.001	25.42	18.49	15.83	14.39	13.49	12.86	12.04	11.54	10.48	9.92	9.33

Denominator Degrees of Freedom, df_2

						Numerator Degrees of Freedom, df_1						
	P	1	2	3	4	5	6	8	10	20	40	∞
9	.25	1.51	1.62	1.63	1.63	1.62	1.61	1.60	1.59	1.56	1.54	1.53
	.10	3.36	3.01	2.81	2.69	2.61	2.55	2.47	2.42	2.30	2.23	2.16
	.05	5.12	4.26	3.86	3.63	3.48	3.37	3.23	3.14	2.94	2.83	2.71
	.01	10.56	8.02	6.99	6.42	6.06	5.80	5.47	5.26	4.81	4.57	4.31
	.001	22.86	16.39	13.90	12.56	11.71	11.13	10.37	9.89	8.90	8.37	7.81
10	.25	1.49	1.60	1.60	1.59	1.59	1.58	1.56	1.55	1.52	1.51	1.48
	.10	3.28	2.92	2.73	2.61	2.52	2.46	2.38	2.32	2.20	2.13	2.06
	.05	4.96	4.10	3.71	3.48	3.33	3.22	3.07	2.98	2.77	2.66	2.54
	.01	10.04	7.56	6.55	5.99	5.64	5.39	5.06	4.85	4.41	4.17	3.91
	.001	21.04	14.91	12.55	11.28	10.48	9.92	9.20	8.75	7.80	7.30	6.76
12	.25	1.46	1.56	1.56	1.55	1.54	1.53	1.51	1.50	1.47	1.45	1.42
	.10	3.18	2.81	2.61	2.48	2.39	2.33	2.24	2.19	2.06	1.99	1.90
	.05	4.75	3.89	3.49	3.26	3.11	3.00	2.85	2.75	2.54	2.43	2.30
	.01	9.33	6.93	5.95	5.41	5.06	4.82	4.50	4.30	3.86	3.62	3.36
	.001	18.64	12.97	10.80	9.63	8.89	8.38	7.71	7.29	6.40	5.93	5.42
14	.25	1.44	1.53	1.53	1.52	1.51	1.50	1.48	1.46	1.43	1.41	1.38
	.10	3.10	2.73	2.52	2.39	2.31	2.24	2.15	2.10	1.96	1.89	1.80
	.05	4.60	3.74	3.34	3.11	2.96	2.85	2.70	2.60	2.39	2.27	2.13
	.01	8.86	5.51	5.56	5.04	4.69	4.46	4.14	3.94	3.51	3.27	3.00
	.001	17.14	11.78	9.73	8.62	7.92	7.43	6.80	6.40	5.56	5.10	4.60
16	.25	1.42	1.51	1.51	1.50	1.48	1.48	1.46	1.45	1.40	1.37	1.34
	.10	3.05	2.67	2.46	2.33	2.24	2.18	2.09	2.03	1.89	1.81	1.72
	.05	4.49	3.63	3.24	3.01	2.85	2.74	2.59	2.49	2.28	2.15	2.01
	.01	8.53	6.23	5.29	4.77	4.44	4.20	3.89	3.69	3.26	3.02	2.75
	.001	16.12	10.97	9.00	7.94	7.27	6.81	6.19	5.81	4.99	4.54	4.06
18	.25	1.41	1.50	1.49	1.48	1.46	1.45	1.43	1.42	1.38	1.35	1.32
	.10	3.01	2.62	2.42	2.29	2.20	2.13	2.04	1.98	1.84	1.75	1.66
	.05	4.41	3.55	3.16	2.93	2.77	2.66	2.51	2.41	2.19	2.06	1.92
	.01	8.29	6.01	5.09	4.58	4.25	4.01	3.71	3.51	3.08	2.84	2.57
	.001	15.38	10.39	8.49	7.46	6.81	6.35	5.76	5.39	4.59	4.15	3.67
20	.25	1.40	1.49	1.48	1.46	1.45	1.44	1.42	1.40	1.36	1.33	1.29
	.10	2.97	2.59	2.38	2.25	2.16	2.09	2.00	1.94	1.79	1.71	1.61
	.05	4.35	3.49	3.10	2.87	2.71	2.60	2.45	2.35	2.12	1.99	1.84
	.01	8.10	5.85	4.94	4.43	4.10	3.87	3.56	3.37	2.94	2.69	2.42
	.001	14.82	9.95	8.10	7.10	6.46	6.02	5.44	5.08	4.29	3.86	3.38
30	.25	1.38	1.45	1.44	1.42	1.41	1.39	1.37	1.35	13.0	1.27	1.23
	.10	2.88	2.49	2.28	2.14	2.05	1.98	1.88	1.82	1.67	1.57	1.46
	.05	4.17	3.32	2.92	2.69	2.53	2.42	2.27	2.16	1.93	1.79	1.62
	.01	7.56	5.39	4.51	4.02	3.70	3.47	3.17	2.98	2.55	2.30	2.01
	.001	13.29	8.77	7.05	6.12	5.53	5.12	4.58	4.24	3.49	3.07	2.59
40	.25	1.36	1.44	1.42	1.40	1.39	1.37	1.35	1.33	1.28	1.24	1.19
	.10	2.84	2.44	2.23	2.09	2.00	1.93	1.83	1.76	1.61	1.51	1.38
	.05	4.08	3.23	2.84	2.61	2.45	2.34	2.18	2.08	1.84	1.69	1.51
	.01	7.31	5.18	4.31	3.83	3.51	3.29	2.99	2.80	2.37	2.11	1.80
	.001	12.61	8.25	6.60	5.70	5.13	4.73	4.21	3.87	3.15	2.73	2.23

Denominator Degrees of Freedom, df_2

(*continued*)

TABLE A.5 (*Continued*)

	P	1	2	3	4	5	6	8	10	20	40	∞
60	.25	1.35	1.42	1.41	1.38	1.37	1.35	1.32	1.30	1.25	1.21	1.15
	.10	2.79	2.39	2.18	2.04	1.95	1.87	1.77	1.71	1.54	1.44	1.29
	.05	4.00	3.15	2.76	2.53	2.37	2.25	2.10	1.99	1.75	1.59	1.39
	.01	7.08	4.98	4.13	3.65	3.34	3.12	2.82	2.63	2.20	1.94	1.60
	.001	11.97	7.76	6.17	5.31	4.76	4.37	3.87	3.54	2.83	2.41	1.89
120	.25	1.34	1.40	1.39	1.37	1.35	1.33	1.30	1.28	1.22	1.18	1.10
	.10	2.75	2.35	2.13	1.99	1.90	1.82	1.72	1.65	1.48	1.37	1.19
	.05	3.92	3.07	2.68	2.45	2.29	2.17	2.02	1.91	1.66	1.50	1.25
	.01	6.85	4.79	3.95	3.48	3.17	2.96	2.66	2.47	2.03	1.76	1.38
	.001	11.38	7.32	5.79	4.95	4.42	4.04	3.55	3.24	2.53	2.11	1.54
∞	.25	1.32	1.39	1.37	1.35	1.33	1.31	1.28	1.25	1.19	1.14	1.00
	.10	2.71	2.30	2.08	1.94	1.85	1.77	1.67	1.60	1.42	1.30	1.00
	.05	3.84	3.00	2.60	2.37	2.21	2.10	1.94	1.83	1.57	1.39	1.00
	.01	6.64	4.61	3.78	3.32	3.02	2.80	2.51	2.32	1.88	1.59	1.00
	.001	10.83	6.91	5.42	4.62	4.10	3.74	3.27	2.96	2.27	1.84	1.00

The table header reads: *Numerator Degrees of Freedom, df_1* (spanning columns 1 through ∞). The left axis label reads: *Denominator Degrees of Freedom, df_2*.

Source: Abridged from Table 18 of *Biometrika Tables for Statisticians*, Vol. 1, edited by E. S. Pearson and H. O. Hartley (1962), London: Cambridge University Press.

Index